THE STATUS OF WORLD SOCIETY

Friedrich Kratochwil's book explores the role of law in the international arena, and the key discourses surrounding it. It explains the increased importance of law for politics – from law-fare to the judicialization of politics, to human rights – and why traditional expectations of progress through law have led to disappointment. Providing an overview of the debates in legal theory, philosophy, international law, and international organizations, Kratochwil reflects on the need to break down disciplinary boundaries and address important issues in both international relations and international law, including deformalization, fragmentation, the role of legal pluralism, the emergence of autonomous autopoietic systems, and the appearance of non-territorial forms of empire. He argues that the pretensions of a positivist theory in social science and of positivism in law are inappropriate for understanding practical problems and formulates an approach for the analysis of praxis based on constructivism and pragmatism.

FRIEDRICH KRATOCHWIL is Emeritus Chair of International Relations at the European University Institute in Florence, Visiting Professor at the Central European University, Budapest, and International Scholar at Kyung Hee University, Seoul.

CAMBRIDGE STUDIES IN INTERNATIONAL RELATIONS: 129

The Status of Law in World Society

Cambridge Studies in International Relations is a joint initiative of Cambridge University Press and the British International Studies Association (BISA). The series will include a wide range of material, from undergraduate textbooks and surveys to research-based monographs and collaborative volumes. The aim of the series is to publish the best new scholarship in International Studies from Europe, North America, and the rest of the world.

CAMBRIDGE STUDIES IN INTERNATIONAL RELATIONS

128 *Michael G. Findley, Daniel L. Nielson and J. C. Sharman*
Global shell games
Experiments in transnational relations, crime, and terrorism

127 *Jordan Branch*
The cartographic state
Maps, territory, and the origins of sovereignty

126 *Thomas Risse, Stephen C. Ropp and Kathryn Sikkink (eds.)*
The persistent power of human rights
From commitment to compliance

125 *K. M. Fierke*
Political self-sacrifice
Agency, body and emotion in international relations

124 *Stefano Guzzini*
The return of geopolitics in Europe?
Social mechanisms and foreign policy identity crises

123 *Bear F. Braumoeller*
The great powers and the international system
Systemic theory in empirical perspective

122 *Jonathan Joseph*
The social in the global
Social theory, governmentality and global politics

121 *Brian C. Rathbun*
Trust in international cooperation
International security institutions, domestic politics and American multilateralism

120 *A. Maurits van der Veen*
Ideas, interests and foreign aid

119 *Emanuel Adler and Vincent Pouliot*
International practices

Series list continues after index

THE STATUS OF LAW IN WORLD SOCIETY

Meditations on the Role and Rule of Law

FRIEDRICH KRATOCHWIL

CAMBRIDGE
UNIVERSITY PRESS

CAMBRIDGE
UNIVERSITY PRESS

University Printing House, Cambridge CB2 8BS, United Kingdom

Published in the United States of America by Cambridge University Press, New York

Cambridge University Press is part of the University of Cambridge.

It furthers the University's mission by disseminating knowledge in the pursuit of education, learning and research at the highest international levels of excellence.

www.cambridge.org
Information on this title: www.cambridge.org/9781107681071

First published 2014

Printed in the United Kingdom by Clays, St Ives plc

A catalogue record for this publication is available from the British Library

Library of Congress Cataloguing in Publication data
Kratochwil, Friedrich V., author.
The status of law in world society : meditations on the role and rule of law / Friedrich Kratochwil.
p. cm. – (Cambridge studies in international relations ; 129)
Includes bibliographical references and index.
ISBN 978-1-107-03728-1 (hardback) – ISBN 978-1-107-68107-1 (paperback)
1. Rule of law. 2. Law–Philosophy. I. Title.
K3171.K73 2014
340′.11–dc23
2013039675

ISBN 978-1-107-03728-1 Hardback
ISBN 978-1-107-68107-1 Paperback

For
Petra Hoelscher
uxori carissimae,
"o et praesidium et dulce decus meum"

ἐὰν μὴ ἔλπηται ἀνέλπιστον οὐκ
ἐξευρήσει, ἀνεξερεύνητον ἐὸν καὶ ἄπορον.
If you do not expect the unexpected, you will not find it;
For it is hard to be sought out and difficult

Heraclitus, frag. 18

_ _ μάχεσθαι χρὴ τὸν δῆμον ὑπὲρ τοῦ
νόμου ὅκωσπερ τείχεος.
The people must fight for its law as for its walls.

Heraclitus, frag.44

CONTENTS

PREFACE

This book is the result of several explorations that are here brought together in a substantially revised form. Thus Meditations 1 through 6 were first delivered as series of lectures at a "winter course" of international law at CEDIN in Belo Horizonte, Brazil in July of 2011. Meditations 7 and 8 were my contribution to the Summer Academy of the European Inter-University Center for Human Rights and Democratization in Venice in the summer of 2012. Meditation 6 was written under the auspices of Kyung Hee University in Seoul, where I was an "International Scholar" in the fall of 2011. The Introduction and Meditation 9 were written while teaching as Visiting Professor at the Central European University at Budapest in 2012.

From its genesis it is clear that this project could not have come to fruition without the great personal and institutional support that I enjoyed while working on this manuscript. My wife put up with me even though I was often grumpier than usual (if people who know me can believe this)! She let me focus on the book while taking care of all the burdens of dealing with workers and authorities that result from running a big house in the Tuscan hills. The European University Institute, my former university, where I taught until April 2011 and where my last seminar on international law provided the first outline of the project, provided me with access to the library during the summer of 2012 when I finished the first draft. At a very decisive point, right at the beginning, Carol Bohmer generously shared some of her research resources when I was suddenly cut off from a research library after my retirement from the Institute, and before I had a new institutional affiliation.

Equally important have been the long conversations and comments I received from Nick Onuf, Oliver Kessler, and Jens Bartelson, who read the manuscript in its entirety and provided me with detailed criticisms. Similarly, Hannes Peltonen and Gulherme Vasconcelos, who had been my untiring research assistants, were also the first critical readers of the initial drafts, providing me with valuable suggestions concerning both content and form of the argument. In addition, I benefited from the comments on different chapters made by Dennis Patterson, Jan Klabbers, Nikolas Rajkovic, Mary Ellen O'Connell, Jean Cohen, Albena Azmanova, Xymena Kurowska, and, above all, from the international research group "Constitutionalism Unbound," assembled by Antje

Wiener in Hamburg. It organized a gruelling day-long workshop in Hamburg, in which both lawyers and social scientists examined each Meditation and gave me valuable feedback. My sincerest thanks to Sigrid Boysen, Julia Fronenberg, Maj Garsten, Hannes Hansen-Magusson, Sarah Imani, Joern Axel Kaemmerer (who also was kind enough to read a further draft), Alexandra Kemmerer, Christine Landfried, Anthony Lang, Philip Liste, Sven Opitz, Almut Schilling-Vacaflor, Joerg Philipp Terhechte, Andreas von Arnault, Antje Vetterlein, and Antje Wiener. Finally, special thanks also to Manuel Mireanu who got the last version of the manuscript in shape. Finally, I owe a great debt of gratitude to Cambridge University Press (John Haslam and Chris Reus-Smit who took an interest in this project) and to Fleur Jones and Rob Wilkinson who saw this manuscript through the editing and production process.

With so much advice and the extensive "canard hunt" by the commentators, the remaining errors of fact or judgment remain, of course, entirely my responsibility. This also concerns the form in which, after careful reflection, I present the material. Some readers remarked (with good reason) that they found the presentation at times confusing, as frequently not a single storyline dominates the discussion, but rather different strands of arguments appear and then "drop" out, only to be taken up again in a different context. They also wondered for which audience this text is written, as the Meditation resembles more an interior monologue than an explicit argument. To that extent I, as the author, seem to engage in a seemingly autistic activity, taking up themes and leaving them after a while unattended, where readers would perhaps have expected other turns.

The latter observation might of course be true, especially when judged against the standard contemporary debates in political science, which are usually as predictable as they are tedious. This is perhaps best exemplified by the mode of exposition in which allegedly "three approaches" frame most dissertations in international relations and explaining the "variance" then takes pride of place. Nevertheless, the above objection deserves some further comments. Actually, contrary to what one would at first suspect, only "demonstrations" are monologic, since universality and necessity unite author and audience and thus, as in the ideal theory of the early Rawls, it makes no difference whether a single person speaks, or a group discusses and discovers the principles of justice. Ultimately the results are justified by universal reason and emerge from what Kant would call "determinative" judgments. But, as we know, even outside of ethics, such as in the sciences, this might be a misleading picture. Normally controversies abound and "debates" rather than demonstrations dominate the different fields. Thus the notion of ideal reason or a universal audience might be a phenomenon that has seen its day, as has the genre of a linear narrative in literature, where an all-knowing author is writing. Actual "thinking," even if done by a single person in the "ivory tower," is, in contrast, hardly ever a monologue, but always consists of an internal dialogue in which (imagined) interlocutors and their arguments – established or controversial – which have become part of the understandings, are scrutinized. Here the various "fields" and traditions constitute the bounds of sense within which we move and within which we locate a problem and perhaps even try to "redraw" the bounds of sense.

Thus engaging in this questioning and participating in the debates and conversations seems particularly appropriate when we deliberate about the practical choices we face, since we are always in the middle of things and cannot withdraw to an absolute point beyond time and the particular situation we are in. Instead, we have to reflect upon the options, largely framed by the institutions within which they are embedded, and the context in which a problem arises, when we try to determine what to do, "all things considered." This means that we have to understand how our choices are linked via the norms and rules to certain practices, but also how our decisions arise from a particular judgment by which we appraise and justify our chosen alternative – or get criticized, perhaps even sanctioned, by others for having selected it – since we usually are not at liberty to follow our idiosyncrasies (*de gustibus est disputandum!*). In addition, in this choice we cannot rely on the criteria of necessity and universality, as the latter might be hollow (and compatible with a variety of choices, even contradictory ones), and different competing necessities (duties) might be at issue. Here the standard modes of presentation quickly run out, as no ultimate foundation offers itself from which we can rigorously derive our conclusions, or show their justifiability by invoking generalizations, as we do in "determinative judgments." Instead, something like a "reflective judgment," as developed by Kant in his *Third Critique*, becomes necessary. Thus, "going back and forth" between facts and norms, falling back on analogies, utilizing metaphors and counter-factuals, and thus "weaving together" different strands of thought, are then the modes in which we try to resolve the issue(s) at hand. Finally, having found a solution, we hope we thereby can "woo" (again a Kantian term) the bystanders to agree with us, instead of apodictically demanding their assent or, in the case of their refusal, of eliminating them from the discourse as they must have violated "universal reason."

To that extent the two fragments of Heraclitus I chose as the *avant propos* capture the two main purposes of this "second journey" (*deuteros plous*) on which I am going to embark, for which the openness for "surprises" and getting rid of preconceived ideas is as important as realizing that law is not a brooding omnipresence in the normative sky or the ethereal sphere of values but an eminently social phenomenon. It is a means for contestation as well as for accommodation, but also of *dominium*, which we all use in order to pursue our personal and political projects. But as such, law has to be cared for and fought for as it will not disclose itself in its "truth" (like Heidegger's *aletheia*) but has to be "made," shaping and being shaped by social forces.

While this latter point has usually been acknowledged even by "non-realist" exponents of jurisprudence – here the topos was that law always pointed "beyond" itself as it is not mere speculation but a social practice – the second notion that knowledge appropriate for practical issues has also had a long tradition, but its reliance on "prudence" has been much contested in modernity. Here, true "knowledge" had to measure up to field independent epistemic standards, as otherwise we would fall into the abyss of errors and relativism. The (implausible) Cartesian doubt could only be assuaged by an equally implausible conception of knowledge exorcizing all doubts by being characterized by clarity, universality, and necessity.

Thus, to let go of the ultimate props of an a-historical universality and necessity might then make for some tough reading and writing, as it is not the familiar canonical form in which we are trained to present our arguments. But it might also provide some new insights that lie outside the tradition of subjecting praxis to a "theoretical" gaze, and even outside the various disciplinary myopias based on such a "prejudice" for "theory." Obviously the proof of the pudding is in the eating. But then again we should also remember that "wisdom" (*spientia*) and "to taste" (*sapere*) spring from the same root, so that there might be perhaps more to it when we say: "*sapere aude*," that is "dare to taste/know," a topos that has inspired our reflections from Horace to Augustine, to Kant, and Foucault.

Introduction: images of law

Images of law

Writing a book about the *Status of Law in World Society* inevitably conjures up certain associations. One is, of course, the perhaps subconscious reference to Richard's Falk *The Status of Law in International Society*,[1] which in turn took its cue from Hersh Lauterpacht's earlier treatise.[2] The other is to the concept of "world society," which could be used analogously to the term "world politics" that once established the research program of one of the first journals in the field, but which consciously adopted a program for analysing both international and comparative politics. Or we could take it in the sense in which Niklas Luhmann and his school are using the term.[3]

It would be tempting to connect the first and the last version and take them as points of reference, thereby constructing a coherent narrative in which the international has been replaced by the global, the state by "society," and international law, formerly merely an adjunct to diplomacy and perhaps of relevance to "international organizations," has finally become one of the main drivers shaping world politics. I shall resist that temptation and stay much closer to the second option, without wanting to deny the impact of globalization on states and societies and the fact that, for better or for worse, "law" and its "lawyers" have arrived as part of the professional class that manages our affairs. To that extent law now provides in large part the vocabulary for contemporary politics. Whether we discuss the "legality" of the second Gulf War, address human rights, the (in)admissibility of certain means of "enhanced interrogation," or trade and development issues, legal concepts figure prominently in all arguments and are made by all sorts of people, be they decision-makers, journalists, public intellectuals, or the proverbial men (and women) in the street.

But if law has become in a way "triumphant," why is it that we do not seem to have realized the "progressive" promise we so ardently hoped for? In a way we seem to experience the same disappointments at the level of public

1 Richard Falk, *The Status of Law in International Society* (Princeton University Press, 1970).

2 Sir Hersch Lauterpacht, *The Function of Law in the International Community* (Oxford: Clarendon, 1933).

3 Niklas Luhmann, *Die Gesellschaft der Gesellschaft*, 2 vols. (Frankfurt: Suhrkamp, 1998).

(international) law as we did domestically, when Watergate exposed the seamier side of the legal "profession," or when, more recently, with the law of "standardized contracts" (contracts of adhesion), which have morphed from an instrument of autonomous agents who freely made agreements into something else. Here not a "few rotten apples" or a specific misuse but the law itself has become problematic. Suddenly, "boilerplate" and "fine print" supersede individual rights and any meaningful concept of "consent" (by "informing" the contracting party e.g. only *ex post* of the "terms and conditions"). "The law" instead protects often questionable business practices through exculpatory clauses and through restrictions on available remedies.[4] Similarly, now that international law has finally emerged from the closet of the state system, not all might have been lost (to paraphrase Kant), but the triumph seems rather stale. True, while it was formerly generals and defence ministers who might have only occasionally paid lip service to the law while ignoring it in practice, now legal professionals[5] decide on retaliatory measures, pinpointing houses in Afghanistan, or persons in Yemen or Gaza,[6] or they give the "go ahead" for striking targets in the former Yugoslavia. The former reasonably clear anti-torture norm, frequently ignored by governments even though its existence was hardly ever doubted, is now being artfully dismantled by inventing new categories, such as "unlawful combatant," and by invoking supreme necessity in the war on terror. Thus the suspicion arises that "law" might have become part of the problem rather than the solution, and this problem requires further analysis

Evidence from other areas reinforces this perception. The continuing global financial crisis had not only to do with the dismantling of a regulatory structure that was derided as an outmoded "control and command" system. While strict supervision certainly has its disadvantages, as it puts high demands on regulators and might create inefficiencies and resistance, the reliance on broad principles in the so-called PBR (principle-based regulation while "deputizing" the institutions to regulate themselves) is unavailable if, in the words of one of the chief regulators in the UK, we deal "with people who have no principles."[7] It made possible the excesses of the "socialization of risk" while privatizing the profits since it was powerfully supported by the intellectual hegemony of

[4] See the indictment of the practice of standardized contracts by Margaret Jane Radin, *The Fine Print, Vanishing Rights and the Rule of Law* (Princeton University Press, 2012).

[5] For an incisive analysis of the changing practices see David Kennedy, *Of War and Law* (Princeton University Press, 2006).

[6] On the problems with long-distance "targeted killings" see Nils Melzer, *Targeted Killings in International Law* (Oxford University Press, 2008).

[7] As quoted in Julia Black, "Paradoxes and Failure: New Governance Techniques and the Financial," *The Modern Law Review*, vol. 75 no. 6 (2012), 1037–63, at 42; see also Kenneth W. Dahm, "The Subprime Crisis and Financial Regulation: International and Comparative Perspectives," *Chicago Journal of International Law*, vol. 10 (2009–2010), 581–638.

certain doctrines about the efficiency of markets. In making "law" the facilitator of market efficiency and in buying into the belief that all risks are calculable, even systemic ones, law seems to have been colonized as exemplified by the "law and economics" or governance approaches that espouse "meta regulation" by relying on the self-regulation of firms and on the "market" itself. Ironically, the inroads into law came at a point when many economists had already abandoned the idea of efficient markets – given the susceptibility of the latter to informational asymmetries and panic reactions. But the "legal professionals" who had been exposed to some "cross-fertilization" by another discipline had participated wholeheartedly in the destruction of the few existing firewalls, with the predictable perverse effects. This is not to say that we can or even should go back to the status quo ante, but it does mean that politics and law will have to find new instruments, instead of treating the market as the ultimate authority.

Finally, the prospects of a global society that moves from segmentary (territorial) to functional differentiation might be good news for law students as more and more specialized services are needed, but not necessarily for the rest of us. Forum shopping, representing clients worldwide, and submitting essentially the same cases to different dispute resolution mechanisms, thereby circumventing the *res judicata* principle, offers the prospect of ever increasing job opportunities. It should not come as a great surprise that these trends are less enticing for those who do not think that the rule of law and the rule of lawyers amount to the same thing.

Although the alternative interpretation sketched here casts a gloomier spell on contemporary developments than we encounter in the usual triumphalist account of progress and cosmopolitan justice, it is not so much at odds with our highly ambivalent attitude towards "the law." This ambivalence becomes visible in a variety of images that we connect with law's "darker" side, serving as an instrument of *dominium*, even repression. I will leave aside in the following the "deeper" psychological interpretations we find, for example in Freud[8] and Lacan,[9] and concentrate more on the images and metaphors by which we commonly capture (some) characteristics of law. Below I inductively listed some typical images and common sayings – some paraphrased for brevity's sake – about the law:

(1) Law is Justice – see the representation of the Goddess of Justice on many court buildings.
(2) An unjust law is no law (Antigone).

[8] Sigmund Freud, *Group Psychology and the Analysis of the Ego*, transl. by James Strachey (London: Hogarth Press, 1945). See also his *Civilization and its Discontent*, transl. by Joan Riviere (London: Hogarth Press, 1946).

[9] Jacques Lacan, *Ecrits*, rev. edn., transl. by Bruce Fink (New York: Norton 2002).

(3) As in nature law is the right of the stronger (Gorgias, Greek sophists).
(4) Among us nobody rules but the law/ The government of ... is one of laws and not of men (Aristotle, Madison-Adams).
(5) It is the law, stupid (American popular saying).
(6) Law is the command of the sovereign (Hobbes, Austin).
(7) The law is an ass (English proverb).
(8) *Summum ius, summa iniuria* (highest law, highest injustice) (Roman proverb quoted by Cicero in *De officiis* Bk. I, 10, 30).
(9) Law and lawyers are hired guns (American proverb).
(10) Law is reason (Cicero).
(11) Law is like a door in an open field. Why would you go through the door? (Bulgarian saying, possibly apocryphal).
(12) Law is what the courts will do (Holmes).
(13) Men are bad and made good by laws (Machiavelli).
(14) Law is a system of norms (rules) (Kelsen, Hart).
(15) Law is the art of the good and the equitable (Celsus).

Let us begin with the image of Justitia, the goddess of justice. She is blindfolded, carrying some scales in one hand while holding a sword in the other. I vividly remember my first encounter with her in a court building in Bavaria when I, as a pre-school kid, accompanied my father to a court. I asked him (a lawyer and soon-to-be judge) who that lady was and why she was blindfolded. He answered that it was the figure of Justice and that she was weighing, for example, the – guilt or innocence – of an accused while not wanting to be distracted. The sword then symbolized the power of punishing wrongdoers. I was impressed and kept silent for quite some time (not my usual behaviour at that age). When we finally left the courthouse, I asked my father how Justitia could know how the weighing came out, since she could not see. My father laughed without giving me an answer and, I guess, that was one of the reasons I tried to find out later how "judging" actually occurs.

But besides inducing my irreverent question, this example also shows the polyvalence of the symbol and the ambivalence of law mediating between opposites. Thus the "equality" of the parties or subjects is created by elevating the law to a goddess "above" the contending parties. The close attention to the facts of the case and their "weight" is paired with keeping other distractions at a distance, symbolized by the blindfold. This impartiality is then linked to "supremacy," symbolized by the sword "besides" the law. But this "blindness" of Justitia also gives rise to the complaint in the Roman saying that "the highest law is the highest injustice," or in the English saw that "the law is an ass." Both complaints are not so much directed against the blindness or bias of a court in appreciating the facts as they are concerned with the construction of the law itself, that is its interpretation, the *callida iuris interpretatio* that Cicero mentions,[10] and that blindly deciding by rules instead of tempering their application with equity leads to absurdities.

Utilizing the disjuncture between foreground and background is another way of resolving the tensions within "the law," as can be seen from the Antigone vs. Gorgias argument about "nature" lending validity to law. The tangible law can then only be understood as a reflection of a deeper order that can be somehow intuited and that serves as its ultimate foundation. It is the "facticity" of the ontological order that permeates the cosmos (as in Antigone) and it is the naturalness of desires (Gorgias) that leads to the opposite conclusion of what "nature" commands. On the one hand we arrive at "natural law" and a notion of law as universal reason, exemplified by the Stoic teachings. On the other hand we encounter here the "realist" position that law is command, either by nature or by public authority, and is not rooted in some universal conception of "justice." "*Ius*" derives from "*iussum*" (the commanded), not from *iustum* (the just), that is Hobbes, Austin's command theory of law. Aristotle and Machiavelli provide some important variations on these positions.

Aristotle points to the importance of practical reason in buttressing arguments when dealing with particular cases. They cannot adduce universality and necessity as guarantors for the validity claims underlying the arguments. Aristotle also "solves" the problem of the inevitably coercive dimension of law by hiding it behind his new version of the traditional topos of *nomos basileus* (the law is king), which in republican thought[11] became the "rule of law" trope, invoked in *Marbury* v. *Madison*.[12] The difference between the ruler and the ruled is effaced by making the law the ruler, rather than any particular person or faction. Instead of "custom," law "rules" now and does so in a different fashion, as we shall see.

Machiavelli – deeply pessimistic about human nature, especially in the absence of functioning political structures which allow for the development of stable expectations – counsels the prince to err on the side of *oderint dum metuant* (they might hate me as long as they fear me), but does not exclude that civic virtues and obedience might develop by contrivance. Men are bad by nature but can be made to act properly by effective laws. In a way, Aristotle and Machiavelli, despite their many differences, develop a distinct political approach to law and legislation.

[10] Cicero, *De officiis*, Bk 1, 33.

[11] For a good discussion especially about the contribution of republican theory to the project of modernity, see Nicholas Onuf, *The Republican Legacy in International Thought* (Cambridge University Press, 1998). For an imaginative use of republican theorizing see Daniel Deudney, *Bounding Power* (Princeton University Press, 2007).

[12] See the interesting discussion in Paul Kahn, *The Reign of Law* (New Haven: Yale University Press, 1997).

The saying "it is the law, stupid" calls attention to the fact that law always attempts to internalize the criterion of its validity, although it can do so only after certain "social facts" are in place that recognize its autonomy. At a minimum, a list of authoritative "sources" becomes necessary, or we assume a normative "system" that allows us to interpret the question of validity as one of the genesis of norm creation. Kelsen's construction of law, as a system derived from a basic norm (*Grundnorm*) that is beyond the law, presupposes the state, not only as a normative idea but also as a "social fact." Hart's somewhat more flexible version of law as a system of primary and secondary rules – also sometimes possessing a "rule of recognition" – follows the same logic. Finally, the notion of law as an autopoietic system (Luhmann, Teubner) based on the code of legal/illegal dispenses with the notion of a "state" as the ultimate source of law. Instead, it focuses on *functionally* organized (rather than segmentary) systems that autonomously create their elements through autopoiesis. Law has now lost much of its power to steer *ex ante* through expectations, but the important sites where law now does its work are the various dispute resolution mechanisms that are part of increasingly "free standing" regimes, particularly in the international arena.

The focus on adjudication and courts as creators of law rather than mere norm appliers has, of course, been an old theme of legal realism. It was reflected in Justice Holmes' dictum that the "law is what the courts will do." It addresses not only the problem of the open texture of rules – and the later controversy concerning rules vs. principles that it spawned – it also radically reduces the notion of legal reasoning to a "theory" of the motivation of judges. While in the former version of reasoning law could still be understood as a craft or "art" – eschewing the hypertrophic pretence of "theory" – in Holmes' realism law's mission is increasingly reduced to a "prediction" of the choices of certain persons in privileged positions sitting in high courts. Thus realism raises questions as to whether issues of interpretation can be reduced without further ado to idiosyncratic psychological factors. After all, Supreme Court judges deciding a case have to argue *the law* in order to get a coalition together, rather than to make wagers on how a bad breakfast or a quarrel at home might influence a judge's vote.

The open texture of legal rules and principles is of course an important issue, particularly when combined with Holmes' "bad man" walking the line. The statements, such as "law being a door in an open field" and of 'law and lawyers being hired guns," belong here. The former is a (probably) apocryphal Bulgarian saying; the latter addresses the perhaps too easily assumed identification of law with justice, returning us to law's "darker" side.

Especially in international relations, many hopes were placed on the "further development" of law that would cure the imperfections of the existing international order. But often the only explanation came from some bad philosophy of history, making short shrift of analysing the possibilities and limitations of law. Now that human rights and the worldwide offering of legal services have become one of the last growth industries of post-modernity, the pious hopes of law "finally" speaking "truth to power" have turned out to be like the former prophesies of communist leaders concerning the date when socialism will mutate into the secular paradise of communism. While we of course hope for the best, we ought to be a bit more attentive to the dangers that the future could resemble more a Foucauldian nightmare than the happy utopia where the lawyer (environmental lawyer, or human rights lawyer, of course) has replaced the businessman as the successful professional, which once was the storyline in American sitcoms.

The allure of "professionalism"

Lawyers are now everywhere, such as in advocacy networks, or in the "disaggregated" networks of states. They even serve as legal counsellors designing policies, circumventing elementary safeguards of the rule of law, as the US "torture memoranda" show.[13] Thus law and its practitioners have arrived and it therefore seems cold comfort to argue, as David Kennedy does, that they should be less defensive but take responsibility for their actions,[14] given the fact that professionals in positions of public power have to contend in an arena in which survival is secured largely through cunning, coalition building, and manipulation.[15] These tendencies are exacerbated by:

> four management practices, which Gabris identifies as a functional organization design, hierarchical authority systems, defensive routines, and socializing forces. To overcome these obstacles the public manager faces formidable risks.[16]

Experiences with whistleblowers have not been too encouraging and even engineers who possessed highly valued technical knowledge had a tough time getting a hearing, as the Columbia Shuttle disaster showed.[17] Besides, as practitioners of law, which is an adversarial system, lawyers can "contribute" only

[13] See the collection of essays by Jeremy Waldron, *Torture, Terror and Trade-Offs* (Oxford University Press, 2010).

[14] David Kennedy: "Reassessing International Humanitarianism" in Ann Orford (ed.), *International Law and Its Others* (Cambridge University Press, 2006), 131–55. See also David Kennedy, *The Dark Sides of Virtue: Reassessing International Humanitarianism* (Princeton University Press, 2004), Chapter 4.

[15] G. T. Gabris, "Beyond Conventional Management Practices: Shifting Organizational Values," in J. S. Bowman (ed.), *Ethical Frontiers in Public Management* (San Francisco: Jossey Bass 1991), 205–24.

[16] April Hajka-Ekins, "Ethics in In-service Training," in Terry Cooper, *Handbook of Administrative Ethics*, 2nd edn. (New York: Marcel Dekker, 2001), 79–103, at 87.

[17] Columbia Accident Investigation Board, *Final Report on the Columbia Space Shuttle Accident* (Washington DC: Government Printing Office, 2003).

according to the "standards" of their profession, which are likely to conflict with their mission as public servants. This means they "contribute" by doing "their job," that is to more or less aggressively manipulate "the facts and the law to suit their clients' purposes."[18] We may well not agree with Lord Brougham's famous remark that a "lawyer by the sacred duty which he owes to his client … knows in the discharge of that office only one person in the world – that client and none other." His interest he must pursue "by all expedient means and reckless of the consequences."[19] Surprisingly, however, there is scant attention paid to this and other "structural" problems in most discussions, which often engage in a nostalgic view of times past[20] despite an ample literature on the problems of the "professions,"[21] some exceptions notwithstanding.[22] Thus, Bruce Ackerman has recently pointed to the rapid growth of the Office of Legal Council in the Justice Department and of the Office of Counsel to the President in the White House and considered it one of the factors that is cutting the US presidency loose from its constitutional moorings and subverting the rule of law by questionable uses of constitutional and international law, bending both to the wishes of the client.[23]

Since judges or juries are of course not constrained in the same way, high hopes were therefore pinned on international tribunals to sort out "who did what to whom," particularly in cases of mass atrocities. But even here the assessment is now, after the experience with the International Criminal Tribunal for the former Yugoslavia (ICTY) and the Milosevic trial, much less optimistic. Even the hope for establishing at least a reliable historical record through court proceedings is no longer a safe assumption, after Nancy Combs'[24] scathing attack on the fact-finding processes of the Criminal Tribunal for Rwanda, the Special Court for Sierra Leone, and the East Timor Special Panels for Serious Crimes. Some of the deeply flawed procedures reported by Combs would be laughable, were they not tragic subversions of elemental procedural justice. Combs still supports international tribunals and "explains" the acceptance

[18] Daniel Markovits, *A Modern Legal Ethics: Adversary Advocacy in a Democratic Age* (Princeton University Press, 2008), 3.

[19] As quoted in *ibid.*, at 7.

[20] See the interesting "Memoirs" of Sol Linowitz, *The Betrayed Profession: Lawyering at the End of the 20th Century* (New York: Charles Scribner's Sons, 1994).

[21] See Andrew Abbot's pathbreaking study, *The Systems of Professions* (University of Chicago Press, 1988). See also Eliot Freidson, *Professionalism* (University of Chicago Press, 2001).

[22] See e.g. Mary Ann Glendon, *A Nation Under Lawyers: How the Crisis of the Legal Profession is Transforming American Society* (New York: Farrar, Straus, Giroux, 1994).

[23] Bruce Ackerman, *The Decline and Fall of the American Republic* (Cambridge, MA: Harvard University Press, 2010), particularly Chapter 4, also calling attention to the dubious practices of "signing statements" and memoranda produced by the Office of Legal Counsel (OLC) of which the torture memoranda became infamous.

[24] Nancy Combs, *Fact Finding Without Facts: The Uncertain Evidentiary Foundations of International Criminal Convictions* (Cambridge University Press, 2010).

of flawed evidence with the continued popularity of the "collective" criminal liability, a notion that was purportedly discredited by the Nuremberg tribunal. But given its powerful hold on our political and legal imagination, what we are likely to get is retribution, but retribution at the price of defeating essential elements of the rule of law.

Besides, "the law," even when applied to less controversial problems, is hardly a neutral tool, as it ensconces specific interests and endows them with privileged status. When, for example, the rule of law is "operationalized" as protection of private property, contract enforcement, and functioning markets, attention is diverted from the "planned misery" of the "business as usual" visited on populations by domestic and international institutions. Naomi Klein has described this phenomenon in the case of Argentina and Chile during the military juntas.[25] Worse still, many of those practices are cemented in the charters of global institutions and imposed on "unruly" subjects, be they failed states, recalcitrant firms, or traditional social arrangements.[26]

By "naturalizing" the ensuing malaise and treating it as "normal" or just like a natural event – such as a catastrophic earthquake rather than a man-made disaster – law and "best practices" become endowed with the aura of universality and necessity. Here the smug accommodation of the "facts" is powerfully reinforced by some theoretical pretences of social science. Both then work as if hand in glove with legal expertise when drafting the proper "policy responses." In this context Susan Marks aptly remarked in regard to human rights: "For all the insistence that human rights abuses and vulnerabilities … are man-made disasters, the drift of our analysis is that natural disaster is the model on which the explanatory effort is imaginatively constructed."[27] This leads not only to a misdiagnosis and policy failure, it also systematically undercuts our ability to "learn." It is indeed cold comfort that legal professionals show only the same pathologies with which other members of the "helping professions," such as administrators, economic advisers (particularly in economic development), and members of humanitarian intervention had to struggle.[28]

[25] Naomi Klein, *The Shock Doctrine* (London: Penguin, 2007).

[26] Thus the tiger states, which were treated nearly as poster children for economic development – and with which "liberal" states like the USA did brisk business – become nearly overnight exemplars of crony capitalism when they refused to open their markets for certain financial instruments. See Rodney Hall, "The Discursive Demolition of the Asian Development Model," *International Studies Quarterly*, vol. 47 no. 1 (2003), 71–99.

[27] Susan Marks, "Human Rights and Root Causes," *Modern Law Review*, vol. 74, no. 1 (2011): 57–78, at 78.

[28] See e.g. Laura Zanotti (who had been part of several UN operations), "Imagining Democracy, Building Unsustainable Institutions: the UN Peace Keeping Operation in Haiti," *Security Dialogue*, vol. 39, no. 5 (2008): 539–61.

A more critical approach – rather than just reiterating the "pure" motives of the humanitarians[29] – involves us in difficult assessments of how action and knowledge interact, how knowledge is produced and separated from the "irrelevant" or even from "non-sense," and how the boundaries of the "known" and the "unknown," the "false" and the "true," of the "mistake," of the "misrepresentation," or of a "lie" are drawn. These distinctions are particularly difficult in the practical world where we do not deal with a fixed reality but with a *World of our Making*.[30] In this world the usual risk models and management practices quickly lose their purchase, because the boundaries between risk assessment and risk management become frequently unclear and interact in complex ways, as the discussions about genetically modified foods before the World Trade Organization (WTO) show.[31] Even more importantly, certain things cannot be known, as Keynes argued in regard to genuine uncertainty, such as the stock prices of one year hence, for example. Nevertheless, the common practice has been to treat uncertainty analogously to natural, but extremely rare events for which nevertheless some distribution exists, or we simply rely on mystic charts and trends. Thus, a probability can be assigned and a specifiable "risk" can be hedged.

If the above thumbnail sketch of some root images and conceptualization of law has shown anything, it is the complexity of the legal *problematique*, which cuts across various disciplinary understandings. Furthermore, given these difficulties, we cannot just clear the ground by some definitional fiat, as all the images are suggestive and necessitate further inquiry. Since neither a Procrustean solution is available, nor a mode of inquiry seems promising that leaves the explication of the concept solely within the remit of "law," we have to face up to this difficulty and opt for a broader interdisciplinary approach, which is admittedly a tricky undertaking.

The second lesson seems to be that we must not err on the other side either, by believing that a new "theory," satisfying the traditional epistemological criteria, will be of much help in understanding the distinct problems of praxis. Here traditional jurisprudence has insisted on both the contextual, contingent nature of action, and on certain important aspects of praxis, such as the ascription of responsibility, and the distinct mode of reasoning arising out of the need to move back and forth between facts and norms. This mode of thinking does not fit the template of either deductive or inductive inferences, but

29 For a critical assessment of humanitarianism as an ideology, see Janice Stein, "Background and Knowledge in the Foreground: Conversations about Competent Practice in 'Sacred Space,'" in Emmanuel Adler and Vincent Pouliot (eds.), *International Practices* (Cambridge University Press, 2011), 87–107.

30 Nicholas Onuf, *World of Our Making* (Columbia: University of South Carolina Press, 1989).

31 See e.g. the interesting account by Mark Pollack and Gregory Shaffer, *When Cooperation Fails: The International Law and Politics of Genetically Modified Foods* (Oxford University Press, 2009).

proceeds according to axiological steps of exclusions, so as to arrive at a conclusion that can muster assent. Pierce spoke in this context once of "abduction," and although I have profited from the American pragmatists,[32] I do not want now just to "apply" their "theory" or approach to law in accordance with the "law of the hammer."

To misconceive this type of reflection on practical matters as an enterprise akin to an ideal theory à la Rawls,[33] or in terms of a "felicific calculus" à la Bentham, or of specifying the "truth conditions" for (legal) assertions (as is the case in the early Habermas[34]), appears to me a problematic undertaking. Despite all of its technical vocabulary, I claim that law proceeds according to the *communication model of ordinary language*. I, therefore, do not think that the puzzles of epistemology that are created by the *Verhexung der Sprache*, as Wittgenstein called it, are susceptible to the logical treatment of meta-languages by Tarski or the early Wittgenstein[35] or the tools of the "scientific method" (whatever that might mean). I rather follow a form of analysis that Wittgenstein develops in his later work, which takes everyday language seriously and employs a mode of reflection that centres on *the use of concepts* rather than on their mere reference.

Since we can never start from an absolute point that allows us a look at the world "from nowhere" - especially the practical and historical world because we are always in the "midst of things" - we have to pay particular attention to context and the pre-understandings or "prejudices," as Hume or Gadamer would call them. Here the narratives of "progress" and 'universality" are of special importance and have traditionally given "law," particularly in the international arena, much of its meaning. Consequently, law and its role have to be examined more critically by also subjecting these *narratives* to scrutiny. This is all the more important since present international legal scholarship has been largely liberated from formalist constraints, and thus can freely speculate and postulate the existence or the "emergence" of norms that allegedly reflect certain "values." However, frequently this speculation is entirely separated from the inquiry into settled practices and the silent assumptions underlying the narrative of progress, or of "emergence," or the alleged universality of values, are then supposed to provide the proof. For example, it is true that the "publicity" of law, has not only been, since Kant,

32 See my "Ten Points to Ponder about Pragmatism," in Harry Bauer and Elisabetta Brighi (eds.), *Pragmatism and International Relations* (London: Routledge, 2008), 11–25; Joerg Friedrichs and Friedrich Kratochwil, "On Acting and Knowing," *International Organization*, vol. 63 (Fall 2009), 701–31.

33 John Rawls, *A Theory of Justice* (Cambridge, MA: Harvard University Press, 1971).

34 Juergen Habermas, *Theory of Communicative Action* (Boston: Beacon 1984).

35 However, one proposition of the *Tractatus* foreshadows the later shift by denying the possibility of getting to "the world" without the mediation of language. Ludwig Wittgenstein, *Tractatus Logico Philosophicus* (New York: Routledge, 2001), at 5.6.2.

one of the fundamental values, but there is also the question that whether the mere publicness, such as promulgation by the media or postings on the Internet, can, in the absence of a genuine "public," measure up to the requirements of "publicity," which remains doubtful – claims of some global administrative law proponents notwithstanding. Similarly, whether this defect can be cured by the co-optation of some non-governmental organizations (NGOs), which assert to speak for "global civil society," remains to be shown rather than merely (silently) assumed, given the unrepresentative character of these mostly one-issue organizations.[36]

The limits of engagement

The intersection between international law, international relations,[37] political theory, and philosophy has certainly become a heavily travelled site. Jean Cohen's broad-based, spirited interdisciplinary engagement with the global governance school[38] and her sombre assessment that the attack on sovereignty might – intentionally or unintentionally – lead to new forms of unchecked and irresponsible hegemony and global hierarchies while invoking the noble purposes of human rights and constitutionalism but missing the actual opportunities for "constitutionalizing" moves, is perhaps the most noteworthy recent example. But any attempt at providing a comprehensive map of this burgeoning field has to be rejected out of hand because of the sheer impossibility of the task. Any cursory look at the catalogues of the major publishing houses for international law, such as the university presses of Oxford and Cambridge, shows that in the last few years the number of books addressing issues of international law, human rights, international trade law, and so on has exploded. The record is not that different in political science or sociology. Even a summary treatment in terms of certain "issue areas" can only be a thumbnail sketch. Thus the brief discussion below has to be limited to some exemplary works of several genres of analysis. In the discussion I use largely political science as my prism in order to look at work in other disciplines, precisely because the focus of the rest of the book is largely on international law, reversing the order of inquiry.

[36] See e.g. Sebastian Mallaby, "NGOs: Fighting Poverty, Hurting the Poor," *Foreign Policy* (Sept/Oct 2004), 50–8; see also the review essays by Kenneth Anderson, "What NGO Accountability Means and Does Not Mean," *American Journal of International Law*, vol. 103, no. 1 (2003), 170–8; Steve Charnovitz "Recent Scholarship on NGOs," *American Journal of International Law*, vol. 103, no. 4 (2009), 777–84.

[37] See e.g. David Armstrong, Theo Farrell and Helene Lambert, *International Law and International Relations* (Cambridge University Press, 2007).

[38] Jean Cohen, *Globalization and Sovereignty: Rethinking Legality, Legitimacy and Constitutionalism* (Cambridge University Press, 2012).

There is on the one hand the perennial issue of how ethics and politics relate to each other, exemplified for example by Cochran[39] and Shapcott,[40] and on the other hand an emerging interest in the historical roots[41] of the conventions of the state system and its transformations. This concern was once largely limited to the English school but has now been broadened to include the history of ideas. Here the two anthologies by Jahn[42] and by Brown, Rengger, and Nardin[43] come to mind, but it also includes more specialized analyses, such as finding the religious roots, or formative ideas underlying the state system, as exemplified by Philipott,[44] Reus-Smit,[45] and Ian Clark,[46] or trace the specific "constitutional moments" (Ikenberry[47]), which add historical detail to a formerly rather crude power transition model of systemic change. These studies have exploded the Westphalian myth by painstaking historical research (Ossiander[48]) or by further conceptual elaboration, as is the case with Beaulac's magisterial study[49] of the historical changes in the meaning of "sovereignty," moving from semantic preoccupations of the meaning of a term, to one of "semiotics," that is focusing on the "social effects of words and expressions."[50]

A second strand concerns the chances and limitations of the cosmopolitan project by either a conceptual analysis of the semantic field, such as that by Walker,[51] or by examining the effectiveness and necessary reforms of existing international institutions, as Held,[52] Archibugi,[53] and others have attempted. This type of work then meets up on certain points with a huge literature on global justice that only recently, after Rawls' *Law of Peoples*,[54] has attended to the

39 Molly Cochran, *Normative Theory in International Relations* (Cambridge University Press, 1999).

40 Richard Shapcott, *International Ethics: A Critical Introduction* (Oxford: Polity, 2007).

41 Jens Bartelson, *A Genealogy of Sovereignty* (Cambridge University Press, 1995).

42 Beate Jahn (ed.), *Classical Theory in International Relations* (Cambridge University Press).

43 Chris Brown, Nicholas Rengger and Terry Nardin, *International Relations in Political Thought: Texts from the Ancient Greeks to the First World War* (Cambridge University Press, 2002).

44 Daniel Philipott, *Revolutions in Sovereignty* (Princeton University Press, 2001).

45 Christian Reus-Smit, *The Moral Purpose of the State* (Princeton University Press, 1999).

46 Ian Clark, *The Post Cold War Order* (Oxford University Press, 2001); see also his *Hegemony in International Society* (Oxford University Press, 2011).

47 John Ikenberry, *After Victory* (Princeton University Press, 2000).

48 Andreas Ossiander, *The States System of Europe 1640–1990* (Oxford: Clarendon, 1994).

49 Stephane Beaulac, *The Power of Language in the Making of International Law* (Leiden: Martinus Nijhoff, 2004).

50 *Ibid.* at 42.

51 R. B. J. Walker, *After the Globe, Before the World* (London: Routledge, 2009).

52 David Held, *Democracy and the Global Order: From the Modern State to Global Governance* (Stanford University Press, 1996).

53 Daniele Archibugi, *The Global Commonwealth of Citizens: Toward Cosmopolitan Democracy* (Princeton University Press, 2008).

54 John Rawls, *The Law of Peoples* (Cambridge, MA: Harvard University Press, 1999).

problem of the appropriate criteria for global institutions. The earlier attempts were largely devoted to distributive issues, such as poverty and subsistence.[55] Here the bridge to the international human rights discourse becomes clear,[56] as do the substantive links to questions of citizenship,[57] the status of refugees[58] and migrants, and the implications of increasingly multicultural societies[59] for personal and collective identities.[60]

The third category comprises writings on the role of force. While formerly issues of the prohibition of the resort to force, of the justifiability of deterrence[61] and questions of the just war,[62] the *ius in bello*, and of "sanctions"[63] took centre stage, now humanitarian intervention[64] and UN peace-keeping figure prominently.[65] Similarly, problematic claims occasioned by scenarios of "ticking bombs"[66] and the war on terror[67] are now used for justifying preventive force.[68] On the one hand, these studies seem to provide a powerful counterpoint to the notion of a "responsibility to protect"[69] that vests the international community with residual rights. On the other hand they also show the recent shift from the

[55] Henry Sue, *Basic Rights: Subsistence, Affluence and US Foreign Policy* (Princeton University Press, 1980). For a useful collection of essays see Thomas Pogge and Darrel Moellendorf (eds.), *Global Justice: Seminal Essays* (St Paul: Paragon, 2008).

[56] See e.g. Philip Alston (ed.), *Peoples' Rights* (Oxford University Press, 2001).

[57] T. Alexander Aleinikoff and Douglas Klusmeyer (eds.), *Citizenship Today: Global Perspectives and Practice* (Washington DC: Carnegie Endowment for International. Peace, 2001).

[58] See Emma Haddad, *The Refugee in International Society* (Cambridge University Press, 2008).

[59] See Will Kymlicka, *Multicultural Citizenship* (Oxford: Clarendon, 1996); Jacob Levy, *The Multiculturalism of Fear* (Oxford University Press, 2000).

[60] See Seyla Benhabib, *The Claims of Culture: Equality and Diversity in the Global Era* (Princeton University Press, 2002); see also Yosef Lapid and Friedrich Kratochwil (eds.), *The Return of Culture and Identity in IR Theory* (Boulder: Lynn Rienner, 1996).

[61] Joseph Nye, *Nuclear Ethics* (New York: Free Press 1986).

[62] Michael Walzer, *Just and Unjust Wars*, 2nd edn. (New York: Basic Books, 1977).

[63] Daniel Drenzer, *The Sanctions Paradox: Economic Statecraft and International Relations* (Cambridge University Press, 1999); Meghan O'Sullivan, *Shrewd Sanctions: Statecraft and State Sponsors of Terrorism* (Washington DC: Brookings, 2003).

[64] See e.g. Nicholas Wheeler, *Saving Strangers: Humanitarian Intervention in International Society* (Oxford University Press, 2002); Terry Nardin and Melissa Williams, *Humanitarian Intervention* (New York; NYU Press, 2005).

[65] Jeremy Farall and Kim Rubinstein (eds.), *Sanctions, Accountability and Governance in a Globalized World* (Cambridge University Press, 2009).

[66] See e.g. Alan Dershowitz, *Shouting Fire: Civil Liberties in a Turbulent Age* (Boston: Little Brown, 2002).

[67] Michael Gross, *Moral Dilemmas of Modern War: Torture, Assassination and Blackmail in an Age of Asymmetric Conflict* (Cambridge University Press, 2010).

[68] Abraham D. Sofaer, *The Best Defense: Legitimacy and Preventive Force* (Stanford: Hoover Institution, 2010).

[69] Alex Bellamy, *The Responsibility to Protect* (Oxford: Polity, 2009).

previous prohibition on the use of force – never, of course, achieved in practice – to the justification for *using force*.

Nevertheless, mainstream international relations (IR) is still largely concerned with the emergence and diffusion of "cosmopolitan" norms and human rights, which is still the predominant but not exclusive domain of constructivists of various stripes. The interaction of global norms and domestic systems usually offers the prism though which the norm dynamic is analysed. Here the work of Keck and Sikkink,[70] Risse *et al.*,[71] Finnemore,[72] Klotz,[73] Burgerman,[74] Price,[75] but also Simmons[76] (looking at domestic mobilization) or Diehl and Ku (examining norm-change systemically in terms of shocks that punctuate the prevailing equilibrium)[77] can be placed.

In a fourth group we could collect those works that focus on specific institutions such as the WTO,[78] or the role of courts as examined by Alter[79] or Stone Sweet,[80] or of governmental networks, which Slaughter[81] or Raustiala[82] investigated.

A fifth cluster, which sometimes overlaps with the cosmopolitan project,[83] rethinks the "state," such as the work of Shaw[84] or, in quite a different fashion,

[70] Margaret Keck and Kathyn Sikkink, *Activists Beyond Borders* (Ithaca: Cornell University Press, 1998). See also Sikkink's more recent work *The Justice Cascade: How Human Rights Prosecutions are Changing World Politics* (New York: Norton, 2011).

[71] Thomas Risse, Stephen Ropp and Kathryn Sikkink (eds.), *The Power of Human Rights: International Norms and Domestic Change* (Cambridge University Press, 1999).

[72] Martha Finnemore, *Rules for the World* (Ithaca: Cornell University Press, 2004).

[73] Audie Klotz, *Norms in International Relations: The Struggle Against Apartheid* (Ithaca: Cornell University Press, 1999).

[74] Susan Burgerman, *Moral Victories: How Activists Provoke Multilateral Action* (Ithaca: Cornell University Press, 2001).

[75] Richard Price, *Moral Limit and Possibility in World Politics* (Cambridge University Press, 2008).

[76] Beth Simmons, *Mobilizing for Human Rights: International Law in Domestic Politics* (Cambridge University Press, 2009).

[77] Paul Diehl and Charlotte Ku, *The Dynamics of International Law* (Cambridge University Press, 2010).

[78] John Barton, Judith Goldstein, Timothy Jostling and Richard Steinberg, *The Evolution of the Trade Regime: Politics, Law and Economics of GATT and the WTO* (Princeton University Press, 2006).

[79] Karen Alter, *The European Court's Political Power* (Oxford University Press, 2010).

[80] See e.g. Alec Stone Sweet, *The Judicial Construction of Europe* (Oxford University Press, 2004).

[81] Ann Marie Slaughter, *A New World Order* (Princeton University Press, 2005).

[82] Kal Raustiala, "Trans-governmental Networks and the Future of International Law," *Virginia Journal of International Law*, vol. 43 no. 1 (2002/2003), 1–93.

[83] See Richard Falk, *On Humane Governance: Towards a New Global Politics* (University Park: Pennsylvania State University Press, 1995).

[84] Martin Shaw, *Theory of the Global State* (Cambridge University Press, 2000).

that of Fraser.[85] Sometimes the authors in this group emphasize new organizational forms and informal processes of law-making,[86] raising issues of global governance,[87] especially also in the context of European multilevel governance.[88] While most proponents seem to adhere to a managerial perspective in which "muddling through" seems the only feasible alternative, some opposition can be seen from the political "right" – stressing the increasing loss of "sovereignty," as exemplified by Rabkin[89] – as well as from the left, which sees the governance in a more Foucauldian fashion (Duffield, Zanotti).[90] The first interpretation is of course hotly contested, not only by mainstream liberals[91] but also by some post-modern scholars who seek ways to "constitutionalize"[92] international interactions precisely because of the frictions produced by the inevitable regime collisions.[93] In addition, important "rule of law" values are at stake when law-making gets captured by (transnational) interests and/or is prescribed by the Kantian nightmare of a "benevolent despot."

Finally, there is a group of works focusing on the role of the USA within the international legal order and the non-territorial form of "empire" it has created. The works of Negri and Hardt[94] belong here, as do some more measured criticisms of the US role in the international system,[95] or some of the direct

[85] Nancy Fraser, *Scales of Justice: Re-imagining Political Space in a Globalizing World* (Oxford: Polity, 2008).

[86] Michael Barnett and Raymond Duvall (eds.), *Power in Global Governance* (Cambridge University Press, 2004).

[87] See Robert O' Brien, Ann Marie Goetz, Jan Aart Scholte and Marc Williams, *Contesting Global Governance* (Cambridge University Press, 2000). See also the anthology edited by Deborah Avant, Martha Finnemore and Susan Sell (eds.), *Who Governs the Globe?* (Cambridge University Press, 2010).

[88] Ian Bache and Matthew Flinders (eds.), *Multi-level Governance* (New York: Oxford University Press, 2004).

[89] Jeremy Rabkin, *Law without Nations? Why Constitutional Government Requires Sovereign States* (Princeton University Press, 2005).

[90] Mark Duffield, *Global Governance and the New Wars* (London/New York: Palgrave, 2001).

[91] Jeffrey Dunoff and Joel Trachtman (eds.), *Ruling the World? Constitutionalism, International Law and Global Governance* (Cambridge University Press, 2009).

[92] See in this context the useful collection of essays by Petra Dobner and Martin Laughlin (eds.), *The Twilight of Constitutionalism* (Oxford University Press, 2010).

[93] Andreas Fischer-Lescano and Guenther Teubner, *Zur Fragmentierung des Globalen Rechts* (Frankfurt: Suhrkamp, 2006), expanded version of their "Regime Collision: The Vain Search for Legal Unity in the Fragmentation of Global Law," *Michigan Journal of International Law*, vol. 35, no. 4 (2004), 999–1046. Nico Krisch, *Beyond Constitutionalism: The Pluralist Structure of Postnational Law* (Oxford University Press, 2010).

[94] Michael Hardt and Antonio Negri, *Empire* (Cambridge, MA: Harvard University Press, 2000).

[95] See e.g. Michael Byers and Georg Nolte (eds.), *United States Hegemony and the Foundations of International Law* (Cambridge University Press, 2003).

indictments of US foreign policies, such as intervention,[96] the Gulf War,[97] the use of drones, illegal detentions, or the use of torture.[98]

Given this wide array of topics, approaches, and methodological orientations, as well as "value-preferences," an attempt to find a point from where one can view everything and reduce the analysis to the usual explanation of the "variance" is tempting, as we then could "talk to the choir." But given the bewildering cacophony of voices, such an undertaking is as disingenuous as it is futile. Thus, laying one's cards on the table becomes necessary, and in that case one has to choose wisely, not only one's friends, but also one's "opponents," because one needs sparring partners. Even though it always is easier to knock down straw men than actually engage with opponents who have something to say, this would be a hollow victory and hardly a contribution to the debate. In this sense Nicholas Onuf and I have recently come in for criticism for our constructivist work.[99] Supposedly both of us, but I in particular, "must"[100] be arguing that norms are neutral. Furthermore, since I want to "study behaviour scientifically," my "technical slant"[101] and liberal orientation prevent me from "analyzing change" and understanding "politics."

Obviously, the author is not familiar with the perhaps most quoted article that I wrote with John Ruggie,[102] which attacks the "scientistic" ideal of explanation using norms as causes. Equally puzzling is the charge that my approach cannot account for transformative change,[103] especially since the author claims to have read the article that explicitly deals with that problem.[104] Most of her argument is, perhaps not surprisingly, predicated on something that the author admits "I never said."[105] But never mind; as in the world of love, reality proves

96 See e.g. Max Hilaire, *International Law and the US Military Intervention in the Western Hemisphere* (The Hague: Kluwer, 1997).

97 See Phil Shiner and Andrew Williams (eds.), *The Iraq War and International Law* (Oxford: Hart, 2008).

98 See Sanford Levinson (ed.), *Torture: A Collection* (Oxford University Press, 2004). See also Vittorio Bufacchi and Jean Maria Arrigo, "Torture, Terrorism and the State: A Refutation of the Ticking Bomb Argument," *Journal of Applied Philosophy*, vol. 23, no. 3 (2006), 355–73.

99 Adriana Sinclair, *International Relations Theory and International Law* (Cambridge University Press, 2010).

100 *Ibid.* at 26, but see also p. 32: "nor are the values of the legal system neutral as Kratochwil himself admits." Oh well, perhaps values are different even though as "principles" they do much work within a legal system, as I tried to show.

101 *Ibid.* at 25.

102 Friedrich Kratochwil and John Ruggie, "International Organization: The State of the Art on the Art of the State," *International Organization*, vol. 40, no. 4 (1986), 753–75.

103 Sinclair, *International Relations Theory and International Law*, 25: "contestation can only happen at the margins, otherwise our social world would become meaningless."

104 See Rey Koslowski and Friedrich Kratochwil, "Understanding Changing International Relations: The Soviet Empire's Demise and the International System," *International Organization*, vol. 48, no. 2 (1994), 215–48.

105 Sinclair, *International Relations Theory and International Law* at ftn 103.

nothing. I just "have" to be a "liberal" (which is a true "first" for me) and those of us who thought that politics and the *res publica* are about something that we all have in common, and that are not "private" (or to use the Greek word, is only a concern for the "*idiotes*" who lives in his private world), have got it wrong all along. It is, therefore, about time that we are told that what is "political is essentially personal."[106] Of course this is quite different from saying – as I always have done – that politics is about making *binding* decisions in the face of inevitable disagreement and the *unavailability of an algorithm* (*pace* Condorcet and Arrow).[107] Were these criticisms just an unfortunate derailment, one would not have to worry about them. Unfortunately, it seems to me symptomatic of a more general "professional" deformation, which has become more pronounced over the last few decades, as the philosopher Harry Frankfurt[108] has argued.

But let me return to the issue of the limits of this book. Given my predicament, decisions about limitations have to be made and must be justified. One limitation emerges from the subject itself, that is the appraisal of the role of law in a globalized world. As such, the debates about fragmentation and constitutionalization, about free-standing regimes, and the emergence of a global administrative law, provide the obvious starting points, as does the growth of the human rights discourse and its transformative impact on constitutional and traditional international law and law-making. Of course, taking these three paired debates as the "stakes" that delimit my field of inquiry does not mean that others could not have been chosen. Thus, one topic certainly short-changed here is the law of

[106] *Ibid.* at 35.

[107] For a good critical discussion of my work see Stefano Guzzini, "De gustibus (valoribus) est disputandum: Friedrich Kratochwil contra Realpolitik without Politics, Theory without Reflexivity, Science without Judgment," in Oliver Kessler, Rodney Hall, Cecilia Lynch and Nicholas Onuf (eds.), *On Rules Politics and Knowledge: Friedrich Kratochwil, International Relations and Domestic Affairs* (Now York: Palgrave-Macmillan, 2010), 23–36.

[108] Harry Frankfurt, *On Bullshit* (Princeton University Press, 2005), at 54f; 56; 63; 65.

> Since bullshit need not be false, it differs from lies in its mis-representational intent. The bullshitter may not deceive us, or even intend to do so, either about the facts or about what he takes the facts to be. What he does necessarily attempt to deceive us about, is his enterprise. His only indispensably distinctive characteristic is that in a certain way he misrepresents what he is up to …
>
> The fact about himself that the bull-shitter hides … is that the truth values of his statements are of no central interest to him … He just picks them out, or makes them up to suit his purpose …
>
> Thus the production of bullshit is stimulated whenever a person's obligations or opportunities to speak about some topic exceed his knowledge of the facts relevant to that topic … This discrepancy is common in public life …
>
> One response to the loss of confidence has been a retreat from the discipline required by dedication to the ideal of correctness, to a quite different sort of discipline, which is imposed by pursuit of an alternative ideal of sincerity. Rather than seeking primarily to arrive at accurate representations of a common world, the individual turns toward trying to provide honest representations of himself.

armed conflict,[109] and another one is the changing law of state and diplomatic immunity (only cursorily treated in Meditation 5), leading directly to the issues of personal responsibility for criminal conduct under international law.

There are two short, although perhaps not very satisfying answers to these queries. One is that raising both issues would have exploded the limits that publishers as well as the attention span of the audience place on an author. It is no accident that traditionally the law of war has been discussed separately. While this separation was largely the result of the traditional dichotomy between war and peace as exclusive "states," the breakdown of this conceptual boundary has certainly not made things easier for the contemporary analyst. But precisely because the traditional justification has lost much of its force – given the various in-between states we face nowadays – the "pragmatic" one, of not opening up all controversies for inspection at the same time, provides a defensible – even if not fully satisfying – rationale. The other "answer" is that the issue of culpability of state representatives has been a topic that I am investigating in my work on practices, on which I have been working for a long time. So rather than duplicating what I want to say there, I save my "last ink" for that work in the hope that it will sometime soon become the companion volume to these Meditations.

An outline of the argument

With these considerations in mind, I want to briefly outline the following meditations and show how they fit into a larger argument. Meditation 1 is devoted to two interrelated points: one, the justification of an interdisciplinary approach and two, the elaboration of a reflective mode of addressing practical problems. Praxis, I argue, cannot be subjected to the traditional theoretical standards articulated in taxonomies, and field-independent epistemological criteria of the "scientific" method, that informs the dominant "unity of science" position.

I begin with a criticism of some interdisciplinary efforts of international law and international relations analysis, and then add a more analytical argument by examining the epistemological ideal that since Descartes has dominated our thinking of how knowledge is produced. I argue that the "epistemological ideal" based on field-independent criteria of "universal" reason cannot make good on its promise for "incontrovertible" foundations. This is borne out not only by the actual production of knowledge that differs from the "epistemological ideal," as Thomas Kuhn and the "science studies" from Bourdieu[110] to Latour[111] and Knorr-Cetina[112] have shown, it also suggests that the realm of praxis differs

[109] For a useful recent compendium of articles on this topic see Tarcisio Gazzini and Nicholas Tsagourias (eds.), *The Use of Force in International Law* (Burlington: Ashgate, 2012).

[110] Pierre Bourdieu, *Outline of a Theory of Practice* (Cambridge University Press, 1977); Pierre Bourdieu, *Distinction: A Social Critique of the Judgment of Taste* (London: Routledge, 1984).

[111] Bruno Latour and Steve Wolgar, *Laboratory Life* (Princeton University Press, 1986).

[112] Karin Knorr-Cetina, *The Manufacture of Knowledge* (Oxford: Pergamon, 1981).

from that of the noumenal world. In the social world the agreements on the proper *use of concepts* rather than on the existence of "things" or objects of the "world out there" are at issue. In addition, time pressure, information deficiencies, and specific duties owed to those represented make a-historical, universal standards inappropriate. This stance then requires the articulation of an alternative yardstick for practical problems. It is here that the "meditation," that is a form of reflection exemplified by Pascal or Montaigne – and more recently revived by pragmatists and philosophers of ordinary language philosophy – provide a mode of thinking that is serious and stringent without the pretences of "scientific theory" (such as "scientific realism" still pandered by some IR ayatollahs) or even of an "ideal theory" based on a-priori assumptions of reason à la Kant, Rawls, or the early Habermas.

Meditation 2 takes up the theme of meaning as "concepts in use" and attempts to ground such an inquiry in the language philosophy of the later Wittgenstein. In his *Philosophical Investigations* he had given up the project of constituting meaning via reference (as in the earlier *Tractatus*) and developed instead the notion of a "family resemblance," a "grammar," and a "form of life." But before I can take up the issue of norm-use, I have to answer to Kripke's criticism[113] and to some of the ambiguities that surround Wittgenstein's notion of rule following. Many of his examples are derived from mathematics or from "drills," which are inappropriate when dealing with norm-use in contexts requiring interpretation. Here the notion of law as a "tradition" provides me with a foil for getting both to the issue of law as a specialized language – which Koskenniemi also stressed in his restatement of *Apology and Utopia* – and of law's looking back to "sources," precedents, and canonical texts, without, however, being constituted by some form of "historical" interests. This provides me, then, with the tools of revisiting the "concept of law" and in particular the interesting parallels of international law and constitutional law as instantiation of "public law."

Meditation 3 (On constitutions and fragmented orders) follows up on this problem by placing constitutionalism in the wider perspective of the "rule of law" argument, as exemplified in *Marbury* v. *Madison* and the development of constitutional review. Showing the paradoxical implications of a "fixed" and uncontroversial constitution that can be applied to "normal" laws, I examine the problems that arise when "the people" have become the authors of their laws and thus constitute the main danger for their own liberties. By examining *Madison's* "political" rather than conceptual "solution" to the problem – arguing both for the need of agreement in a society, and for the use of "factions" for preventing a tyranny of the majority – I approach the "constitutionalization" debate in international law. Here both the "fragmentation" debate focusing on

[113] See Saul Kripke, *Wittgenstein on Rules and Private Language* (Oxford: Blackwell, 1982).

"free-standing" regimes and the embarrassment of riches created by the multiple dispute resolution forums serve as my focal points. I examine proposals for making the UN Charter or the WTO (through the incorporation of human rights) into some constitution-like framework that would impart some coherence to the international legal order. My sceptical gloss here is that the problem of "incoherence" is less due to the flaws of international legal process, but rather to the poorly institutionalized *political process*. Thus we do not have institutions that could make important choices on priorities in the pursuit of global common goods. Instead, we leave those problems largely to specialized courts or organizations, which necessarily are "bound" by their narrow charts and the specific tasks entrusted to them. Attempts to expand their remit then meets stiff resistance not only from states but also from other courts.

In Meditation 4 (Of experts, helpers, and enthusiasts) I examine the changes in both the practices of law-making and in the role of helpers, experts, and activists who attempt to translate those normative "visions' into actual practice. In this context I deal with norm entrepreneurs and experts who have become participants in normative networks, engaged in monitoring and in law-making, but who increasingly also administer certain programs. I use the traditional categories of the Weberian enthusiast (charismatic leader) and expert (bureaucrat) as my foil in order to show which role they play in contemporary processes of soft law-making, in the case of "sustainable development," and in the area of administering "humanitarian aid" in complex emergencies (East Timor, Haiti, and Kosovo). This then sets the stage for examining the role of "judges" in international courts, in particular the ICTY, in dealing with the "development" of international law by tribunals.

The theme of law-making is continued when in Meditation 5 (The power of metaphors and narratives: systems, teleology, evolution, and the issue of the "global community") I analyse the influence of activist legal scholars on the development of legal doctrine. What interests me here is less the drafted documents, but rather the "frames" that they use and the metaphors that they invoke, in order to provide the normative pull. I argue that the political projects contained in the narratives of a "from–to," or in the focus on "breaks," or in observing "progress," either take some secularized version of Christian eschatology, or Kant's argument of deciphering "nature's plan" (for those having lost faith) as their template.

In this context Luhmann's "system theory" has a special place since it focuses on autonomous autopoietic systems, but also places the development of these systems in the larger narrative of social development from segmented orders to a world society. By unpacking his approach to law and society I try to show that Luhmann uses problematic metaphors and fundamental concepts, such as "function," "evolution," or "communication." He also fails to deal adequately with the issue of why and how the "logic" of the legal code (legal/illegal), which is potentially applicable anywhere, has apparently failed to "win" the hegemonic struggle with the "economy" (based on the code of payment/non-payment), as the "efficient market hypothesis" has attained "moral" authority in neo-liberalism. Thus something more than "structural coupling"[114] seems to be required to explain these developments. I argue that here we encounter the historical political struggles and settlements that define "normalcy" in the way the bounds of sense are drawn and we are enabled to "go on" with our practical life (or prevented from doing so).

Meditation 6 (Cosmopolitanism, publicity, and the emergence of a "global administrative law") is devoted to the global administrative law project that emerged at the intersection of the constitutionalization debate and discussions concerning the autonomous logic of sectors or systems. Three problems arose in this context. First, there was the question of whether a set of quasi free-standing administrative law principles can be identified and used in the absence of constitutional structures that inform administrative law domestically. Some adherents argued that it is "publicity," and the norms supporting this value that can give the Kantian ideal new traction at the global level. But even if non-retroactivity, publication of the laws, and transparency satisfy important rule of law values, the further question arises whether such principles are "democracy- or autonomy-enhancing." Otherwise they could equally well serve Kant's benign despot, whom he so abhorred. Only in the former case can the democratic deficit of many of the supranational law-making processes be remedied through the involvement of groups from civil society.[115] Sometimes the expectations concerning "civil society" involvement are, however, more narrowly conceived and focus only on efficiency and effectiveness gains, as policy implementation should be easier when the "regulated" have a voice in making the rules to which they are subjected.

I examine here participation of civil society groups in some international organizations and at the EU level and show some of their shortcomings. Not only do most civil society groups lack legitimization (aside from ascribing to themselves noble intentions and "good values"), they also serve at the pleasure of the respective bureaucracies and thus *need not be* heard. Two further problems arise. As these organizations are mostly focused on a single issue, they fail to tackle the various trade-offs between for example welfare, labour or environmental issues, human rights and free trade, and so on, which are crucial for policy-making. Furthermore, the notion of "stakeholders" derived from corporatism sits uneasily with the idea of a general "public" that has to be represented when such choices are made. Although some welfare gains can be expected from admitting certain groups to law-making, this inclusion does not

[114] Niklas Luhmann, "Operational Closure and Structural Coupling: the Differentiation of the Legal System," *Cardozo Law Review*, vol. 13 (1992), 1419–41, at 1430.

[115] For a good collection of essays on "global governance" see Edgar Grade and Louis Pauly (eds.), *Complex Sovereignty* (University of Toronto Press, 2005).

necessarily satisfy the democracy-enhancing notion of "publicity," but comes indeed rather close to Kant's benign despot.

The issue of "rights" and in particular human rights is the subject of Meditations 7 (The politics of rights) and 8 (The limits and burdens of rights). Meditation 7 provides the historical background by tracing the emergence of "rights talk" and bringing together several historically distinct strands, the most important being the conjunction of "natural law" with the assertion of "subjective" rights. The latter originally conceived as "birth rights" – in virtue of being a member of a historically constituted society – develop their transforming potential during the US and French Revolutions. They eventually become "human rights" that constitute us as free agents. These rights cannot be "made," but since they are antecedent to any political association, they can only be intuited or "declared," although their connection with particular political projects is clearly visible. I examine this co-constitution of the modern subject and of the political project of founding "rule" on the consent of the governed. I follow this line of argument to show how "human rights" became connected with transnational movements after the Cold War, and how the shift from civil to *human* rights constituted a decisive step in delegitimizing the "communist" utopia, thus preparing the ground for the "silent" revolutions and, more recently, the Arab Spring.

Meditation 8 (The limits and burdens of rights) takes on some of the *conceptual issues* of the rights talk, which sees rights as "trumps" and attempts even (as in Dworkin's case) to build an entire legal and moral theory on them.[116] Such an approach presupposes that the traditional schools of rights, called the "will theory" of rights, which emphasizes individual autonomy and freedom, and the other theory of rights, focusing upon certain important "interests," can be made to fit within the larger Dworkian framework. But not only can this be shown to be an illusion, it also raises the issue of the continuously expanding catalogues or "generations" of rights. They supposedly are of "the same quality, mutually supporting and indivisible," as the Vienna Declaration on Human Rights asserts.[117] That this is, of course, a tall order to fill can be demonstrated by the simple example of two conflicting rights when no "lexical ordering" or appeals to the "natural order of things" are possible. Rights must then be "weighted" by a procedure that shifts considerable power to the courts, away from the legislator, *and from the individual* who no longer can simply "stand" on his right.

116 For a criticism see the review of Dworkin's *Justice in Robes* (2006) by Richard Nobles and David Schiff, "The Emperor's New Clothes," *Modern Law Review*, vol. 70, no. 1 (2007), 139–60.

117 Vienna Declaration on Human Rights, Part 1, para. 5: "All human rights are universal, indivisible, and interdependent and interrelated." UN General Assembly A/Conf. 157/23 of July 12, 1993.

There also remains the issue whether certain interests regarding for example communal goods, such as living in a free society or having a clean environment, can be sensibly construed as individual, subjective rights. While this is, of course, often done (*vide* the "right to peace" or the "right to democracy"), such constructions quickly become incoherent. Here I engage on the one hand with Waldron's political conception of a "right to rights" – echoing, in a way, Hannah Arendt's position – and on the other hand with the problem that even an extensive theory of "rights," as suggested by Mackie and Dworkin, cannot substitute for morality *tout court*, or for a theory of justice.

Meditation 9 addresses issues that arise from the paradox that courts have to "apply" the law, but what the law "is" can only be ascertained by the courts. On the one hand it follows up on the previous discussions of judicial review and of "grounding" law in some incontrovertible foundation, while at the same time emphasizing the self-referential character of law. This paradox leads us back to our discussion at the beginning – Kelsen's theory of law resting on a *Grundnorm* "beyond" the law, but which allows for the "internalization" of all other validity claims by the legal system, as they are simple derivations. Now we encounter the same problem in the more radicalized version by Derrida, who claims that the "groundlessness of law" shows that law is rooted in arbitrariness and "violence without ground."[118] Thus while law is supposedly helping us to decide practical questions, it is itself not free of paradoxes and problems of undecidability – which is exactly why there always remains an element of "fiat." This "gap" cannot be resolved cognitively, but depends on the decision of a court, which possesses the "power" to make such determinations and on the "reasons" that can be advanced and are found acceptable for the decision rendered.

This raises the more general problems of how practical reason and action relate to each other; how knowledge is "produced," and finally what type of knowledge is appropriate for the realm of praxis. As we have seen, self-reference creates not only a problem for the law but also appears in other areas. It is especially worrisome in logic, precisely because logic is so central to our conception of knowledge. If logic becomes incoherent, it not only defeats the "epistemological project," but seems to suggest that this indeterminacy must lead to "relativism" and to an "anything goes" attitude. While this is a hasty conclusion, as I will try to show, it *does* impose upon me the task of investigating more closely various strategies of "de-paradoxification." Thus the issue is no longer one of the distinction of "truth" vs. "falsity," whose "correction" is the first step on which the de-paradoxification in logic centres, but the realization that something more is "going on."

One way of not being stymied when we encounter paradoxes is to rely on "training." In this way we can adapt to new situations, by "knowing how" rather

[118] Jacques Derrida, "The Force of Law: The Mystical Foundation of Authority," *Cardozo Law Review*, Vol. 11 (1989–1990): 920–1045, at 943.

than "knowing what," such as when we ride a bicycle, or learn a language by using it without being aware of the complexities of grammar, for example. The aim is not an exact reproduction of actions governed by cognitive criteria only, but rather the provision of certain skills that we can "use" in situations we might have never encountered before. As the "skill" of language use shows, the bounds of sense seem to be more complex than when we focus on "correctness" in following the rules of grammar. But since no grammar can make us speak or decide what to say, language use also comprises issues of "invention," a problem that in the standard epistemology of logical positivism remains exogenous. It is treated as a purely "psychological" problem, as there is no "logic of discovery" but only one of justification (corroboration). However, there is no reason to privilege the demonstration in this way, especially when we deal with practical matters. Here "figures of speech," comparisons, reasoning from case to case, changing the links to other concepts in a semantic field, all of these "tricks" allow us to recombine and "discover" new ways of finding our way in the world. Most of these moves are more like "trying out" or play, rather than making generalizing inferences or following strict algorithms. This leads me to the third question stated above: the appropriateness of knowledge for praxis.

I begin, therefore, with a critical look at "ideal theory," that is the traditional way of generating knowledge for practical purposes: via assumptions (clear definitions) and deductive reasoning that are then put to a "test." This ideal theorizing – and here I take Rawls as well as economic models as my foil – proceeds with providing first idealized (or even non-realistic assumptions) that yield, after proper procedures, the principles that can then be "applied" to the "real world." Then I outline a different mode of analysis that relies on a "second best" approach, sometimes used in heterodox economics, but which also informed casuistic reasoning and legal argumentation. Criticizing ideal theory, I try to make the case for a "diagnostics" and for relying on "criticism" of concrete "ills," instead of engaging in ideal theorizing or endless deconstruction.

It should come as no surprise that this book does not contain a "conclusion" in which all arguments fit into a new theoretical synthesis. But if what I have argued is true, that *use and "doing"* things are the proof of the pudding, then I would commit a performative contradiction if I ended up with a new comprehensive "theory." Thus, "buyer beware"! If that is what you expected, you certainly will be disappointed. But for those who are willing to engage with the argument, I hope I can contribute to understanding our predicament, which, in turn, could enable us to change the way "things are."

Meditation 1

Inter-disciplinarity, the epistemological ideal of incontrovertible foundations, and the problem of praxis

Introduction

To examine the status of law in the international arena does not seem to require any special justification. We see law everywhere, ranging from the exponentially growing number of treaties to the informal arrangements of soft law, to attempts of subjecting the actions of public and private actors to further scrutiny through a global administrative law. For some observers this represents success, as it gives the "rule of law" some further bite; for others a Foucauldian dystopia is just around the corner. Yet such an omnipresence of law might be a mixed blessing for purposes of analysis. As in the case of "power," which is fundamental for the study of politics, the concept itself seems to have mutated from an agency-related notion, in which A makes B act in a way which he would not do otherwise (Weber), to a pervasive force penetrating all social relations. Foucault's analysis suggested at least that much.[1] Law seems to share the same fate. But something that we find everywhere might escape our conceptual grids, as it no longer allows us to discriminate, to distinguish.

The solution to this puzzle, we are told by traditional logic and epistemology, consists in finding the firm foundations and proper method that lead us to secure knowledge. This is what the Cartesian quest was all about, on which both the *Meditations* and the *Discourse on Method* elaborated.[2] It was this foundation, and the Humean and Kantian challenge to it,[3] that later resulted in the epistemology of logical positivism.[4] In law this engagement gave rise to the project of a "pure theory of law" à la Kelsen.[5] In the social sciences it resulted in

[1] Michel Foucault, *Security, Territory, Peoples: Lectures at the College de France* (New York: Palgrave Macmillan, 2007).

[2] Rene Descartes, *Meditations and other Related Writings* (London: Penguin, 1999).

[3] See David Hume, *Treatise On Human Nature*, On Morals, sec. ii, in *David Hume The Philosophical Works*, vol. II, pp. 105ff., reprinted Aalen: Scientia, 1964).

[4] For a still useful discussion of the Vienna Circle and its influence on the epistemological debates in the social sciences see Paul Diesing, *How Social Science Works* (Pittsburgh University Press, 1991).

[5] Hans Kelsen, *The Pure Theory of the State*, transl. by Max Knight (Berkeley: University of California Press, 1967).

various methodologically driven research programs of political "science" and international relations that, as academic disciplines, aspired to scientific status. Thus, both disciplines, traditionally firmly placed in the area of praxis – as they were relying on prudence rather than theoretical knowledge – had apparently, for reasons of respectability, rather gladly parted with their former moorings and now sought to satisfy the epistemological ideal.

The vagaries of the discussions in the two fields need not preoccupy us here, but anyone who engages with these debates cannot but feel a certain frustration.[6] If power were such a multifaceted phenomenon, "taking care of it" by nominal definitions would hardly qualify as progress.[7] Similarly, if law can be found in so many places, all definitional exercises (notwithstanding the attempts of limiting it to "the command of the sovereign" à la Austin, or to some specific formality) will deliver so much less than they promise, as the theoretical discussions on the "nature of law" in the twentieth century show. It might have been one thing to write international law out of existence by the stroke of a pen. It was quite another to argue that, for instance, medieval society, which did not know a sovereign able to claim legislative power, or the "common law," or all the societies that sociologists from Durkheim[8] to Weber[9] and Malinowski,[10] or legal theorists such as Llewellyn and Hoebel,[11] had studied, simply possessed no "law."

These problems were of course intensified by modern developments, such as the legal pluralism challenge, the development of "soft law," and the erasure of systemic boundaries between the "national" legal systems themselves. The latter trend is observable most clearly in Europe, but has also been noticed in the USA. The recent American discussion on "multiple points of entry"[12] for other legal systems, such as EU law, has focused on the transformation of US environmental law because of the concurring jurisdiction between state and federal government, which provides "foreign" law with surprising access to shaping at least part of the US domestic legal order. To that extent a traditional image of

6 Yosef Lapid, "The Third Debate," *International Studies Quarterly*, vol. 33 no. 3 (1989): 235–54. Mark Neufeld, *The Restructuring of IR Theory* (Cambridge University Press, 1995).

7 See Gianfranco Poggi, *Forms of Power* (Cambridge: Polity Press, 2001). Michael Barnett and Raymond Duvall, "Power in International Relations," *International Organization*, vol. 59 (2005), 39–75.

8 Emile Durkheim, *The Elementary Forms of Religious Life* (New York: Free Press, 1965).

9 Max Weber, *Economy and Society*, ed. by Guenther Roth and Claus Wittich (Berkeley: University of California Press, 1978).

10 See e.g. Bronislaw Malinowski, *Crime and Custom in Savage Society* (London: Kegan Paul, Trench, Truber, 1926).

11 Karl Llewellyn and Adamson Hoebel, *The Cheyenne Way* (Norman: University of Oklahoma Press, 1941).

12 See Judith Resnik, "Law's Migration: American Exceptionalism, Silent Dialogues, and Federalism's Multiple Ports of Entry," *The Yale Law Journal*, vol. 115, no. 7 (2009), 1574–670.

a closed legal system no longer provides an adequate representation of social reality; rather such a "map" is conducive to a systematic misreading of the situation and not helping us to orient ourselves.

Things become even more complicated when we consider the proposals of modern system theories, such as those of Luhmann[13] and Teubner.[14] Both use an open systems approach for explaining the reproduction (autopoiesis) of functionally differentiated systems that irritate each other but create their own boundaries and elements by means of specific codes: in the case of law, by the root distinction of legal/illegal that operationally closes the system. But such a conceptualization is problematic, as I try to show in Meditation 3. It fails to explain how, for example, economics and its cost–benefit analysis has been able to colonize "the law" by undermining its *proprium*, but also how "rule of law" might have become an imperial project even without a change in territorial boundaries (as the emphasis on "best practices" and the EU neighbourhood policy shows).

There are indeed many puzzles, both practical and epistemic, which threaten to derail the attempt to understand the role of law before this project can get off the ground. If we want to cast our net wider and approach the problem via interdisciplinarity, we must face the problem that all of our knowledge is based on disciplinary understandings, even if we thereby do not have to accept the proposition that there is only *one* method we can use. For example, as important as "justice" might be, the question of a "just price" is simply a non-question for an economist, and an interdisciplinary dialogue is not likely to succeed. This does not mean that such efforts must always fail, as some concerns, such as the environment or education, can enter the economic paradigm if they are appropriately reformulated as "collective goods" (as problematic as this notion is, as I will try to show), as "externalities," or as "human capital." Similarly, while poverty did not exist as a distinct problem in the neo-classical vocabulary – it resulted from trade distortions and inefficient markets – as of late, it has made the agenda of the post Washington consensus.[15] Some problems transcend disciplinary understandings because they simply cannot be ignored, even though they do not fit the disciplinary agendas. After all, even disciplines themselves

[13] Niklas Luhmann, *Social Systems*, transl. by John Bednarz Jr and Dirk Baecker (Stanford University Press, 1996).

[14] Gunther Teubner, *Global Law without the State* (Aldershot: Dartmouth, 1997).

[15] The "break" with the old orthodoxy became evident when the World Bank issued its World Development Report in 2001, released in 2004, where poverty was now identified as a distinct problem that needed to be addressed by policy. See World Bank, *The World Bank Development Report 1990* (New York: Oxford University Press, 1990) and also World Bank, *The World Bank Development Report: Attacking Poverty 2000/2001* (release April 2004) (Washington DC: World Bank, 2004). For an insightful discussion of the debates and the emergence of a new consensus see Antje Vetterlein, *The Politics of the Development Discourse* (Florence: Ph.D. Dissertation of the European University Institute, 2006).

are subject to change. Thus, as in the case of war, which is too important to be left to the military, politics might be too important to be entrusted to realists, and law to jurists, bureaucrats, or administrators.

The pitfalls of interdisciplinarity

It is for this reason that I begin this series of "meditations" on the status of law in world society with a critical inquiry regarding the nature of knowledge and how disciplinary understandings are made and unmade. Rather than focusing on the "inside" of disciplinary understandings – which of course are surrounded by other "islands of knowledge" – or by examining the "bridges" that might connect these islands, I focus on the *processes by which these boundaries of "sense" are drawn and redrawn* so that different elements can be included, reconfigured, or excluded.

Given the bounded nature of knowledge and the inexhaustible ways in which the world can be described, the idea that we somehow could get to the "right" description by simply aggregating all different "islands" or disciplines seems futile indeed. This explains why interdisciplinarity is somehow a little bit like virginity – a state that many, if not all of us, appreciate, but which we do not maintain. Otherwise we, and the people around us, would not be here. On the other hand, like Monsieur Jourdain we all should also realize that we speak prose and that this prose is always "interdisciplinary" for two reasons. One reason is not only that disciplines, as assemblies of discourses and practices, are not like natural kinds, such as rocks or planets, chemical elements, or species. This might sound, very "constructivist" and postmodern, but even the hard sciences are increasingly moving away from their old orthodoxies. Some objects representing "natural kinds," such as planets and species, have been reclassified, as the various reformulations of the Linnaean system and the discussions about the status of Pluto have demonstrated.[16] Under such circumstances communication among scientists is more like a debate and less of a "demonstration."[17] And in those debates the price will most likely go to those who can use a variety of "vocabularies" and bridge the gaps or circumvent the impasses created by disagreements. This requires a different notion of communication than one based on stringent "models" or on the logic of "autonomous systems," as I shall show. For now those few remarks might suffice.

[16] See my "Constructivism: What It Is (Not) and How It Matters," in Donatella della Porta and Michael Keating (eds.), *Approaches and Methodologies in the Social Sciences* (Cambridge University Press, 2008), 80–99.

[17] For a further discussion see my "Evidence, Inference and Truth as Problems of Theory Building in the Social Sciences," in Richard Lebow and Mark Lichbach (eds.), *Theory and Evidence in Comparative Politics and International Relations* (New York: Palgrave Macmillan, 2007), Chapter 2.

The second reason has to do with the "wider" audience within which scientific disciplines are embedded. When our understandings of how the world works have been shaken, we tend to invite "experts" to tell us what happened. Understanding the problem is, after all, the precondition of how it can be fixed. But in order to be effective, these experts cannot communicate simply in terms of their usual conceptual tools and practices. Instead, they must be able to "translate" the complicated theoretical propositions in "understandable" language. To that extent the Wittgensteinian position, which I espouse, and which emphasizes the importance of *everyday language* (rather than relying upon artificial languages and calculi), is a bias to which I admit. But this bias can be justified, particularly when one deals with questions of praxis. Here paradigmatic examples become important for moulding common understandings, even though they can be tricky and misfire. Sometimes they "stick," but the point they were supposed to illustrate gets lost. Instead, they lead to flights of fancy, such as when the relativity of time and space gives rise to fantasies of time travel, providing a never-ending slew of scripts for Hollywood B-movies. Sometimes, however, these translations and the debates they engender lead to a discovery of significant blind spots in the existing disciplinary understandings, and hence to serious criticism. The discussion of the economic understanding of development as potentially unlimited "growth" and the substitution of "sustainable development" can serve here as an example.[18]

In such conceptual shifts ordinary language plays an important part by mediating the various disciplinary discourses. The new problems, which emerge at the edge of disciplines, can get picked up by ordinary language before they engender new "policies" that then are fed back again into the particular disciplines. In the area of law the *scandalum* of officially perpetrated torture, or the disappearance of regime critics comes to mind, which led in international law to a reformulation of the immunity *problematique*, exemplified by the *Pinochet* case.[19] Similarly, the Faustian bargain with atomic energy was cast in sharp relief by Chernobyl and linked to the criticism of "modernity" developed by Beck in his "risk society,"[20] in that the incalculability of certain risks was diagnosed. It led not only to public debates and policy choices eschewing atomic energy but also fed back to various disciplines that began to search for various renewable forms of energy.

Of course, there is no assurance that such feedback loops will actually come into existence. Thus the failure of breaking the intellectual hegemony in neoliberal thinking concerning the causes of the financial crisis is evidenced by the fact that the current reform proposals largely address the risk of particular

[18] That this proved to be a pyrrhic victory, however, is discussed in below in Meditation 4.

[19] For a discussion of Pinochet see Andrea Bianchi, "The Pinochet Case: Immunity vs. Human Rights," *European Journal of International Law*, vol. 10, no. 2 (1999), 217–77.

[20] Ulrich Beck, *Risk Society* (Beverly Hills: Sage, 1992).

market instruments, but pay insufficient attention to systemic risks, quite aside from the fact that opinions as to how the various factors leading to the crisis are to be weighted diverge widely.[21] The "instruments," supposedly securitizing debts through a spreading of risk, are still considered part of the "self-regulation" of markets and most of the time they are not recognized as systemic causes for panics and market failures. Nor is this only a recent development, since debts as promissory notes have a long history, through "sale," becoming of increasingly anonymous and in-transparent and of shifting the default burden ultimately to the public.[22]

In the latter case everyday language was evidently not able to break the lock of certain intellectual hegemonies, even though some "heterodox" economists have long pointed out that markets are efficient and frictionless only under very special conditions, and that bubbles are not simply exogenous but often endogenously generated, such as by information asymmetries.[23] Consequently, the herd behaviour that markets foster in crisis situations is not just a fluke or an aberration that can be modelled by analogies to such rare events in nature as earthquakes,[24] it results instead from the "working" of the very system. The fact that the present crisis does not result just from greedy bankers who have lost their sense of shame – although that might also be true – but that it has been a long-term process involving fundamental changes in law and politics seems, however, cold comfort.

These remarks highlight several points on which I shall elaborate below. However, for the moment I am interested in why most interdisciplinary projects fail to render the expected results, although the disciplinary competence of the researchers is hardly ever at issue. Something more seems to be going on. Perhaps it has to do with the way we usually proceed and with our conception of method. Let us remember that "doing" science is a social enterprise.[25] Thus, in order to get such an interdisciplinary undertaking off the ground, we obviously need to know some researchers in the other fields. Knowing somebody in law, or sociology, who shares certain interests and whom we like (precisely also because we need not fear for our turf) is surely the necessary but not sufficient condition for having a good conversation. Even then it is not always clear whether we talk with each other or at each other.

[21] Since there is much blame to spread around, Howard Davies has analysed thirty-nine "causes" that have contributed to the 2007 to 2009 episode of the still ongoing financial crisis. See Howard Davies, *The Financial Crisis – Who Is to Blame* (Cambridge: Polity Press, 2010).

[22] See the fascinating discussion in Joseph Vogl, *Das Gespenst des Kapitals*, 4th edn. (Zurich: Diaphanes, 2010/2011).

[23] See e.g. Joseph Stiglitz and Bruce Greenwald, *Towards a New Paradigm for Monetary Policy* (Cambridge University Press, 2003).

[24] Fischer Black and Myron Scholes, "The Pricing of Options and Corporate Liabilities," *Journal of Political Economy*, vol. 81 (May/June 1973), 637–54.

[25] See e.g. Karen Knorr-Cetina, *Epistemic Cultures: How the Sciences Make Knowledge* (Cambridge, MA: Harvard University Press, 1999); Bruno Latour and Steven Wolgar, *The Social Construction of Scientific Facts* (London: Sage, 1979).

But never mind! As in a Judy Garland movie where some teenagers, who lack the means for realizing their different projects, decide to finance them by putting on a show, the script is rather similar. So it goes: "I do the stage, which we put up in my cousin's barn," Nick says. "Cynthia, you do the costumes, Bob does the flyers, and Bill can bring his uncle to help with the electricity. Dan and his quartet do the music and Emily sells the tickets. Jessica, Dave, Rose, and Paul do the song and dance. Anything left out? Oh yeah, Greg can lead through the program as master of ceremonies." Since all of these teens are, of course, simply "fabulous," the show is a huge success and everybody can ride into the sunset with some fame and money to boot.

Yet, contrary to this script, people engaged in real interdisciplinary groups quickly become aware that they speak different languages, and that the problems of one discipline are often of no real interest to outsiders. This can cause either heated debates or mutual boredom (depending how long one has been "at it"). Thus a "preliminary operational definition" needs to be found! It is usually a compromise that does not offend some important members of the group, but it might satisfy none of the participants. At least some progress seems to have been made by moving the issues to "neutral" territory, that is to logic, taxonomy, and epistemology.

However, such a gloss on the events might be highly optimistic, as the myopias created by the respective disciplines can actually work in tandem instead of correcting each other. For example, a political scientist, steeped in the standard epistemology of positivism, will insist on "precision" and argue that precise norms are likely to influence behaviour more strongly – hence neatly reducing the problem of obligation to one of the influence of an independent variable on the dependent one. Law students will remember that "vagueness" is also a standard gambit for winning interpretive battles in court. But the remedies for this defect will differ significantly in each discipline, and thus the consensus, which has been reached, probably misdiagnoses the problem.

Consider in this context the interdisciplinary project that a few years ago brought together international lawyers and international relations specialists. They settled on three elements (variables?) that were supposed explain the "legalization" trend in world politics.[26] Those three elements were: precision, delegation (third-party dispute resolution), and obligation. While this choice was neither explicitly justified nor derived from any identified theory, one had to wonder whether we had here only an assembly of some categories rather than an explicit framework,[27] or even only a few pigeonholes for the stories that different authors contributed.

[26] Ken Abbot, Robert Keohane, Andrew Morawcik, Ann-Marie Slaughter and Duncan Snidal, "The Concept of Legalization," *International Organization*, vol. 54 (Summer 2000), 17–35.

[27] Martha Finnemore and Stephen Toope, "Alternatives to Legalization: Richer Views of Law and Politics," *International Organization*, vol. 55 (2001), 743–56.

Since the concepts of delegation and obligation are part and parcel of law, it had to fall on "precision" to provide the added value in this project. For positivists following the scientific canon, "precision" lies in increasing the sharpness of the conceptual boundaries, thus fitting the concept more closely to the phenomenon in the "world out there." Here the question immediately arises whether such a method is appropriate for the appraisal of the normative pull of a rule or principle. The suspicion is heightened by recognizing that concepts are not simply accurate descriptions of independently existing facts, since this notion is based on a rather misleading conception of language.

As can be shown, the descriptivist ideal of language, which takes "reference" as its main yardstick, very quickly falls down, even in non-normative contexts. Many supposedly straightforward descriptive terms actually function quite differently from what we expect. Consider such attributes as "small" or "big," which seem pretty straightforward descriptive terms. But what is a small deviation for a watchmaker, or for a computer chip producer, will differ from that of an architect, who is building a fifty-story office tower. While 1 millimetre is a "big" deviation for the former two, it is not even worth mentioning when we evaluate the precision of an elevator shaft built by the architect. Thus, even in the constative mode of language, what a term "means" cannot be decided by simply looking at "reality." There is no free-standing "fact of the matter" as the philosopher would say. Instead, we have to relate these terms to the standards and practices in the various professions, which will obviously use different yardsticks and which would not be helped by any attempt of defining once and for all what "big" or "small" means.

The lawyer, on the other hand, should not forget that many of the norms that do most of the work in his field are not precise at all. Such principles as good faith, due process, and *mens rea* do not specify their range of application and they cannot be stated in an "if – then" form either, which is one way to arrive at precision. Consequently, the problem of vagueness in law is quite different. It attains its meaning from how the term functions within a particular mode of reasoning using rules and norms, which arrives at a decision through a process of exclusions. Here, reasoning from case to case (as in common law), the use of paradigmatic cases, or the distinctions among them that justify giving preference to one reading of the relevant facts rather than to another, attain importance. Consequently, such modes of reasoning are far from a simple subsumption under a norm, or even from the *enthymeme* of Aristotle, where the major premise in a practical syllogism consists of a norm.[28] Rather, legal reasoning requires a constant going back between facts and norms in which various trade-offs between conflicting values, protected by law, are made. All this is a far cry from both deduction or from simply fitting the norms to fact patterns,

[28] Henrik von Wright, *Norm and Action* (London: Routledge, Kegan Paul, 1963).

as the "precision" argument suggests. Rather, the procedure follows *axiological* rather than purely logical or theoretical standards.

Another significant point calls into question the argument that the legalization of world politics had much to do with either precision or delegation[29] and, on second thought, even with the classical notion of obligation. I am speaking here of the growth of "soft law" exemplified by, for example, the "Global Compact,"[30] and the non-enforceable non-legal commitments contained in the conditionality agreements of the International Monetary Fund (IMF) with countries receiving stabilization funds. Also in this category are such creations as the *lex mercatoria* and the *codex alimentarius*. Be their legal status what it may – or whatever it may *become* when *used* by supranational or "domestic" institutions – one thing seems clear: soft law represents an observable countertrend to the formalistic criteria of precision and perhaps also to judicialization, since alternative modes of dispute resolution have become increasingly popular.

Strangely enough, we observe a similar "deformalization" even in some International Court of Justice (ICJ) decisions – where equitable considerations rather than strict obligations and state responsibility are invoked[31] – and in some International Law Commission (ILC) drafts.[32] Again, whatever we might think of these indicators, they are too important to be left out of the picture, and obviously some further conceptual work is needed. In addition, adopting a strategy of disengagement with the ongoing debates in favour of a ground-clearing exercise, which starts with an "operational definition," is likely to lead to an outcome that researchers do what they are doing anyway. They just sprinkle their allegedly interdisciplinary research with some of the agreed upon terms, and thus engage in an effort of, at best, recasting their findings in a different terminology, instead of opening up a new set of puzzles.

There is still another danger in interdisciplinary research that is connected with the problem of operational definitions but actually goes well beyond it. It is the danger of settling on a specific methodology in accordance with the maxim "one size fits all." It "works" largely by silencing some of the problems that are specific to a particular field. Adhering to the theoretical ideal that holds that only statements that are universally or by necessity "true" can contribute to knowledge, some characteristic elements of praxis are simply passed over. As Aristotle already pointed out, politics is about the *particular* and not the

[29] For a measured assessment of the role of international courts see Jose Alvarez, "The New Dispute Settlers: (Half) Truths and Consequences," *Texas International Law Journal*, vol. 38 (2003), 405–44.

[30] Gerard Ruggie, "Business and Human Rights: The Evolving International Agenda," *American Journal of International Law*, vol. 101 (Oct 2007), 819–40.

[31] Here boundary delimitations of continental shelves and issues of sharing common resources provide the examples (North Sea, Malta, Lybia, Gabcikovo cases).

[32] See GA Res. 63/12, 4th Suppl., Dec. 10, 2008.

universal. It is about things that "can be otherwise" rather than about those that are "by necessity" so.[33] About the latter one need not deliberate, or make choices, he laconically remarks. Similarly, in law norms are counter-factually valid so that "breaches" do not refute their validity. To that extent the term "validity" contributes to confusion, as it is used equivocally. In the first case, "laws" describe physical regularities and validity has to specify the "truth" conditions that an assertion has to meet. In the other case, when the deontic force of a statement is at issue, validity concerns, for example, the issue of "sources." Here, of course, the argument for a hierarchy of norms (or sources), that is of a normativity of varying degrees (*jus cogens*!), sits uneasily on top of the categorical distinction between facts and norms.

The understandable tendency is then to declare everything a matter of "degree," as the misnomer of "soft law" suggests. While I will deal with this problem below, here I only want to point out that such a strategy will not do. Sartori[34] has shown in his criticism of "operationalism" that a strategy of dissolving everything into a one-dimensional "more" or "less" is unviable, even if we move solely at the factual level. Consequently, there is prima facie no reason to believe that the same does not also hold at the normative level. After all, any judgment about "more" or "less" presupposes antecedent categorical distinctions among different dimensions that cannot be flattened out to one of quantity (save that one believes in a given ontological order, or in the ubiquity of "prices").

Thus, in law the question of normativity cannot be reduced to the "operational" problem of "compliance," or what people presumably do in the "real world." There we encounter, instead, interacting reasons, some of which concern preferences and interests, while others relate to the normative status of the prescriptions. The myopia of the legalist who explains everything in terms of normative force is then simply reproduced by the myopia of the realist (or liberal) who thinks that individual interests are simply given and beyond debate (*de gustibus non est disputandum*), and can, therefore, remain outside the scope of the analysis. This leads to rather scholastic debates instead of answering the original, albeit naïve question of whether "interests" or "norms" are "real" and determine outcomes in a "causal" fashion.

Consider in this context the recent attempt by Goldsmith and Posner to enter this IR debate and use some of the "insights" of rational choice in order to determine the *Limits of International Law*.[35] Here non-cooperative game

[33] See Aristotle's distinction of scientific (theoretical) knowledge, of "art," and of prudential action in his *Nichomachen Ethics*, Book VI, transl. by J. A. K. Thompson (Harmondsworth: Penguin, 1953), especially Chapters 1–10, at 171–85.

[34] Giovanni Sartori, "Concept Misformation in Comparative Politics," *American Political Science Review*, vol. 64, no. 4 (1970), 1033–53.

[35] Jack Goldsmith and Eric A. Posner, *The Limits of International Law* (Oxford University Press, 2005).

theory is supposed to be the "methodology" that has allowed IR scholars to approach the problem of compliance with more sophisticated tools, as they claim its puzzles "have been solved there." This comes, of course, as a great surprise to someone like me who has watched the fights in the fraternity of the IR profession over several decades. The first thing to note is that Goldsmith and Posner use rather elemental game theory, never achieving the sophistication of, for example, Schelling, who already suspected in the 1960s that the really interesting problems fall outside of this approach.[36] Similarly, Eric Posner, as one of the exponents of the "law and economics approach" who had examined the same game-theoretical literature before, admitted that the tendered "explanations are primitive"[37] and "even a complete game theoretic account would miss some of the essential aspects of norms,"[38] in particular the problem of "obligation."

Thus, to understand actual state practice we need to do more than look at hard and fast rules, as clarity, predictability, and consistency requirements stand in complex trade-off relations with values and rights, a situation familiar from administrative law or constitutional law where "balancing" is common. It simply does not follow, then, that elementary game theory and a heavy dose of armchair "realism" is helpful for the admittedly more controversial case of international law. As a matter of fact, the refusal of the authors to engage with any of the existing legal approaches, ranging from the modern process school to postmodern approaches, or even to the old Austinian argument of international law being, like constitutional law, only some form of "public morality,"[39] makes one wonder what the intellectual and political agenda of the authors actually is, since they ignore the major debates in their own field while engaging in some trivial dabbling in social "science."

Second, considering that the project of finding solutions to the problem of multiple equilibria in games of coordination (under conditions where individual and collective rationality do not diverge) has run into heavy water,[40] one has to ask whether the diamonds Goldsmith and Posner parade before us are nothing more than some pieces of broken glass, left over from the last food fight in the fraternity house of international relations students.

Finally, since some games have no rational solution (such as "chicken") and since the discussion about global public goods has shown that many of the assumptions driving the original debate on the global commons were

[36] Thomas Schelling, *Strategy of Conflict* (Oxford University Press, 1961).

[37] See Eric Posner, "Law, Economics, and Inefficient Norms," *University of Pennsylvania Law Review*, vol. 144 (1996), 1697–744, at 1708.

[38] *Ibid.* at 1709.

[39] See e.g. John Austin, *The Province of Jurisprudence Determined* (1832), ed. by Wilfrid E. Rumble (Cambridge University Press, 1995), 141–3 and 254–64.

[40] Donald Green and Ian Shapiro, *Pathologies of Rational Choice Theory* (New Haven: Yale University Press, 2004).

mistaken, one would like to know why these authors think that a "method" has been discovered here that solves our problems. This is all the more surprising, since virtually all work in this area has established that there is no "one size fits all solution," as contextual factors, information deficiencies, sequencing, and imperfect substitutability of contributions, and so on, decisively shape the outcomes.[41]

This leads me to a more general problem. What is truly astonishing is that lawyers, for whom "contracts" have to be a central concern, now suddenly pretend that one can "contract out" of the proper methodology in one's own field. But this creates a serious problem for law as well as for what we accept as evidence, or as an "explanation." Thus the legal institution of contract entails past commitments, intended to shape future outcomes. Rational choice approaches, on the other hand, are based on purely forward-looking reasons, as past commitments and promises have no force in selecting a rational player's strategy.[42] This means that the "binding" character of contracts cannot be explained in this way. It has often been remarked that the Hobbesian solution to the n-person prisoners' dilemma is incoherent and that it can only be remedied by a more institutionally oriented analysis, in which both the uptake of an obligation and the existence of institutional rules matter. If in the state of nature promises are just "mere words," then the social contract can never get off the ground, as every "rational" player has to defect. Although the move from a mutual defect to a cooperative strategy might be, in a way, "rational" as it provides higher pay-offs for all players, it is not "reachable" for the players, given the narrow specification of rationality and motivation.

This does not mean that we have now to assume that "morality" must do all the explaining, but the above recognition does change the research agenda considerably, even for rational choice approaches. The crucial question then is no longer the identification of a strategy in a one-shot dilemma, but how rational agents in iterative plays are able to choose actors who are likely to cooperate – so that a "virtuous circle" of cooperation can commence. Otherwise, they must defect and will remain hostage to the situation. But even in this extension the problem still remains largely a cognitive one and thus distinguishing cooperators (through signalling, audience costs, and so on) take pride of place; the hoped for "solution" escapes us since disseminating information (or searching for it) is costly and thus gives rise to a new collective action problem. Furthermore, while iteration of the games and "learning" do certainly widen the scope of inquiry, the question remains why "signalling" – which is such a truncated form of "communication" whose pitfalls Jervis analysed years

[41] Todd Sandler, *Global Collective Action* (Cambridge University Press, 2004).

[42] See Christine Chwaszcza, "Gametheory" in Donatella della Porta and Michael Keating (eds.), *Approaches and Methodologies in the Social Sciences* (Cambridge University Press, 2008), Chapter 8.

ago[43] – is supposed to provide the appropriate template. This can remain an open question, but I am sceptical that either international relations analysis or law will be able to profit much from it.

Two mutually reinforcing problems seem particularly important for such an assessment. The first is the underlying assumption that difficulties of communication arise out of the vague nature of ordinary language and second, that this defect can be overcome only through "clear and distinct" ideas (concepts) and rigorous modes of inference according to the Cartesian ideal. After all, it was Descartes who offered epistemology as a new foundation, after scepticism had undermined the belief in an ontological order. In the end he was, of course, unable to solve the problem of how the *res cogitans* and the *res extensa*, that is concept and "thing," could be brought together, except through the introduction of a benign God guaranteeing their coincidence. Particularly troubling was the later discovery that even formal logic seemed to violate its own criteria, as Russell's paradox showed,[44] and that "basic sentences," which allegedly record "pure observations" and thus provide "empirical" evidence for the "truth" of our propositions, created more problems than they solved. Let us consider the latter problem in more detail.

Why is the sentence "There is a broom in the corner" not a "basic sentence" that records a pure observation? One the one hand, it seems basic enough, as its meaning seems to be given by clear reference. On the other hand, it is not basic at all since I "see" a broom, rather than a wooden stick with some bristles, held together at one end by some wire. In other words, how far down do we have to go in our observations so that we can reach the "basic" or "indubitable" level? There is an answer to this query, but it does not arise out of cognition or "perception" by taking sensory impressions as "basic." Rather, the solution comes from the realization of how sense-perception and conceptualization interact and from the acknowledgement that this interaction is more complicated than the account of the reliability of observation suggests. After all, I correctly assign the concept of "broom" to the assembly in the corner, if I understand the *use of this contraption, and, therefore, there is no point of looking further for simpler descriptions*. Second, the focus on meaning as *use* rather than *reference* also relieves us of the impossible task of finding some "essences" when we bring different things under a common concept. Thus, the "real" description of "money" cannot be fathomed by trying to find the common denominator between the various things in the outer world that have served as money. Here we would have to find a common element that all share despite the fact that we are dealing here with salt (*salaire*), gold, silver, iron, sea shells, little animals

[43] Robert Jervis, *The Logic of Images in International Relations* (New York: Columbia University Press, 1989).

[44] For the explication of the Russell Paradox see Meditation 9, ftn. 1.

(*pecunia*), plastic cards, or blips on a computer screen. But what makes these things "money" is how they are *used*, not what they *are*.

This recognition has important implications for meaning and communication in general. For the moment I shall focus only on one implication justifying my scepticism about the epistemological ideal. The latter entails a silent and a rather dogmatic assertion that the world of practice is best studied in the same way as nature and that we must, therefore, find universally valid "laws," or at least generalizations; however, this raises Hume's hoary problem of induction.

While this argument might already be problematic for giving a coherent account of natural "science,"[45] we know that, different from nature, the human world is one of artifice, as Aristotle has pointed out. Human sociality is not programmed by nature through genetic coding, as is the case in other "gregarious animals," such as bees.[46] The formation of human societies depends rather on language and the use of common concepts that not only free us from the here and now, and the stimulus/response limitations of efficient causality, but also enables us to make choices, communicate with others, and engage in discourses of justice and responsibility, which ground our individual and common political projects.

The question then is whether the type of "knowledge" appropriate for informing actions must satisfy "theoretical" standards, or whether such an endeavour fundamentally misunderstands what is at stake. Since I believe that a good case can be made for the latter hunch, I have to provide an account of both the traditional scientific discourse and its limitations, and of how the "bounds of sense" informing praxis can be reconceptualized. Such attempts have been made by Toulmin[47] and Bourdieu among others. But often these examinations ended up with just another attempt of a "theory of practice," as Bourdieu's earlier work shows.[48] His later *Pascalian Meditations*[49] suggest, however, that a much more fundamental change in conceptualization is required, for which he takes Pascal as his inspiration. In this way Bourdieu called attention to a different way of disciplining thought that differs from that which Descartes expounded in his *Meditationes de Prima Philosophia*.[50]

In these Meditations I try to use this largely forgotten mode of reasoning about practical problems, reappropriating it from Descartes and directing it *against* the Cartesian ideal. To that extent my approach is also quite different

[45] See e.g. Stephen Toulmin, *Return to Reason* (Cambridge, MA: Harvard University Press, 2001), Chapters 3–5.

[46] Aristotle, *Politics*, Book I, Chapter 2.

[47] See Stephen Toulmin, *An Examination of the Place of Reason in Ethics* (Cambridge University Press, 1950).

[48] See Pierre Bourdieu, *Outline of a Theory of Practice*, transl. by Richard Nice (Cambridge University Press, 1977).

[49] Pierre Bourdieu, *Pascalian Meditations* (Stanford University Press, 2000).

[50] René Descartes, *Meditationes de Prima Philosophia* (Hamburg: Felix Meiner, 1959).

from Husserl's in his *Cartesian Meditations*,[51] in which he wanted to radicalize and perfect the Cartesian project, thus overcoming the "crisis of the European sciences through a new transcendental phenomenology."[52] Similarly, I shall not follow up here on Robert Brandom's impressive attempt[53] at rethinking the norm/action problem by exploiting the "discursive exit transitions in action and discursive entry transitions in perception," introducing thereby a non-Humean way (non-conventional way) of reflecting upon practical reason that links both to Wittgenstein and language philosophy and to Kant's "free will as a rational faculty of practical reason."[54] I shall resist this temptation, since I am here mainly interested in "unearthing" the realm of praxis and much less interested with creating a coherent "theory" that resolves the conceptual tensions that have arisen in the Western philosophical tradition. Precisely because this tradition has always given pride of place to "theory," which I consider problematic for reasons developed throughout these Meditations, I am not convinced that we can solve our practical problems requiring judgment by some "inferential semantics" linking doxastic commitments (beliefs) with practical commitments (intentions), even if the "inferences" are not limited to "formally valid inferences."

From my comments above, it also should be clear that the driving force for my effort here is not some historical interest in a largely forgotten tradition, but rather a hunch that understanding action can thereby be pursued in a more satisfactory way. We neither need to rely on endless deconstructions, nor opt for the hegemonic project of importing a methodology from a different field in the naïve hope that it will serve as the key that magically opens the doors to an overarching "theory." Rather, we work things "through," as in the talking cure that Freud – among others – suggested, and for that we need some "others" and not some monologues.

In explicating this approach I shall draw freely on ordinary language philosophy, as well as on the writings of American pragmatists such as Pierce and Dewey.[55] They were taking issue with the "quest for certainty" that is bound to derail the analysis of the social world in the pursuit of an untenable

[51] Edmund Husserl, *Cartesian Meditations*, transl. by Dorion Cairns (The Hague: Martinus Nijhoff, 1973).

[52] Edmund Husserl, *The Crisis of European Sciences and Transcendental Phenomenology*, transl. by David Carr (Evanston: Northwestern University Press, 1970). For an informative discussion of this attempt see A. D. Smith, *Husserl and the Cartesian Meditations* (London: Routledge, 2003).

[53] Robert Brandom: *Reasoning, Representing and Discursive Commitment* (Cambridge, MA: Harvard University Press, 1994).

[54] See also Robert Brandom, "Action, Norms and Practical Reasoning," *Philosophical Perspectives*, vol. 12 (1998), 127–39, at 127 and 129.

[55] Emmanuel Adler and Vincent Pouliot (eds.), *International Practices* (Cambridge University Press, 2011), 36–60.

idea.[56] I am also deeply influenced by Wittgenstein's later work and owe an intellectual debt to the constructivism of Luckmann and Berger,[57] as well as to Searle,[58] and – with some critical distance – to Luhmann[59] and his school. Finally, my thinking about law was shaped by exposure to the writings of Kelsen,[60] Hart,[61] Fuller,[62] and Dworkin,[63] the "critical studies movement," the legal process school (New Haven school and follow-ups), and the writings of legal pluralists and their critics.

The problems of praxis

What are some of the important characteristics of action? One is that it takes place in irreversible time and that it is brought about by an agent who, in the pursuit of a goal, exercises his or her choice. This latter criterion distinguishes actions from events and places them in a particular situation, but also makes timeliness and time pressure important elements of analysis – something that was possible yesterday, for example, is no longer possible today. In addition, by having to act *now*, I am not only foreclosing other options, but I also have to decide on the basis of incomplete information. Both elements have been discussed in terms of Aristotle's right moment (*kairos*), and as the sense of "timing" (in the strategic literature), as well as in crisis decision-making in international relations analysis. There both time pressures and cognitive and emotional distortions impairing decisions have been addressed.[64]

This leads us to a second important element of the situatedness of practical choices. We never start from scratch, be it from a real or hypothetical contract, or from some other contraption that tries to divide the flow of time into a mythical "before" and "after." We always start in the middle of things. Thus the appropriate metaphor for this situation is not the rupture of time, the contract, or the revolution leading to a revaluation of all values. Rather, the fitting metaphor is that of the "drama" where the actors enter the stage and where we soon realize

[56] For a further discussion see my "Making Sense of International Practices," in Emmanuel Adler and Vincent Pouliot (eds.), *International Practices* (Cambridge University Press, 2011), Chapter 2.

[57] Peter Berger and Thomas Luckmann, *The Social Construction of Reality* (Garden City: Doubleday, 1967).

[58] John Searle, *The Construction of Social Reality* (London: Penguin, 1995).

[59] Niklas Luhmann, *Rechtstheorie*, 2nd edn. (Reinbeck: Rohwolt, 1972); appeared in English as: *A Sociological Theory of Law*, transl. by Elisabeth King-Utz and Martin Albrow (London; Routledge and Kegan Paul, 1985).

[60] Hans Kelsen, *A General Theory of Law and the State* (New York: Russell and Russell, 1961); Hans Kelsen, *Principles of International Law* (New York: Holt, 1966).

[61] H. L. A. Hart, *The Concept of Law* (Oxford: Clarendon, 1961).

[62] Leon Fuller, *The Morality of Law*, rev. edn. (New Haven: Yale University Press, 1964).

[63] Ronald Dworkin, *Taking Rights Seriously* (Cambridge, MA: Harvard University Press, 1977); Ronald Dworkin, *Law's Empire* (Cambridge, MA, Harvard University Press, 1986).

[64] See e.g. James Richardson, *Crisis Diplomacy* (Cambridge University Press, 1994).

that what is being played in front of us has its roots in actions and events that occurred long before but which have shaped us and are part of our predicament. The search for the break, for beginning from scratch, for the construction of an absolute point – the "view from nowhere"[65] – from where we, instead of being historical creatures, can finally see things as *they are*, is as understandable as it is futile. We had also better remember that the Cartesian search for un-controvertible foundations follows from an equally implausible general doubt. It is not surprising that such a discovery might then engender a feeling of power, even of omnipotence, especially if we have been stymied for so long. But such foundations do not help us master our individual and collective lives, which are always shaped powerfully by contingency, (moral) luck,[66] and limits to the feasibility (not the "truth" or potential universalizability) of our projects.

Here a third important characteristic of praxis comes to the fore. Social action takes place in a strategic environment in which the outcome is determined by the double contingency of the actors' choices. Consequently, norms play a decisive role in stabilizing expectations and making the coordination of actions possible. However, as in any halfway realistic situation, not only do two players with two strategies meet, but many players also interact and many possible solutions might exist.[67] Here "rationality" is often of no avail, since there is either no solution, or the only reachable one is "socially" destructive (as in a general "prisoners' dilemma" (PD) game), or many points of convergence exist that are logically equivalent (multiple equilibriums in coordination games). But since these equilibriums might also favour different interests, different parties prefer different "solutions." Thus the decision problem is not simply one of cognition, but also consists in getting the actors to settle on one such point and in making this choice stick. Here politics raises its ugly head, as it is supposed to find a solution to the collective action problem by either using persuasion or coercion, and it is here that the role of law as an instrument of both *argumentum* and *dominium* becomes visible.

Finally, practical choices are frequently made for or on behalf of others, such as clients, citizens, or patients. This imposes particularly important "responsibilities" on those acting on their behalf. These duties cannot be justified by universal reasons. They rather result from the specific undertaking of protecting certain interests over others,[68] even vis-à-vis some universal ones,[69] as can be seen in

[65] Thomas Nagel, *The View from Nowhere* (Oxford University Press, 1986).

[66] Bernard Williams, *Moral Luck* (Cambridge University Press, 1981).

[67] In this context, see the so-called Arrow's Theorem first published in Kenneth J. Arrow, "A Difficulty in the Concept of Social Welfare," *The Journal of Political Economy*, vol. 58 (1950), 328–46.

[68] This is the case in property law, which "privileges" claims based on titles while the issue of the original assignment of titles is left outside its scope, thus for example "favouring" capital over labour.

[69] Here the lawyer/client privilege comes to mind or the right of refusing to give testimony against family members.

the client/lawyer privilege, or in the right not to testify against another family member.

With these considerations in mind, one can see that a different set of criteria emerges for assessing "practical" knowledge. Traditionally the epistemic distinction has been drawn between theoretical knowledge – aiming at the universal and at "truth" – and "prudence," which supports choices where an actor has to come to terms with the constraints imposed by a particular situation. While this distinction provides a good first cut, it needs further unpacking. Consider in this context how we understand a simple action. The scientific understanding would argue for a causally efficient account in which the antecedent cause brings about the subsequent result. Hume talks in this context of the "constant" conjunction that has to be established between the two. But that will not do, as the following example shows.

The playing of the national anthem at baseball games does not "cause" the baseball game. Why not? Because we understand actions finalistically, that is in terms of an intended goal (Aristotle's *hou heneka*)[70] rather than through antecedent, independent causes. Although the independence condition is met in the above example, the playing of the anthem is not "part" of the game and cannot establish a plausible link that we require from an explanation (rather than a simple "before" and "after" of two events). True, an efficient causal explanation of action uses the "end" as the antecedent "motive" (cause) or employs simply "desires" that remain exogenous. Neither gambit, however, solves the problem.

In the finalistic explanation the "end" (outcome) and the antecedent cause (motive) are precisely not *independent* of each other, which is the logical requirement that characterizes (efficient) causal explanations. In the second case – using "desires" as causes – we do not fare much better. In that case, contrary to the usual "rational" explanation, no "*expected* utility" maximization would be possible, because desires are "immediate" and can only in this way be causally efficient. Reason can only calculate the means to an end, but is unable to choose among "ends." Given these conceptual difficulties, finalistic explanations do pretty well, and this is what we *are doing when we explain* an action. In short, there is nothing wrong with explaining an action finalistically. We see this in the case where the goal is not reached and the explanation fails the efficient causality test. For example, we would not consider our explanation as "refuted," if a person running after a bus could not hop on. Rather than revising our account, we hold on to it and simply treat it as a "failed" attempt, unless further evidence impels us to "dig deeper." Thus, the reason why finalistic explanations employing "purposes" seem to have gotten a bad name has probably more to do with Aristotle also applying them to *nature*, than with their alleged flaws in explaining actions.[71]

[70] See Aristotle, *Nicomachean Ethics*, transl. by J. K. A. Thompson, Book 6, Chapter 5, at 176f.

[71] The *entelecheia* of e.g. the acorn in which the oak is prefigured, or even more problematically in his *Physics*, where the first mover can exert force at a distance akin to the lover

Furthermore, since practical questions address what shall be done, not what is "true," truth-criteria are not determinative for both logical and "realizability" reasons. Since I shall deal with the realizability issue in Meditation 9, I want to say a few words here about the logical reasons. Consider the following cases. If the assertion that "nearly all A's are B's" is true, then it is wrong to say that "all A's are B's." But practically we are "probably" not getting into hot water if we act accordingly. Similarly, while the assertion "all knowledge claims are problematic" involves a performative self-contradiction, the logically equivalent rule of thumb – "Never make dogmatic knowledge claims" – does not seem to be untenable.[72]

What becomes clear from the first example is that the heuristic "in which situation am I?" provides the decisive first step for analysis, since otherwise even the pious hope of a probability assessment fails. Finding quick cognitive short cuts is now more important than rigor, parsimony, or generalizability.[73] Furthermore, because I know that things are not only risky, but they might also not work out due to unforeseen – even unforeseeable reasons – worrying about "optimal" strategies and equilibria is of lesser importance than having a fall-back position, or a viable exit strategy. This point was powerfully made by Clausewitz in his controversy with von Bülow,[74] who wanted to make grand strategy a "science" where victory could be calculated. But Clausewitz's insight seems to have been lost on those who want to wear the mantle of "science."

It is also important to note that in the case of assertions a decision concerning their "truth" follows the binary code (true/false) with no third (logical) possibility. In practical matters, however, compromises are sometimes possible, as logically impossible solutions to dilemmas can be found through introducing time, or through spatial separation schemes. Thus a "rotating" presidency, as was used in some post-Westphalian corporate arrangements for governance, gives each party a chance to rule. Another (spatial) example is provided by the antebellum compromise in the USA concerning slavery and the admission of new states to the Union.

Finally, in multi-party interactions, that is situations that involve potential n-person's prisoner's dilemmas or coordination games with asymmetric

who "moves" his partner. While the genetic code (but not mutation and evolution) could be made compatible with such an explanation scheme, the second example quite clearly projects anthropomorphic metaphors onto nature. See also Aristotle, *On Becoming to Be and Passing Away*, ed. by Marwan Rashed (Paris: Les Belles Lettres, 2005), where he deals with the "four causes."

[72] Nicholas Rescher, "Ueber einen zentralen Unterschied zwischen Theorie und Praxis," *Deutsche Zeitschrift fuer Philosophie*, vol. 47, no. 2 (1990), 171–82.

[73] For a further discussion see Joerg Friedrichs and Friedrich Kratochwil, "On Acting and Knowing," *International Organization*, vol. 63 (Fall 2009), 701–31.

[74] Peter Paret, "Clausewitz," in Peter Paret (ed.), *Makers of Modern Strategy* (Oxford University Press, 1986), 186–216.

multiple equilibria, expectations are not stabilized by private preferences or by personal experience and communication about non-cooperators (since this puts just another PD dilemma on top of the first one). Rather, such expectations are established by "*generalized presumptions*," or expectations about which expectations ought to be upheld, and by credible assurances as to their maintenance through a variety of measures. This is what we mean when we speak not only of the *counterfactual validity* of norms but also of their *institutionalization*.

If we acted only on established facts, only bilateral sequential deals would be possible, since there would be no general "credit" on which we could rely to fill the gap between my action and that of many others to which it is connected. Of course, classical game theory takes bilateral interactions as its paradigm and assumes simultaneity of choice and complete information. In this way the above-mentioned difficulties are assumed away, as non-simultaneity could be dangerous. Hobbes focused particularly on the difficulties that arise from the fact that one party has to perform first and the other is left in the lurch.[75] Another example are drug deals or black market transactions that can only get off the ground if one actor holds in one hand the money that he releases as soon as the "bag" or item is captured by the other hand.

Breaking up the exchange into sequential episodes might sometimes become necessary, however. For instance, the Mafia requires a to-be-initiated member to commit a crime first in order to prevent the novice from becoming a turncoat and selling out his new partners to the police. But a further test might then be required that proves that the new member has now made the gang his ongoing concern. The novice might be required to do a heinous act that might not be against the law but that is fundamentally against his interests. An example could be that he must kill his own beloved dog.

Diego Gambetta has conducted some very interesting studies on "trust" among criminal associations.[76] On closer inspection his analysis deals, however, with problems of private contract enforcement – in that appeals to the public authorities are unlikely (because of self-incrimination) – rather than with the general problem of social trust. Furthermore, incriminating evidence alone might not suffice to provide the necessary social "glue" among the gang members since the state might pass a key witness program that undermines the threat of self-incrimination. This is why an equally important part of the socialization program in criminal gangs depends upon changing the novice's self-conception, which provides an important anchor for loyalty to the group as the "dog test" above illustrates.

[75] Thomas Hobbes, *Leviathan*, ed. C. B. Macpherson (London: Penguin, 1985), Chapter 14 at 191–6.

[76] Diego Gambetta, *Codes of the Underworld: How Criminals Communicate* (Princeton University Press, 2009); see also his *The Sicilian Mafia* (Cambridge, MA: Harvard University Press, 1996).

These examples show that in the absence of general trust, interactions would be severely curtailed. But we must and do rely on some generalized expectations that facilitate the ongoing multiple transactions, as well as our future undertakings on which we have, however, to count *now* when making our choices.[77] There is no reason why we should exclude this general reliance from our explanations of actions only because these expectations cannot be person-based or be derived from direct personal experience (in a mistaken deference to an extreme stance of methodological individualism).

The point is simply that I have to presume that not only an *alter*, with whom I have never dealt with before, will be doing "his part" when I, for example, order a book, but that the choices of innumerable others will also be coordinated so that my transaction can go through. I have to assume that I can rely that the telephone or that the Internet works when I place an order, that the plane carrying the goods will be properly serviced and not crash, that a courier service will work in delivering the parcel, that the roads will be cleared of snow by the city to make delivery possible and so on. If all of these expectations had to be formed and reinforced by personal experience, which I then have somehow to transmit to others, none of our actions could ever get off the ground.

As this example illustrates, it is through institutions that we create and maintain these generalized expectations. This problem is poorly understood if the generalized trust is considered to be "emerging" directly from the interactions themselves. Two reasons speak against such an interpretation. First, as the discussion on custom in international law has shown, we need not only bilateral reiteration but also accretion (many members have to act similarly in specified situations). In addition, we also need the *opinio juris* that embodies the general presumption.

Second, in order to maintain and firm up these "presumptions," it is necessary that each actor *does not "learn"* from her last transaction with others and that she does not adjust her strategy accordingly. If Allan has been burned by Bill, he cannot use this experience as a reason for making up for his losses by taking advantage of Christine. Even if we stress the importance of self-help in systems where transgressions are not centrally sanctioned, the international arena is not really an example of anarchy in the Hobbesian sense of an anomy, where anything goes and where I have to rely on worst-case analysis. To that extent self-help systems usually are quite explicit about which form this "private" enforcement may take. The most important point, especially for the "bystanders," is that the retaliatory action has to be *publicly* related to the injury suffered by the claimant – thus ruling out acts of revenge that remain secret – and that the execution of the sanctions follows certain rules. Otherwise the self-help measures would be indistinguishable from random acts of violence

[77] Heinrich Popitz, *Die Normative Konstruktion der Gesellschaft* (Tübingen: J. C. B. Mohr, 1980).

and could not be recognized as "sanctions." Here the actual examination of the medieval *Fehde* (feud) in the Holy Roman Empire, which Otto Brunner presented,[78] is much more illuminating than much of a-priori reasoning of rational choice approaches.

These preliminary remarks, placing the study of norms in a wider framework of social action, make it clear that instrumental rationality is insufficient to account for what norms do. Thus, we do have to think of norms not only in terms of external constraints and costs; we must also recognize their capacity of moulding pre-dispositions, which in turn enable actors to pursue their individual and collective projects. To that extent the "constraint view" of (legal) norms seems too narrow for two reasons. When norms are merely "prices," then opportunistically driven actors will adjust their behaviour accordingly, very much in line with Posner's argument that a "norm constrains attempts by people to satisfy their preferences."[79] This does not mean that all incentives have to be "material," as naming and shaming might be a quite effective strategy, even in the absence of further sanctions. Nevertheless, the cost of these "sanctions" will be quite high when compared to the case where actors accept certain standards as "normal" and follow them out of habit or self-respect, since transgressions would entail internal guilt rather than externally imposed shame.

There is a second, perhaps even more important reason why the constraint view is problematic. As Martti Koskenniemi has pointed out, the distinctive character of law is that, unlike claims of interest or privilege, legal claims entail the recognition that their violation is a matter of community concern:

> In law benefits and burdens that belong to particular individuals or groups are universalized by reference to membership rules. What otherwise would be a mere private violation, a wrong done to me, a violation to my interest, is transformed by law into a violation against everyone in my position, a matter of concern for the political community itself.[80]

This community concern in "developed" societies is accompanied by central sanctions, but as the above example of self-help showed, it need not be. Self-help is not the situation in which "all bets are off" – as in a Hobbesian war of all against all – even though this danger exists. Self-help is a normatively constituted and circumscribed institution, and also exists in the domestic arena, as shown by the "repossession" man of numerous movies, or the "stopping" of a cheque (possible in the USA but not in many European jurisdictions). It requires a specific reference to the unredressed injuries and to

[78] Otto Brunner, *Land und Herrschaft* (Darmstadt: Wissenschaftliche Buchgesellschaft, 1990), reprint of the 5th edition of 1939.

[79] See Posner, "Law, Economics and Inefficient Norms," note 37 at 1699.

[80] Martti Koskenniemi, "International Law and Hegemony: A Reconfiguration," *Cambridge Review of International Affairs*, vol. 17, no. 2 (2004), 197–218, at 214.

the norms that have been violated. It presupposes not only the existence of some "public" (yet the "state" only residually), but also a language that goes far beyond that of "signalling."

It is indeed as difficult to imagine how the reproduction of social order could be explained in terms of the minimax strategies of purely self-interested individual actors. This would be similar to studying the phenomenon of language by aggregating individual utterances only, as only individuals can "speak." Here both the extreme individualism underlying the concept of rationality and the fallacy of misplaced concreteness (such as in: "states do not act, only people do") are a hindrance to understanding what we are doing. This leads me to a further shortcoming: the dichotomy between "interests," which are supposedly self-explanatory, and "norms," which are not, that is hardly ever critically examined. Not only do we have to know a bit more about where the interests come from – instead of leaving them outside the model of rational action – we also do need to know that what "counts" as an interest, and this in turn crucially depends on the situation or "game" in which we find ourselves, as this recognition also determines what "counts" as a resource. Thus, being big and heavy might be a resource a line backer has to have in football, but it will be of no use to someone playing chess.

To the extent that "interests" are also not like idiosyncratic personal preferences or desires, as in the old notion of *de gustibus*, but need to be reflected upon and placed in context, this does not mean that we have to assume benevolence or that altruism abounds in social life, but we do have to see that the really interesting problems lie far beyond the confines of theories of action relying on instrumental rationality. In addition, the notion of "theory," and the unquestioned assumption that what might be appropriate for the production of knowledge in one area will ipso facto also apply in all others, is not helpful, since some distinct problems of praxis are thereby passed over, as I have shown.

Conclusion

In a way I seem to have returned to my point of departure. I began by undermining the old orthodoxies in order to create some space for fresh reflection. This led me to a critical examination of the problems of interdisciplinarity. Such an approach seemed promising given the disappearance of the classical international law and the emergence of all types of law that mix public and private sources, lack formality (soft law), and deal with certain internationalized aspects of the environment, of taxation, of trade, or with human rights and responsibilities of international organization. This made it necessary to wrestle with the paradox that on the one hand knowledge is always disciplinary, as it is there that the bounds of sense are drawn, while, on the other hand, certain questions are ruled out of bounds even if some old, or newly emerging problems fit poorly into the old disciplinary templates.

My investigation moved at two levels. On one level I approached the problem through a critique of some existing interdisciplinary projects in international law. This critique led me to the more abstract problem on the second level: the assumption that disciplinary understandings have to satisfy the criteria of "theory" in order to provide warranted knowledge. Here I argued that such a subjection of the field of praxis to theoretical standards is problematic, as praxis has different needs and therefore requires criteria that are adequate for assessing the knowledge that informs action. Thus, the often-contested disciplinary division between politics and law can be shown to replicate a more fundamental chasm that has been papered over by the belief in the uniformity of all "true" knowledge. This belief emerged from the Cartesian quest and its epistemological project. To this day it characterizes the "unity of science" position and accounts for the emphasis on methodology in the social sciences. For a long time only law provided a fully articulated alternative, based on "prudence," even though law is now also increasingly colonized by the social sciences, particularly by economics.

Furthermore, I maintained that the "epistemological project" is not able to make good on its promises. To that extent, efforts to establish theoretical standards as canonical in the realm of practice are likely to derail analysis. Finally, I attempted to clarify some of the specific requirements of the analysis of practice. I took here the "meditation" as my genre for reflection, linking my discussion not only to the pre-Cartesians (Pascal and Montaigne) but also to such newer approaches as those by Toulmin[81] and Searle,[82] as well as to ordinary language philosophy.

Although I believe I showed several of the shortcomings of existing disciplinary and interdisciplinary approaches to law, I have not yet demonstrated how the initial paradox of disciplinary knowledge and genuine interdisciplinary analysis can be overcome. I provided only a hint that since these paradoxes cannot be "solved" – as attempts to do so lead to exacting logical requirements of various language levels (meta-languages) that only displace the paradoxes – the only way is to circumvent them. This can be done by retracing the conceptual steps that lead to the paradox and take then a different conceptual path. This leads to a therapeutic reconceptualization, which Wittgenstein and also some pragmatists suggested, in order to escape the "*Verhexung der Welt*" through language.

[81] Toulmin, *Return to Reason.* (Cambridge, MA: Harvard University Press, 2001).
[82] John Searle, *Rationality in Action* (Cambridge, MA: MIT Press, 2001).

Meditation 2

On the concept of law

Introduction

That nations dwell in anarchy has been the mainstay lore of realists of different stripes. Yet even Hobbes realized that things are not that simple. He distinguished the "misery" of the state of nature among individuals from that which prevails among "persons of sovereign authority."[1] Contrary to the necessity of transcending the war of all against all, states can counteract the dangers that arise in the case of individual vulnerability. They can organize police forces and a military, and contract alliances, thereby providing at least a modicum of security. Moreover, through establishing a public order, states create incentives for the development of a "commodious living" that comes to a naught when no sovereign keeps all of his subjects "in awe."

Those realists, who were not captured by certain "assumptions" by which the *homo politicus* has to maximize power analogous to the *homo economicus*' amassing of revenue,[2] but who were more historically inclined, as they were interested in the *actual functioning* of the (European) state system, paid close attention to the conventions and institutions facilitating the relations among "persons of sovereign authority."[3] Thus the institution of treaty making (bilaterally or in congresses), of the acquisition of titles and their transfers, and the attempts to regulate the use of force (*ius ad bellum* and *in bello*) emerged quickly as core concerns for a systematic analysis.[4] Hume had already considered these norms and institutions as fundamental in the sense that without the establish-

[1] See Thomas Hobbes, *Leviathan*, ed. by C. B. Macpherson (London: Penguin, 1985), Chapter 13, at 188: "But because they [the persons of Sovereign Authority] uphold thereby the Industry of their Subjects, there does not follow from it that misery, which accompanies the Liberty of particular Men."

[2] See Hans Morgenthau, *Politics Among Nations*, 4th edition (New York: Knopf, 1967), 6th principle of realism, at 11.

[3] This is the term Hobbes uses for describing the "international." See Hobbes, *Leviathan*, Chapter 13, at 187.

[4] See e.g. Hedley Bull, *The Anarchical Society* (New York: Columbia University Press, 1970), Chapter 2.

ment of certain normative expectations in regard to those concerns, no social system can reproduce itself.[5]

From this, the English School[6] developed a research program focusing on an "anarchical society" and on comparisons of historical systems of states, which in turn raised further questions as to the embeddedness of these institutions in the wider context of "civilizations," cultures, or traditions. This was a problem that Arnold Toynbee, Martin Wight,[7] and more recently Christian Reus-Smit have addressed.[8] But the question whether these rules were really proper "law" or just part of some vague international "morality" remained problematic. "Law," as opposed to other types of prescriptions, seemed to be tightly linked to the state, as was shown by the foundational myth of the social contract that established the sovereign and his subjects, but only the sovereign was authorized to make law as an exercise of *dominium*.

Ironically, the English School reopened that debate at a time when the classical "society of states" was already coming under pressure from transformative processes of change.[9] Although states were not being replaced by other actors, even an international organization, of universal scope, could not shoulder the tasks for which it was designed, as the Cold War showed, for example. This failure to establish a new universal order therefore provided a grim reminder that "block politics," while transcending the state, looked nevertheless quite similar to the Hobbesian state of nature among individual men. However, states were no longer the only members of the club determining the rules of the game. Even long before the human rights revolution, and before obligations "*erga omnes*" ignited the discussions, the emergence of *transnational* law made the notion that international law was the "body of rules binding upon states" appear to be out of touch with actual praxis. An even more challenging development was that of "soft law," which was showing its bite not only in the cases of various conditionality agreements of the IMF, but – after the Helsinki Accords – it also empowered domestic groups to claim their rights from their government. It initiated a fundamental

[5] David Hume, *A Treatise of Human Nature*, Book II, section "On Morals," in Thomas H. Gree and Thomas H. Grose (eds.), *The Philosophical Works* (Aalen: Scientia 1886, reprinted 1964).

[6] See Tim Dunne, "The English School," in Christian Reus-Smit and Duncan Snidal (eds.), *The Oxford Handbook on International Relations* (Oxford University Press, 2008), 267–85. For the European State system see also Hedley Bull, Benedict Kingsbury and Adam Roberts (eds.), *Hugo Grotius and International Relations* (Oxford: Clarendon, 1992).

[7] See Martin Wight, *Systems of States* (Leicester University Press, 1977).

[8] See e.g. Christian Reus-Smit, "Constitutional Structure of International Society and the Nature of Fundamental Institutions," *International Organization*, vol. 51, no. 4 (1997), 555–89; see also his "Struggles for Individual Rights and the Expansion of the International System," *International Organization*, vol. 65, no. 2 (2011), 207–42.

[9] See Barry Buzan, *From International to World Society? English School Theory and the Social Structure of Globalization* (Cambridge University Press, 2004).

transformation of the international system that eventually contributed to the demise of the Soviet bloc.[10] It also exploded the myth that the neat distinction between soft and hard law followed the familiar distinction between more or less unimportant functional areas, while matters of high politics could only be handled – if at all – by "hard law" (the "law of coexistence"[11]).

In short, formality was no longer neatly correlated with "obligation" as the dichotomy of "law/non-law," or the Kelsenian "sanction/non-sanction" distinction had implied. Similarly, courts, supposed to apply *legal* rules (namely those that have a pedigree and can be traced to their authorizing source), soon found these limitations too confining. As the ICJ in the *North Sea Continental Shelf* case suggested,[12] rules of positive law might exist, yet applying them would lead to unsatisfactory outcomes. For that reason equity principles, rather than strict rules, had to be invoked for arriving at a decision.

Of course, one could be tempted to turn these arguments around, arguing that "therefore" the ICJ was not a "real" court, and also that international law was nothing more than some mouthpiece of international morality. But these gambits would be too easy, taking for granted that the traditional criteria for law were indeed establishing a conceptually distinct and exclusive set of norms, that is those that contained sanctions. However, not all legal norms have sanctions attached to them. For example, a constitutional proviso stipulating that "there shall be ten courts of appeal" functions quite well within the legal system without a sanction. Similarly, equity has been part of common law for quite some time, but nobody doubts that common law is genuine law and its courts are "real" courts. Thus, neither the "character tag" theory à la Kelsen, which assumed that all legal rules must have something in common,[13] nor viewing legal rules as part of a system of primary and secondary rules, as suggested by Hart, seemed to do justice to the complexity of "rule-handling."

On the other hand, insisting on the "indeterminacy of rules" and pointing instead to the importance of "principles" was not that helpful either, since it seemed to make law into an ethics at basement prices. After all, we need hard and fast rules at the domestic level as well as at the international level. There is no moral reason that justifies the rule of driving on the right side of the road, or setting time limits for appeals, aside from making the case that a hard and fast rule has to exist as otherwise the legal enterprise would come to a screeching halt. Similarly morality cannot tell us what the width of the territorial sea is, or the number of days a belligerent vessel might stay for repair or refuelling in a

[10] See the discussion in Meditation 7 on the "Politics of Rights."

[11] See Wolfgang Friedmann, *The Changing Structure of International Law* (New York: Columbia University Press, 1964).

[12] *North Sea Continental Shelf* (*Germany* v. *Denmark and Netherlands*) (1969) ICJ Reports, 3.

[13] Hans Kelsen, *Principles of International Law* (New York: Holt, 1966).

neutral port. As in municipal orders, we need something like statutes so that law can resolve our quandaries.[14]

Not deterred by those rebuttals, one could again take a quick escape and claim that international law possessed no "rule of recognition" (which would have to be a tertiary rule), and that it was, therefore, not law. But it is doubtful whether most of the historical legal orders had such a clear-cut hierarchy. Moreover, as Hart pointed out, a rule of recognition was a "luxury" not a "necessity"[15] for a system of law.

These puzzles show that something more is amiss. Perhaps it is the idea, criticized in the previous Meditation, that in order to belong to a "class," all exemplars of a given "type" must show one common characteristic. This gives rise to attempts at designing exclusive categories and of separating "essential" properties from accidental ones. But what if these attempts derive from a false notion of language as a simple mirror of the "world out there"?[16] They thus mistakenly assume that concepts "work" by reference rather than by their link to other concepts and to practices that authorize, forbid, or require a certain conduct. What if "the law" consists of rules and norms that can have more than one characteristic, which several of them but not all of them share? Here Wittgenstein's notion of family resemblances and language games comes into play. In this context he also uses the example of a rope that is made up of many strings without one string, representing the core, going through the whole length.

Let us briefly look at the famous paragraph 66 of the *Philosophical Investigations* where the notion of a game is explicated:

> Consider for example the proceedings we call "games." I mean board games, card games, ball games, Olympic games, and so on. What is common to them all? – Don't say: "There *must* be something common, or they would not be called "games" – but *look and see* whether there is anything common to all. – For if you look at them you will not see something that is common to *all*, but similarities, relationships, and a whole series of them at that … And the result of this examination is: we see a complicated network of similarities overlapping and criss-crossing: sometimes overall similarities, sometimes similarities of detail.[17]

In paragraph 67 Wittgenstein introduces the notion of family resemblances:

> I can think of no better expression to characterize these similarities than "family resemblances"; for the various resemblances between members of

[14] H. L. A. Hart, *The Concept of Law* (New York/Oxford: Oxford University Press, 1961), 224.

[15] *Ibid.*, at 229.

[16] See Richard Rorty, *Philosophy and the Mirror of Nature* (Princeton University Press, 1979).

[17] Ludwig Wittgenstein, *Philosophical Investigations*, transl. by Elisabeth Anscombe (New York: Macmillan, 1953), para. 66.

> a family: build, features, colour of eyes, gait, temperament, etc. etc. overlap and criss-cross in the same way. – And I shall say: "games" form a family.[18]

Given these thoughts, our puzzle seems to result from a problematic view of how our concepts and language function. For one, a theory of language based on a purely referential notion of meaning (specified by "truth conditions") would presuppose that we have direct, unmediated access to reality – an echo of a Cartesian coincidence of the *res cogitans* with the *res extensa*. Second, this has some important implications for the way we think of how norms function in moulding our choices. Given the unstated assumption of the epistemological ideal, norms would simply have to be "external constraints" that function analogous to efficient causes.

But we know that this is false due to the already discussed problematic nature of the "epistemological ideal" and, therefore, we need to clarify what we are doing when we use rules and norms. We do not need a "truer" description but a clarification of how we actually proceed when we use norms and relate them to actions. This requires an "internal" point of view of rule-following, but not a psychological report on the individual's mind and its "mechanisms." Rather, what we need is an account of the "competent performance" of a common practice.[19]

In his inaugural lecture at Oxford H. L. A. Hart, relying on Bentham, suggested that "what is" questions when directed at "law" are not very useful, since norms are not "matters of fact."[20] Thus, to understand what the law *is*, we must comprehend what it *does*, namely how it functions. To this we might also add that since law addresses actions that do not take place in space but in time, it does not lend itself well to spatial representation, as is suggested by the architectonics or the "structure" of a system. True, different norms might be arranged in super- or sub-ordination, but which of the (sometimes) conflicting rules will be chosen, in the light of higher order principles and of the facts of the case, cannot be read off the norms themselves or their "structure." Instead, norms have to be interpreted and related to the facts of the case. Thus, the (logical) closure of a legal system might be an illusion resulting from a lack of awareness that closure obtains only through the act of judging. Finally, these judgments are not "true," but they have to be *justifiable* in terms of certain criteria. However, the latter are not field-independently specifiable once and for all, so that they can be later "applied" to a specific domain, as the predominant conception of "ideal theory" and analytical ethics suggests.[21] Rather, they are

[18] *Ibid.* at para. 67.

[19] See the recent anthology by Emanuel Adler and Vincent Pouliot (eds.), *International Practices* (Cambridge University Press, 2011).

[20] H. L. A. Hart, "Definition and Theory in Jurisprudence," *Law Quarterly Review*, vol. 70 (1954), 37–60.

[21] By ideal theory I mean attempts such as those by Rawls or building models based on idealized assumptions. For a criticism of this approach see Meditation 10.

part of a common practice shared by the competent performers in the field. As Brunée and Toope have pointed out, a "richer understanding of legal obligation emerges when the focus is shifted from the formal manifestations of law to the interplay between internal markers and the practices that sustain legality."[22]

The move from the intrinsic characteristics of rules to the concept of a *system* and to the realization of closure obtaining not for logical but axiological reasons has advanced our understanding. But it shows at the same time the limits for an inter-disciplinary dialogue, because, in the case of law, such issues as the ascription of responsibility, or of rights, cannot be reduced to "causal" action accounts or to the pursuit of "interests" by rational actors without neglecting fundamental characteristics of the legal enterprise. On the other hand, the change in perspective helps us to see how law, as a practical discipline, cannot remain in splendid isolation, as other disciplines also concerned with action provide the "material" for law's ordering function in social life. Here the links to ethics (free will), medicine (when does life end), and economics (perverse incentives, allocation of risks) and so on come to mind. These interactions of disciplinary understandings create dilemmas that cannot be solved in a straightforward fashion by "assuming" that a method can provide us with a universal algorithm, or a one-to-one translation. Nevertheless, many dilemmas can be circumvented by engaging with the understandings articulated in different "disciplines." In this way we might also become aware that the most vexing puzzles arise out of certain conceptual befuddlements, which we usually do not see because they are so ingrained.[23] This new awareness is then not simply cognitive. It is also practical. It has not eliminated all puzzles, but at least it has set us free to "go on" in spite of the persistence of those puzzles.

Two problems are now of particular import when we want to understand how a rule is followed and take our cues from Wittgenstein's later work. One concerns Kripke's rule-sceptic interpretation of Wittgenstein,[24] according to which nothing follows from rules since no rule specifies its range of application. How then do we go on? It seems that we need rules about rules, leading to an infinite regress. But how can we then say that we are following rules? Usually we think that we have to find an explanation in terms of how the "independent" variable, the norm, affects the "dependent" variable, the action, and thus the chase is on for finding how the norms got into "the mind" of an actor and

[22] Jutta Brunée and Stephen Toope "Interactional International Law and the Practice of Legality," in Emmanuel Adler and Vincent Pouliot (eds.), *International Practices* (Cambridge University Press, 2011), 108–36, at 109. See also the further elaboration on their distinct approach, which is indebted to both constructivism and Fuller's teachings on legality in Jutta Brunée and Stephen Toope, *Legitimacy and Legality in International Law: an Interactional Account* (Cambridge University Press, 2010).

[23] Wittgenstein, *Philosophical Investigations*, at 340.

[24] Saul Kripke, *Wittgenstein on Rules and Private Language* (Cambridge, MA: Harvard University Press, 1982).

affect her actions in a causal way. Since this usually leads to some murky arguments of "compliance," we frequently look rather quickly for some more reliable "predictors," such as structural constraints or "interests" that can explain more of the "variance" and thus provide us with a "truer" description of what is going on. But this, as I shall argue below, amounts to a giant misstep that prevents us from understanding and analysing the realm of practice. In short, I shall argue that we do not need a truer "description," but a clarification of how we actually proceed when we use norms for making decisions and link norms to action. As I have already argued, this requires an "internal" point of view of rule-following, but not a psychological report on the individual's mind and its "mechanisms." This has important implications not only for law, but also for any interdisciplinary dialogue in which we might want to engage.

The second problem concerns the applicability of Wittgenstein's examples, because they are largely derived from mathematics[25] and from "drills" that teach us a way of "learning" in terms of "knowing how" – like having learned how to ride a bicycle so that we can perform the required actions nearly automatically.[26] However, this might indeed be a highly problematic analogy to following rules in a legal context, where disagreements are rife. After all, in mathematics, disputes "do not break out … over the question whether a rule has been obeyed or not."[27]

These objections seem grist to the mill for legal realists as well as for postmodernists. The former explain actual choices, including judicial decisions, in terms of constraints (Holmes, "bad man"), or individual idiosyncrasies, or the ideologies prevalent in a society.[28] For some postmodernists such as Derrida, law does not result from rule following, but it is by its very nature a "site of repression," where a line is drawn so that the "mystical foundation" of the "authority of laws"[29] are hidden, and "the operation that consists of founding, inaugurating, justifying law (*droit*), making law, would consist of a *coup de force*, of a performative and therefore interpretative violence."[30] In this way, laws can appear as just and legitimate, while claiming that they "can't by definition rest on anything but themselves, they are themselves a violence without ground."[31]

It is to these two issues that I turn in the next two sections before I propose an alternative account indebted to ordinary language philosophy. Moreover,

[25] See Wittgenstein, *Philosophical Investigations*, para. 240.
[26] On the notion of "knowing how" and implicit knowledge see Michael Polanyi, *Personal Knowledge* (University of Chicago Press, 1958).
[27] Wittgenstein, *Philosophical Investigations*, para. 240.
[28] See Brian Leitner, "American Legal Realism," in Martin Golding and William Edmunson (eds.), *The Blackwell Guide to the Philosophy of Law and Legal Theory* (Oxford: Blackwell, 2003), 50–62.
[29] Jacques Derrida, "Force of Law," *Cardozo Law Review*, vol. 11 (1989–1990), 920–1045, at 939–41.
[30] *Ibid.* at 941. [31] *Ibid.* at 943.

my approach also incorporates pragmatic elements and notions of reasoning about praxis similar to hermeneutic approaches. Although these remarks sound highly abstract and philosophical, they are of considerable importance for the understanding of law and its role in social life.

Reflections on "obeying rules blindly"

Some of the remarks in Wittgenstein's *Philosophical Investigations* seem to come close to a purely cognitivist account of action, such as when he says: "When I obey a rule I do not choose. I obey the rule blindly."[32] To that extent "rules" seem to work like external causes that inevitably call forth an action. The rules that somehow have "gotten in the actor's mind,"[33] either through "socialization" or "emulation," are then supposed to work in a causal fashion. Since, however, no rule "makes" one behave in a certain way, as rules or norms are not causes, but provide reasons for actions,[34] there is a tendency, as we have seen, to treat rules as epiphenomenal, as rationalizations of some deeper and more reliable explanatory factors. Here "interests" or "desires" are supposed to fill the gap. But when we explain, as I have adumbrated above, what we are doing is to appeal to common practices that we use as templates, we do not refer to our private psychological states, but place our actions within the publicly known rules underlying our practices. "In other words, the chronic problem of both social theory and cognitive science is that they suppose that explanation requires a new explanatory mechanism, when in truth, explanation of a clarificatory kind will suffice to solve (or rather dissolve) their problems."[35]

Since Wittgenstein's main effort was precisely to undermine the classical dualism between the inside and the outside, between mind and body, by showing that "action" has its own logic and justification, amalgamating his approach to a "causal" inference is misleading. We know what we are doing – and so does everybody else – by being able "to go on." The sceptic's complaint is, therefore, unwarranted – at least for the easy cases. This is what Wittgenstein highlights in his aphorism 217: "If I have exhausted the justifications I have reached bedrock and my spade is turned. Then I am inclined to say: 'this is simply what I do.'"[36] This does not mean that Wittgenstein suggests that we *follow rules automatically in all contexts* as his examples of games show, where some of them

[32] Wittgenstein *Philosophical Investigations*, para. 219.

[33] See e.g. the implausible account of Stephen Turner, *The Social Theory of Practices: Tradition, Tacit Knowledge, and Presuppositions* (University of Chicago Press, 1994).

[34] Friedrich Kratochwil and John Ruggie, "The State of the Art on the Art of the State," *International Organization*, vol. 40 (Fall 1986), 753–76.

[35] Wes Sharrock and Alex Dennis, "That We Obey Rules Blindly Does Not Mean that We Are Blindly Subservient to Rules," *Theory, Culture and Society*, vol. 25 no. 2 (2008), 33–50, at 35.

[36] Wittgenstein, *Philosophical Investigations*, para. 217.

are strictly defined by rules (such as chess), some are rule-flexible and need a referee, and in some, as in improvisations or in children's plays, we seem to make them up, or modify them, as we go along.

Against the theoretical ideal that looks for external factors causing actions, Wittgenstein stresses practice; against the notion of concepts fitting objects, he emphasizes their "use" in a language. But "use" depends on a "form of life" and on publicly shared criteria or grammars (and not on private preferences – vide Wittgenstein's rejection of "private languages") by which we establish the proper use of the terms. In this way we can also communicate about sensations and feelings that seem at first entirely idiosyncratic expressions. As Wittgenstein points out:

> There doesn't seem to be any problem here; don't we talk about sensations every day, and give them names? But how is the connection between the name and the thing named set up? The question is the same as: how does a human being learn the meaning of the names of sensations? – of the word "pain" for example. Here is one possibility: words are connected with the primitive, the natural, expressions of the sensation are used in their place. A child has hurt himself and he cries; and then adults talk to him and teach him exclamations and, later, sentences. They teach the child new pain-behaviour.[37]

Here no deictic procedure, no feeling of empathy, has to be invoked. To understand means to understand an intersubjective language and to understand a language "means to master a technique."[38] Thus meanings can be established without direct intuition or "perception" of "things" leaving their marks on the *tabula rasa* of the mind.[39] The whole apparatus of epistemological standards and of a scientific method are of little use here. And neither can such a stance be construed as the result of a mere coincidence of opinion or as an "agreement." It is rather the way we have learned to use the terms in accordance with certain "grammars" and criteria embedded in a "form of life."[40]

> "So you are saying that human agreement decides what is true and what is false?" – It is what human beings *say* that is true and false; and they agree in the *language* they use. This is not an agreement in opinion but in form of life.[41]

Such a stance rules out idiosyncrasies, but it also eschews appeals to transcendent verities, such as Platonic ideas. When, for instance, someone says "this is a

[37] *Ibid.* at para. 244. [38] *Ibid.* at para. 199.

[39] See John Locke, *An Essay Concerning Human Understanding*, ed. by Kenneth Winkler (Indianapolis: Hackett, 1996), Book II.

[40] Here the use of form of life (*Lebensform*) in the singular means the general way in which humans function and use language while the plural *Lebensformen* is used more for specific "communities of practice" such as lawyers, doctors etc., whereby the former is the enabling condition for different, more specific forms of life to emerge.

[41] Wittgenstein, *Philosophical Investigations*, para. 241.

good car" or "this is a good fountain pen" or this is a "good person," we can ask for reasons why this term "good" was used. Although it is the "same" in all three cases, this sameness cannot be understood as some essence or participation in the idea of goodness. Yet it is not a mere statement of personal preferences either, because it is governed by the criteria of proper use of the term. If we say "this car is good" and we are challenged to give reasons, we could say "because it goes fast," or "it is comfortable," or "it does a lot of miles per gallon." In those cases we use "good" properly, although we might point to different reasons by which we buttress our claim. If we were to say it is "good" because it is "blue," we obviously would not understand the use of the term, or we would be pulling the leg of our audience. And it would then not even matter whether we got agreement among the bystanders (who might want to pull our leg in turn).

This general discussion has important implications not only for communication and the problem of interpretation, but also for judgments that command assent because they are not mere indications of personal preferences, as suggested by the conventional accounts of "normative" statements. The latter stance leaves us with either the problem of *de gustibus non est disputandum* or with an implausible "theory" of judgment that assumes, à la early Dworkin, that failing to come to the same conclusion, our judgments are somehow faulty. This is not only problematic for law, but also as a general proposition. It is problematic for the simple logical reason that determinacy and uniqueness are different criteria that do not necessarily coincide. The "multiple equilibria" problem in game theory suggests that determined outcomes (equilibria) need not be unique. But how can we claim on non-idiosyncratic grounds that our solution to a practical problem can marshal assent? Let us begin with the problem of interpretation, because something more and something less than assumed seems to be required.

From what was said, it should be clear that interpretation emerges as a "second order, reflective enterprise" as Dennis Patterson called it. It arises when our interactions are interrupted and we can no longer "go on."

> For example, one evinces understanding of the request "please pass the salt" by passing the salt, or by explaining why it is impossible to do so. Understanding is made manifest in the *act* of passing the salt, and the act is a criterion for having understood the utterance. Understanding is acting properly in response to the request. If the request is vague or otherwise opaque, interpretations of the request are necessary, otherwise not ... Thus interpretation is best thought of ... as an activity of clarification – we take the utterance in question and appraise competing construals or interpretations in an effort to clarify its meaning.[42]

[42] Dennis Patterson, "The Poverty of Interpretive Universalism: Toward the Reconstruction of Legal Theory," *Texas Law Review*, vol. 72 (1993), 1–56 at 54f.

In this way our interpretations always presuppose that something is already in place that can be used as a background for dealing with the ruptures in our interaction. This means that our communications might have to include not only certain well-understood practices but also paradigmatic cases based on judgments, as Wittgenstein points out.[43] While in law these "precedents" might let us go on with greater ease, they are seldom so clear as to recommend a way to proceed to a single outcome. The reason is not simply that precedents might be countered with other precedents, or that the controversy might be susceptible to different readings. Whether an issue should be dealt with as a national security issue, as an issue of human rights, or as one falling under the laws of war regulating occupation, has vexed not only the ICJ judges and the commentators of the *Wall* case.[44] In short, Dworkin's early argument for unique right decisions in constitutional cases simply assumes too much, as does his later yardstick of the chain novel, written by many authors over time but thereby requiring a consistency, or at least the "followability" of a storyline.[45] Indeed, the judges of Appellate or Supreme Courts have then to be some kind of Herculi, endowed with superhuman powers, which is also probably why they can be found, in a good right-Hegelian fashion, only at the highest courts! Moreover, we are led to believe that the question of determinacy and of uniqueness is the same, which, for the above reasons, is simply mistaken.

Ultimately we might have to fall back on some other method for justifying our judgments if – not surprisingly – no agreement emerges. Such alternative methods could be majority voting, as is common in higher courts, the avoidance of a decision by not taking on the case (denial of certiorari) – despite the inadmissibility of the *non liquet* presumption enshrined in legal systems – or the use of other "avoidance techniques." Thus, there is ineluctably some "indeterminacy" or arbitrariness in law, even though this is much less than, for instance, in moral debates. This indeterminacy has little to do with the reasons advanced by rule sceptics, legal realists, or de-constructionists, however. The question is not, as Derrida maintains, that "the absence of the transcendental signified" can be understood as the "destruction of … the metaphysics of presence," and that the *différance* is not simply a concept but rather "the possibility of conceptuality, of a conceptual process and system in general."[46] Rather, the

[43] Wittgenstein, *Philosophical Investigations*, para. 242.

[44] See the Advisory Opinion "On the Legal Consequences of a Wall in the Occupied Palestinian Territory" (2004) ICJ Reports, 136.

[45] See Ronald Dworkin, *Taking Rights Seriously* (Cambridge, MA: Harvard, 1977), Chapter 4. See also his *Law's Empire* (Cambridge, MA: Harvard, 1986), Chapter 6. Whether Dworkin has in the meantime given up on his earlier thesis, as Raz suggests, can here remain unresolved. For another argument that Dworkin has changed his position in *Law's Empire*, see also N. E. Simmons, "Imperial Visions and Mundane Practices," *Cambridge Law Journal*, vol. 46 (Nov 1987), 465–88.

[46] Derrida, "Force of Law."

problem is what to do about it. The issue is whether we should be satisfied with endless rounds of deconstruction, which Derrida calls "play," thereby falling again and again into the theoretical traps that reinscribe a metaphysics of presence that deconstruction was supposed to undermine, or whether we should search for new ways to "go on" with our lives and political projects, despite the fact that there is no ultimate foundation.

Similarly one has to wonder whether Martti Koskenniemi's original post-modern deconstruction of the international legal discourse, encountering thereby a seemingly endless spiral of arguments that meander between apology and utopia, does not result from his conceptual framework. If you start out with conceptual tools that distinguish clearly between the "is" and the "ought" that are rooted in the tradition of "theory" – after all Kant still wanted to reform metaphysics so that philosophy could become a "science" – then what we are seeing is exactly what this distinction lets us see, because everything else is left out. But we know – and Wittgenstein took great pains to make us aware of it – that this is not what we are after *when we act or argue*. It is therefore perhaps not accidental that Koskenniemi more recently emphasized the elements of *a practice of legal arguing* that modifies (or clarifies) considerably[47] his earlier indeterminacy argument and the characterization of international law as "useless." He still maintains that "law" is all "about lifting idiosyncratic (subjective) interests and preferences from the realm of the special to that of the general (objective)," which, by this very procedure of "making" the law, loses much of the idiosyncratic character as the rules seem now "natural, necessary or pragmatic."[48]

Thus the imagery of a meandering between two poles is now largely displaced by the metaphor of "competence." As in the case of the well-formed sentences of a native speaker,[49] this competency is not directly derivable from what he says. Nor do the ingrained structures of the grammar "make" him utter certain sentences, or advocate certain "solutions," as "international law is not necessarily representative of what is good in the world."[50] This leaves the indeterminacy thesis standing, but at the same time casts doubt on the implication that in the absence of firm guidance or foundations nothing significant can be said.

> The indeterminacy treated in *From Apology to Utopia* is then not about semantic openness of legal speech. There is nothing necessarily unclear about "if an armed attack occurs" or "territorial inviolability" or "right to life." The indeterminacy is about the relationship of those expressions to their

[47] See Marti Koskenniemi, *From Apology to Utopia* (Cambridge University Press, 2005), 67.

[48] *Ibid.* at 597.

[49] Koskenniemi states in his Epilogue: "The descriptive project of *From Apology to Utopia* was to reconstruct the argumentative architecture of international law … so as to produce an account of it as a language and a professional competence." *Ibid.* at 589.

[50] *Ibid.* at 568.

> underlying reasons and to other rules and principles that make it sometimes seem necessary to deviate from a formally unambiguous provision in view of new information or a new circumstance, to sacrifice a smaller good (abstract legality) in view of realizing a larger one. The deformalization of international law we have surveyed … points to the apparent necessity of applying the reasons for the rule over the empty form of the rule (e.g. allowing self-defence even where no proper attack has occurred) or finding a pragmatic balance between various rules and principles and other normative materials (most frequently "rights") and choosing between rules and exceptions.[51]

There are not only bridges between "is" and "ought" in praxis – as institutional rules, for example, allow us to derive from such seemingly factual premises, such as "this is a contract," prima facie obligations – that are neither apologetic nor utopian. The fact that there is no *logically* compelling bridge – if one applies the traditional criteria of a two-valued logic – does not mean, however, that *no bridge* exists at all, as the principle of the excluded middle in classical logic postulates. Here the attempts to bridge the gap in a Kantian fashion by focusing on his *Third Critique* have to be mentioned. They are exemplified by the works of Lyotard,[52] Korsgaard,[53] and Ferrara.[54] The early work of Habermas on a "transcendental pragmatics" represents another instance of such an effort.[55] But ultimately the quest for a "theoretical" solution of these conundrums might not be available since it does not concern a theoretical problem to begin with, as the last Meditation will suggest. Koskenniemi intimates this much when he states that the criticism of (international) law not being able to provide for its own foundation had lost much of its power when he realized that:

> International law is not a theoretical discipline. Its basis or "core" does not lie in theory but in practice … [and] seeking an abstract grounding has never been its strength … This is the inherent weakness of internal or "immanent" critique – a demonstration that a practice does not live up to its justifying explanations has no force when the practitioners themselves do not take those explanations seriously.[56]

It is only when we leave this perspective behind, and focus on what we are doing, that the interesting problems become visible. Terms such as "soft law" or "relative normativity" might seem oxymorons when viewed from the old perspective of theory. But they are far from nonsensical in the world of praxis. Instead, nonsensical are the attempts at arriving at incontrovertible foundations, unique

[51] *Ibid.* at 595.

[52] Jean François Lyotard, "Sensus Communis," in Andrew Benjamin (ed.), *Judging Lyotard* (London: Routledge, 1992), 1–25.

[53] Christine Korsgaard, *The Sources of Normativity* (Cambridge University Press, 1996).

[54] Alessandro Ferrara, *Justice and Judgement* (London: Sage, 1999).

[55] Juergen Habermas, *Theorie des Kommunikativen Handelns* (Frankfurt: Suhrkamp, 1981).

[56] Koskenniemi, *From Apology to Utopia*, at 600.

solutions, or at the point from where we can view the natural and historical world as it "actually" is, when viewed from "nowhere" (in the parlance of the philosopher Nagel). It is here that Wittgenstein's reflections help us dispel what he calls *Verhexungen*, or "bewitchments of our intelligence by language,"[57] and proposes to focus on "perspicuous representations": "A perspicuous representation produces just this understanding which consists of finding and inventing intermediate cases."[58] While Wittgenstein has certainly not worked out a set of such perspicuous representations for law, his approach is nevertheless useful as a first move, since it points us in a new direction of how rules and practices function and how we find our way through language.

Thus by following his pointers, we have not only moved from the notion of legal norms that are allegedly all of one order by possessing a character tag (Kelsen's sanctions), to a notion of law as a system of rules (Hart), and to a notion that such representations still do not do justice to what goes on when we use norms since we use them for a variety of communicative acts: for making demands, for justifying choices, or for empowering someone to decide authoritatively a case and controversy, and thereby also saying what the law is. It is this problem that I try to address in the next two sections, which will show that "law," even domestic law, is much more heterogeneous than most legal theories suggest. Here Wittgenstein's idea of family resemblance and of law as a "language game" is helpful. But before I can address these issues, I examine more closely what the notion of "meaning is use" implies for law.

Law as norm-use

If it is true that law is badly conceived as an abstract system of norms, or even as a generative system of rules, why not emphasize the process-character as various approaches have done? These range from the attempts of the New Haven School around Myres McDougal, to the managerial approach characteristic of the "new process" approach.[59] Both share a rejection of formalism and both tend to emphasize the law's goal-oriented character, be it "human dignity," common solutions to public goods problems,[60] or – here process meets realism – the national interest.[61] A difference exists, however, in that McDougal

[57] Wittgenstein, *Philosophical Investigations*, para. 109.

[58] *Ibid.* at para. 122.

[59] See e.g. Abram Chayes and Antonia Handler Chayes, *The New Sovereignty: Compliance with International Regulatory Agreements* (Princeton University Press, 1995).

[60] See e.g. Inge Kaul, *et al.*, *Providing Public Goods* (New York: Oxford, 2003). Here economic analysis is clearly the driving force and legal norms are just to enable the actors to achieve their goals by providing transparency for choices, securing property rights, and allowing for dispute settlement.

[61] See e.g. Goldsmith and Posner, who prefer an "instrumental account" of international law and consequently suggest that compliance with international law will depend on the "price"

and Lasswell still emphasized the bounded nature of a system of public order that includes "both the identity and the preferred distribution pattern of basic goal values and implementing institutions that are accorded protection by the legal process."[62] Most of the more recent approaches, however, have lowered the bar for participation in this process. Although McDougal basically remains a statist, despite his emphasis on the informality of norms, in the more modern versions of the process school the law-making process is characterized by a further informality, as new actors have made their appearance and shaped this process decisively.

These remarks have important implications for law. First, while law certainly is a process, not all processes in which normative claims are made and answered by counterclaims are legal. In this context debates and bargaining comes to mind. They almost always contain appeals to norms and values that are used as argumentative "trumps." One need only think of the references to Kant's argument for human emancipation with which most people invoking the "liberal peace" are probably familiar. But as the bargaining literature suggests, even particular facts to which some "precedential" value gets attached, such as a wage agreement in a different city, might provide some normative pull in an audience and thus might contribute to ending a strike. Second, the above remarks also draw attention to norms that have a constitutive status, such as those determining who is an "authoritative" decision-maker, or what the rules are underlying the practice of diplomacy. Different from the first type of norms (which are often vague because they involve principles or values), the latter have to be precise, although their application might be highly contested. Here the controversy concerning the representation of China at the UN of the 1950s comes to mind.

Finally, one can also see that the problem of "delegation," or letting a third party decide a controversy, does not necessarily get us to the "law." Historically we know of arbitral decision, such as in Ancient Greece[63] or in Islam around

in relation to other goods. This argument is on the one hand nonsensical since the whole point of making categorical distinctions is precisely to avoid the formation of "prices" (see the endless but rather conclusive debate about the non-fungibility of power in international relations and why a universal means of exchange would mean the end of individual liberties and the "separation of powers"). On the other hand, it recognizes that this does not absolve us from the difficulties of weighing various goods and accepting trade-offs. But these processes do not function like the price mechanism in a market. Here of course we quickly run into difficulties, which explains the tendency to "solve" the problem "by fiat," i.e. assumption. Jack Goldsmith and Eric A Posner, *The Limits of International Law* (Oxford University Press, 2005), 15.

[62] See Myres McDougall and Harold Lasswell, "The Identification and Appraisal of Diverse Systems of Public Order," in Richard Falk and Saul Mendlovitz (eds.), *The Strategy of World Order*, vol. II, *International Law* (New York: World Law Fund, 1966), 45–74, at 54.

[63] See e.g. the "award" by Periander of Achileum, a colony that was claimed by both Athens and Mytilene, to the Athenians, as recorded in Herodot, *Histories*, vol. III, trans. by A. D.

the time of the Prophet, where the contending parties submitted their "case" to a third party and swore to uphold his decision, no matter what. How much such a "judge" was constrained by law is unclear. Weber considers such phenomena as instances of "*kadi*" justice.[64] Obviously, the arbitrator – here its etymological link to *arbitrium* becomes visible – could not decide by simple fiat alone. Instead, he had to render his judgment on the basis of some common background assumptions. Yet how the "facts" of the case and the rules and norms interacted in such situations seems neither clear nor predictable.[65]

Nevertheless, the development of third-party settlement and a class of official rule-handlers is a precondition for the emergence of law. If, however, the norms of consistency, of treating like cases alike, and the practice of explicitly ascertaining this comparability across controversies do not also emerge, it is difficult to argue that we have a settled practice of *juris dictio*, of "finding," "declaring," or "making" the law. Again, mere institutionalization of a decision process seems insufficient, as it could still involve magic, rites, or ordeals, which we usually do not associate with the proper working of "law," despite their historical importance. Significant in this context is that such procedures largely concerned issues of evidence, which is the "is" part of law and which – perhaps this is what Fuller considers the "inner morality of law" – was over time brought in line with the above-mentioned normative requirements. Thus, evidence was no longer simply obtained by a simple proof, for example through a trial by combat, or through other "crucial experiments" such as throwing witches into water. Instead, obtaining valid evidence became subject to criteria of appraisal that included the credibility of witnesses, procedural corroboration (cross-examination), and imputing motives (*dolus specialis*, *mens rea*), as well as counterfactual reasoning ruling out some otherwise plausible possibilities.

In sum, while the discussion has shown that no once and for all "definition" of law is useful given the historical diversity, we can now spell out some criteria that in *our society* are part of the language game of law. One such criterion is that law concerns a choice process that is characterized by the principled nature of norm-use in arriving at a decision through reasoning. What the law "is" cannot, therefore, be decided by a quick look at statutes, treaties, or codes,

Godley, Loeb Classical Library (Cambridge, MA: Harvard University Press, 1938), book V, para. 95, p. 117.

64 The term was used by Max Weber in distinguishing formal rational law from informal ways of dispensing justice. See Max Weber: "Of Law and in Economy and Society," in Max Rheinstein and Max Weber, *Of Law in Economy and Society* (Cambridge, MA: Harvard University Press, 1954). Weber's treatment of Islamic law is not uncontroversial; see Lawrence Rosen, "Equity and Discretion in Islamic Law," in Lawrence Rosen, *The Justice of Islam* (New York: Oxford University Press, 2000).

65 Strangely enough the same difficulties arise when we consider the exact opposite of the *kadi*, i.e. the charismatic leader who has a new message and overturns old law and customs cannot simply engage in a speech act, as the latter will only have perlocutionary force if it is recognized by the audience.

but it can only be ascertained through the performance of rule application to a controversy and the appraisal of the reasons offered in defence of such a decision. A second criterion is that the reasons are circumscribed by law itself. Here reference is limited to authorized "sources," not to the totality of "good reasons," even though the boundaries are not watertight. They cannot be watertight for the reasons pointed out above, namely that law is always embedded in wider social understandings and in a life-world that includes philosophical speculations (social contract, bioethics, and so on), individual and collective life-projects (liberalism and democracy), disciplinary understandings (expert witnesses), and so on. Yet the law provides that these external reasons enter through specified paths.

Finally, the language game of "law" seems to require that there exists a group of authorized persons deciding what the law "is." This "authority" has two implications. The first is that their decisions are "binding" and that obligations to abide by these decisions are owed to the "law" in whose name a case and controversy is decided. This means that their decisions are "valid" even if they are mistaken and will "stand" unless overridden by another "authorized" decision. The other connected issue has to do with the problem of discretion vested in such an institution. As Raz put it, courts are bound to apply laws:

> and are not at liberty to disregard [them] whenever they find their application undesirable, all things considered. It does not follow that courts are to be regarded as computing machines always applying pre-existing rules regardless of their own views … But it does follow that they are to apply a certain body of laws regardless of their views on its merits and are allowed to act on their views only to the extent that this is allowed by those laws.[66]

While the realists are right to point to the importance of adjudication (the law is what the court says the law is), they are wrong when they intimate thereby that these choices are not "constrained" in specific ways. In a way, they commit the opposite error of Dworkin, who sees only unique and right choices, while they argue for virtually unlimited discretion. Similarly problematic are attempts to subject law to the instrumental logic of economic rationality – the felicific calculus that had already animated Bentham – that has gotten another lease on life in the "law and economics" movement.

In order to flesh out better what I mean by *legal* (rather than by political or "rational") reasoning styles, a discussion about "tradition" and hermeneutics is useful. This goes beyond the account I tried to give a couple of decades back in my book *Rules, Norms and Decisions*. Let us begin with the observation that "thinking like a lawyer" entails learning a new language. People in a legal discourse do not simply walk or step over a fence; they trespass, they commit a tort when they let their animals escape which trample the fields of the neighbour, or

[66] Joseph Raz, *The Authority of Law* (Oxford: Clarendon, 1997), 113.

they "defraud" someone by acting with guile. This language contains not only a jural ontology, but also allows for recognizing similarities among different situations. Furthermore, it highlights *which* features of the situation are to be taken into consideration.

It is, therefore, also evident that while such language use entails reasoning by analogy, typification, and the creation of sub-types through further distinctions, it involves more than cognitive factors, as no simple description is at work here. Stepping over a fence is a "violation" of rights, while acting with guile involves an attribution of a motive, and "negligence" occasions perhaps some counterfactual reasoning of what one could expect from a circumspect person in such a situation; or it calls for an appeal to a precedent or a statute that allocates risks and responsibilities. The language here is one of appraisal, not of description.

This becomes even clearer when one moves from single concepts to larger units, such as to sentences that are part of a "story" or fact patterns. When Macbeth stabs Duncan and thereby becomes king, the case might be redescribed as "Macbeth killed Duncan" but not as "Macbeth succeeded Duncan," even though this is what happened. Similarly, the truth – the "whole truth" the law is after – would not be "whole" even if it contained a surplus of "irrelevant" information, which could be, for instance, the type of knife, its make, or colour – although the knife might be an "exhibit" for everyone to see in a trial. Rather, truth becomes "whole" only by not allowing one to conceal the nature of the act by *simply focusing on outcomes*. If Macbeth, different from the Shakespearian story, could argue that the stabbing was an accident, because he wanted to cut loose some game tied to Duncan's saddle, or because he fell over a branch and thereby killed Duncan, things could be different. If that were the case, questions as to the *mens rea* would arise, as well as to the credibility of the excuses tendered and to the description of facts offered. What "counts" as a relevant "fact" is not established by observational accuracy but rather by the intersubjective validity of the characterization of an action upon which reasonable people could agree: what matters is not "truth" but what is to be held to be true (*pro veritate habetur*).

Learning such a language and speaking about the world in such a way means to participate in a practice, a shared form of life, as Wittgenstein has called it. It involves reasoning, but much of what goes on is more a "knowing how" than just a "knowing what" (namely, the rules). It is a skill that has been "handed down" as it is transmitted by training from generation to generation. But while this seems to be the case with most practices – even those in the trades, where secrets are transmitted in the workshops and studios of artisans – something more is going on in the case of law. After all, the point of traditional trade secrets is that, as soon as someone makes a better mousetrap, or applies colour to fresh plaster, the old ways will most probably be discarded. In law, in contrast, precedents and statutes stand until amended or overruled by duly authorized agents.

Here a second, and much more important, point emerges that is clouded if one focuses solely on the written manifestation of legal rules and the skills for applying them. As I have argued, legal rules are not just "commands" or general standing orders. They are treated as issuing from sources, such as legislation, custom, or precedent, all of which lie in the past. To that extent Aristotle's distinctions of different genres of speech,[67] attributing the *enkomion* to the present, political speech to the future, and legal argument to the past, make an important point but leave us in the dark of how this temporal element entering as a characteristic of legal discourse matters. In other words, Aristotle's classification deals with the attribution of genre to a time frame, but it fails to explain why the "past" plays such an important role in law, aside from pointing out that the "facts" of the case must lie in the past. But the legal proceedings before a court have to do not only with ascertaining "who did it" but, in statutory or constitutional interpretation, they must also ascertain the legislators' or the Founding Fathers' will or original intent. In this manner the past casts a highly significant shadow over the present and informs our future choices.

Pointing to "history" does not explain, however, why such excursions into the past tell us something about the reasons for the normative force of certain historical "facts" connected to law. One becomes even more puzzled when one realizes that it is not historical interest that drives legal explorations. Most of the traces and sources a historian would consider significant in telling her story are not even looked at by lawyers. Similarly, some of the things that still mould the present, such as past wars, or wise and foolish policies, whose consequences we enjoy or now have to suffer, do not usually enter into legal inquiry. Here Maitland gives us a valuable hint: it is not the past per se that interests us in law, but it is the past that is "present." It is the past that is not only remembered – hence escaping the fate of most actions and events, which are forgotten as soon as they are over – but it is a past that frames the way in which we approach the present. As Maitland suggests, "what is really required of the practising lawyer is not, save in the rarest cases, knowledge of medieval law, as it was in the middle ages, but rather a knowledge of medieval law as interpreted by modern courts to suit modern facts."[68] Such a method of putting a straight line between two points might make for bad history and for the smugness that often attaches to such interpretations of the past, which Herbert Butterfield has criticized as the "Whig interpretation of history."[69] Nevertheless, it is part and parcel of approaches to the past that are informed by "traditions," law, particularly common law, being one of them.

[67] Aristotle, *The Art of Rhetoric* (Cambridge, MA: Harvard University Press, 1956).

[68] See Fredrick Maitland, "Why the History of English Law is not Written," in *The Collected Papers of Fredrick Maitland*, 3 vols., ed. by H. A. L. Fisher (Cambridge University Press, 1911), vol. I, p. 491.

[69] Herbert Butterfield, *The Whig Interpretation of History* (New York: Norton, 1965).

In short, what is "handed down" and remembered of the past is not simply part of a "historical" past. Rather, it is in significant ways part of the present by providing authoritative sources and materials for the resolution of the problems at hand. Thus "traditions" are always "productions" rather than simple storehouses for things when they slip from the present. Traditions are not simply "there" as is suggested by the large collection of "data," for instance, in the Correlates of War project in international relations.[70] They are "facts" and thus "made" (from *facere*) in the double sense of the word. They record *actions* rather than mere events, and they are "made" in the sense that they are "recollected" or remembered rather than just found.

Both recollection and remembrance involve a much more active participation of the subject than just "seeing" what is out there. They involve choices and selections, exclusions and inclusions, remembering and forgetting. We can see this in "histories," which are always written from a certain point of view, fitting problems, events, and actions into a narrative that shows their significance while downplaying the significance of others or simply omitting them.[71] Traditions share this constructed character of the past and its facts with history, but they accord significance to facts by fitting them within a framework of meaning that is institutionalized in *an authentic canon of records*. Both give special importance to this present/past conundrum, but the analogy is here less to "history" as a form of remembrance, than to *religion* that emphasizes a "canon" and the interpretation of "sacred" texts. As Krygier points out:

> Record keeping allows more of the past to speak to the present and can help lend a sense of inter-generational continuity and coherence to traditions ... Also where records are kept, those who fashion and/or implement the criteria for selecting what to record, have a means to edit the past and control the future ... In societies which have developed institutions of sacred and/or secular authority, castes of experts – kings, priests, judges, scholars – are frequently granted an official monopoly in the authorized interpretation of recorded texts. Where the authority is un-appealable or ultimate, their interpretations ... become what their tradition is officially taken to mean. This gives these interpreters also, power over the past and the future. Such power, however, is rarely absolute, but must conform to canons of coherence and plausibility known to and accepted by participants in the tradition.[72]

[70] The Correlates of War project was started by David Singer in 1963 and provides comprehensive data sets. See www.correlatesofwar.org/datasets.htm (accessed September 19, 2013).

[71] Thus the significant omission of the peace of Kallias and the probably invented Melian dialogue has raised the question of the "objectivity" of the Thucydidean account (even though this might come as a shock to realists). Together with the changing fortunes of the battle of Bouvines in French historiography so well researched and told by Duby, imply that histories are always (re)constructions, not reports of how to assemble egg beaters or fix television sets. On the problem of Thucydides see e.g. Wight, *Systems of States*. On the battle of Bouvines see Georges Duby, *Le Dimanche de Bouvines* (Paris: Gallimard, 1973).

[72] Martin Krygier, "Law as a Tradition," *Law and Philosophy*, vol. 5 no. 2 (1986), 237–62, at 251.

The last few remarks also reveal why the absolute dichotomy of persistence and change is less of a problem for law than what it is usually made out to be. First, using rules is not meant to cover instances of reproducing identical exemplars as with cookie cutters or hole punchers. The notion of rule and the "same" might be interwoven, as Wittgenstein remarked, but it does not imply identical reproduction. Rather than stressing the observable regularities that rules might create when looked on from the outside, seen from the inside they are "flexible" – some more than others – and they allow us to "go on" rather than to stay in place and become frustrated. As a matter of fact, taking rules as instructions to always act in exactly the same way, irrespective of circumstances, is one of the most effective strategies of resistance, demonstrated by "the going by the book" strategy of air controllers, policemen, or garbage collectors during their salary negotiations. Since these officials are often not allowed to strike, they take "job action" and do "exactly" what the rules provide. So much for the belief that codifying "best practices" is a short cut to achieving both efficiency and responsibility! Rules might solve certain problems, but they are also a source of officially sanctioned stupidity, as one can see from bureaucracies and how frequently the latter thereby shirk their responsibilities. After all, if I have gone by the book, I cannot be blamed!

Second, "traditions" are hardly ever of one cloth. For example, the "theological tradition" contains "free will," "grace," "faith," and the need for informed choice, all of which point to genuine dilemmas. Ethics experiences similar difficulties in formulating once and for all universally applicable and usable criteria for practical choices, since deontological and consequentialist approaches point in different directions. Compared to them, the legal tradition is both more limited and more useful. It is more limited because its claims are usually limited to a concrete historical society and its own sedimented practices. Here Weiler's geological metaphor for understanding law and its development shows its heuristic purchase.[73] It also throws some light on the fact that law realizes that because of its specific configuration of the "strata" and its historical situatedness, it cannot command universal assent, even though traditions can inspire (imperial) political projects or universal fantasies. In another sense, though, law is more useful than ethics, since it provides answers to concrete problems and ways of resolving them instead of believing that concrete questions can be solved by ascending to ever-higher levels of abstraction or even to one overarching value. What is often forgotten by philosophers who "do" ethics and are fascinated by the universalizability criterion, the more ethereal the concepts become, the more they are in need of interpretation and of a community of interpreters rooted in a particular social order or tradition!

[73] J. H. H. Weiler, "The Geology of International Law: Governance, Democracy and Legitimacy," *Zeitschrift für ausländisches öffentliches Recht und Vöelkerrecht*, vol. 64 (2004), 547–62.

I return to this dialectic between understanding the particular and the universal later in the Meditations on universal human rights and the "bounds of (non)-sense" (Meditations 8 and 9). For the moment I only want to point out the alleged incompatibility of change and tradition, which all revolutionaries preach, and which they quickly forget after they have gained power: remember Trotsky, who planned to close up the shop after the revolution! Such a stance does not simply result from cynical rascality, but it is based on a deep misunderstanding of action since even the "newness" of the revolutions has to be communicated and a frame of reference is, therefore, needed by which people are able to assess the changes. Thus, if for example the notion of a subjective right is absent in a particular tradition, a program that everybody has "rights" is likely to misfire, or result in something different than expected. Similarly, we can be at loggerheads as to who the sovereign is – the crowned heads of the traditional dynasties, or "the people" – but in the absence of a shared understanding of sovereignty, cries for popular sovereignty will not make much sense.

The attempt to fix the meaning of the past in the present through "printed" (fixed) text is likely to bear the seeds of its own subversion. This is because the "past" then becomes more available for controversy, as Luther came to realize after making the "true" scripture available to all (instead of reserving it for the class of designated interpreters). It did not take long for the peasants, and Thomas Müntzer to boot, to read the Bible as a document for social egalitarianism. And it did not take Luther long either to side with the nobility and charge them with authority in matters of faith! Of course, such controversies are the nightmares of irenic textualists, since the very text that is supposed to prevent, or at least to mediate, the conflict leads instead to violence and suppression.

These remarks highlight three important lessons: that no text is simply the property of the author, that it can be approached directly without mediation, and that, instead, every age has to appropriate a text in its own way. Gadamer put it aptly:

> The real meaning of a text, as it speaks to the interpreter, does not depend on the contingencies of the author and for whom he originally wrote it. It certainly is not identical with them, for it is always partly determined also by the historical situation of the interpreter and hence by the totality … of history … Not occasionally only, but always, the meaning of a text goes beyond its author. That is why understanding it is not merely reproductive, but always a productive attitude as well.[74]

What do these considerations mean for our understanding of law and for the age-old question of whether international law is "really" law? While this topic

[74] Hands Georg Gadamer, *Truth and Method*, 2nd edn. (London: Sheed and Ward, 1979), p. 263f.

will be an ongoing engagement in all Meditations, the next section draws out some of the implications of this change in perspective.

The concept of law reconsidered

After the legal pluralism of ancient and medieval times, in which law comprised the law of God, of nature, of different nations, and of custom,[75] the last 500 years have defined law increasingly in terms of the "state" project. Law was not law because it derived its status from justice – as one etymological link suggested, *ius* comes from *iustitia* – but because it was "commanded" (*ius* from *iussum*). Although this was an old controversy, to which Bodin, and more so Hobbes contributed, the "pleasure of the prince to legislate" (*quod placuit principi legis habet vigorem*) reached back to Roman law. Now the "command of the sovereign" became the characteristic that distinguished "true" law from morals, or any other type of norm claiming validity. The paradigmatic example of true law became the general command issuing from the sovereign (or parliament). Law addressed each citizen who had an obligation to obey it. Controversies or infringements were to be adjudicated by courts, whose decisions were, in turn, to be "executed" by the sovereign.

This gave rise to understanding the realm of the "international" simply as the negative flip side of domestic political orders. While in the domestic arena we had hierarchy and a set of institutions that could declare what the law is and how it is made (even if contested, and applied), "out there" could be found only anarchy: no legislation, no compulsory jurisdiction, no shared purposes and values enshrined in a constitution, and no (centralized) enforcement of legal rights.[76]

Since international law seemed deficient in regard to any of those dimensions, attempts to safeguard the *legal* character of international law were mainly concerned with showing that, different from morality or some other normative preferences, international law could somehow measure up to the "usual" criteria of law by being, a "sanctioning order" or a "primitive system" relying on self-help, but clearly specifying "delicts" and "sanctions."[77] Yet such views, informed by the domestic analogy, were increasingly at odds with actual political practice. The focus on "sanctions" was not helpful either, because it narrowed the concept of law even further. Now neither criminal law, nor even public law supplied the paradigm of what law "really" was.

[75] See David Kennedy, "Primitive Legal Scholarship," *Harvard International Law Journal*, vol. 27, no. 1 (1986), 1–98.

[76] Here Waltz's conception of anarchy vs. hierarchy has (mis)informed several generations of graduate students. See Kenneth Waltz, *Theory of International Politics* (Reading, MA: Addison Wesley, 1979).

[77] See Kelsen, *Principles of International Law*, at 5.

Hart's move from norms to a system of rules opened (again) the *problématique* of law and allowed for the inclusion of international law, while simultaneously holding on to key tenets of positivism. As is the case of Hart's engagement with language philosophy that remained somewhat sparse, Hart's interest in Austin's jurisprudence also overlooked – or avoided seeing – the implications of Austin's argument regarding constitutional law. For the positivist Austin, both international law and constitutional law consisted of norms of "positive morality" but were not actually law.[78] This is all the more surprising in that a "branch" of law, whose character as "true" law few of us doubt, is thereby placed in the same category as international law.

The crucial point here is simply that both international law and constitutional law, as versions of public law, exhibit specific problems of legitimacy and of enforcement, since both systems have to rely on the institution of the state(s) that they supposedly control. But if we follow the categorization of public law, then this attribution casts some doubt on the proposition that constitutional law is actually able to provide an effective restraint on governments and on populist law-making. The idea that constitutional law is "settled" and, contrary to the weak institutionalization of international law, is also easily enforceable, might indeed need some correction. The problem of enforcement also brings to mind President Jackson's quip that "Justice John Marshall [who wrote the decision in *Worchester* v. *Georgia*,[79] which Jackson refused to execute] has made a decision, now let him enforce it." It seems, however, cold comfort indeed when we now have to discover that much of the "firmness" of constitutional law may turn out to be induced by a certain myopia rather than critical analysis. As Goldsmith and Levinson point out:

> problems of uncertainty create special challenges for constitutional and international law that ordinary domestic legal systems do not face. Domestic legal systems can rely on the authoritative legal and judicial institutions of the state to identify and specify legal norms. But because systems of public law aspire to stand outside of, and govern, the state, they cannot fully rely on the international apparatus of the state itself. Public law can only institutionalize the legislative and judicial functions by consciously conscripting state institutions to play a meta-governance role, or by building new institutions outside of the state or its conventional governance structure. Both international and constitutional law have used a combination of these strategies with some success in reducing legal uncertainty. Still the challenges of institutionalizing the secondary rules of a legal system outside of the institutional apparatus of the state remain daunting in both areas of law.[80]

[78] See John Austin, *The Province of Jurisprudence Determined*, ed. by Wilfrid E. Rumble (Cambridge University Press (1832) 1995), 141–3 and 254–64.

[79] *Worcester* v. *Georgia*, 31 US (6.Pet) 515 (1832).

[80] Jack Goldsmith and Daryl Levinson, "Law for States: International Law, Constitutional Law, Public Law," *Harvard Law Review*, vol. 122 (May 2009), 1791–868, at 1803.

The upshot of the above arguments is that clear-cut definitions of law might not be useful for understanding *what law does* by making a certain part of law an "essential" requisite of law in general. Rather "law" is indeed a language game in which different exemplars exhibit different features rather than one "essential characteristic." It will be the task of the next Meditation to examine these problems more extensively.

Meditation 3

On constitutions and fragmented orders

Introduction

We use the term "constitution" in a variety of ways. Probably the oldest use was that applied to someone who was in good stead, who could do the things he or she wanted and was able to handle the concomitant physical problems, such as fatigue and exertion. This usage points to a further implication. We can speak of such a constitution only if all the bodily parts fulfil their functions properly. Here architectural and functional biological metaphors often overlap, such as in the notion of "weight" and "counterweight," familiar from "republican" political theory, or from some realist thinking. However, the roots of the term both in nature and in action transcend simple functional or design associations, and also place the concept in a historical and practical context. The latter point is driven home by the famous Aesopian fable of the quarrels among the different parts of the body that go on strike. They refuse to feed the "idle" stomach while they are doing all the work. Of course, very soon they had to realize that without digestion they would wither away.[1]

That fable supposedly ended one of the constitutional crises of early Roman history, when the *plebs* had moved to a different hill and refused to cooperate with the nobles. It later became one of the important lessons to be understood by all if the "body politic" was to flourish. Similarly, Aristotle's teachings about the advantages of mixed forms of government and his collection of dozens of different constitutions – well exemplified by his *Constitution of Athens*[2] and the references in his *Politics*[3] – subordinated abstract "design" questions to an assessment of what actually "works," given the social compositions of

[1] There are two versions, one by Livy and one by Plutarch, which Shakespeare uses in his play Coriolanus. They give differing accounts for the revolt of the *plebs*. In both Menenius Agrippa is, however, credited with bringing the insurrection to an end by telling the *plebs* the Aesopian fable. See Titus Livius, *The History of Rome*, vol. I (Books 1–5), transl. by Aubrey de Selincourt (London: Penguin) 2002. Book 2, 32; *Plutarch's Lives*, transl. by Dryden, ed. by Arthur Hugh Clough (New York: Modern Library, 2001), 291–321.

[2] Aristotle, *The Politics and the Constitution of Athens*, transl. by Stephen Everson (Cambridge University Press, 1996).

[3] See Aristotle. *Politics*, transl. by T. A. Sinclair (Harmondsworth: Penguin, 1962) where in Book II he first criticizes Plato and other "ideal theories" and then discusses "successful" constitutions.

the "the people" (*politeuma*), and the different political traditions. He thereby emphasized the problematic nature of an "ideal theory" that attempts to derive everything from assumptions about human nature. Since there is always a gap between the "good man" and the "good citizen"[4] – the latter depending on the particular form of regime – the dangers of revolution (*stasis*) in a polis can only be banned when people accept a constitutional arrangement that incorporates the various accepted notions of justice and that provides for the pursuit of common political projects.

It is in this context that the role of law in its "constitutive" dimension can be appreciated. Historically, its role can be seen in the coming together of different families and clans under a new law, Aristotle's *synoikismos*. But, as we learn from some Greek tragedies (Oresteia, Antigone), the new law often remained contested and ineffective in establishing the new association and in inculcating a new loyalty to the city rather than to kin. Furthermore, law was no longer simply "found" through a reflection on custom and tradition, as was the case with the old law-givers such as Solon, but it was now able to create *new social facts*. Thus, even though many of the old terms remained, they now had an entirely new meaning. This radically new idea is observable in the Cleisthenic reforms, where the old *phyle* changes from a tribal association to a territorially defined administrative unit. Another example is the "dis-empowering" of the Aeropagus, which provides the subtext for Aeschylus' *Eumenides* (the last part of the *Oresteia*). It shows that a conscious creation of law by political means could now substitute for the old custom of blood revenge which had been entrusted to the clans.[5] Finally, we can also trace these developments in the significant change of the traditional *nomos basileus* (law is king) argument, that is "law" is now neither just custom, nor "rule" by any particular person or coterie.[6] The *locus classicus* for this new conception is provided by Aristotle's treatment in his *Politics*:

> It follows that it is preferable that laws should rule rather than any single one of the citizens. And following this same line of reasoning … these persons should be appointed as guardians of the law and as its servants … Therefore, he who asks law to rule, is asking God and intelligence and no others to rule, while he who asks for the rule of a human being is importing a wild beast … for desire is like a wild beast and anger perverts rulers and the very best of men. Hence law is intelligence without appetite.[7]

[4] See Aristotle, *Politics*, Book III, Chapter IV (1276b–1277b32).

[5] For a further discussion and the discovery of "law" as a result of a conscious political decision rather than as a function of custom, see Christian Maier, *Die Entstehung des Politischen bei den Griechen* (Frankfurt: Suhrkamp, 1995).

[6] For a further argument see my "Has the Rule of Law become a Rule of Lawyers?," in Gianluigi Palombella and Neil Walker (eds.), *Relocating the Rule of Law* (Oxford: Hart, 2009), 171–96.

[7] Aristotle, *Politics*, Book III, Chapter 16: 1287 a25–32.

This new conception thereby becomes part and parcel of the "rule of law" argument, as it migrated via Venice to England and the New World and was celebrated in *Marbury* v. *Madison*.[8] In the *Federalist Papers*[9] it becomes explicitly part of the constitutional endeavour to deal with the dangers of anarchy and hierarchy, both internally and externally. This leads to a constitutional set-up that is designed to cope simultaneously with four threats:[10] internally with the problem of stasis (anarchy) or despotism, externally with that of anarchy (annihilative war), and with the dangers of imperial rule.

In the civil law tradition this *topos* is mostly concerned with the constitutive function of legislation (Bodin) – of creating new rights and obligations through acts of the sovereign – or with the *pouvoir constituante*. In this context the "rule of law" focuses more on the internal systematization and hierarchization of legal rules, particularly those of *empowering* the sovereign to become active and address clear and present dangers through "police powers," or later on to intervene through legislation in society to rectify specific social ills.[11] Consequently, the rule of law and the constitutional discourse amalgamate different themes and present us with a *bricolage* of different semantics rather than with an unequivocal and clearly structured program or corpus of rules and principles, sometimes hinted at in discussions on global administrative law,[12] or in debates on the constitutionalization of international law.[13]

In the following I want to concentrate on the issue of how the "constitutional discourse" is related to the problem of change and to the role of law that is to provide us with an authoritative "map" for orienting ourselves and then acting collectively. As we can see historically, "constitutional" moments arise in crisis situations, as exemplified in Athens, or in the Glorious Revolution in England where the centralizing tendencies of the Stuart monarchs were successfully resisted by Parliament and common lawyers discovered the "ancient freedoms of Englishmen," or in the USA in the War of Independence, or the French Revolution, or in the case of the transitional regimes that emerged from

[8] See *Marbury* v. *Madison*, 5 US (1Cranch) 137 at 163: "The government of the United States has been termed a government of laws and not of men."

[9] *The Federalist Papers*, ed. by Clinton Rossiter (New York: Mentor, 1961).

[10] See e.g. Daniel Deudney, *Bounding Power: Republican Security Theory from the Polis to the Global Village* (Princeton University Press, 2007).

[11] For a good discussion of some of the differences between the common law and civil law systems as reflected in different conceptions about the status of administrative law, see Oliver Lepsius, *Verwaltungsrecht unter dem Common Law* (Tübingen: Mohr-Siebeck, 1997).

[12] On the notion of the emergence of a global administrative law see Benedict Kingsbury, Nico Krisch and Richard Stewart, "The Emergence of Global Administrative Law", *Law and Contemporary Problems*, vol. 68 (2004/2005), 14–62.

[13] See e.g. Anne Peters, "Compensatory Constitutionalism: The Function and Potential of International Norms and Structures," *Leiden Journal of International Law*, vol. 19, no. 3 (2006), 579–610.

the collapse of the Soviet Empire. Such changes lead to "constitution making" in the sense of drafting a new instrument that authoritatively sets forth who is entitled to act under which circumstances and which rules have to be followed in making, changing, or applying the rules to the resolution of conflicts. But nothing in the historical record suggests that this is the only, or perhaps even the predominant way of deciding constitutional questions.

Many laws and documents might have constitutional standing without explicit systematization, as the British constitution shows,[14] and even when a clear and systematic exposition of the principles is intended – as in written constitutions –some of the hoariest problems might actually remain outside the constitutional framework.[15] Here the "compromises" in the *ante bellum* United States come to mind. But contrary to the common belief, it was not the failure to address these issues in the US Constitution that eventually created havoc. When the question of slavery was finally addressed and "decided" by the Supreme Court in the notorious *Dred Scott* case,[16] a civil war ensued. Similarly, the subsequent abolition of slavery did not really come about by the envisaged amendment procedure of the Constitution, but resulted from the imposition of a new regime on the South by the victorious North.

But saying that constitutional arguments are voiced in crisis situations does not mean that they necessarily have to be the result of traumatic experiences. Thus the silent revolution of gender equality was accomplished with much constitutional talk, but again without using the envisaged amendment process and *despite* widespread hostility in the USA to such an amendment! Nor do these phenomena seem unique to the United States. In Europe calls for a European Constitution became stronger precisely because of the success of the European project, both in terms of "deepening" and "widening." Furthermore, the failure of the European Constitution to win approval has not derailed the European project – as one could have suspected – or stopped the constitutional talk, even if it has changed its register. This leads to the rather strange phenomenon that, on the one hand, European integration is proceeding rather nicely – establishing the free movement of goods and persons (less so of services) through case law and intergovernmental "deals" – but attempts to "codify" what happens on the ground curiously fail.

There are also areas of integration that are lacking in progress, of course, and neither the "de-pillarization," nor the artificiality of, for example, declaring the economy a self-contained "system" with its own logic, seem to be able to cope with some emerging problems. Here different social policies, different "models" of

[14] See e.g. Badgehot's famous study published first in 1867 at the height of the parliamentary reforms: Walter Badgehot, *The English Constitution* (Oxford University Press, 2001).

[15] This point is powerfully made by Andrew Glencross in his comparisons of the *ante bellum* US and the European Union; see Andrew Glencross, *What Makes the EU Viable? European Integration in the Light of the Ante-bellum US* (Basingstoke: Palgrave, 2009).

[16] *Dred Scott* v. *Sanford*, 60 US393 (1857).

economic growth (vide Ireland), of bank regulation, of energy policy, and of disciplining the "sovereign" from indebting itself, make themselves felt. They feed scepticism, perhaps even raise questions about the way in which we have been proceeding all along by postponing some critical choices. This not only creates constitutional talk among integrationists in their controversies with the Eurosceptiks, it also generates debate among constitutional lawyers and some of the constitutional courts in the different countries, as the Maastricht[17] and Lisbon judgments[18] of the German Bundesverfassungsgericht show.

Finally, when we look at the level of the international system, we also observe that when the UN was confronted with increasingly complicated "peace(-keeping) missions" that exceeded the original authorizations, "organizational innovation" at first took the route of experimental and incremental change, always invoking "exceptional circumstances" in order *not* to set any precedent.[19] But in the end it resulted in constitutional talk, as evidenced by comprehensive reports entitled *In Larger Freedom*,[20] *The Responsibility to Protect*,[21] and the Outcome Document of 2005.[22] The authorization for the mission for Haiti marks the beginning in this respect. When several of those missions were carried out, a deeper conceptual adjustment became necessary. The broader interpretation of Article 39 of the UN Charter (threat to peace) in the aftermath of the Cold War served as a powerful attractor for several new "themes" in the discourse.

The problem of incoherence also arose at the intersect of the UN Charter and the many free-standing regimes, which raised the issue of super- and subordination, as otherwise the "fragmentation" of the international legal order could seriously impair the ability of law to serve as an authoritative map and provide guidance for decisions. These concerns, which had been articulated by two presidents of the ICJ and scholars alike,[23] were finally addressed by a

[17] German Constitutional Court, Maastricht decision, at BVerf.Ge., 89, 155, October 12, 1993.

[18] German Constitutional Court, Lisbon decision, at BVerf.Ge. 123, 267, June 30, 2009.

[19] See e.g. the invocation of "special circumstances" in the case of the Haiti mission by the then Secretary-General Boutros-Ghali and President Clinton. See Laura Zanotti, "Taming Chaos: A Foucauldian View of UN Peacekeeping, Democracy and Normalization," *International Peacekeeping*, vol. 13, no. 2 (2006), 150–67.

[20] See the Secretary-General's Report *In Larger Freedom*, UN General Assembly 59th Session (A59/2005).

[21] See International Commission on Intervention and State Sovereignty, *The Responsibility to Protect* (Ottawa: International Development Research Centre, 2001).

[22] See the Outcome Document, UN General Assembly, 60th Session (A/60/L1).

[23] See e.g. the addresses by the former President of the ICJ Stephen Schwebel (October 26, 1999 before the General Assembly of the UN) and Gilbert Guillaume (October 26, 2000 before the General Assembly), as discussed by Martti Koskenniemi and Paeivi Leino, "Fragmentation of International Law? Post-modern Anxieties," *Leiden Journal of International Law*, vol. 15 (2002), 553–79; see also Bruno Simma and Dirk Pulkowski, "Of Planets and the Universe:

study group of the International Law Commission on the "Fragmentation of International Law."[24] In a way, these two "deliberative processes" exhibited constitutional quality even though they differed quite markedly in their tone and the remedies they advocated.

In regard to the constitutional reformulation of UN activities, Laura Zanotti points out that the report *In Larger Freedom* wanted to provide a new normative anchor for interpreting a variety of activities, rooted in several, up to then largely independent discourses of development, security, and peacekeeping:

> the novelty of his [Annan's] approach lies in the systematic reorganization, under the umbrella of security, of discursive practices that were previously considered separate. Idioms that emerged in the context of UN debates about a variety of matters, including peace-keeping, disaster-management, sustainable development, and gender, are now reorganized as part of a political rationale that intensifies international interventionism and bio-political management of populations.[25]

Thus while the report by the Secretary General seems much more "visionary," tapping into the energies that characterize "constitutional moments" by focusing on the common predicament,[26] the report of the ILC sounded a more cautious note. It relied more on legal technique than on new departures. As the report stated, the solution to the problems could not be found in a grand design for a new "general" international law, but in the application of the principles enumerated in the Vienna Convention on the Law of Treaties (VCLT), such as *lex specialis, lex posterior* and so on, and in applying the principle of harmonization in cases where some norms conflict with obligations *erga omnes* or *ius cogens*.[27] In particular, it suggested a restatement of international law rather

Self-contained Regimes in International Law, *European Journal of International Law*, vol. 17 (2006), 483–529; Guenther Teubner and Andres Fischer Lescano, "Regime Collisions: The Vain Search for Legal Unity in the Fragmentation of Global Law," *Michigan Journal of International Law*, vol. 25 (2004), 999–1046; Rosalyn Higgins, "Respecting the Sovereignty of States Running a Tight Courtroom," *International Comparative Law Journal*, vol. 50 (2001), 122–32, taking issue with some of Guillaume's ideas as already expressed before his UN speech (see Gilbert Guillaume, "The Future of International Judicial Institutions," *International Comparative Law Quarterly*, vol. 44 (1995), 848–62).

[24] Martti Koskenniemi, *Fragmentation of International Law: Difficulties Arising from the Diversification and Expansion of International Law* (Helsinki: Erik Castren Institute Research Report 21, 2007).

[25] Laura Zanotti, *Governing Disorder* (University Park: University of Pennsylvania Press, 2011), 64.

[26] For a discussion of "constitutional moments" see Bruce Ackerman, "The Storrs Lectures," *Yale Law Journal*, vol. 93 (1983/84), 1013–72; see also his *We the People* (Cambridge, MA: Harvard University Press, 1991).

[27] See para. 42 of the Report of the Study Group of the ILC, July 18, 2006 (UNGA A/cn.4L702) (hereafter *Fragmentation Report*), as reprinted in Koskenniemi, *Fragmentation of International Law*, at 281.

than codification[28] or progressive development, while claiming at the same time that such a stance was neither denying the need for the "systemic integration" of international law, nor was it claiming that in the fragmented environment of the international "public sphere" no constitutional order existed:

> In an increasingly specialized legal environment, few institutions are left to speak the language of general international law … The International Law Commission is such an institution. The work for codification and development it has carried out has been precisely about elucidating the content of "general international law" as an aspect of what can only be understood as a kind of an international public realm. The fact that it has been possible in this study to develop an overarching standpoint by taking the perspective of the Vienna Convention has shown that general international law speaks to present concerns not so much in terms of substantive rules and principles … but as a formal argumentative technique. In an important sense, it is that technique that represents what is "general" in a world of proliferating technical particularisms.[29]

One could be inclined to see in these two responses reflections of the prototypical differences between the "politician" (Kofi Annan) and the "lawyer" (Koskenniemi), the former mobilizing support through appeals to common political projects, the latter trying to find solutions through the judicious use of certain techniques. But such an interpretation might be overdrawn, even though differences of temperament and professional sensibilities do matter. That things are not as simple is evidenced by the fact that Koskenniemi expects ultimately viable answers to our common problems – following Kant – not from lawyers (whom the latter had dismissed as "pathetic comforters"), and not even from "moralists" engaged in the clarification of moral principles, but rather from *moral politicians*.[30]

While again Koskenniemi's stance might be too easily dismissed as an idiosyncratic preference, most lawyers are well aware that part and parcel of their "technique" is to appeal to political projects. Thus, if the traditional rules of interpretation no longer suffice in sustaining their argument, pleas for more "holistic solutions" are entered. In the international sphere we notice then the invocations of ultimate values, such as "human dignity" or human rights, since the standing of these principles seems to put them beyond debate. The hope is that these values or principles will lend not only their persuasive power to a particular position, but that values also provide us in general with an opportunity to "de-fragment" again the shattered unity of the international legal system.[31]

[28] *Ibid.* at 256. [29] *Ibid.* at 255.

[30] Martti Koskenniemi, "Constitutionalism as a Mindset," *Theoretical Inquiries in Law*, vol. 8 (2007), 1–36.

[31] See e.g. the attempt by Anne von Aaken to put the Humpty-Dumpty of the fragmented international legal order together again by a wide reading of Article 31(3)(c) of the Vienna

Such "sacralizing" moves invoking ultimate foundations are pervasive in law, as exemplified by the quote from Aristotle above with its identification of God and law (which later morph into appeals to nature, humanity, universality, and so on).

In general, placing an issue in the "right" frame is endemic to arguing with rules, as thereby the "bounds of sense" are delineated, showing how a certain issue is instantiating a "case" of a legal concept. As Julius Cohen once pointed out:

> when a lawyer, jockeying for a favourable position for his client, urges the court to delineate a conflict situation as, say "free speech" instead of "picketing" he is urging a decision and not a reason for arriving at it. The capturing of the symbol by the lawyer is tantamount to capturing the decision itself.[32]

Of course, even judges will use principles in a purposive fashion, especially in constitutional interpretation as the field is less settled than some other areas of law, where rules allow for a broad range of "routine" decisions. Such is the case in the courts of first instance, where the taking of pleas and ruling on motions concerning admissible evidence are the dominant activities. Issues can be handled on the basis of applying general rules, as here usually no complicated deliberations concerning a choice among competing principles and values are necessary. Even at the appellate level much remains routine, although here "the law," rather than the "facts," plays a larger role and the scope of decision making widens. Still, the process is guided by the provisions of allowing appeals, by the trial court's handling of the case, and by the lawyers' framing of their appeals. Only the most controversial cases make it beyond these confines, where the politics of constitutional decision-making then comes into play. Here the constraints might lie less in the controversy and the "law" itself than in the role the "constitution" attributes to judges by placing their activities within a system of meaning.

It is here that the "constitutional" problem arises, that is when we try to bridge the gap between controversial laws that are tested against the presumably less contested constitutional principles. The latter allegedly allow us to decide whether a specific law is not only valid – since the formal test of its pedigree must have been applied long before the appeal could reach the high court – but that it is also legitimate in terms of the broader principles embodied in the constitutional order.

Convention of Treaties. Anne von Aaken, "De-fragmentation of Public International Law Through Interpretation: A Methodological Proposal," *Indiana Journal of Global Legal Studies*, vol. 16 (Summer 2009), 483–512.

32 Julius Cohen, "Value Symbols in Law," in *Essays on Jurisprudence from the Columbia Law Review* (in homage to Karl N. Llewellyn) (New York: Columbia University Press, 1963), 332–9, at 335.

In the following I want to address two interconnected problems, that is the public law character of constitutional law (section two) and its peculiar problems for securing adherence. This allows me critically to evaluate some of the arguments in the constitutionalization debate in international law, which I take up in section three. But since constitutionalization is in a way a response to the fragmentation issue in international law, this question is developed by a reprise of the regime debate and of "free-standing" regimes (section four). In section five I return to the issue of constitutionalization, but approach it this time mainly via the problem of legal pluralism, addressing the notion of constitutional orders from a different angle.

The problem of "public law"

The above observations call into question some of the most dearly held beliefs about how constitutions do or do not function – especially when the finality and completeness of their decisions come into focus. The questions raised above also provide the justification for considering that the notion of a constitution in international politics is not the oxymoron that "realism," in both its legal[33] and international relations theory version, has made it out to be. Focusing on the similarities of international and constitutional law does not, of course, dispose of significant and undeniable differences, but this is a common problem of any classification. True, apples and oranges *are* different; however, they are also "the same" when they are compared to birds or stones. Since both observations are obviously true, the traditional way of resolving the apparent paradox is to argue in terms of "levels," either of abstractions or of values, such as between higher order "principles" and lower norms cast in rule form. These differences are then supposed to be mediated by a technique, that is by applying the higher norms competently to the case at hand. But this is precisely what legal realists called into question. As Justice Holmes laconically pointed out in *Lochner*,[34] "general principles do not decide concrete cases," thereby zeroing in on the gap between concrete rules and principles that no canon of interpretive rules can logically close. This is why additional props are usually adduced, such as

[33] For the dismissal of constitutional and public law in general in the debates among realists and formalists alike, see Thomas Grey, "Langdell's Orthodoxy," *University of Pittsburgh Law Review*, vol. 45 (1983/84), 1–53, at 34:

> The classicist did not regard public law including constitutional law as amenable to scientific study at all. Thus Langdell's Harvard colleagues and disciples Beale and Ames threatened to withdraw their offer to help the new University of Chicago Law School get started, because its organizers proposed to teach a substantial number of public law courses thus violating the Harvard curricular dogma that students must be exposed to scientific "pure law" courses. Constitutional law was unscientific because hopelessly vague, as typified by the police power doctrine; the question whether a statute was "reasonably related to safety health or morals" could not be treated formally.

[34] *Lochner* v. *New York*, 198US, 45 (1905), at 76.

an "observable trend" in court decisions that observers detect, allegedly heralding a change in the law, or serving even as an indicator of more deep-seated value-changes in a society. But even with such a move we are not in the clear since more than one principle might apply and they themselves might conflict. The emphasis on norm application and of a "competent" performance draws, therefore, our attention to the importance of the "practice" of legal decision-making, although it is questionable whether the problem can be reduced to one of technique. A more detailed discussion seems in order.

As we have seen, constitutional arguments allow people to "bracket" their disagreements, which a full-fledged decision "on the merits," or of "all things considered," might engender. This was after all what Sunstein's argument concerning "incompletely theorized agreements" suggested.[35] In short, the "constitutional" argument rests on two beliefs that have to work in conjunction. As Michelman points out:

> [One is that] a law was enacted by constitutionally specified procedures. [The] second [is], that the law is innocent of transgression against substantive limits and constraints on government powers, that the constitution also lays down, presumably as assurances of basic justice and decency in the exercise of democratic rule.
>
> We start to see what is generally alluring about the idea of constitutional legitimation. It offers a way of combining one's ethical impulse of allegiance owed to the decisions of procedurally fair majorities of fellow citizens with one's moral sense of there being limits on acceptable uses of the law-making and other coercive powers of the state. Constitutional legitimation offers an apparent place of refuge from the tug of war between our loyalties to majorities and to justice.[36]

In a way the constitutional argument promises a solution to a genuine dilemma, but can do so only by displacing it. The duality of "laws," that is the constitutional law on the one hand, and the "normal" law that is being "tested" on the other, presupposes a clear separation of the constitutional part that is fixed in advance of the decision concerning the constitutionality of the acts or laws that are being tested. This separation creates the logical conundrum that "constitutionality" cannot serve as a test for the obligatory character of the constitutional part of law, as we face here either the problem of infinite regress, or have to resort to justifications that transcend the avoidance-minded proceduralist ideal. At this point the "authorization" part comes into play, that is the role of "the people" as authors of the law and of their acceptance of the

[35] See Cass Sunstein, *Designing Democracy: What Constitutions Do* (Oxford University Press, 2002).

[36] Frank I. Michelman, "Constitutional Legitimation for Political Acts," *The Modern Law Review*, vol. 66 (Jan. 2003), 1–15, at 5.

decisions rendered. The issue is the how these different principles can work in conjunction rather than singly. As Michelman remarks:

> For the avoidance-minded proceduralist idea possibly to work, it seems it will have to be tied … to an author-based or acceptance-based conception of the binding virtue of constitutions … The … point … is that avoidance-minded constitutional legitimation for political acts is possible – if at all – only insofar as we are open to an author-based or acceptance-based conception of the grounds of constitutional bindingness. May be that could help account for why author-based and acceptance-based conception get any respect at all, considering how unattractive they look (to liberals) in just about every other way.[37]

There is still a further point that deserves attention, which is the issue between "theory" and "practice" that we have already encountered several times and that here reappeared in the distinction of a "content-based" vs. an "author-based" conception of legitimation. While theoretical arguments are governed by the criteria of truth, that is entailment, the principle of the excluded middle, truth conditionality and so on, practical arguments are different, as John Wisdom reminded us. Even singly inconclusive arguments can provide a viable justification if they "work" in conjunction. They are more like the legs of a chair, which support a seat jointly, rather than the links of a chain, which have to be of independent and near equal strength if the chain is to remain in existence.[38]

The idea of mutual support of different parts – not only in terms of logical "coherence," which would be requiring too much (logically) and at the same time too little (practically), but also in *order to sustain common practical projects*, has of course been part and parcel of "republican thinking." The static or the "design" part finds its dynamic correspondence in the *process* in which "checks and balances" work themselves out in practice. Here the American discussion among Federalists and Anti-federalists, especially Madison 10 and 51,[39] provide important clues. The fundamental idea, though, is that "the people" – which concept is of course a political "myth" – are both the authors and enforcers of their constitution, and that in this way a written document or agreement on a "higher law" can be taken as the incontrovertible "foundation." Thus law directly points to the political process and its institutional design. It is the only guarantee for the viability of a constitution, able to insure both identity and change. The "success" of a constitution does not therefore lie in its logical form or in the coherence of its underlying values – as values will always conflict and only temporary solutions are possible – but in its ability to institutionalize both a common concern and a generation-transcending endeavour,

[37] *Ibid.* at 14f.

[38] See John Wisdom, "Gods," *Proceedings of the Aristotelian Society*, vol. 45 (1944/45), 185–206, at 194.

[39] See Clinton Rossiter (ed.), *The Federalist Papers* (New York: Mentor, 1961).

while taking care of the twin dangers that any polity faces: that of anarchy and of despotism.

The former concern is echoed in the debate concerning the inclusion or exclusion of a bill of rights in the US Constitution, which claims to be based on popular consent. Here the problem arises that such an insurance against "our own encroachment on ourselves" amounts, according to Daniel Webster, to "a curiosity in government"[40] that would not only be ineffective but would also send the wrong signal. A similar note is struck by Jefferson's warnings concerning the second problem: "no society can make a perpetual constitution … The earth always belongs to the living generation."[41] Finally, the problem of the institutionalization of the political process as a "solution" for this conundrum is addressed in Madison's famous re-evaluation of "factions" – not as aberrations, detracting from the *salus publica* – but rather as the institutional guarantee of freedom. Since factions are ubiquitous and are constantly formed and transformed, the challenge for an effective constitutional design consists in creating the proper checks and balances for a process in which no one faction can get a hold of the governmental apparatus throughout the land. Here the separation of powers, as well as the division of federal – and state – governments make such an eventuality unlikely in the "extended republic" of the USA. Madison elaborates in Federalist 51:

> In framing a government which is to be administered by men over men the great difficulty lies in this: you must first enable the government to control the governed; and in the next place oblige it to control itself. A dependence on the people is no doubt the primary control on the government; but experience has taught mankind the necessity of auxiliary precautions …
>
> Ambition must be made to counteract ambition. The interest of the man must be connected with constitutional rights of the place.[42]

How much the constitutional problem is not a simple legal one but a *social and political* one can be seen from his further remarks directed against tyrannical majorities and against attempts of creating "a will in the community independent of the majority – that is of society itself."[43]

> It is of great importance in a republic not only to guard the society against the oppression of its rulers, but to guard one part of the society against the injustice of the other part … If a majority is united by a common interest, the rights of the minority will be insecure. There are but two methods

[40] See Gordon S. Wood, *The Creation of the American Republic 1776–1787* (Chapel Hill: University of North Carolina Press, 1998), quoting Daniel Webster, Government.

[41] Jefferson's letter to Madison of September 6, 1789 in Adrienne Koch and William Peden (eds.), *The Life and Selected Writings of Thomas Jefferson* (New York: Random House, 1944), at 488 and 491.

[42] Madison 51 (Publius) in *The Federalist Papers*, at 322. [43] *Ibid.* at 323.

> of providing against this evil: the one by creating a will in the community independent of the majority – that is of the society itself; the other by comprehending in the society so many descriptions of citizens as will render an unjust combination of a majority of the whole very improbable, if not impracticable. The first method prevails in governments possessing a hereditary or self-appointed authority … The second method will be exemplified in the federal republic of the United States. Whilst all authority in it will be derived from and dependent on the society, the society itself will be broken in so many parts … that the rights of individuals or of the minority, will be in little danger from interested combinations of the majority. In a free government the security of civil rights must be the same as that for religious rights. It consists in one case in the multiplicity of interests, and in the other in the multiplicity of sects …
>
> In the extended republic of the United States … whilst there being thus less danger to a minor from the will of a major party, there must be less pretext also to provide for the security of the former by introducing into the government a will not dependent on the latter, or in other words, a will independent of the society itself.[44]

These remarks could be interpreted as a cautionary tale regarding judicial review – the development that began with the famous Supreme Court decision of *Marbury* v. *Madison*[45] – and that failed to resolve the fundamental issue of slavery despite the notorious *Dred Scott* decision. The latter in a way "solved" the legal issue, but did not resolve the underlying political problems, carefully hedged by extra-constitutional compromises that had been undermined by the Jacksonian revolution that had transformed American society and politics.

Today again Madison's remarks resonate in some recent controversies between Judge Scalia and other members of the judiciary about the injections of "foreign" elements into the US domestic legal process, showing that the controversy between the value-based constitutionalist vs. an authorization-based notion of constitutionalism is still with us.[46] Most constitutional lawyers, though, doubt that that the Supreme Court can for long stay out of synch with the "policy views dominant among the law making majorities of the United States."[47] Indeed, with the exception of the Court's resistance to the New Deal, it is surprising how close politics and constitutional law as interpreted by the Supreme Court have moved in tandem, although the reasons for this synchronization are much less clear.

[44] *Ibid.* at 324f. [45] *Marbury* v. *Madison*, 5 US (1Cranch) 137 (1803).

[46] For a fundamental discussion that widens the scope of the debate by identifying both substantive and methodological problems that arise from piecemeal comparison, from selection biases (looking only at points of convergence), or by using misplaced analogies (foreign law as the *ius gentium*), see Vlad Perju, "The Puzzling Parameters of the Foreign Law Debate," *Utah Law Review* (2007), 167–214.

[47] See Larry Alexander and Fred Schauer, "On Extrajudicial Constitutional Interpretation," *Harvard Law Review*, vol. 110 (1997), 1359–87, at 1368.

This might be, on the one hand, the result of prudential restraints by the Supreme Court, which has, different from many purely constitutional courts, no right to examine constitutional questions outside of a concrete case and controversy. The Court also has exacting standing requirements and has developed various avoidance techniques and doctrines (political questions doctrine) not to appropriate the powers of other branches. But in spite of these doctrinal considerations, the brunt of the Court's criticism goes to the legislative branch while the Court usually defers – especially in foreign affairs – to the executive. This is a far cry from the "constitutional court" that Kelsen had advocated in the Weimar period, or of the powers that have been exercised by the European Courts and that are sometimes the envy of lawyers from other jurisdictions. It is not surprising that in the absence of functioning representative political institutions in the EU and of transparent processes of governance, we encounter here the same phenomenon as in the social world where the one-eyed person becomes the leader of the lame. Whether judicial supremacy is desirable under such circumstances can be doubted.

On the other hand, the above rosy picture of constitutional review might also be the result of a particular myopia of a Whig-interpretation of history. In that view the present state of affairs is the result of having gotten it "just right," thereby blocking out disconfirming evidence (such as substantive noncompliance, reversals and so on) and mistaking doctrinal announcements for actual practice.[48] Although constitutional review is not uniform and different modi exist, ranging from near judicial supremacy to more accommodating arrangements, a good case could be made that the notion itself is at odds with democratic theory and that courts are not the appropriate institutions for "protecting" the constitutional order.[49] In the absence of effective checks and balances – as today's political reality is much less federal and much more unitary when compared to its inception – the once "least dangerous branch" has mutated. Constitutional litigation can now result in protecting vested interests that – contrary to Madison's hope – have gotten a hold of the most important governmental mechanism, which is invoked to protect "private rights" against political and societal "infringements." Similar issues are raised by "pluralists" who favour contestation and fragmented rather than unitary public law systems, as the latter tend to suppress weakly articulated interests and certain legitimate differences among groups and people. For some pluralists it is exactly the decentralized nature of international law rather than the template of a unitary

[48] For a further discussion see Michael Klarman, "Brown and Lawrence (and Goodrich)," *Michigan Law Review*, vol. 104 (2005), 431–89.

[49] See Jeremy Waldron, "The Core Case against Judicial Review," *Yale Law Journal*, vol. 115, no. 6 (2006), 1346–406.

state (with its established hierarchy of courts) that provides the paradigm for legal ordering, particularly in the postnational era.[50]

We need not take any position concerning the alleged advantages of such a "system," especially before we have discussed the problems for the international legal order that arise out of its fragmentation. Nevertheless, it is interesting that international law has suddenly taken pride of place in legal thought. This might also be a result of the fact that the postnational condition creates new opportunities for activist politics, and that doing "good" might sometimes be better than doing "right" – as a matter of fact that was precisely the starting point for this section on constitutionalism. In addition, any measure might be construed as enhancing democracy – or autonomy – if one has a somewhat more complex understanding of democracy than the one that has been narrowed down to "contested elections." What is thereby not shown, however, is whether this type of "politics" allows for the pursuit of common projects by creating reliable levers for common action.

Resorting to constitutional litigation is certainly a contentious form of politics, using judicial means and the rhetoric of rights in order to push a particular agenda. But it is also often a politics of dependency in which the actors and citizens frequently have become "clients" who need (legal) help to plead their case and invoke the "protection" by "professionals," as they are no longer in charge. And it is also a largely doctrinaire politics, since even after courts have spoken, actual implementation is not an idle side issue that can be neglected. This latter observation contains an important lesson for international politics, since the implementation of "cosmopolitan law" cannot be left hanging by being charged to an "international community as a whole," or even a "humanity" that cannot act. It would indeed be fatal if, with the demise of the state and its sovereignty, "the people" – admittedly a historically contingent and non-universal but politically real magnitude – have now also been left behind. Then we would face the mere "parchment barriers" of a constitution of which Madison and Jefferson warned.[51] It is the task of the next section to address some of these issues.

International law and the uses of "constitutionalization"

What gives the constitutionalization discourse in international law a certain identity is the claim – sometimes well articulated and sometimes only

[50] See e.g. Paul Schiff Berman, "A Pluralist Approach to International Law," *Yale Journal of International Law*, vol. 32 (2007), 301–29; William Burke White, "International Legal Pluralism," *Michigan Journal of International Law*, vol. 25 (2004), 963–79.

[51] See my "Leaving Sovereignty Behind?" in Richard Falk, Mark Juergensmeyer and Vesselin Popovski (eds.), *Legality and Legitimacy in Global Politics* (New York: Oxford University Press, 2011), 127–48.

indirectly alluded to – that international law can (no longer) be understood within the traditional contractual paradigm. The traditional notion of a "practical association" already had to assume certain "customary" practices – such as mutual recognition and the institutional rules establishing treaties as a source of obligations. But the largely bilateral conception that framed the transactions of sovereigns – putting a legal gloss on power politics[52] – should be better conceived as a "field" in Bourdieu's sense,[53] rather than as a set of simple bilateral undertakings. Thus the "field" of international law united various practices but with all the accoutrements of struggle and conflict. Here even "peace" became the sturdy child of the balance of power, while the irenic ideal, or the notion of humanity as the *civitas maxima*, was left to philosophers such as Wolff, or later to a dubious philosophy of history à la Kant. In this sense it was perhaps not accidental that one of the fathers of international law, Grotius, named "war" first, and "peace" (only) second in his magisterial work, while these two parts were uneasily held together by the legal project of articulating the rules for both war and peace.

The notion of an "order" requires something more than recognition and a set of practices, however. It emphasizes the systematic and "transcendental" conditions for the functioning of the rules that constitute our practices. Furthermore, we need some help in "applying" these rules to a case at hand in a process of interpretation, and some hints for how to decide on priorities among rules in cases of conflict. Here the principle of *lex specialis*, *lex posterior*, of *changed circumstances*, and so on come into play. Thus, even without the invocation of common "purposes" or of notions of a *civitas maxima*, or of constitutionalization as a "mindset" – to use Koskenniemi's term[54] – law begins its transformative work.

"Postmodern" international law receives its dynamism from three further developments: first, from the entry of new actors who are "founded" by the original participants in the international game through chartering international organizations; second, from the proliferation of issue areas that have became a matter of public concern because of their externalities; and third, from the introduction of new instruments, such as "soft" law.

While the effects of the first factor, that is the creation and proliferation of international organizations, are obvious, the other two developments deserve

[52] This is well in line with Philip Allott's characterization: "The role of international law within international society has been marginal, residual and intermittent … It has seemed to be little more than neutralized diplomacy, international relations half set in amber, a more or less safe refuge within so much international turbulence … the modest voice of common sense in the midst of rampant unreason." Philip Allott, *Eunomia: New Order for a New World* (New York: Oxford University Press, 1990), at 296f.

[53] See e.g. Pierre Bourdieu, "The Force of Law: Towards a Sociology of the Juridical Field," *Hastings Law Review*, vol. 38 (1987), 805–53.

[54] Koskenniemi, "Constitutionalism as a Mindset."

some brief discussion. Consider in this context the growth of state concerns that Foucault mentions in the context of the observed shift from a disciplinary politics to biopolitics. It occurs when the management of populations and of "risks" becomes an explicit state task, and when later the practices developed for internal management are transferred to the international level. The use of passports in the Holy Roman Empire provides a striking example. The issuance of passports began as a response to internal population movements, caused by differences in economic development and welfare provisions in various towns and regions. It gave rise to the principle that one had to return these "non-members" of the community to their original home, instead of just pawning them off to the next neighbour if one was no longer willing to provide them with work or welfare.[55] Later, when passports were used for controlling entry and exit at the state borders, this practice informed refugee law.

As to the third element, that is the invention of different "instruments" by which states and "other actors" attempt to regulate their relations, we notice the emergence of transnational and "soft law" instruments. The first developed out of the disparities between the status of the "sovereign" on the one hand and of a "private" entity, such as a corporation with whom the sovereign contracted. Since the public actor could easily abuse its power by changing the terms of a contract it had entered into with an inferior partner, new standards had to be articulated, which became part of "transnational law." It undermined the legislative monopoly claimed by states[56] and strengthened the powers of non-state actors and of "courts" such as the International Centre for Settlement of Investment Disputes (ICSID).

Furthermore, new synergies developed between the first and the second element, that is between international organizations and the "softening" of the supremacy of states. It led to the growth of non-formal instruments, such as the "conditionality" agreements of the IMF. Strangely enough, the three elements in conjunction seem to account for the latest trend, that is the trend of deformalization of law and the preference for "alternative forms of dispute settlement." While firms might for a variety of reasons prefer "private" arbitration,[57] it is significant that states involved in investment disputes[58] have now

[55] See Ursula Münch, *Sozialpolitik und Föderalismus: Zur Dynamic der Aufgabenverteilung im sozialen Bundesstaat*, Habilitationsschrift im Fachbereich Sozialwissenschaft der LMU Munich, 1996.

[56] See e.g. the Texaco–Lybian arbitration (Award of January 19, 1977), *International Legal Materials*, vol. 17 (1978), 1–37.

[57] For a general discussion see Yves Dezalay and Bryant G. Garth, *Dealing in Virtue: International Commercial Arbitration and the Construction of a Transnational Legal Order* (University of Chicago Press, 1996).

[58] The first instance of today's investment dispute arbitration seems to have been a case where a corporation submitted a claim against a state for arbitration. See *Radio Corporation of America* v. *National Government of China*, (1935) Permanent Court of Arbitration, The

also chosen that route, and most recently have even considered arbitration for the resolution of tax disputes.[59]

These developments are usually adduced as proofs of the "growth" of international law, of the increasing judicialization of politics, as a move from "bilateralism" to community interest, or even to a common emerging "value consensus." While the "growth" argument is certainly right quantitatively, we had better be careful of the underlying premise that this is something "good" as it accords with the liberal principle that more is better than less. After all, not all growths need to be good, as some of them kill their host! Nevertheless, all these elements feed back into the doctrinal development of law and engender various debates: which of the existing regimes should be considered the overarching one; whether the relative normativity of soft law[60] can be fitted within the classical categorical distinction law/non-law; whether *jus cogens* and obligations *erga omnes* function really as "higher" norms;[61] whether some constitutional principles, such as subsidiarity and margin of appreciation, or principles of administrative law could provide some help in dealing with conflicts; whether a constitutionalism "lite,"[62] or one informed by a full-blown commitment to "values" is the right strategy to pursue; and whether "interlegality"[63] (which legal pluralists emphasize) provides some clues for the configuration of law in a postnational setting.[64] Whatever position one takes on these issues, it is clear that the constitutionalization debate takes a central place in linking to both the fragmentation debate in international law[65] and to the pluralism and

Hague, available at: www.pca-cpa.org/showfile.asp?fil_id=1144 (accessed September 24, 2013).

59 See e.g. OECD: Committee on Fiscal Affairs Report, *Improving the Resolution of Tax Treaty Disputes*, adopted January 30, 2007 (published February 2007). See also the OECD Model Tax Convention as discussed in Marcus Desax and Marc Veit, "Arbitration of Tax Treaty Disputes: The OECD Proposal," *Arbitration International*, vol. 23, no. 3 (2007), 405–30.

60 For a brief discussion of soft law see Dinah Shelton, "Soft Law," in David Armstrong (ed.), *Routledge Handbook of International Law* (London: Routledge, 2009), 68–80.

61 J. H. H. Weiler and Andreas Paulus, "The Structure of Change in International Law, or Is There a Hierarchy of Norms in International Law, *European Journal of International Law*, vol. 8, no. 4 (1997), 545–65.

62 Jan Klabbers, "Constitutionalism Lite," *International Organizations Law Review*, vol. 1 (2004), 31–58.

63 See e.g. Bonaventura de Sousa Santos, *Towards a New Legal Common Sense: Law, Globalization and Emancipation*, 2nd edn. (London: Butterworth, 2002).

64 Roderick Macdonald and Martha M. Kleinhans, "What is Critical Legal Pluralism," *Canadian Journal of Law and Society*, vol. 12 (1997), 25–46; see also the special issue on Pluralizing Discourses of Law and Governance, *Northern Ireland Legal Quarterly*, vol. 57, no. 4 (Winter 2006).

65 To name just a few examples: Bruno Simma, "From Bilateralism to Community Interest," *Recueil des Cours*, vol. 250 (1994-VI); Jan Klabbers, Ann Peters and Geir Ulfstein, *The Constitutionalization of International Law* (New York: Oxford University Press, 2009); Jean Marie Dupuy, "The Constitutional Character of the United Nations revisited," *Max Planck Yearbook of United Nations Law*, vol. 1 (1997), 33; Bardo Fassbender, "The United

globalization debates, whereby "regimes" serve as an important conceptual bridge.[66]

Free-standing regimes

Consider in this context the notion of a "regime" that has been one of the foci of attention in international relations dating back to the special issue of *International Organization*[67] and finding its echo in the recent collection of detailed studies in *Who Governs the Globe*.[68] The concept itself actually originated at the Congress of Vienna, where it concerned the internationalization of rivers, such as the Rhine or Danube. It also marked the birth of the first international Unions, that is organizations that are vested by states with some regulatory powers.

The notion of a "free-standing" regime appeared first in the *Wimbledon*[69] case in the inter-war period, where the Permanent Court of International Justice (PCIJ) had to decide whether the rules (appended to the Treaty of Versailles) regulating the use of the Kiel Canal were sufficient, or needed to be supplemented by general international law. The Court came to the conclusion that the regime was sufficient and therefore represented a "free-standing regime." Although, of course, no regime can be entirely free-standing[70] since the general norms of treaty law (nowadays the Vienna Convention) are obviously part of any regime, the term "free-standing" meant originally only that certain primary rules existed. On the other hand, the problem of the "free-standing regimes" in more recent times, which fuels the fragmentation debate, is quite different in that the relative isolation of the regime results *from its unity of primary and secondary rules*, that is results from the existence of autonomous dispute resolution mechanisms.

Nations Charter as the Constitution of the International Community," *Columbia Journal of Transnational Law*, vol. 36 (1998), 529–619; Neil Walker, "The Idea of Constitutional Pluralism," *Modern Law Review*, vol. 65 (2002), 317–59; Werner Wouter, "The Never-ending Closure: Constitutionalism and International Law," in Nicholas Tsagourias (ed.), *Transnational Constitutionalism: International and European Perspectives* (Cambridge University Press, 2007), 329–67; Erika de Wet, "The International Constitutional Order," *International Comparative Law Quarterly*, vol. 55 (2006), 51–76; Peters, "Compensatory Constitutionalism; Jeffrey Dunoff and Joel Trachtman (eds.), *Ruling the World? Constitutionalism, International Law and Global Governance* (Cambridge University Press, 2009).

66 See William Twining, *Globalization and Legal Theory*, 2nd edn. (Cambridge University Press, 2006).

67 See the reprint in Stephen Krasner (ed.), *International Regimes* (Ithaca: Cornell University Press, 1983).

68 For a sophisticated analysis of various contemporary regimes see Deborah Avant, Martha Finnemore and Susan Sell (eds.), *Who Governs the Globe?* (Cambridge University Press, 2010).

69 *SS Wimbledon (UK* v. *Germany)* 1923 PCIJ (ser. A) No. 1 (June 28).

70 See the discussion by Simma and Pulkowski, "Of Planets and the Universe."

Thus the WTO, devoted to free trade, is a free-standing regime. It "sees" or phrases an issue in terms of its charter and thus has to rule out trade restrictions based on, for example, human rights, labour standards, or environmental concerns. China's push for becoming a member of the WTO was largely due to the advantage it expected from WTO membership, despite some new duties such as having to take measures against the "copycats" in many of its industries. Chinese human rights violations, which had been closely monitored by Washington and which mandated sanctions in case of gross violations, could, however, no longer be used for "punishing" China.

Similarly, in the *MOX* case[71] – where Ireland sued Great Britain in three courts for its placement of a nuclear facility on the Irish Sea – the issue arose whether a complaint fell under general international law, under a special environmental regime to which the two countries had acceded, or was a matter of European Community law. The case gave rise to hegemonic claims among different courts, as exemplified by the European Court, which excoriated the Irish for not having considered the issue to be solely a European one. Furthermore, since in such cases each "court" conceptualizes the problem differently, they are also in their rulings more or less "free-standing" – as the Appeals Chamber of the International Tribunal for the former Yugoslavia explicitly stated in the *Tadič* case.[72] The downside of this circumstance is that decisions have no precedent value. This reinforces the already existing limitations of Article 59 of the ICJ statute for shaping the legal process in a systematic fashion. The plurality and proliferation of courts is not only likely to result in conflicting and incoherent decisions, but "law" is no longer able to do its job of *prospective* ordering, despite the existence, or rather precisely *because* of the existence, of "binding" dispute settlement institutions. Thus "fragmentation" dissolves the notion of an even halfway integrated international legal order and stimulates – at least potentially – legal competition, not only among territorial states, but across issue areas and regimes. In the worst case, it leads to the absurdities that became notorious in the *Lauder* cases where two panels of the same institution (the United Nations Commission on International Trade Law/UNCITRAL), one in London and one in Stockholm, decided respectively that the same act – an expropriation by the Czech Republic – did and did not violate fair and equitable treatment, and did and did not deny the investor full protection and security.[73]

[71] *MOX Plant* case, Request for Provisional Measures Order (*Ireland* v. *the United Kingdom*), December, 3, 2001), International Tribunal for the Law of the Sea (2005) 126 ILR, vol. 273, at 50. Judgement of the Court of Justice in Case C-459/03 *Commission of the European Communities* v. *Ireland*, Press Release No 45/06.

[72] ICTY: *The Prosecutor* v. *Dusko Tadič*, Judgment of 15 July 1999 (1999) ILM 1518.

[73] See UNCITRAL Final Award (September 3, 2001) by the London panel and UNCITRAL, Final Award (March 14, 2003), Stockholm panel, as discussed in Jeffrey Dunoff and Joel Trachtman, "A Functional Approach to Constitutionalization," in Jeffrey Dunoff and

If it is true that "law" differs from expectations emerging out of interactions, and that it differs even from expectations *about* expectations – since differences among these secondary expectations must be adjudicated by a court – it is also true that courts are again bound by (much looser) expectations of how such conflicts are to be settled. Clearly, for the development of such tertiary expectations, which are supposed to stem the tide of forum-shopping or endless litigation, certain rules of regulating jurisdictional competences and discretion have to exist. Only in this way can the competing readings of a case as a tax or environmental case, as a zoning or civil rights issue, be decided. But it is precisely this function that cannot be served by free-standing regimes. Their adjudicative pronouncements, even if the "mutual supportiveness"[74] criterion is used as an interpretive principle, lack the *ex ante* ordering function that is an important part of law's effectiveness.

In a way, the principle of mutual supportiveness exceeds the traditional standard of harmonious interpretation, or of a conflict clause, since it also charges the parties to seek jointly cooperative solutions.[75] It was put to good use by the WTO Appellate Body in the 1998 *Shrimp–Turtle* case.[76] There the US import ban on shrimps caught by procedures that harmed sea turtles – an environmental concern that the USA quoted in support of its trade-restricting measures – was considered illegal, but not simply because it restricted free trade. Taking note of environmental concerns and the goal of sustainable development, the Appellate Body used the principle of mutual supportiveness

Joel Trachtman (eds.) *Ruling the World? Constitutionalism, International Law and Global Governance* (Cambridge University Press, 2009), 3–36, at 7f. For a more general discussion of the problem of inconsistent arbitration awards see Susan Franck, "The Legitimacy Crisis in Investment Treaty Arbitration," *Fordham, Law Review*, vol. 73 (2005), 1521–626.

[74] The principle emerged from the discussions on the compatibility of multilateral environmental agreements (MEAs), human rights concerns and WTO rules particularly when applied by the dispute settlement mechanism of the WTO. It made its appearance in the Agenda 21, which was adopted at the 1992 UN Conference on Environment and Development. A few years later the WTO adopted a report of its Committee on Trade and Environment endorsing the principle of mutual supportiveness as an internal WTO standard. The Ministerial Declaration at Doha (2001) acknowledged that the protection of private property rights enshrined in the Agreement on Trade Related Aspects of Intellectual Property Rights (TRIPS Agreement) "should be interpreted and implemented in a manner supportive of WTO members' right to protect public health and in particular, to promote access to medicine for all." Finally, the principle made it into the body of rules in the 2005 United Nations Educational, Scientific and Cultural Organization (UNESCO) Cultural Diversity Conventions (Article 20). Different from preamble statements of intent, which can be used as an aid to interpretation, Article 20 conceives mutual supportiveness "in terms of state obligations."

[75] See Nele Matz Lueck, "Harmonization, Systemic Integration and 'Mutual Supportiveness' as Conflict Solution Techniques: Different Modes of Interpretation as a Challenge to Negative Effects of Fragmentation," *Finnish Yearbook of International Law*, vol. 17 (2006), 39–53.

[76] United States – Import Prohibition of Certain Shrimp Products WT/DS58/AB/R (October 12, 1998).

for its construction of the chapeau to Article XX of the General Agreement on Tariffs and Trade (GATT). The latter provides that exceptions to the free trade principle must be the least restrictive measure available, and that the measures cannot be used in an arbitrary or discriminatory fashion. In this instance the Appellate Body found that the USA violated the chapeau's non-discrimination clause because it had *unilaterally* imposed restrictions, instead of engaging in meaningful *multilateral negotiations* in order to find a common position on the species protection problem.

Thus while a more "holistic approach" to interpretation and the resort to soft law might be able to finesse some problems, the question remains how malleable such instruments really are and whether they can create those tertiary expectations necessary for the prospective ordering function of law. Here doubts are indeed justified. For one, even in the well-established dispute settlement arena of the WTO, the "recommendations and rulings … cannot add to or diminish the rights and obligations provided in the covered agreements,"[77] so that the room for manoeuvre seems rather limited. "In the light of this, any hardening of soft law that occurs in the course of a WTO settlement may well be regarded, at least by some WTO members, as illegitimate law making."[78] The subsequent decision of the WTO in the *EU– Biotech*[79] case shows what complications arise when "third-party" effects have to be assessed, when for example some states are party to only one of the competing treaties and when it is precisely this regime that would have to be changed if the mutual support principle is adduced for giving effect to the essential norms embodied in the other treaties. Since the Panel did not take into account any unratified treaty by any of the disputing parties, it could not apply *a fortiori* the mutual support principle.[80]

[77] GATT: Multilateral Trade Negotiations, Final Act Embodying the Results of the Uruguay Round of Negotiations, April 15, 1994, Annex 2 Understanding on the Rules and Procedures Governing the Settlement of Disputes, reprinted in *International Legal Materials*, vol. 33 (1994), 1125, quote from Article 3(2).

[78] Jose Alvarez, "The New Dispute Settlers: (Half) Truths and Consequences", *Texas International Law Journal*, vol. 38 (2003), 405–44, at 424.

[79] See EC – Measures Affecting the Approval and Marketing of Biotech Products, Panel Report WT/DS 291/R and Panel Report WT/DS.293/R of September 29, 2006.

[80] See the Report of the panel: European Communities – Measures Affecting the Approval and Marketing of Biotech products (September 26, 2006) available at www.wto.org/english/tratop_e/dispu_e/cases_e/ds293_e.htm (accessed September 24, 2013) The European Commission had argued that the 1992 Convention on Biological Diversity and the related Biosafety Protocol should be consulted for deciding the dispute, which arose out of the EU ban of genetically modified organisms. But since the USA was not a party to the Biosafety Protocol, the Panel rejected the suggestion (see para. 7.68) and construed narrowly what was "part of the WTO law." Similarly, it rejected any intimation that the precautionary principle had become part of customary law or a "general principle" of public international law (para. 7.89).

Similarly, the Fragmentation Report of the ILC rejected the mutual support principle since its open-ended structure tends "to support the primacy of the treaty that is part of the law applier's regime." The group opted instead for regime-independent third-party settlement.[81] This proposal, however, addresses only half of the problem, because it is not clear whether such third-party settlements are to be given to the "functionalist" dispute settlement mechanism of a regime, or to a court with jurisdiction in several areas. The latter would indeed create a type of "world court." If such institutionalization of disputes is most unlikely, then in what relation do the decisions of various dispute settlement institutions stand vis-à-vis each other and vis-à-vis the decisions of, for example, the ICJ?

Constitutionalizing the world?

It is therefore not surprising that a full "constitutionalization" is in large part a "knee-jerk response to the existential anxiety arising out of fragmentation."[82] Here several contenders for becoming a "constitution" are in the wings, the most prominent being the UN and the WTO. The bitter truth, however, is that neither the WTO Charter nor the UN Charter comes even close to embodying the basic elements of "constitutionalism" with which we are familiar, namely the separation of powers, checks and balances, democratic representation and participation, an emphasis on individual rights, and governmental restraint in the exercise of power.

One could perhaps "constitutionalize" the UN[83] through a teleological reading of the Charter and its purposes – eliding thereby the difficulties of "original intent" of how much weight is to be given to the text and to subsequent practice, also brushing aside the problem that the big power concert was cemented by constitutional means and by an exacting amendment procedure. By a conceptual stretch we could even argue for implied powers, which are no longer limited only to the "necessary" and "essential" performance of the organization's duties, as was held in the *Reparations* case;[84] a wider reading could now perhaps also include those powers that are "desirable" and "consistent" with those duties. This stretch in turn could be justified by relying on the "trend" of the recent expansive interpretations of Article 39 of the UN Charter. Assuming that we could pass these hurdles, a new constitutional "blueprint" could, however, provide true guidance only if these purposes were well ordered and were clearly perceptible by all – similar to Descartes' clear and distinct ideas. But it

[81] See *Fragmentation Report*, para. 280.
[82] Klabbers, "Constitutionalism Lite," at 49.
[83] See e.g. Fassbender, "The United Nations Charter."
[84] Reparations for Injuries Suffered in the Service of the United Nations (1949) ICJ Reports, 177ff., at 182.

was precisely such an uncontested and incontestable appeal to "nature," God's will, or to "reason" that a constitution was supposed to curb – quite aside from the fact that making such intuitionist arguments in the international arena is even more difficult to sustain, given the far more heterogonous cultural environment. The appeal to fundamental principles or ultimate values simply will not do, since values not only often conflict, but are also compatible with conflicting specific rules that usually privilege certain interests over others. As Jan Klabbers points out:

> The very idea of constitutionalism presumes that constitutionalism helps mankind into an a-political, a-ideological space, a realm somewhere beyond politics where people would no longer disagree with each other. Such a realm does not exist, cannot exist, and would be abhorrent at any rate. The idea of overcoming politics by insisting on adhering to certain fixed values is bound to fail, because reference to those values itself is intensely political.[85]

It is therefore not surprising that such a move does not enjoy much support outside of academia, particularly since the representative credentials of the Security Council are quite "underwhelming"[86] and the "federal analogy"[87] has been subject to well-taken criticisms. Furthermore, as the *Kadi* case[88] showed, some of the "sanctioning practices" of the UN Security Council – blacklisting private persons on the basis of non-vetted information – violate fundamental principles of the rule of law. Although the now established appeals procedure[89] alleviates some of the most problematic effects of the "smart" sanctions, it still seems a far cry from an effective remedy, as the *Sayadi* case demonstrates.[90] While a more active ICJ could review the actions of the Security Council and

85 Klabbers, "Constitutionalism Lite."

86 For an important discussion of the constitutionalization move in international law see Klabbers *et al.*, *The Constitutionalization of International Law*, Chapter 1.

87 See e.g. G. Arangio-Ruiz, "The Federal Analogy and UN Charter Interpretation: A Crucial Issue," *European Journal of International Law*, vol. 8 (1997), 1–28; see also Jose Alvarez, "Constitutional Interpretation in International Organizations," in Jean Marc Coicaud and Veijo Heiskanen (eds.), *The Legitimacy of International Organizations* (Tokyo/New York: UN University Press, 2001): 104–54.

88 See the ECJ decision of September 3, 2008 in the joint cases of *Kadi* and *Al Barakaat* (C-402/05 and C-415/5).

89 By Resolution 1904 of December 2009 an Office of an Ombudsperson was created to which persons contesting the listing of the Sanction Committee can appeal and which can assist them before the Sanctioning Committee. Alternatively those persons can appeal to their state, which will, after review, bring the case to the Sanctioning Committee.

90 In October 2008 the Human Rights Committee decided to go along with the decision of the UN Sanctioning Committee, which had refused Belgium's request for a delisting of two of its nationals who had been blacklisted by the UN Sanctioning Committee. The Sayadis then filed a complaint to the Human Rights Committee alleging the violation of several Articles of the International Covenant on Civil and Political Rights (ICCPR) including the denial of due process in their listing by the UN Sanctioning Committee. This complaint was dismissed by the Human Rights Committee on the basis of Articles 25 and 103 of the

prevent blatant cases of *ultra vires* decisions, there is nothing in the history of the UN to suggest that the permanent members would agree to such an arrangement, nor is there much interest in the World Court for such a "law job." Given the heterogeneity of the international community, the great power disparities, and the fact that human beings remain "creatures of limited generosity" as Hume suggested, such expectations seem unrealistic. Even if the Court, or some courts, were empowered to render such judgments, they could not count on much support or link their decisions to any viable political processes that could jump-start a reform similar to the US Supreme Court impulse in *Brown* v. *Board of Education*,[91] which resulted in the Civil Rights Act of 1964.[92]

Writing about the European experience, Antje Wiener sounds another cautious note:

> the potential for conflict caused by moving constitutional norms outside the bounded territory of states, i.e. outside the domestic polity and away from the inevitable link with methodological nationalism lies in the de-coupling of the customary from the organizational. It is through this transfer between context that the meaning of norms becomes contested, as differently socialized actors, such as politicians, civil servants, parliamentarians or lawyers, trained in different legal traditions seek to interpret them. In other words, while in supranational contexts actors might well agree on the importance of a particular norm, such as the proposition that human rights matter, the agreement about a specific norm based on formal agreement (formal validity) does not allow for conclusion about the meaning of norms. As in different domestic contexts that meaning is likely to differ according to experience with "norm-use," it is important to recover the crucial interrelation between both types of social practices, i.e. the cultural practices that generate the customary, on the one hand and organizational practices facilitated by public performance interpreting the norm for political and legal use.[93]

Since the UN has one other serious competitor, one could perhaps give priority to the WTO and its effective dispute resolution system. But even the most ardent advocates of such a move have to admit that this, at a minimum, would require the incorporation of human rights – never mind ecological, or basic distributional concerns. This seems far beyond existing possibilities, as Boyle and Chinkin' s careful study of international law-making confirms.[94]

UN Charter as, in case of a conflict of obligations derived from different agreement, the "Charter shall prevail." See CCPR/C/94/D 1472/2006.

[91] *Brown* v. *Board of Education of Topeka*, 347 US 483 (1954).

[92] See Publ. L 88–352, 78 Stat. 241, enacted July 2, 1964.

[93] Antje Wiener, *The Invisible Constitution of Politics* (Cambridge University Press, 2008), at 33f.

[94] Alan Boyle and Christine Chinkin, *The Making of International Law* (Oxford University Press, 2007).

Finally, there exists the non-enticing prospect that greater "constitutionalism" at the international level might be undermining constitutionalism domestically. Proponents of proposals that are difficult to get through the domestic constitutional processes might opt for an "international solution" that is negotiated out of the limelight of public scrutiny by "informal networks." In that case a state would have to enforce such an agreement, even if that means that it thereby has to uphold a "law" that might violate elementary constitutional principles. These problems would not be less, but probably even more severe when such a regime was no longer only "free-standing" but now, in addition, possessed the new cloak of constitutional legitimacy. It will be the task of the next two Meditations to probe these issues further, by first addressing the problem of functionalism, regime collisions, and legal pluralism in greater detail, and finally by probing more deeply the concept of the international community.

Meditation 4

Of experts, helpers, and enthusiasts

Introduction

The upshot of the previous discussions was that the weakness of the international legal order is due to the feeble institutionalization of *the political processes* rather than to the lack of laws, conventions, or "courts," as it is often suggested. Indeed, as the discussion of free-standing regimes showed, there is an awful lot of law out there, and the proliferation of legal norms and dispute resolution is part of the problem, not of its solution. In the absence of an authoritative decision, in which priorities of policy can be determined, trade-offs can be agreed upon, and broad powers can be delegated, dispute settlement and judicial control – while certainly not irrelevant – can play only a limited role. This is why we frequently observe a struggle over which discourse shall become the hegemonic one: whether an issue should be phrased as a trade or an environmental issue, as a labour question, or as one involving human rights.

It is unsurprising that with increasing complexity "norm collisions" are difficult to handle. Moreover, agencies determining policy often resort to informal norms or dispute settlements outside the legal sphere. Such developments are not limited to the international sphere where "soft" law and "best practices" have become a trend (or rather a counter-trend to the argument of the legalization or judicialization). A similar phenomenon has been noticed in domestic legal orders, where both the preference for "private ordering" and for alternative dispute settlement procedures (ADS) have been noted by sociologists, and law and economics lawyers alike.[1] Cost considerations are certainly one reason why firms and investors prefer arbitration to lengthy litigation, or to the even more cumbersome procedures of diplomatic protection. Within the domestic sphere the preference for private ordering is, however, also fuelled by a troubling loss of faith in regulation and in the

[1] See Eric Posner, *Law and Social Norms* (Cambridge, MA: Harvard University Press, 2000).

social engineering by courts that resulted from the "rights" revolution a few decades ago.[2]

Sometimes this trend of searching for alternatives to law is explained in terms of the deep-seated changes that have transformed societies and that have eroded the state's ability to preserve its law-making monopoly. As Robert Cooter remarked: "A post-industrial society must discover ways to decentralize not only commodity production, but also significant ways of law-making."[3] Why this should be so Cooter does not say, but he does point to a problem that legal pluralists had already identified some time ago and that has become even more pronounced through globalization. As opposed to the monolithic notion of "the law," identified with the state, legal pluralists had always argued that several sets of norms usually exist in a society and that legal orders resort to the fiction of "incorporation" in order to give the appearance of unity.

That this is a more general pattern can be seen from other historical examples. In Roman law *aequitas* was originally a principle outside of normal law. It provided for the resolution of conflicts where the formal rigidities of the *ius civile* would lead to an "unjust" result.[4] In England, "equity" courts developed alongside the common law, and were incorporated into the common law system by the 1873–75 Judicature Act. In cases where jurisdictional problems arose, such as among medieval merchants of different jurisdictions, they developed a separate system for dealing with disputes. It was based on equitable principles and common practices and developed into the old *lex mercatoria*. Similarly, if the new "law merchant" of today were to become "law," which is hotly debated,[5] we could see it when the decisions of its conflict resolution mechanisms are quoted by other "courts," be they national or supra-national.

The last observation is also important for understanding the emergence and growth of "soft law," which is generated outside the usual legal "sources" but attains legal standing if used in a principled fashion by "normal" courts. Furthermore, this trend toward deformalization has even reached the courts themselves and traditional law-making institutions, as the spirited discussions in the ILC and the twists and turns of the Draft Convention on State

[2] See e.g. Cass Sunstein, *After the Rights Revolution* (Cambridge, MA: Harvard University Press, 1995).

[3] Robert Cooter, "Against Legal Centrism," *California Law Review*, vol. 81 (1993), 417–29, at 418.

[4] Franz Wieacker, *Roemische Rechtsgeschichte* (Munich: Beck 1988).

[5] See e.g. Gunther Teubner, who considers it a "phantom" promulgated by a "few speculative Sorbonne professors" in Gunther Teubner, *Global Law without a State* (Dartmouth: Aldershot, 1997), at 12. See also Gralf-Peter Calliess and Moritz Renner "Between Law and Social Norms," *Ratio Juris*, vol. 22 (June 2009), 260–80.

Responsibility show.[6] In the latter case no consensus has emerged of making these articles into a formal treaty. Yet only a few members seem to consider this a serious problem. International financial institutions, as we have seen, have traditionally relied on "soft" rather than black letter law in drawing up their conditionality understandings, as draconic as the substantive provisos might have been otherwise. Similarly, instead of speaking the language of state responsibility and sanctions, some treaties now provide for "capacity-building" measures as responses to treaty violations.[7]

Finally, considering the increasing interdependencies and their externalities, and given the loss of steering capacity by states confronting the "denationalization" of politics, neither transnational nor national regulation appears to suffice for managing global problems. This deficiency involves, however, more than the managerial issues that have dominated the discussions in the field. It concerns the legitimacy and the ability of inducing the habitual obedience that once accrued to law in general as a product of the state. One indication for this change is the loss of deference to traditional arguments that formerly shielded the state from too close a scrutiny of its practices. This development has a "bright side" when issues of human rights are at issue, since sovereignty and domestic jurisdiction no longer serve as exclusionary reasons. But this also comes at a cost, particularly since other forms of authority have become part of the game: be it the market or "value-based" arguments promulgated largely by "cosmopolitan" publicists, or *jus cogens* and obligations *erga omnes* that try to square the circle by claiming a special normative status.[8]

The problem of legitimate authority engenders fundamental order issues at the individual, state, and interstate level, as Rob Walker has pointed out.[9] In the international legal writings those problems are addressed in a variety of ways: as an issue of legal "style," when David Kennedy contrasted pre-modern, modern, and postmodern legal arguments in terms of legitimate sources, or when Koskenniemi draws from different authoritative sources a "mindset"[10] that is to bring the enlightenment project to fruition, or when we are treated to historical

6 The ILC seems divided on the issue of whether or not to make its draft articles a multilateral convention. After several attempts it decided in 2011 again to postpone a decision and take it up again in 2013, but as of November 2013 nothing seems to have happened.

7 On the history and execution of the capacity-building program of the UN, see Roger Macormick (ed.), *Capacity Building for Poverty Eradication* (New York: United Nations, 2002).

8 For an interesting account on different sources of "private" authority, see Rodney Bruce Hall and Thomas Biersteker (eds.), *The Emergence of Private Authority in Global Governance* (Cambridge University Press, 2002).

9 R. B. J. Walker, *After the Globe, Before the World* (London: Routledge, 2010).

10 Martti Koskenniemi, "Constitutionalization as a Mindset," *Theoretical Inquiries in Law*, vol. 8 (2007), article 2.

narratives of an "evolving" international community, so familiar from the writings of Kelsen,[11] Allott,[12] Falk,[13] Tomuschat,[14] or Simma.[15]

While the narrative of the "international community" will be the topic of the next Meditation, here I examine more closely the problem of deformalization of law. Thus, questions of the "origin" of this phenomenon and the "responses" to it will serve as the focal points in my discussion. I shall argue below that the examination of "origins" has to do with new problems on the political agenda, and with the new quasi-legal instruments, while the "responses" concern the emergence of new actors and the increasing role of legal writings in the law-making process.[16]

Let us begin with the "origins" of these problems. In a way, it is not just that nowadays we have "more" problems. As any consultation of newspapers will tell us, there were always plenty of problems around,[17] and many important issues that ought to be addressed today either do not even make the papers, or

[11] See e.g. Hans Kelsen, *Das Problem der Souveraenitaet und die Theorie des Voelkerrechts* (Ann Arbor: Reprint of The University of Michigan Library, 1920). See also his later *Peace Through Law* (Chapel Hill: University of North Carolina Press, 1944) in which he outlines a full-fledged system of a compulsory jurisdiction and individual responsibility for violations of international law, parallel to an institutionalization of the Great Powers improving on the League of Nations model. Whether this represents a break with his "pure theory" is debatable as most of his "cosmopolitan ideals were derived from Wolff and Kant and can already be found in his earlier work on Sovereignty. The problematic assumption of a universal peace system guaranteed by law is in typical Kantian fashion left to history. It is only temporarily, by no means forever, that contemporary humanity is divided into states … Its legal unity, that is the *civitas maxima* as organization of the world: this is the political core of the primacy of international law." Danilo Zolo, "Hans Kelsen, Peace Though International Law," *European Journal of International Law*, vol. 9 (1998), 306–24, at 310. As Danilo Zolo points out, this is the argument about the "evolution of the international legal community from its primitive condition imposed by the dogma of state sovereignty to a universal organization of mankind: within this framework, morality, politics and economics should converge and be integrated under the aegis of law." *Ibid.*

[12] Philip Allott, *Eunomia: New Order for a New World* (New York: Oxford University Press, 1990).

[13] Richard Falk, *A Study of Future Worlds* (New York: Free Press 1975).

[14] Christian Tomuschat, *International Law: Ensuring the Survival of Mankind at the End of the New Century* (The Hague: Martinus Nijhoff, 2001).

[15] Bruno Simma, "From Bilateralism to Community Interest," *Recueil des Cours*, vol. 250 (1994-VI).

[16] Joost Pauwelyn, Ramses Wessel and Wouter Werner, *Informal International Law Making* (Oxford University Press, 2012).

[17] As a matter of fact, look nowadays at, for example, the once standard-setting newspapers, such as the London *Times* that has become nearly indistinguishable from the "infotainment" that is globally advancing and that addresses questions of what (might) interest us "privately" (such as gossip or celebrities), while reports on "public" issues that ought to be addressed, from poverty to financial regulation to resource use and so on, are simply relegated to oblivion.

are treated there at best episodically and superficially. The issue is, rather, that many of the identified "problems" are part of deeper conceptual changes and thus their "gravity" and not only their sheer "number" is at issue.

Take for example the eradication of the line separating natural from man-made disasters. As global warming demonstrates, human actions in the aggregate can be the cause of "natural" catastrophes. Similarly, the *Responsibility to Protect* is part and parcel of a new and wider political project of how to mediate the tensions between autonomy and accountability, not only within, but also among states. Finally, the claims for the superiority of private ordering, for free markets and the "rule of law" (largely reduced to the protection of property rights, contract enforcement, and dispute resolution) are the not so innocent attempts of ensconcing particular interests and exempting them from political challenges. This was, after all, a rather successful move in the eighteenth and nineteenth centuries, when "property" was nearly exclusively assigned to the "private" realm where it was shielded from public order concerns. The move mystified this form of private power, which then could be exercised without much interference, while being able to rely on the state's public power for protection.[18]

These considerations also turn our attention to the issue of agenda-building and to the "responses" to these changes. With new actors entering the political arena and claiming a "voice,"[19] it is not an exaggeration to say that the emergence of NGOs as "spokespersons" has been one of the decisive changes in world politics. It was itself the result of the confluence of various long-term trends. One of them had its roots in the earlier "reformist" movements of internationalists, or world federalists, who had pushed for the establishment of the League of Nations and the UN.[20] Another precursor were the "functionalists," who argued that with science and technology a new intelligentsia would become empowered to make the decisions on "neutral grounds" instead of simply deferring to the national interest. Politics, always contentious and inefficient, could then be dissolved into technique and administration.

But it was probably the First World War and the need for economic planning and inter-allied collaboration in the execution of the war that transported this idea from the desk of philosophers and sociologists, such as Comte and St Simon (or later even Dewey), to the national bureaucracies and to the offices of various "boards." What counted were results, not formalistic games or diplomatic procedures. The emphasis had to be on transparency, comparability, reliance on "numbers," and, if they were unavailable or problematic, on "best

[18] See Justin Rosenberg, *The Empire of Civil Society* (New York/London: Verso, 1994).

[19] See Albert O. Hirschman, *Exit, Voice and Loyalty* (Cambridge, MA: Harvard University Press, 1970).

[20] See David Kennedy, "The Move to Institutions," *Cardozo Law Review*, vol. 8, no. 4 (1987), 841–988.

practices" (even though the introduction of "rule books" stands in clear tension with effectiveness and efficiency, as we will see). Knowledge and organizational know-how also explain why many NGOs can now claim a "voice" in global debates, and why they are consulted by governments and international organizations.

Sometimes they have even become partners in policy execution, as for instance in the delivery of international aid, which is now increasingly channelled through NGOs.[21] This has important implications for both states and "civil society" that go far beyond the usual "capture" argument typical of corporatism on the one hand, and of the illusion that civil society is replacing the state in "global governance." Instead a new form of "governmentality" is emerging. As Sending and Neumann point out, after having studied in detail the "contractual implications" of NGO involvement in two cases (landmines and population policy):

> these actors are not brought into the fold and as such deprived of their autonomy and as recognized representatives of "civil society." Rather it is precisely their status as actors that possess [*sic*] expertise central to the task of governing and, much more importantly, the fact that they appear to be autonomous political subjects with a capacity for political will formation that makes them key subjects of, and allies in governmental tasks. It is thus not the functional role of the state that has changed as such, but the intermeshing of the networks which has become so much denser that is qualitatively changing how the state goes about minding that function – how it recruits its personnel, organizes its work and shapes in different ways the plethora of actors central to governmental functions.[22]

Finally, as this quote hints at, part of this "confluence" is also the "revolutionary" heritage of not only "naming and shaming" but also of speaking for "all" and being involved in projects that stand for human emancipation and progress. Here the link of many NGOs to social movements becomes visible, as "movements" live off their capacity for taking things out of the ordinary and of mobilizing the public through dramatic, emblematic action[23] that has important organizational and "ideological" implications.

[21] On the explosion of distributing aid through NGOs and its problems see Briana Yontcheva, Gilles Nancy, *Does NGO Aid go to the Poor?* (Washington DC: IMF, 2006), Working Paper WP/06/39; Dirk Koch, Alex Dreher, Peter Nonnenkamp and Rainer Thiele, "Keeping a Low Profile: What Determines the Allocation of Aid by NGOs," *World Development*, vol. 37 no. 5 (2009), 902–18. For a discussion of the normative issue and the praxis of humanitarianism see Janice Gross Stein, "Background Knowledge in the Foreground: Conversations about Competent Practices in 'Sacred Space,'" in Emmanuel Adler and Vincent Pouliot (eds.), *International Practices* (Cambridge University Press, 2011), 87–107.

[22] Ole Jacob Sending and Iver B. Neumann, "Governance to Governmentality: Analyzing NGOs, States, and Power," *International Studies Quarterly*, vol. 50 (2006), 651–72, at 668.

[23] See Douglas McAdam, Sidney Tarrow and Charles Tilly, *Dynamics of Contention* (Cambridge University Press, 2001).

Let us look at the "ideological" issue of enthusiasm first. If the effervescence is to be sustained, however, the trans-valuation of all values has to be posited. Not the past, not the look to tradition and precedent, but the future, and above all "action," now becomes a consumption good. Hanna Arendt has elaborated on this transformation of the notion of revolution from an understanding of a return to the origins, to one in which only the future matters.[24] These two meanings of revolution are well exemplified by the Glorious Revolution on the one hand, and by the American Revolution, French Revolution, and later the Russian Revolution, on the other hand. Particularly in the latter two cases conviction and sacrifice rather than questions of conforming to conventions provided the yardstick for evaluation. Loyalty was constantly being questioned and treason was suspected everywhere. These suspicions could be assuaged only by outrageous actions that proved the "virtue" of the revolutionary (Robespierre), or that could be taken as indications of sound "class consciousness." Law, for the enthusiast, can be at best an instrument to be used when it is getting him nearer to the future goal, but which has to be discarded when it is not.

But, of course, "the future" is not a book open to all for inspection and for thereby ending all disagreements. Conflict is rife among enthusiasts, and it is hardly surprising that the bitterest fights break out among true believers. Sects and splinter groups arise, as differences are quickly translated into the existential choice of belonging "in" or "out," of being "for" or "against." Thus leaving the fold is often the only way of saving one's life or sanity, since such revolutions have a tendency of devouring their children.

It is here that often a new group of "high priests" forms and steps in. Of course, their commitment and credentials and, beyond that, their character and their "politics" have to pass muster, but they also bring to the fold the ability to limit the damage from conflicts. They do so by inventing a "tradition." A canon of "authoritative" texts is established, paradigmatic examples for action are assembled, interpretations are given, cases decided, and the revitalization of enthusiasm is left for the high holidays, when rites are enacted, memories are invoked, and enthusiasm is managed by ritualization and the careful staging of "revival" meetings. The true believers have metamorphosed from enthusiasts into sectarians – if not into a "church"[25] that uses hierarchies, offices, and laws.[26]

[24] Hannah Arendt, *On Revolution* (New York: Viking, 1965).

[25] I am using here Weber's distinction. Weber elaborated on and modified the argument of Ernst Troeltsch, *The Social Teachings of the Christian Churches* (New York: Macmillan, 1931); a translation of Weber's paper, presented at the 1910 meeting of the Deutsche Gesellschaft für Soziologie (with Troeltsch, Simmel, Toennies, and Jellinek participating) can be found in Max Weber, "On Church, Sect, and Mysticism," *Sociological Analysis*, vol. 34 (1073), 140–9.

[26] See also Peter Berger, "The Sociological Study of Sectarianism," *Social Research*, vol. 21 (1954), 467–85.

In the following I use three "ideal types" as my foil. I do not want to imply (as was perhaps done by Weber and perhaps also in my brief narrative above) that there is a necessary development from enthusiasts (Weber's charismatic leaders) via "tradition" to the bureaucratic apparatus of modern formal law and its concomitant Herculi. After all, ideal types are not essential descriptions but heuristic tools, and actors might at different times fit one or the other type, or even exhibit elements of all of them. Instead, I want to use these "caricatures" to understand several problems. There is, first, the problem of formalism and the deformalization of contemporary international law. Beyond that, I am interested in the roles of different forms of expertise in the legal process and in providing "professional" help in complex emergencies.

With these considerations in mind my argument will take the following steps. In the next section I address the problem of "soft law" and probe the puzzles that the dimension of hardness/softness generates (addressing the "origin" question mentioned above). The third section (on experts and enthusiasts) is devoted to "best practices" and the role of new actors in both law-making processes and in the execution of interventions in crisis situations, before I address the role of "courts" in these interventions.

What is "soft" in soft law?

According to the taxonomic ideal, categorical distinctions have to be exclusive and they require that all members of the class share at least one common characteristic. To that extent the categorical distinction between the "is" and the "ought," between normative and assertoric statements, seems clear enough. Unfortunately, some of the inferences based on this distinction are much less clear. Here one is reminded of the debate about "relative" normativity that arose in conjunction with the discovery of "soft law," that is the informal instruments containing promissory commitments by states receiving loans from the IMF. These commitments were explicitly *not* considered to have legal character.[27]

One can of course understand that the notion of relative normativity was disconcerting for lawyers, for whom much of their professional skill consists in having a clear answer to questions of whether an obligation or instrument is "legal" or not. Issues of "obligation" can then be decided rather easily. Yet the language game of obligation is obviously much wider than that of legal obligation, and, even in the latter case, something which might not clearly oblige "legally," *might become* such an obligation, such as when one party "relies" on the declarations of the other party, thereby showing the protean character of this supposed fixed dichotomy.

[27] See J. Gold, "Strengthening the Soft Law of International Exchange Arrangements," *American Journal of International Law*, vol. 77 (1983), 443–89.

The *Eastern Greenland* case provides the *locus classicus* in international law. Here reliance (on the unilateral declaration by the Norwegian Minister of Foreign Affairs) and "consideration" (Denmark had indicated that it would not oppose Norwegian claims to Spitzbergen) created a legal obligation that would not have existed otherwise. Thus, while most of the discussion in the literature has focused on the "speech act" of the Norwegian minister Ihlen, the interesting point is that it was actually the later Danish request for a confirmation, and the construal of a *quid pro quo* by the Court (mutual non-interference with the respective claims to Greenland and Spitzbergen), that had made a legal obligation out of an informal deal.[28] In a similar fashion, the ICJ construed more recently in the *Pulp Mills* case a joint press communiqué issued by Argentina and Uruguay as an "agreement," despite the fact that the instrument was neither a treaty, nor even signed by the respective ministers.[29]

This raises the general problem of how we decide on the "sameness" in classical taxonomies and what this implies for law. Thus apples and oranges, or even tomatoes, are the "same," namely "fruits," when compared to stones or animals, but they are certainly not the "same" in all respects. One could now object that this example does not seem to take care of the alleged possibility of "gradation" in normativity, since, after all, the different fruits are the "same" qua fruits (even if most of us might have difficulty in counting tomatoes as such and may "downgrade" them despite their properties). For law, however, a trivial example clarifies the problem of graded normativity. If someone has the right of way but another driver disregards the traffic rules, the right holder is not simply entitled to "stand on his right" and thereby "rub out" the law-breaker. Here the "right" of having the right of way is trumped by the "higher" norm of safeguarding life and limb, despite the non-conformist actions of the "law-breaker."[30] On the other hand, as we shall see in the next Meditation, which takes up *ius cogens* and obligations *erga omnes*, normative hierarchies do not – contrary to the hopes placed in them – provide for a near automatic "override" by the "universal" norms (as exceptions and exemptions might exist), and the existing state practice and case law are far from settled. Such a state of affairs is then conducive to attempts at "closing the gaps" by bold doctrinal statements – such as announcing the end of traditional state immunity, or construing claims

[28] See *Denmark* v. *Norway*, PCIJ 1933 PCIJ Series A/B No 53, 3; Hudson World Court Rep. 148 (1938) (*Eastern Greenland* case).

[29] *Case Concerning Pulp Mills on the River Uruguay* (*Argentina* v. *Uruguay*) (2010) ICJ Reports, paras. 132–50.

[30] For a further discussion, see Martti Koskenniemi, "Hierarchy in International Law: A Sketch," *European Journal of International Law*, vol. 8 (1997), 566–82; J. H. H. Weiler and Andreas Paulus, "The Structure of Change in International Law or Is There a Hierarchy of Norms in International Law," *European Journal of International Law*, vol. 8 (1997), 545–65.

to universal jurisdiction in both civil and criminal matters,[31] and asserting the standing of non-injured parties for violation of *erga omnes* obligations and so on. Unfortunately, many of these arguments run afoul of both logic – as they seem to involve a logical *petitio principii*, that is they presuppose what they want to prove – and actual practice, as the example of Belgium's abandonment of its law for universal jurisdiction for prosecuting violations of international law shows.[32]

From these brief remarks, it should be clear that "relative" normativity exists and thus the one exemplified by "soft" law is not simply an oxymoron,[33] despite some puzzling problems, and the recognition that the classical distinction of *lex lata* and *de lege ferenda* (bringing soft law under the latter category) is not particularly illuminating. For positivists and some non-positivists alike,[34] any attempt to tamper with the dichotomy engenders fears of confusing law and politics, a move that is, in their view, "counterproductive" since it allegedly dissuades people from taking international law seriously.

Such a stance might have some merit without, however, addressing the larger problem of the dynamics of law creation and settled practices. We observe similar phenomena in domestic law. If, for example, the German Civil Code (BGB) refers to certain accepted trade practices, it seems that the latter have become part of the law, even though these provisions cannot be found as fully formulated rules in the respective codes that are supposedly exhaustive of "the law." Furthermore, whether and how these "unwritten rules" will be used again in the future remains somewhat uncertain, as civil law systems are not based on case law and precedent (although even this distinction is losing much of its discriminatory power). Nevertheless, it seems rather uncontroversial that legality is bestowed through "incorporation" by court decisions.

Consider in this context the Agreement on Technical Barriers to Trade, which became part of GATT in 1994. It incorporated the Environmental Management Standards of ISO 14001, and it committed "central governments to ensure that their standard setting bodies comply with GATT national treatment and least restrictive requirements." When, in addition, a code of conduct was attached, these standards became part of international trade law. As Naomi Roht-Arriaza pointed out:

[31] See the critical discussion of Andreas Zimmermann, "Violations of Fundamental Norms of International Law and the Exercise of Universal Jurisdiction in Criminal Matters," in Christian Tomuschat and Jean-Marc Thouvenin (eds.), *The Fundamental Rules of the International Legal Order* (Leiden: Martinus Nijhoff, 2006), 335–53.

[32] See Steve Ratner, "Belgium's War Crime Statute: A Postmortem," *American Journal of International Law*, vol. 97 (2003), 888–97.

[33] Prosper Weil, "Towards Relative Normativity in International Law?" *American Journal of International Law*, vol. 77 (1983), 413–42.

[34] See e.g. the critical assessment by Jan Klabbers, "The Redundancy of Soft Law," *Nordic Journal of International Law*, vol. 65 (1996), 167–82.

> [The] rules created by ISO and its sister bodies have privileged status in trade law, a status not conferred on voluntary standards created by intergovernmental bodies. ISO standards help define what is meant by a "standard" in a given area … States that impose or allow standards differing from existing (or draft) ISO ones on the same topic bear the burden of justifying the departure.[35]

While this case seems pretty uncontroversial, the term "soft law" is also used in other contexts. Indeed, if one examines the types of norms that are said to be "soft," one is inclined, at first blush, to share the misgivings of positivists. Christine Chinkin includes here norms that are vague or imprecise, articulated in non-binding form, originate in bodies not endowed with law-making authority, are addressed to non-state actors whose practice cannot create "custom," or represent voluntary norms, or norms that do not contain specific obligations whose violation would raise issues of responsibility.[36]

It needs no further elaboration that the term "soft" is used equivocally, and Kal Raustiala's proposal to unpack this notion and distinguish between several dimensions is to be welcomed. One such dimension concerns the "form" of the undertaking (distinguishing between contracts and pledges, which involve the legal/non-legal dimension). Another relates to "substance" (that is the behavioural "deviation from the status quo which an agreement demands," thereby distinguishing between "deep" and shallow commitments) and yet another refers to implementing "structure" (monitoring vs. sanctioning).[37] These distinctions allow us to see the various trade-offs that are possible and that are only insufficiently captured by the one-dimensional hardness/softness criterion.

The fact remains that, despite the different dimensions of "softness," an increasing number of norms have become part and parcel of international practice, their doubtful pedigree or their lack of "sanctions" notwithstanding. States have resorted to such soft agreements for a variety of reasons: to shorten negotiation time, especially in complex multilateral contexts; to retain control of implementation; to mitigate the effects of domestic dissent at the ratification stage; to have more flexible instruments recognizing the differing conditions prevailing in different countries; to avail themselves of the know-how and collaboration of actors who have no international standing but to whom the norms are addressed; and to prevent or pre-empt regulation of a field, or to retain the flexibility for norm adjustments when circumstances change.

[35] Naomi Roht-Arriaza, "Soft Law in a Hybrid Organization: The International Organization for Standardization," in Dinah Shelton (ed.), *Commitment and Compliance* (Oxford University Press, 2000), 263–81, at 271.

[36] Christine Chinkin, "Normative Development in the International Legal System," in Dinah Shelton (ed.), *Commitment and Compliance* (Oxford University Press, 2000), 21–42.

[37] Kal Raustiala, "Form and Substance in International Agreements," *American Journal of International Law*, vol. 99 (2005), 581–614.

To that extent any elucidation of practice is far more complex than approaching the problem with clear-cut taxonomies *ex ante* and by stretching them afterwards, insisting thereby on traditional clear red lines for doctrinal reasons, even though the distinctions "mark a difference that makes little or no difference," as Dewey would have said. Again, this does not necessarily mean that the debates are simply navel-gazing exercises,[38] but rather that they confront us with complicated appraisals for which no "final answer" seems possible, at least not when we want to "solve" the problem by a taxonomic exercise without paying attention to the underlying issues. The difficulties we encounter rather point us to important problems, such as, for example, the *cui bono* question of who is empowered or disempowered by where the lines are drawn, or whether the "intent" of the parties or some more intersubjective consensus should govern our "line-drawing," whether we should place a higher value on "problem-solving" or (input) "legitimacy," and so on.[39]

Again, some "soft" norms are less controversial than others, depending on the type of softness they instantiate. "Unspecific" or hortatory principles, often invoked in the preambles of treaties, do not specify duties, but they do not thereby lose their legal character. They are part of a legal undertaking and one can resort to them when interpreting the "purpose" of a treaty in accordance with the Vienna Convention on Treaties. In the dismissal of "unspecific" norms we encounter again the "descriptivist" fallacy that wants to derive the normative pull of a norm from its "precision." Yet most of the reasons for "softness" concern *practical* problems, such as retaining flexibility while still wanting to benefit from stabilization. This is in a way the old "Goldilocks" problem and not a theoretical issue. As in the tale, the norm, like the mattress, has to be "just right," neither too soft nor too hard.

Finally, sometimes it is the subject matter – such as we frequently encounter in multilateral treaties of the environmental domain[40] – that does not lend itself to the classic treatment of responding with "sanctions" (another "essentialist" attempt of classification!) to the failure of others to live up to their promises. Little is to be gained by starting to pollute again in retaliation for other parties having exceeded their quotas! Here it does make sense – even if there is a clear

[38] For a seminal treatment of the empirical and conceptual difficulties involved, see the collection of essays combining case studies and analytical chapters, edited by Joost Pauwelyn, Ramses Wessel and Wouter Werner, *Informal International Law Making* (Oxford University Press, 2012).

[39] For a thoughtful treatment see Joost Pauwelyn, "Is It International Law or Not, and Does it Even Matter?" in Pauwelyn *et al.*, *Informal International Law Making*, 125–61.

[40] For a general discussion see Pierre Dupuy, "Soft Law and the International Law of the Environment," *Michigan Journal of International Law*, vol. 12 (1990/91), 420–35; O. Yoshida, "Soft Enforcement of Treaties: The Montreal Non-Compliance Procedure and the Functions of Internal International Institutions," *Colorado Journal of Environmental Law and Policy*, vol. 10 (1999), 95–141.

danger of a moral hazard – to offer "capacity-building" measures instead, and avoid the legal terminology of state responsibility and of "countermeasures."

Thus the binary opposition of law/non-law seems ill-suited for managing the growing complexity of contemporary international relations. Consequently, additional normative instruments are necessary for tackling the respective governance problems. What the discussion has also shown is that there are several sources of "softness," of which two are explainable in terms of Roman law's distinction between *instrumentum* and *negotium*. The third can be explained in terms of the changing discipline of law itself. Here I have in mind the changing role of law in dealing with policy issues instead of the restricted set of questions of classical "public" international law. This not only moves the focus of inquiry away from "sanctions" and the bilateral deals of states, it also creates a need for new (legal) expertise, but thereby also opens up law to colonization attempts by other disciplines.

As to the first two sources of softness, Jean d'Aspremont suggests that:

> A legal act contains what its author(s) have/has wished. This is classically called the *negotium*. This will is usually recorded in a document or an instrument which is classically called the *instrumentum*. The *instrumentum* is the "container." The authors of the legal act have full control of both the *negotium* and the *instrumentum*.[41]
>
> The *instrumentum* is soft when the parties decide to resort to an instrument other than a formal treaty … or a binding unilateral declaration … It is undisputed even by positivists that acts with a soft *instrumentum* still produce legal effects … and many scholars continue to qualify these acts as law, despite their soft *instrumentum*.[42]

Parties can, however, decide to soften the *content* while choosing a full-fledged formal contract. They may not specify precise obligations, or include opt-out clauses, or they can leave the implementation more or less to the parties themselves. After all, Article 2 of the Vienna Convention of the Law of Treaties[43] does not require a specification of duties as a constitutive requirement for a treaty. Similarly, in the *Oil Platform* case[44] the ICJ decided that the 1955 Treaty of Amity, Economic Relations and Consular Rights between Iran and the USA could not be construed as implying specific obligations (following therein the reasoning in the *Nicaragua* case concerning the nature of Article 3(d) of the Charter of the American States).[45]

[41] Of course subject to public order requirements and constitutive limitations (capacity to contract, authorization, titles etc.).

[42] Jean d'Aspremont, "Softness in International Law: A Self-Serving quest for New Legal Materials," *European Journal of International Law*, vol. 19 (2008), 1075–93, at 1081f.

[43] (1996) ICJ Reports, 803 at paras. 28 and 31.

[44] *Case Concerning the Oil Platforms (Iran* v. *USA)*, Merits [2003] ICJ Reports 161.

[45] See *Military and Paramilitary Activities in Nicaragua* (1986) ICJ Reports, 14 at paras. 259–61.

Similarly, so-called "framework conventions" always require complementary instruments (*pacta de contrahendo* or *de negotiando*) for defining their scope and for fleshing out the basic directives of the convention. Here environmental treaties and Article III of the 1968 Treaty on the Non-proliferation of Nuclear Weapons (referring to the safeguarding regime to be negotiated) come to mind.[46] Thus, while there might be a trend toward more flexible legal instruments, their "softness" should not be overstated. Even if treaties contain no specific obligations, or the latter are left vague, as when reference is made to measures "within the available resources," or "as far as possible," or "to the extent possible," they clearly direct the parties to act in good faith. Interestingly enough, these phrases are also not simple self-denying ordinances, since a third party could actually determine whether these criteria have been met, as problematic as such assessments appear. Courts generally have had no great difficulties in determining what "unreasonable searches and seizures" are, or what "good faith" or "deliberate speed" means, even when these determinations turned out to be controversial.

These two meanings of "soft" are quite different from the construal of norms on the basis of an alleged "emergence," or of certain "trends," even if these phenomena exist only in the eye of the beholder. Such perceptions usually result from policy preferences and doctrinal considerations for which some sprinkles of "empirical" proof, implying acceptance, is adduced. But there is a problem with "confirmatory evidence," even in the hard sciences, and in law there remains the hoary problem of the *opinio juris* character in customary law that cannot that easily be "foxed." As, for instance, the endless re-recitations of UN resolutions based on certain political agendas show, no "custom" is thereby established, since not frequency but a certain "quality" of the consensus must be met before such resolutions can be interpreted as an articulation of *opinio juris*. Similarly, the cross-referencing of citation cartels in books and scholarly journals has little to do with the emergence of a norm that mutates from soft into hard law, even if a whole industry has a stake in pretending otherwise.

This phenomenon alerts us to the increasing role of legal *scholarship* in law-making, for which there are two reasons. One is the increasing specialization of the field. Thus we encounter – to name just a few – tax law, corporation law, environmental law, refugee law, intellectual property law, all of which can take the prefix "international." Admittedly, both components, the "international" and the "law" part, seem sometimes negligible, since it is the issue area, or the "nature" of things, requiring "solutions" such as optimizing welfare, wealth, or even "freedom" (for example in Milton Friedman's sense), for which the allegedly best standards have been developed in other

[46] Treaty on the Nonproliferation of Nuclear Weapons of July 1, 1968, 729 UNTS 161, reprinted in Burns H. Weston, Richard Falk and Anthony d'Amato (eds.), *Basic Documents in International Law and World Order* (St Paul: West Publ. Co, 1980), 126–7 at 126.

disciplines. This challenge to formal law is not new, as it is the credo of functionalism that has thrown down the gauntlet to politics and law alike. Over the years this functionalist credo has gone through several reincarnations and mutations. Irrespective of whether such functional prescriptions are based on best design, on market efficiency, on managerial lore, on law and economics standards, or on modern systems theory, the fact remains that opening up the formal legal process makes law, at least potentially, an object for colonization.

Another root is the reformist bent animating much of legal scholarship. Many "reformist" scholars share the conviction that the state is not the answer but the problem. Confirmatory evidence for this proposition can always be found, of course, and traditional criteria count for little when the "emancipatory" impulse takes over. Enthusiasts are then able to preach to the choir and communicate with each other in an echo chamber, thereby establishing a "dominant opinion" (*herrschende Meinung*). Thus the pen shows itself to be not only mightier than the sword, it even outperforms the gavel! As in a badly mistaken characterization of "constructivism" – where everything is allegedly possible since everything is "constructed" – people have apparently only to sit around a table and confirm to each other that they are rich in order to be rich! All that seems necessary in order to "sing" this new reality into existence is the "progressive development" of law by following the logic of "the more, the better."[47]

The result is rather astounding, as can be seen in the human rights area where the catalogue of such presumably "indivisible and mutually reinforcing rights" is constantly expanding. Anything deemed desirable becomes a "right," without much concern for specifying the corresponding duty holders. No wonder that the newest human right is, according to a recent announcement by the UN, the "right to internet access."[48] But why stop there and reinforce our "species chauvinism"? Let's think big and argue with some environmentalists for an "emerging right to life by whales."[49]

As opposed to this type of "legalism" celebrated by scholars, activist "norm entrepreneurs" of course know that "norm cascades" do not happen by themselves, even though restatements of "truths" might be helpful.[50] As in the case when spectacular actions mobilize the public but fail to translate this potential

[47] See Steve Smith's "Singing Our World Into Existence," *International Studies Quarterly*, vol. 48 no. 3 (2004), 499–515.

[48] See the vote by the Human Rights Council of July 6, 2012.

[49] See e.g. Anthony D'Amato and S. K. Chopra, "Whales: Their Emerging Right to Life," *American Journal of International Law*, vol. 85 (1991), 21–62. D'Amato and Chopra make their "presentation" (*sic*! at 22 fn. 14), which is supposed to "bring the future into the present" by arguing for an emerging "humanist right in international law" (at 61).

[50] See Martha Finnemore and Kathryn Sikkink, "International Norm Dynamics and Political Change," *International Organization*, vol. 52, no. 4 (1998), 887–917).

into actual influence, the existing institutions must be worked on, and a more "professional" approach seems necessary. Unfortunately, there is also always the danger of a "sell out." Thus activists might be a bit savvier in their politics, but they also need to know that they are on the "right" side, helping the good cause. In the absence of God, nature, and the will of the people – which traditionally served as foundational myths – a nearly sacred notion of "humanity's law" now has to fill this gap.[51] Of course, what we end up with seems, despite good intentions, more like an *Ersatz* of what we hoped for, as real people and historical nations, or "peoples," which provide the institutions and levers for realizing political projects, have disappeared from the screen. The result is that largely ready-made solutions are now in search of problems, instead of concrete problems being analysed in order to find solutions.[52]

The disappearance of concrete "peoples" or "people" is no accident. If they appear at all in treatises, they do so no longer as autonomous, historically situated actors, but as clients, perpetrators, as avatars of universal values, or as holders of bundles of rights that are unrelated to concrete social or political contexts. Nowhere does this become more obvious than in the increasingly problematic interventions, justified on humanitarian grounds and carried out by "professional" helpers. These follow "best practices," ranging from book-keeping to peace-keeping, in the vain hope that the metaphysical principle of the continuity in nature also holds in the social world, and that what works "here" also has to work "there." The next two sections address this problem.

Experts and enthusiasts

At first blush experts and enthusiasts could not be more different. Not only do they occupy different places – consulting offices and international organizations, as opposed to social movements, which organize spectacular actions in order to raise consciousness and undermine the Gramscian hegemony of the "normal." Both groups also engage in different discourses, making communication across the divide difficult. Both are exponents of different conceptions of legitimacy, the first claiming their status on the basis of some special "knowledge" (often sanctioned by the authority of science), the other as a representative of something "even bigger," be it the environment, global civil society, humanity, or even "life" itself (forgoing all "species chauvinism"). It is cold

[51] Although this term is a neologism by Ruthi Teitel, it is characteristic for a good many non-positivist and postmodern scholars. It postulates a new source of legitimacy that, like Kelsen's *Grundnorm*, bestows legitimacy on "the law," uniting the notions of subjective human rights and an encompassing "community" of mankind. See Ruthi Teitel, *Humanity's Law* (Oxford University Press, 2011), particularly Chapters 2, 3 and 7.

[52] See Michael Cohen, James March and Johan Olsen "A Garbage Can Model of Organizational Choice," *Administrative Science Quarterly*, vol. 17, no. 1 (1972), 1–25.

comfort indeed that both are critical of, or even opposed to, "officials" who derive their legitimacy from the consent of particular historical peoples, serving them either as political representatives or as bureaucrats.

Understandably, there is usually not much love lost between experts and enthusiasts, even though they need each other not only as sparring partners, but also for purposes of affirming their respective identities. After all, enthusiasts who get involved locally may possess information or "local knowledge" that experts lack. They can also make life easier, if they can be dissuaded from performing stunts or protests that interfere with normal, "rational" policies. Enthusiasts might thus be enticed, if not to join forces, at least to become part of a process in which they can make their influence felt. Thus, the prospects for having a "voice" in some form, before decisions are made, may have some appeal and provide the incentives for a move toward "professionalism." It offers itself as a middle ground, but changes on both sides are, therefore, necessary. Experts have to forgo the notion that they know everything (or even that they know everything *better*); enthusiasts have to reduce "direct action" and engage in writing reports, create coherent and empirically or normatively supported position papers (rather than recite only their commitment to the "cause"), and both parties have to find new and civil ways of dealing with each other, in spite of mistrust and continuing deep-seated disagreements.

Such moves are helped when the "scientific" consensus among experts is being challenged internally by dissidents,[53] or when the more or less uncontested evidence proves that things are not working as they are supposed to. Then the "aura" of science and of expertise is lost, and new ways have to be found.[54] Not surprisingly, both elements were present when the World Bank and the IMF finally grappled with the issue that half of the World Bank projects were not meeting the internal requirements, and that "poverty" was not simply a result of market inefficiencies, as the "Washington consensus" had suggested.[55]

A similar dynamic occurs on the other side when enthusiasts begin to build organizations lobbying for certain policies. As activist professionals they have to forge issue-transcending coalitions, such as pushing for "sustainable" development, rather than nurturing only some pet project, such as saving pandas. The hope of getting invited to the table at different "rounds" of

[53] See Ha Joon Chung, *The Rebel Within: Joseph Stiglitz and the World Bank* (London: Anthem, 2001).

[54] See e.g. the lessons learned from the various crises beginning with the East Asian crisis in Joseph Stiglitz and Bruce Furman: "Economic Crises: Evidence and Insights from East Asia," in *Papers on Economic Activity 1998* (2) (Washington DC: Brookings Institution, 1998), 1–114.

[55] See the account of Antje Vetterlein, *The Politics of the Development Discourse* (Florence: Ph.D. dissertation of the European University Institute, 2006).

GATT and WTO meetings, of submitting an *amicus curiae* brief,[56] of becoming accredited to the UN's Economic and Social Council (ECOSOC), or of becoming a "participant" in UN conferences and global forums, provides further incentives. Finally, when movements become "parties," they have to develop a coherent program on all "public" issues, whereby, of course, some fights between "Fundis" and "Realos" (fundamentalists and realists) within the caucus are not excluded.[57]

When this happens, some changes quickly become noticeable. For example some international institutions begin to share their information more freely by placing position papers, agendas, and supporting evidence on websites. When things are good, some delegations of NGOs are even marched into the inner sanctum at decisive meetings, only to be escorted out when the real business starts. After all, being allowed to speak does not mean that one has to be heard, or that attention should be paid to one. These are rights that are structured in an ascending order and are contained in the status of citizenship, but they are, all cosmopolitan or governance rhetoric notwithstanding, not institutionalized at the global level, as Boyle and Chinkin[58] rightly point out.

The actual problem of international governance is thus not primarily a lack of transparency – even if we could be doing better on this score. It is also not primarily one of participation, in view of the number of people who are nowadays involved, even though they are frequently self-appointed or co-opted rather than having been "empowered" in any meaningful sense. It is perhaps not even one of ideological hegemony, although the hijacking of the policy agendas by neo-cons and neo-liberals is rather obvious. The problem is rather that in all these multilevel governance structures nobody seems to be in charge of or able to set clear priorities. Thus, a variety of processes coexist uneasily, but the left hand frequently does not know what the right hand is doing. The result is that the governance game often takes on Kafkaesque features. A slew of contradictory rules exist, which would lead to different outcomes even if the "issue area" that they "govern" is well defined, but nobody can fathom which norms are to be applied and how those deciding could be held accountable by the general public. As David Kennedy has remarked:

> What is needed is not openness or transparency, as that term is understood by even the most aggressive proposal to render intergovernmental institutions transparent … If there is a problem of participation or voice in international governance, it seems a far more profound one: an almost complete

[56] See WTO, *United States – Import Prohibition of Certain Shrimp Products*, ILM 38 (1999), 145ff; at 146 line 9. But it limits the access to its disputes settlement clearly to the members of the WTO agreement: *ibid.* at 146 line 101.

[57] The names are taken from the German Green Party, which has these two "wings."

[58] See their careful study on NGO participation in law-making in Alan Boyle and Christine Chinkin, *The Making of International Law* (Oxford University Press, 2007), Chapter 2.

> absence of politics in the sense of collective contestation among groups over the allocation of power, wealth, services or status. Legal structures for governance abound and an extremely wide array of people participate in global governance. But an overt and conscious global political process is altogether absent, replaced by conversations and struggles with limited policy vernacular.[59]

This sombre assessment is an important corrective to some high-flying expectations that the legitimization deficit of governance institutions is easy to fix by a boot-strapping exercise of enrolling, in an inconsequential way, some parts of civil society and by relying increasingly on "output" rather than "input legitimacy." This latter move sits well with professionals since they seldom feel comfortable with politics anyway. Operating at some place "above" the politics they know – the "bad" national politics of log-rolling, deceit, corruption, and pork barrel – and focusing on "policy" rather than representation, applying efficiency and "best practices" criteria rather than focusing on issues of positioning, all seem to provide a less ideological approach to problem-solving.

But again a moment's reflection shows that things are a bit more complicated than this picture painted in chiaroscuro suggests. First, fixing legitimacy deficits by relying on equally deficiently legitimized elements of "civil society" is hardly convincing, as two times zero still remains zero. Second, while outcome legitimacy certainly has its merits, one must realize that *ex post* legitimization has a distinct tint of the end justifying the means. Even if we look at successful policy initiatives that have gotten ensconced in a variety of legal documents, such as *sustainable development*, it is unclear whether the episteme on which this inclusion was founded has meanwhile created a normative consensus that is robust enough to sustain certain policies.

Let us take a closer look at this particular concept and its genealogy. The ideas shaping this notion emerged out of a criticism of Western development policy. Traditionally, economic theory had identified "development" simply with growth and had paid little attention to the impact of such policies on the biosphere. The criticism that emerged in the late 1970s and 1980s suggested that there actually might be "limits to growth." Given resource shortages and population dynamics and the concomitant severe negative externalities imposed on the environment, the very notion of "growth" through ever-increasing consumption was unsustainable.[60] In short, development strategies based on such presuppositions courted disaster, because of the costs involved.

59 David Kennedy, "The Politics of the Invisible College: International Governance and the Politics of Expertise," in Doris Fuchs and Friedrich Kratochwil (eds.), *Transformative Change and Global Order* (Münster: Lit; New Brunswick: Transaction Publishers, 2002), 83–133.

60 Donella Meadows *et al.*, *The Limits to Growth: A Report for the Club of Rome* (New York: Universe Books, 1972).

The counter paradigm of a "sustainable development" was then spelled out in the Brundtland Commission's report in 1987.[61]

The subsequent popularity of this concept in policy-making circles was, however, somewhat different from what one would expect. As Duffield has shown,[62] sustainable development evolved as an alternative to state-led development and was indebted to Ernst Schumacher's ideas of "small is beautiful,"[63] and of self-reliance in achieving economic well-being and social stability. But with the onslaught of neo-liberalism it was neither the ecological theme, nor that of communal stability (highly problematic in war-torn societies, such as Mozambique where it was tried out), but the indictment of state-led development that caught the attention of neo-liberal critics. As Julian Reid suggested,[64] the message for neo-liberals was quite clear: sustainable economic development could only happen when people gave up on state-led growth policies and relied on themselves and the virtues of free markets. The subtext was that the pursuit of wealth in a free market would also further ecological goals. Why have costly regulation, if pollution certificates traded on the market are more efficient!

The problem with such arguments is not that they cannot be true, given certain assumptions and factual circumstances. The problem is instead that the argument relies on unarticulated "background" conditions whose "externalities" often haunt us later with a vengeance. To mention just a few: the different kinds and duration of toxicity, incalculable risks for catastrophic "singular events," such as Chernobyl and Fukushima; perverse effects, and the blindness that social action takes place in a strategic environment where often self-fulfilling prophesies rather than objective "nature" is at work. This can lead to "virtuous cycles" but also to panics, as exemplified by the financial crisis.[65]

The problem is not that using models that are based on such assumptions might get it wrong, as that happens to all of us (and not so infrequently either). The key issue is rather that no "learning" can take place if crucial problems remain unaddressed, as they are outside the model. They just become (theoretically speaking) "invisible" through heroic "assumptions," and thus contrary evidence can easily be dismissed as a fluke. The resistance to learn from these "non-confirmatory" experiences is, therefore, no accident. Models and theories

[61] See World Commission on Environment and Development, *Our Common Future* (Oxford University Press, 1987).

[62] See Mark Duffield, *Development, Security and Unending War: Governing the World of Peoples* (Cambridge: Polity, 2008), Chapters 3 and 4.

[63] See Ernst Friedrich Schumacher, *Small is Beautiful: A Study of Economics as if People Mattered* (London: Blond and Briggs, 1973).

[64] Julian Reid, "The Neoliberal Biopolitics and the Specter of the Ecofascist State," Paper for the Conference on *The State and State Building: Theory and Practice in Retrospect*, Belgrade May 2011, at 14.

[65] See the fundamental discussion in Oliver Kessler, *Die internationale politische Oekonomie des Risikos* (Wiesbaden: VS Verlag, 2008).

then become immunized from criticism as their "bounds of sense" abort critical questions, a problem to which I shall return in the last Meditation.

Furthermore, there is a second theme in the modern version of sustainable development that remains in the background but that is responsible for skewing the program. It is the notion of "resilience." Taking its cue from evolutionary theory that only "resilient" species have a chance at survival, it repeats a social Darwinist argument of yesteryear, although now in a new, individualist garb. While social Darwinists at least recognized that "selection" takes place at the level of the species (although liberally substituting nations or states for "species"), the extreme methodological individualism of contemporary (neo)-liberal theory holds that the exposure to threats and the capacity to buffer external shocks is part and parcel of all living systems.

The upshot of this argument is that now *the individual* has to deal with those shocks. Put simply: he or she has to adapt instead of waiting for some collective solution adopted by the government. No wonder that "markets" now attain such prominence. After all, markets, "proven to be one of the most resilient institutions,"[66] have become the generators and selectors of diversity. As Julian Reid points out, it was this conceptual move of linking resiliency with sustainable development – interpreted in the narrowest terms of a neo-classical *homo economicus* theory – that created in the post-Johannesburg period (after the World Summit on Sustainable Development in 2002) "explicitly neo-liberal prescriptions for institutional reform."[67] The task was now one of "getting the incentives right":

> Resilience began to be conceived not simply as an inherent property of the biosphere, in need of protection ... but as a property within human populations which now needed promoting through the increase of their economic options. As remarkably, the biosphere itself began to be conceived not as an extra-economic domain, distinct and vulnerable to the economic practices of human populations, but as an economy of "services" which humanity receives ... The absence of prices and price signals in ecological services is a major threat to resilience UNEP argues because it means that "changes in their conditions have gone unnoticed."[68]

This has some interesting implications for the poor who, around the same time, had figured in some treatises on "security and development" as objects of concern. Since security without development seemed impossible, and since development without security is not viable, the search had been on for "mutually

[66] P. Pingali, L. Alinovi and J. Sutton, "Food Security in Complex Emergencies: Enhancing Food System Resilience," *Disasters*, vol. 29 (2005), 5–24, at 18, as quoted by Reid: "The Neoliberal Biopolitics."

[67] Reid, "The Neoliberal Biopolitics," at 13.

[68] *Ibid.* at 14, the quote comes from UNEP: *Exploring the Links: Human Well-Being, Poverty and Ecosystem Services* (Nairobi: UN Publications, 2004), at 13.

supportive" policies. But after the above-mentioned "turn," the world ecological disasters were suddenly no longer viewed as the deplorable results of industrialization and its externalities, for example of industrial farming relying on abundant energy, water, and pesticides, or of the accelerating desertification brought on by CO_2 emissions and global warming. Rather, they were the result of the ecological *ignorance of the poor* "who use the ecosystem system in non-sustainable ways by over-harvesting, over-use, misuse, or excessive conversion of eco-systems into human artificial systems."[69]

In an unwitting similarity to Swift's *Modest Proposal*, the author of the quoted UNEP report does not recommend directly the consumption of the poor by the rich, but suggests that the next best thing to making "sustainable management decisions" was to respect "natural resources and enable the achievement of a sustainable income stream."[70] Traditionally such prescriptions would have meant the assignment of exclusive property rights, or their reform, or even the adoption of redistributive policies. But here we are left with a recommendation to let the individuals themselves cope with the disasters looming on the horizon. We are even advised to use such disasters as "windows of opportunity" for developing our resilience, which will be tested by functioning markets.

Whatever one might think of such proposals, one point seems clear: the alleged "consensus" on sustainable development and the epistemic community, supposed to provide the shared interpretive background understandings, hardly exists. What remains is a ritual invocation of empty verbal shells that everybody can bandy about as s/he sees fit. To call this a non-ideological and pragmatic, problem-oriented community of practice is hardly sensible.

This leads me to the wider problem of whether the often advocated move from "law" to "policy" is as promising as it is often made out to be, particularly if we face complicated problems of praxis and do not move within the special confines of a scholarly discourse or the legal setting of courts.[71] Legal systems usually deal with such vexing problems through grants of authority to "agencies," subject perhaps to judicial review of their actions or policies. But this often has the effect that the same indeterminacy characterizing abstract principles now also applies to policy, particularly if the grant of authority is broadly conceived and "control" is limited to *ex post* litigation. Agencies have, therefore, to develop their own rules.

Yet the move from the formalism of law to "best practices," which an agency might adopt for carrying out its mission, turns out to be quite perplexing. True, best practices might be nearer to the ground and they also might be more flexible and enshrine some of the "lessons" learned. But they also have *to be applied*, and thus they are based on judgments whether or not the situation at hand is

[69] *Ibid.* at 20. [70] *Ibid.* at 5.

[71] See Mary Ellen O'Connell, "The New International Legal Process," *American Journal of International Law*, vol. 93, no. 2 (1999), 334–51.

sufficiently similar, so that what worked "there" applies also "here." This already creates great difficulties in the domestic arena when concrete "cases" have to be standardized. But there "authority," "administrative" styles" – or, in the private sector, a "corporate culture" or informal traditions – provide some help when working *with* and, as importantly, "*around*" the rules.

Such props are hard to come by in international policy-making and administration.[72] There the most diverse elements interact in complex ways so that the expert knowledge of any single person comes quickly to an end – unless one blindly trusts the "law of the hammer" where anything we encounter can be nailed down. "Doing things," or rather "getting them done," faces then several problems. First, some important features of the case at hand might not be in the "rule book," as such problems may never have emerged before (or were not noticed, at least not in this configuration). While this is still a familiar issue calling for innovation and creativity, a second problem interacts with the first one. Professionals are, of course, aware that there are multiple ways of "understanding" a problem, and that several criteria exist for identifying affected values, which, in turn, might differ significantly from culture to culture. Again, this might not be unique to international collaborative problems, since "national cultures" or styles are seldom homogeneous, but those problems are considerably heightened when we move to the supranational level.

Since one has to work in a team, the different traditions of "doing things" might clash and raise "political" problems. Frequently, the "consensus" for the mission is not robust enough to begin with, so as not raise legitimacy questions at every turn, and this encourages either denial or blind reliance on rules. The widening gap between reality and the mission's goals can later be papered over by reports and post-mortems that declare the mission a "success" with, of course, "some problems" that need to be addressed in the future. But such criticism is usually taken care of by adding a new lesson to the "recognized" best practices.

Third, despite such comforting tales of organizational learning, the "professionals" on the ground are keenly aware that they operate in an environment of great volatility, which has perverse side effects. Especially if the situation is complicated and involves contestable judgment calls, insuring oneself by doing things "by the book," rather than searching for an effective solution, is a "rational" strategy in the face of uncertainty. It is no wonder that the maxim of "better safe than sorry" becomes the default position. Thus, even though one might know that things on the ground do not fit the template, one had better stick to it, since inventing a new one would require, at a minimum, new information. This, in turn, might entail knowledge of the local language, not to speak of the difficulties of getting one's hands on data that might not be available, as

72 For an illuminating discussion see Cass Sunstein, *Legal Reasoning and Political Conflict* (Oxford University Press, 1996), particularly Chapters 5 and 6.

none has been collected. It would probably also necessitate fresh manoeuvrings concerning the authority within the team for setting priorities. All such tasks are, however, frequently beyond the capacities of the policy implementers on the ground, or even the policy-makers at, for example, UN headquarters.

Fourth, an equally problematic reason for the lack of success and the failure to learn is the usually unstated assumption that the professionals who come to intervene can remain objective outsiders who just administer "help," instead of becoming part of the problem. The continuance of this assumption is all the more surprising because we have ample evidence that such effects can obtain even *when no direct intervention* by outside personnel occurs. Examples abound: the importing of cheap food as "humanitarian aid" after disasters (or as part of an enduring program of "feeding the hungry") has nearly always had the effect of ruining local small farmers, or of making large sectors of the population dependent on charity from abroad. Nowadays we have the additional problem of tying the farmer to a supplier of seeds for which royalty payments can be due. The gift of Monsanto to Haiti after the last earthquake is just one of the more recent instances of this familiar pattern.

In the event that experts and helpers actually descend upon a society, the image that such an intervention resembles a "surgical" procedure, in which the cancer is being removed while leaving the body (politic) the same but better off, is entirely inappropriate. True, there might be some analogies that fit the medical metaphor, but the similarities are superficial at best. The use by the military of the term "surgical strikes" shows what is problematic in such an analogy. It suggests precision and minimal invasion that do not rend the social fabric, even though experience tells us that such strikes are hardly ever possible and are obfuscated by the euphemism of "collateral damage." Thus, bringing in a few thousand experts and helpers inevitably changes the ongoing political, economic, and social processes of the local society that is now handed over to the "helpers."

Consider some other repercussions. Right off the bat, the income differential between the locals and the "helpers" will disrupt the local economy, or what is left of it. For instance the per diem paid to United Nations Transitional Authority in Cambodia (UNTAC) officials in Cambodia was $145 – certainly not excessive by Western standards – but when it met the local economy where the average *annual* income was at that time about $160 a year, not much imagination is necessary for realizing what such an influx does to an already torn society. Inflation, corruption, prostitution, and nepotism became rampant, and many civil servants left their jobs in order to benefit from the "economic boom" of the "private sector." After all, UN drivers made more than government ministers![73]

[73] Nicolas Lemay-Hebert, "The Bifurcation of the Two Worlds: Assessing the Gap Between International and Locals in State Building Processes," *Third World Quarterly*, vol. 32, no. 10 (2011), 1823–41, at 1833.

Other impacts were equally severe. Cases of AIDS increased tenfold, and UNTAC became known among the "locals" as the "UN Transmission of Aids to Cambodians." Furthermore, having to deal with a motley crew of helpers from all over the world created distinct control and command problems. As Steve Heder and Judy Ledgerwood, who were working for UNTAC, had to admit: "UNTAC was seen more as an occupying army." One had to be subservient in order:

> to be on the safe side. As stories of outrageous acts by individual, ill-disciplined soldiers piled up, and were told and retold, UNTAC was also seen with horror as a horde of drinking, whoring, half-naked drivers who ran over people and could not care less.[74]

All of these experiences strongly suggest that the medical metaphor is inappropriate. It hides important differences between these two types of interventions. Putting oneself under the care of a doctor, whose expertise is beyond doubt, is rational for the individual, even though she might still not be in an enviable position. Plans for treating the disease might be controversial, risks have to be weighed, and the individual's physical and psychological capacities have to be assessed. But, most importantly, both the patient and the doctor share a rough idea what constitutes "health" and agree on the intervention.

The problem in humanitarian interventions is entirely different. In this case, the "cure" – and the need for it – is virtually exclusively determined by outsiders, since they are the ones "in the know." Allegedly, they will bring democracy, human rights, and the rule of law – and who could object to that? – despite the rather dismal experiences of similar former operations. Local wishes can be passed over, precisely because most social and political processes have broken down. But things are not getting better when "the locals" get organized. Then the jockeying for positions with the new overlords begins, making the helpers part of the new political process, hence undermining their "neutrality." Thus we get two poxes for the price of one: perceptions of unresponsiveness to local wishes, and compromised neutrality.

Hun Sen, the Premier of Cambodia, who spoke from experience, told the Timorese in September of 1999: "The UN will come with their white cars and their high salaries and they will run around busily for two or three years, then their mandate will expire, they will leave, and you will be left with almost nothing."[75] It is rather ironic that even the UN representative in East Timor understood that something was "clearly not right" when the UN Transitional

[74] Steve. Heder and Judy Ledgerwood, "Politics of Violence," in Steve Heder and Judy Ledgerwood (eds.), *Propaganda, Politics and Violence in Cambodia: Democratic Transition under UN Peacekeeping* (Armonk: M. E. Sharpe, 1996), 32.

[75] Lemay-Hebert, "The Bifurcation of the Two Worlds," which also provides a general discussion of these problems from a participant observer perspective (East Timor and Kosovo).

Administration in East Timor (UNTAET)'s budget was $692 million, while that of East Timor was $59 million. The difference in pay between locals, whose pay-roll amounted to about 1 per cent of the UNTAET budget, and international staff was 1:20–30, despite the fact that the locals were paid about double what those locals who were not employed by the UN earned!

Despite all good intentions and promises by UNTAET administrators of not repeating the errors of Cambodia in East Timor, the results there were not that different. Food rations came from Singapore and Australia, so that the local economy could hardly profit or be jump-started from this influx of capital. Not surprisingly the old market in Dili decayed and the Australian-owned supermarket "Hallo Mister," which imported "what was needed" by the UN personnel, became the symbol of foreign domination. It was promptly ransacked when violent protests by "locals" broke out in 2002.

The other symbol, increasingly spawning local resistance, was the "floating hotels" that housed the UN personnel. Actually they were not hotels but ships with up to four stacks of air-conditioned containers mounted on them. They solved the UNTAET's housing and later "entertainment" problems for its staff, when a disco opened on the top of the freighter *Olympia*. Although these boats were by no means luxury liners, for a population facing severe depravation, they seemed to be so. Similarly, for some Western observers the ships were the perfect indication of the "transitional" intent of UNTAET, but for the locals, who had access to them only as waiters and cleaning personnel, it drove home the message that they were "off limits." Things did not take a turn for the better when the administration decided to leave the unloved abode and move to the palace of the former Portuguese and Indonesian "administrators." UNTAET's chief de Mello even occupied the same office as the much-hated former Indonesian governor![76]

These problems did not escape the notice of the administrators in place and created much soul-searching in New York. One attempt was made to reduce personnel. Critical voices such as those of Chopra,[77] Harland,[78] and

[76] *Ibid.* at 1829f.; see also James Traub, "Inventing East Timor," *Foreign Affairs*, vol. 79 (summer 2000), 74–89.

[77] Chopra, himself part of the East Timor administration, resigned his job. See Jarat Chopra, "Building State Failure in East Timor," *Development and Change*, vol. 33 no. 5 (2002), 979–1000. See also Jarat Chopra and Tanja Hohe, "Participatory Intervention," *Global Governance*, vol. 10 (2004), 289–306; Jarat Chopra, "The UN's Kingdom in East Timor," *Survival*, vol. 42 (Fall 2000), 27–39.

[78] David Harland, head of the UN Best Practices Unit, who had worked for UNTAET, put his finger right on the sore spot by noting "all international administration, however benign, is to some extent illegitimate … fundamental political illegitimacy of an administration mandated from the outside poses some unique problems, with which the UN continues to wrestle." David Harland, "Legitimacy and Effectiveness in International Administration," *Global Governance*, vol. 10 no. 1 (2004), 15–20, at 15.

Ignatieff[79] openly faced what David Kennedy has called humanitarianism's "dark side."[80] Internal discussion at the UN and various post-mortems[81] led to the announcement of a "light footprint approach," a term coined during the preparations for the UN mission in Afghanistan (UNAMA) and associated with the work of the UN official Lakhdar Brahimi.[82] But as we, with the benefit of hindsight, can see, whatever lessons had been learned, the "footprint" had definitely not become lighter, neither there nor in Kosovo.

In the latter case we observe how the "white car" syndrome attained the same symbolic importance as the *Olympia* had in East Timor. The white Land Cruisers with "UN" painted in big block letters had been part of many missions. By 1996 they had become a status symbol for "foreign professionals" (as with black BMWs for drug lords, or Mercedes for state officials in Africa, the "Benzis" as they are called). In Kosovo the aura of colonialism began to stick to the "white cars" when they were used in a poster protesting the UN presence. As Nicolas Lemay-Hebert, on whose "participatory observations" I draw, states:

> The Vetevendosje! Movement (Albanian resistance) has specifically targeted UN vehicles for their contestation. For instance, the activists modified the traditional UN logo on the vehicles, adding and "F" and a "D" to UN, making it "FUND," loosely meaning "end" in Albanian. Always faithful to their theatrical practices, the movement distributed parking tickets to UN vehicles for "parking at the wrong spot – Kosovo" and deflating the tires of the vehicles for the purposes that "people can breathe freely only when this unjust regime dies. This is why we have released the air from the tires of their vehicles."[83]

In short, while local reactions in both cases might be the result of considerable misperceptions, they point to a real problem. After all, the hiring of the ships in Timor was a "rational" response to the urgency of finding housing for the staff in a city that had been devastated and did not have sufficient living space. Similarly, the use of four-wheel drive vehicles in the rugged terrains and harsh weather conditions during winter in the Balkan mountains is again not a capricious choice. The question remains, nevertheless, why virtually all missions end so unsatisfactorily. In an unusual case of candour the

79 See the critical remarks in Michael Ignatieff, "State Failure and Nation Building," in J. L. Holzgrefe and Robert Keohane (eds.), *Humanitarian Intervention: Ethical, Legal, and Political Dilemmas* (Cambridge University Press, 2003).

80 David Kennedy, *The Dark Side of Virtue: Reassessing International Humanitarianism* (Princeton University Press, 2004).

81 See e.g. Chiyuki Aoi, Cedrik de Coing and Ramesh Thakur (eds.), *Unintended Consequences of Peacekeeping Operations* (Tokyo: United Nation's University Press, 2007).

82 Lakhdar Brahimi, "State Building in Crisis and Post-conflict Situations," lecture at the 7th Global Forum of Reinventing Government, Vienna, June 26–29, 2007 at p. 3.

83 Lemay-Hebert, " The Bifurcation of the Two Worlds," at 1835.

Secretary-General himself asked on November 9, 2000 for a discontinuation of the International Civilian Support Mission in Haiti (MICAH),[84] which was supposed to consolidate the gains from various previous civilian and military operations. The reason for this decision was the mission's readily admitted lack of success. Nevertheless the UN was back in Haiti after the second ousting of Aristide. Although we can say that for some missions the jury is still out, it is an open secret that Afghanistan went badly and the Balkans have now become a permanent problem for the European Union.

Perhaps things are not that bad, as life goes on. This is certainly true, but it is equally true that in the end we are all dead. To make these truisms the criteria for assessment of what we should do is hardly sound advice. What is so surprising is that we seem to "learn" very little, despite our dedication to best practices and the slew of critical scholarly articles and books that inform us about the widening gap between plans and reality. Part of the answer is, of course, that we do have to deal here with virtually intractable problems. Dilemmas do exist in practical life, and no "technique" or expert can deny this. But there are, on the other hand, clearly *some* things that could be changed, if so desired.

Thus approaching the problem of "logistics" as one of getting "things" from here to there, without considering the impact on the local economy, is one such area. Here the "military" frame of mind concerned with the "efficient" movement of men and materiel still dominates our discussions. Nowadays that means: canned and frozen food, produced and packed according to ISO norms (after all, members of civil society have worked on the *Codex Alimentarius* and procured those "soft" norms!), so that you know what you are getting (you can even read the table of contents and look up the ingredients in your chemistry textbook on food safety). This makes any engagement with the local economy, with a foreign "cuisine," and with the question of "what to cook" superfluous. After all, the "market" indicates that frozen pizza and burgers *are* king anytime and anywhere (another victory for "universality"!).

As to the logistics of housing and supplies, different sequencing, more direct involvement of rebuilding the local infrastructures that could then provide housing for the officials, contracting with local producers for food, helping to set up cooperatives that could be used for "quality control," are all proposals that offer some alternatives if one is ready to give up the "hammer" and not view the entire world only as a nail.

But why should one do this? This leads me to my fifth point. After all, what we do is based on "science," be it chemistry, physics, economics, or management. And what is true "here" has to be true everywhere. We all seem to fear that all hell might break loose if we let go of this belief. This tendency is powerfully reinforced by another deeply held conviction that it is not only the area of

[84] See Laura Zanotti, *Governing Disorder* (University Park: Pennsylvania State University Press, 2011), 81ff.

technology and production, but also that *our way of life* that has shown itself superior. *Our* approach to organizing societies has been born out and tested by "history." Yet it is easy to forget the contingencies and historical struggles from which "our" institutions resulted and it seems heroic to assume that Western modalities of governing are easily transferable with predictable effects, because all people everywhere basically want "the same."

Thus, a cult of the "universality" of norms prevails (point six), as if the latter were ready for direct intuition and application by all those who are "reasonable" and "civilized." The attitude this cult produces is not only oblivious of the historicity of institutions, but prevents us from seeing their embeddedness in a wide variety of specific "local" practices and understandings. As Laura Zanotti, a thoughtful participant in one of the Haiti missions, writes:

> Ideas of individual liberties, human rights and justice as they are understood from the Enlightenment on are tightly linked with disciplinarity and codified modalities of … control and punishment. Human rights and discipline are twins. Liberal-democratic regimes operate in conjunction with the bodies of knowledge and power that operate in the disciplinarization and domestication of citizenship. These processes played a key role in establishing the power of the state as a main modality … of political life in Europe. However, institutions do not work in isolation from domestic and international politics and from the economy, and the effects of transplanting them are not universally predictable but case specific. In attempting to carry out state building through the blue-print traced by the Enlightenment reformers, the UN intervention in Haiti precipitated instead the disintegration of the capacity of local administrations to govern.[85]

When everything is said and done, we cannot shake a feeling of unease, as the gap between the outcomes and our expectations is glaring. Visions based on technical prowess and near omnipotence of the "designs" – *never actually "tested" in any Western society* – are suddenly taken to promise success when administered in a foreign country. Perhaps we *should* take the analogy to medicine more seriously, but not in the sense of being lured by the metaphor of the surgeon and her ability and detachment, but rather in the sense of putting the whole practice under the cautelary maxim of the Hippocratic oath: above all, do no harm.

Tales from the temples

When enthusiasts, experts, and professionals have failed, and the threat of the revival of conflict, or of despair, casts its ominous shadows, there is still one narrative that holds out hope. It is distinct from tragedy, which, according to Aristotle's *Poetics* turns in the third act into either a tragedy (as the

[85] *Ibid.* at 105.

"catastrophe" becomes inevitable), or into comedy (which arrives at a happy ending).[86] Rather, it relies for deliverance on the pronouncements and decisions of some heroes or protagonists who, through their travail, are able to save us (romance).

Calls for a more activist judiciary are then heard. Courts and judges are supposed to fill in the gaps of the fragmented international legal order. They are to serve the international community through bold pronouncements, thereby becoming the symbol for a more cosmopolitan order that is in the offing, but which most of us fail to see, because we do not read the tell-tale signs correctly. These exhortations have a certain attraction especially after crises that "prove" the outmoded nature of the existing order.

Thus, in the wake of September 11, the prominent French international lawyer Mireille Delmas-Marty called for a new ad hoc tribunal created by the UN Security Council in order to deal with those crimes against humanity. Under the title "Global Crime calls for Global Justice,"[87] she defended the view that only a new international tribunal was, for symbolic and practical reasons, capable of tackling this task. Such a court, armed with an international arrest warrant guaranteed by the Security Council, could bring those perpetrators to justice. After all, the attacks of September 11 no longer fitted the paradigm of a crime under national law; it was an assault on humanity itself. Consequently, only a tribunal located "above" the state could command the respect of an even-handed dispenser of justice and serve as a symbol for moving toward a global order envisaged by the "cosmopolitan model of Kant."[88]

One can seriously doubt that such a court could have gotten a hold of the perpetrators, since neither the binding Security Council resolutions concerning the apprehension of the terrorists of 9/11, nor the forceful intervention in the subsequent war on terror were able to do so. This failure led, then, to some "unilateral" measures of highly questionable political and legal standing. One can also be quite sceptical about the proposition that supranational enforcement action is what Kant had in mind.[89] What is surprising, though, is how here a host of unexamined half-truths are assembled and paraded as the solution to very difficult normative and practical problems. Take the question of legitimacy as an example. For good positivists and "cosmopolitans" alike (admittedly some rather odd bedfellows), legitimacy derives from an action of the Security Council. But if we are interested in the symbolic value of such an authorization, it seems that in a good number of countries it will be more like a kiss of death

[86] See Aristotle, *The Poetics*, transl. by Malcolm Heath (London: Penguin, 1997).

[87] Mireille Delmas-Marty, "Global Crimes Calls For Global Justice," *European Journal for Crime and Criminal Justice*, vol. 10, no. 4 (2002), 286–93.

[88] *Ibid.*

[89] See Immanuel Kant, "Perpetual Peace," in *Political Writings*, ed. by Hans Reiss (Cambridge University Press, 1970), 93–130.

(this is why the Security Council decisions were not implemented in the first place). Furthermore, there is the problem whether all of al-Qaeda's actions on September 11 really were crimes against "humanity," as were those systemic attacks on the civilian populations at Ground Zero. Arguably, the misfired mission against the White House or the one against the Pentagon might have been aimed at "legitimate" military targets.[90]

Furthermore, take the general proposition that through a proliferation of ad hoc tribunals – we are asked to install yet another court! – the rule of law is strengthened, an argument whose questionable validity emerged in the "fragmentation" debate. Some of those problems might have been mitigated by the creation of the International Criminal Court, but its less than distinguished record suggests that the expectations that law will from now on be speaking truth to power have been grossly exaggerated. Indeed, given the lack of all the prerequisites that a functioning legal process needs – as discussed above – such a record is not surprising. To that extent, all the appeals for filling the gaps and becoming the crucial voice for the global community have to be taken with a grain of salt.[91] Here the attempts to come to terms with the tragedy of the former Yugoslavia by legal means are again not encouraging.

Consider in this context both the *Tadič* case and the "resolution" of the "control" controversy by the ICJ in its decision in *Bosnia–Herzegovina* v. *Serbia*. The latter was sharply criticized by some academic commentators[92] for having stopped a "progressive" development of international law and instead returned to the more restrictive "control" standard of the ICJ's *Nicaragua* decision. Thus, while some might consider this progress,[93] others were not happy about the outcome on "substantive grounds,"[94] although the problem of inconsistency

[90] This presupposes of course that the laws of war apply here.

[91] Perhaps this is one of the reasons why recent research focuses again more on the role of domestic courts, especially constitutional courts, in their role as participants in international law-making. For a good review of the recent publications see Karen Alter, *The European Court's Political Power* (New York: Oxford University Press, 2009); George Vanberg, *The Politics of Constitutional Review in Germany* (Cambridge University Press, 2005); Gretchen Helmke, *Courts Under Constraints: Judges, Generals and Presidents in Argentina* (Cambridge University Press, 2005); Andrew Guzman, *How International Law Works* (New York: Oxford University Press, 2008); Jeffrey Stanton and Will Moore, "Judicial Power in Domestic and International Politics," *International Organization*, vol. 65 (Summer 2011), 553–67.

[92] See Antonio Cassese, "The Nicaragua and Tadic Tests Revisited in the Light of the ICJ Judgement on Genocide in Bosnia," *European Journal of International Law*, vol. 18, no. 4 (2007), 649–68. For a measured assessment, see Marko Milanovich, "State Responsibility for Genocide: A Follow-Up," *European Journal of International Law*, vol. 17, no. 4 (2007), 669–94.

[93] See *Case Concerning the Application on the Prevention and Punishment of the Crime of Genocide (Bosnia and Herzegovina, Serbia and Montenegro)*, February 26, 2007.

[94] See e.g. David Luban, "Timid Justice: The ICJ Should Have Been Harder on Serbia," *Slate Magazine*, February 28, 2007, available at www.slate.com/articles/news_and_politics/jurisprudence/2007/02/timid_justice.html (accessed October 14, 2013). See Martin

(after *Tadič*) in assessing command responsibility has been mitigated by a subsequent ICJ decision reaffirming the old standard.

Yet the "progressive" jurisprudence of the ICTY concerning command responsibility was also based on a doctrine of *mens rea* that seems contrary not only to civil law but has been also discredited in common law – after a brief episode of having enjoyed precedential value in England. However, there the British Parliament corrected the Law Lords rather swiftly.[95] International Tribunals are, however, not so constrained politically because "humanitarians" – in an ironic twist of the traditional sovereign's defence – apparently "can do no wrong." They can formulate their own standards and impose them on others, although they may run afoul of the "principles recognized by civilized nations."

In *Prosecutor* v. *Tadič* the Appeals Chamber had to determine whether the conflict in Bosnia–Herzegovina, resulting from the dissolution of the Yugoslav Federation, was an internal or an international war. In the latter case the defendant could be charged with the crimes, as listed in Article 2 of the ICTY statute (grave breaches of the Geneva Conventions). In the first round the Chamber of the Tribunal had classified the conflict as an internal one, thus exempting the Bosnian Serb Army fighting in Bosnia–Herzegovina from the charge that it was an agent of the Federal Republic of Yugoslavia (or what had been left of it). In coming to this conclusion the chamber used the "effective control" standard enunciated by the ICJ in its *Nicaragua* decision. Under this test "agency" could be established only if the state in question supervised and controlled the group by giving specific instructions.

The Appeals Chamber, however, reversed this finding by using a new test, namely the "overall control standard," which was satisfied if the foreign state somehow coordinated the planning of the warring group. In deviating from the existing standard the majority justified its "innovation" by a rather unsupported argument that the effective control standard was "contrary to state and judicial practice." As "proof" the Tribunal cited decisions of the US–Mexican Claims

Shaw, "The International Court of Justice: Serbia, Bosnia, and Genocide," Open Democracy, February 28, 2007, available at www.opendemocracy.net/node/4392/print (accessed September 25, 2013).

95 Traditionally criminal law in both common law and civil law required a special subjective intention (*dolus specialis, mens rea*) from the perpetrator of a crime. This subjective criterion for assessing the motive differs from the more "objective reasonable man" standard used in tort law, which makes an attribution on the basis of what an actor "must have known," given general experience. In 1961 the House of Lords tried to establish an objective version of *mens rea* by overriding the well-established precedent base on the subjective version (Director of Public Prosecutions v. Smith [1961] AC 290 (HL)). At issue was the killing of a police constable who had tried to ticket the defendant (Smith), who sped away with his car although the officer was still clinging to it. The officer was killed by oncoming traffic. Against precedent Smith was convicted at first instance for capital murder, which was changed on appeal to manslaughter (in line with precedents, but reversed again to capital murder by the Law Lords). The case caused an uproar in all common law countries, which all preferred the traditional subjective *mens rea* doctrine and Parliament reversed the Law Lords again through legislation in 1967. See Roozbeh B. Baker, "Customary International Law in the 21st Century: Old Challenges and New Debates," *European Journal of International Law*, vol. 21, no. 1 (2010): 173–204, at 193–96.

Tribunal, the Iran–US Claims Tribunal, and the European Court of Human Rights (ECtHR). Unfortunately, the US–Mexican Claims Tribunal decisions were made decades before, the US–Iran Claims Tribunal was an arbitration body, hardly having the same authority as the ICJ, and the fact pattern in the ECtHR cases seems to satisfy the criteria of the effective control standard.[96]

Things are no better if we examine the criticism concerning the ICJ decision in the *Bosnia–Herzegovina* v. *Serbia* case. Although the ICJ clearly stated that Serbia failed to prevent genocidal incidents (Srebrenica), and that it had not adequately cooperated with the ICTY, in the words of a former member of the ICTY, it missed an opportunity to extend "the rule of law into international politics."[97] Falling back on the "effective control test" instead of using the more flexible standard developed by his former court, Antonio Cassese criticized that "effective control delivers effective immunity for those groups and state-sponsors too clever (or incompetent) to keep scrupulous records. Instead, the less stringent standard of over-all control developed by this court is the way to prevent disaster in a time where terrorist networks like al-Qaeda threaten us all."[98]

Why this should be so is never spelled out, since al-Qaeda is not even a state and lives from its lack of an "over-all" control, so that this standard would be inapplicable precisely in the case that is adduced to justify it. Thus, a clear preference for a particular normative position is developed by a former member of the ICTY and is made plausible by some (faulty) backward reasoning, instead of analysing why in that particular case a high level of "control" might have made sense in the case before the court. Of course, relying on the more stringent higher test disturbed the simple story of "good" and "bad" guys, of "victims" and "perpetrators," but, unfortunately, in this story there was enough evil on both sides. The fact that the Court did not find a "smoking gun"[99] in the hands of the Belgrade government might have had something to do with the actual conflicts between the Serbian command and the Serbian part of the Bosnian Army. And it had something to do with the fact that the only massacre *held to be genocidal* occurred several years *after* the Court had been asked to declare the conflict a genocide perpetrated on the Bosnian Muslims. In the meantime the ICTY had convicted the Bosnian Serbs Tadič and Kristič (the latter for genocide proper in Srebrenica), but it had also convicted a Bosnian

[96] See Davis Tyner, "The Internationalization of War Crimes Prosecutions: Correcting the International Criminal Tribunal for Former Yugoslavia's Folly in Tadic," *Florida Journal of International Law*, vol. 18 (2006), 843–86, Opening statement at para. 2, as quoted in Nikolas Rajkovic, "On 'Bad Law' and 'Good Politics': The Politics of the ICJ Genocide Case and its Interpretation," *Leiden Journal of International Law*, vol. 21 (2008), 885–91 at 859, n. 91.

[97] Cassese, "The Nicaragua and Tadic Tests Revisited."

[98] Rajkovic, "Of 'Bad Law' and 'Good Politics,'" at 897.

[99] See William Schabas, "Whither Genocide: The International Court of Justice Finally Pronounces," *Journal of Genocide Research*, vol. 9, no. 2 (2007), 183–92, at 184.

Croat and three Bosnian Muslims for beating, sexual assault, and murder of Bosnian Serbs in the Celebiči camp.[100]

This is not to open up a counter-narrative of "who suffered more," so popular in Belgrade as it is also in other places. It only shows the complexity of the situation in which the Sarajevo government found itself, and of the "politics" of international law. Apparently convinced that a "maximum strategy" was likely to pin the opprobrium of genocide on the other side, Sarajevo had hoped to rally international support to its cause. As the situation had degenerated into a civil war, it also wanted to get out of the Dayton Accords and circumvent the weapons embargo, so as to counteract the advances of the Bosnian Serbs on the battlefield. Filing suit (March 10, 1993) was, of course, under such circumstances not only a legitimate but also a promising strategy. As Bosnia's representative, Barrister Phon van Biesen, suggested in his opening statement at the trial: "We will have to present to this Court a story of prolonged, ugly, extremely vicious, genocidal assault on people whose only mistake apparently was not to be born as a member of the Serbian nation."[101]

There is no need to speculate further what the consequences would result from the articulation of more "progressive" standards. After all, the UN peacekeepers were under the "control" of the UN and had been tasked to set up "safe havens" at Srebrenica, only to deliver the people there to the one massacre that does fulfil the criterion of genocide. Would they also have to be charged as accomplices to genocide? What about their predicament and the problem of how this would affect the willingness of others to shoulder peacekeeping responsibilities in the future? What about NATO or other "onlookers"? *Ruat coelum …?*

The possibilities for even further "progress" by prosecuting half the world might be enticing for some, but probably only for those with an activist bent, who are also suffering from a legalist myopia. The point is not that clever lawyers could not sort out some of these problems. It is rather that broad-based political support for such far-reaching changes is not likely to be forthcoming (aside from some parts of the bench, or from writers in law journals who, different from national decision-makers, do not even bear any responsibility for the consequences of their speculation!).

Yet irrespective of the worthiness of the goal and the purity with which we set out to reach it, there is a virtue in being reined in by such "formalities" as having to decide a "case" according to precedent and existing rules of law, rather than saving "humanity" *tout court* through heroic doctrinal pronouncements.

[100] See *Prosecutor* v. *Delalic*, Case No. IT-96–A (February 20, 2001); see also *Prosecutor* v. *Hadzihasanovic and Kubura*, Case No IT 01–47.

[101] See his opening statement at para. 2, as quoted in Rajkovic, "On 'Bad Law' and 'Good Politics,'" at 893.

Meditation 5

The power of metaphors and narratives: systems, teleology, evolution, and the issue of the "global community"

Introduction

The previous Meditation dealt with the problem of "soft" law and with the role of expertise. It also mentioned in passing a counter-trend in international law, namely the emergence of a new type of norms that "trump" all others, since no derogation is possible from *jus cogens*, and *erga omnes* obligations are owed to the international community as a whole.[1] In terms of the soft/hard continuum, *jus cogens* norms are definitely on the "hard" side since they can be limited or changed only by a norm of the same character. This somewhat sibylline and formal definition of *jus cogens* by the Vienna Convention on the Law of Treaties[2] has given rise to extensive discussions concerning which substantive norms would qualify for that status. In this context the general injunction against the use of force (with the exception of self-defence in cases of armed attack or under Security Council authorization), perhaps some of the requirements establishing an *ordre public* in international relations, or even a very "thick" notion of human rights have been mentioned.

Different from the functionalist logic of "soft" law, here the *proprium* of law is defended, not by experts or technocrats, but by scholars and judges, preferably those at various courts "above" the state. Functioning like a squadron of Herculi they are entrusted with bringing this new legal order into existence by pen and gavel. Similarly, "values" rather than technical necessity or function are supposed to serve as the *gluons* for the new cosmopolitan "community." Of course, if one does not want to be an outright prophet, one has to note the slow pace and the resistance to embracing this new utopia. Usually, however, such disconfirming evidence does not undermine the faith in the goal and in the conviction that we are all on the right bus, even if there are many fits and

[1] For a fundamental discussion of similarities and differences, the former arising out of the law of treaties establishing the peremptory character of certain norms, the latter protecting certain fundamental interests imposing duties on an actor that are owed to the international community as a whole, see Maurizio Ragazzi, *The Concept of International Obligations Erga Omnes* (Oxford: Clarendon, 1997).

[2] See Art. 53 of the Vienna Convention on Treaties, 8 ILM 679 (1969).

new starts and the journey is far from being a smooth joyride. This was at least the storyline from Oppenheim[3] to Kelsen,[4] Lauterpacht,[5] and Friedmann,[6] and, in more recent times and with a different accent on "community values," to Tomuschat[7] and Simma.[8]

There are, however, some well-founded doubts whether we are indeed on this metaphorical bus, given that history is open-ended and that it has no clear teleology. In former times one could still fall back on the natural order and determine, like Aristotle, the "end" or *telos* of each form of association, ranging from the family (reproduction), to the village (exchange), and to the polis enabling the "good life." Interestingly enough, Dante added, with the help of this logic, the universal "*imperium*" whose purpose was the pacification of the Earth *(orbis terrarum)*. Obviously both the Roman example and the subsequent *translatio imperii* to the Holy Roman Empire had become part of this elaboration. The task of creating peace among all people was for Dante embedded *in nature*. And since it was based on nature's design, it needed no further justification. The universality of the church was thereby replicated in the universality of a co-equal political order, which in accordance with the medieval "two swords" theory could be subordinated neither to the church – claiming that its "higher" values (the *spiritualia)* trump the lower ones (the *temporalia*) – nor to an agreement among the princes.[9]

The references to a cosmopolitan order in modernity usually have a Kantian ring, although Kant was quite wary of new encompassing orders and wanted to limit the cosmopolitan law – at least in one version – to a right of visit.[10] Yet of course there is also the notion that the *Rechtsstaat* had to be perfected through the renunciation of war and legal dispute resolution. Kant therefore appealed to the "cunning of nature" and its secret plan that pushed mankind through ever-costlier wars towards enlightenment. In a thicker version of contemporary cosmopolitanism, the "community" encompassing "humanity" has not

3 Lassa Oppenheim, *International Law*, vol. I, 4th edn. (London/New York: Longmans, Green and Co, 1928).

4 For an illuminating discussion of both authors *inter alia* see Martti Koskenniemi, *The Gentle Civilizer of Nations: The Rise and Fall of International Law* (Cambridge University Press, 2004).

5 Sir Hersch Lauterpacht, *International Law and Human Rights* (Hamden, CT: Archen 1968).

6 Wolfgang Friedmann, *The Changing Structure of International Law* (New York: Columbia University Press, 1964).

7 Christian Tomuschat, "International Law: Ensuring the Survival of Mankind at the Eve of the New Century," *Recueil des Cours*, vol. 281-IV (1999), 9–438.

8 Bruno Simma, "From Bilateralism to Community Interest in International Law," *Recueil des Cours*, vol. 250 (1994-VI), 217–389.

9 For a further discussion see Jens Bartelson, *Visions of World Community* (Cambridge University Press, 2009).

10 See the 3rd Definitive Article in his "Perpetual Peace," in Immanuel Kant, *Political Writings*, ed. by Hans Reis (Cambridge University Press, 1971), 93–130 at 105.

only common interests in maintaining the global public order – exemplified in the prohibition of the use of force – but it also rests on recognized substantive values enshrined in human rights.

The visions mentioned above emphasize different elements of social order and entail different political projects, which range from reformist to "revolutionary" ones. Sometimes the revolution is supposed to occur in our minds only and not in actual political struggle (as this might imply a resort to violence). Conflicts are not necessarily denied but they are considered resolvable through a commitment to law and through a reflection upon man[11] and/or the common needs of mankind as a whole.[12] It is here that "law" is treated like a "revelation" that is exalted above all mundane doubts. Law is not only a mode of arguing with norms that always points beyond law, but it also contains, supposedly, "the answers" that will become obvious if we allow ourselves to be guided by "law's spirit" or "integrity" rather than by its mere letters. In this way, it seems, we can enter the "kingdom of ends" and escape the *agora* of politics.

While such hopes might be unfounded, investigating the role of law within these different accounts is heuristically fruitful because it highlights the role law plays in our attempts to draw and redraw the bounds of sense in the light of our historical experiences. This dimension usually remains out of sight when we focus on law's role in dispute resolution or in managerial problems. In order to investigate this problem more closely, I follow up here on some of the remarks that I made in the previous Meditation about the influence of literary *genres* within which certain activities – in that case it was judicial activities – are recorded.

For this purpose, I examine the great Enlightenment narrative whence much of the scholarly production at the intersection of international law and international politics derives its plausibility. In this context I examine alternative accounts that might sound more "technical" or functionalist, such as modern system theory, or more legalist, such as the account of the "emergence" of obligations *erga omnes* or of *jus cogens*. Nevertheless, their normative pull derives largely from the same source. In this context the notion of universality and its opposition to the merely "particular" becomes important, as demonstrated for example in the argument of obligations *erga omnes*, owed to "the international community as a whole." I claim that all these arguments are justified by the narrative of progress that informed the Enlightenment project, even though the mediation between universality and particularity can vary markedly in different projects.

[11] Here Philip Allott in his *Eunomia*, imitating Wittgenstein's *Philosophical Investigations*, is perhaps the most pronounced. See Philip Allott, *Eunomia: New Order for a New World* (New York: Oxford University Press, 1990). See also his *The Health of Nations* (Cambridge University Press, 2002).

[12] See e.g. René Dupuy, *L'humanitee dans l'imaginaire des nations* (Paris: Julliard, 1991).

I shall treat the Enlightenment narrative in greater detail in the next section by showing that it is the New Testamentarian narrative of redemption in a secular garb. The third section is devoted to the discussion of "systems" owing much of their power to architectural and biological roots (functionalism), whereby the notion of "design" seems to provide a bridge between a static view of natural "elements," and the dynamic notion of an "evolution." In the fourth section I investigate the contribution of Luhmann and his school to legal analysis in times of globalization where the traditional analytical distinction between domestic and international, and between the private and the public have lost their discriminatory power. In the final section I place the problem of emerging norms such as *ius cogens* within the wider narrative of progress.

Tales of breaks, purposes, and history: probing the narrative of the Enlightenment

A typical feature of teleological accounts is that they all not only negate the reality of deep-seated value conflicts – which Weber likened to a war[13] among mythical giants – but also that they embrace a strange longing for "community" in which individual interests are simply subordinated to those of the community. Oddly enough this trope actually represents a move towards a form of association that in the story of "progress" was supposed to be overcome by the emergence of a "society." The latter was integrated through exchanges and a different pattern of solidarity, rather than through a (potentially oppressive) community based on common values.

The organizing principle for this narrative is often further elaborated by the notion of sharp breaks that separate the "before" and the "after," thus implying a transformative change, as in the New Testamentarian break of the Final Judgement, which brings the historical time to an end. In the discourse of modernity the Westphalian myth plays a similar role,[14] as does the "before" and "after" of the League of Nations, analysed by David Kennedy.[15] Another, less pointed way of conceiving of this process is that of steadily advancing development that leads either semi-automatically, or even by necessity, to the "end of history." There are also other elements at work in these narratives that lend

[13] See Max Weber, "Politik als Beruf," in Max Weber, *Gesammelte Politische Schriften*, ed. by Johannes Winckelmann, 5th edn. (Tübingen: Mohr, 1988), 505–60.

[14] See Leo Gross, "The Peace of Westphalia 1648–1948," *American Journal of International Law*, vol. 42, no. 1 (1948), 20–41. See also the criticism of this position in Andreas Ossiander, "Sovereignty, International Relations, and the Westphalian Myth," *International Organization*, vol. 55, no. 2 (2001), 251–87; see also Benno Teschke, "Theorizing the Westphalian System of States: International Relations from Absolutism to Capitalism," *European Journal of International Relations*, vol. 8, no. 2 (2002), 5–48.

[15] David Kennedy, "The Move to Institutions," *Cardozo Law Review*, vol. 8, no. 5 (1987), 841–988.

additional persuasiveness to the teleological irreversibility, sounding some apocalyptical themes, such as the "quickening" with which disasters befall mankind before deliverance can occur, or the sequence of "empires" (Third Rome, the End of History) on which I do not want to elaborate further here. I think that a good prima facie case can be made that we are here encountering a secularized version of the eschatological "end of times" argument of the New Testament.[16]

But even if such an interpretation is considered too speculative, there is little reason to object to the observation that the modern conception of a "universal history" provides an encompassing frame by assigning a place to all particular *histories*, be they those of cities, wars, empires, families, and great men (biographies) or deeds (*res gestae*), all of which have been traditional genres of historiography. The invention of a "universal history" in the eighteenth century, that is a "History" in the collective singular[17] (as "Geschichte," "Histoire," "History") provided not only the last horizon for endowing actions and events with meaning, it also had as its subject "humanity" in its march through time. Ironically, this eighteenth-century invention of a "universal history" also led to the great works of particular *national histories*, ranging from Hume's and Carlyle's histories of England, to Michelet's and Ranke's works on French and German history, a development which at first seems somewhat strange.

One can draw several lessons from this observation. First, narrative frames are potent conveyors of meaning that go far beyond those of "systemic" considerations. They also confer conceptual "trumps." For instance, calling an action or a judicial decision "progressive" immediately puts someone opposing this choice on the defensive. Given the principle of the excluded middle, the opponent, by logical necessity, has then to be a "reactionary" or, at best, one of those "old moss heads" who does not understand modern life. The second lesson is that framing the account of our social life in this way allows us to skirt the difficulties we face in the practical task of organizing groups and societies for collective action. Violent conflicts are thus no longer part of the human predicament but result from irrational resistance to enlightenment. These defects, then, must be cured through "education" – literally by "pulling someone out"[18] of his state of ignorance, à la Kant[19] – and by opening up a vista of "nature's secret design" so that freedom and necessity can be reconciled.[20]

The attractiveness of this story is, however, undermined by the realization that conflicts are inevitable (and not just a result of ignorance or lack

[16] See Karl Loewith, *Weltgeschichte und Heilsgeschehen* (Stuttgart: Kohlhammer, 1990).

[17] For a searching discussion of these new framings see Reinhart Koselleck, *Futures Past: On the Semantic of Historical Time* (Cambridge, MA: MIT Press, 1985).

[18] After all, "educare" is the "intensivum" of "educere," i.e. "leading out" (in that case: pulling) someone out of ignorance.

[19] Immanuel Kant, *Political Writings*.

[20] See Kant, "Perpetual Peace," at 108.

of information), although their trajectory might be subject to intervention. Furthermore, conflicts are not necessarily the result of the "*natura corrupta*" à la St Augustin and some early realists (Niebuhr). Even perfect altruists would face some of the same (prisoners') dilemmas in situations in which individual and collective rationality diverges. Since the issue is also one of logic and not only of intention, altruists too would face the collective action problem of defining a common (and "binding") ordering meshing their individual plans into a common strategy.

These short reflections seem to indicate that something more is required for praxis than knowledge, information, or even good intentions and insight. Whatever the ultimate boundaries of "sense" might be, they do not automatically provide us with viable strategies for getting from "here" to "there," unless we forget the "will" problematic in action, and human freedom. This freedom defines us – in our parlance – as "agents" with certain rights and responsibilities, but not as beings with unlimited capacities so that we can become universal respondents when made aware of the ills of the world. Thus it is just not true, as Allott suggests, that we have no idea of a common humanity, or that we suppress it.[21] In both a religious (children of God) and secularized version (humanity) we do have such a "universal" conception. But this universality does little in telling us what to do in particular circumstances. This is probably also the reason why the religious or secular panorama of "humanity" becomes quickly overtaken by "national" histories. The tales of the historically contingent and limited attempts of organizing social life resonate precisely because they give depth and concreteness to the efforts of constituting individuals, citizens, and even "cosmopolitans." Visions on of an all-encompassing order, be it the cosmos, or "only" the globe, on the other hand, often resemble the fantasies

[21] See e.g. Allott's remarks concerning the "others" that are not part of "us": "They share with us the species characteristics of human beings. They think and want and hope and suffer and despair and laugh and weep as human beings … And yet somehow we stop ourselves from feeling responsibility for them. They are aliens. As human beings, we know that we are morally responsible for all what we do, and do not do to and for other human beings, a responsibility which we cannot think away, a responsibility which we owe to a billion human beings as we owe to one human being. Every alien is also our neighbour. And yet as citizens, we have somehow been led to believe that we are not socially responsible for them." Allott, *The Health of Nations*, at 405. First, one is perhaps surprised by this picture of breadth, but then again why stop at humans when feeling pain and pleasure is the criterion for the ascription of responsibility. If you want to think big, then think big. So, enough of species chauvinism! The second observation is that we invented law precisely for the reason that saddling everybody with duties towards everybody else is an impossible task, as Aristotle had already pointed out. If one rejects this thought for the love of humanity, then one obviously has left the ground on which law rests. The new teaching then has to be some new form of religion, since even in the Christian teachings the Commandment "love your neighbour" is predicated on self-love (Kant would, in a more sourpuss version of this Commandment, talk about "duties towards oneself") that forms the basis of "love" and of extending oneself to others.

of omnipotence, which Freud describes as a compensatory mechanism for powerlessness.

This realization of course does not entail that "nations" are real and that "humanity" is not, since both are constructions. But it does mean in making them real, problems of power and force cannot be ignored by relying on moral appeals or the pious hope that "in the future" law will be able to substitute for politics, and that conflicts will be abated, as the lion shall sit next to the lamb and we will forge swords into ploughshares.

It was precisely this potential of universalist speculations to engender millenarian politics or crusades – be they cloaked in the garb of a mandate from heaven, sold as the "end of history," or of serving "human dignity" – from which the notion of a "society" was supposed to deliver us. Kant fathomed the danger of projects wanting to organize humanity, which instead could end up in a (universal) despotic regime. It made him wary of plans of a world government or even of federal arrangements (instead of just a "league" of republics), and it made Hegel suspicious of claims of universal morality supplanting *Sittlichkeit*. One need not be an adherent of Carl Schmitt either to suspect that those who, in his words, "invoke humanity, cheat" – even though his argument might not be free of a performative contradiction itself. Nevertheless, as R. B. J. Walker points out:

> It is in this context that we can understand what is at stake in the way the primary contradictions of modern political life appear to be set out spatially on the territorial ground of the sovereign state: here inside and there the system of … states … and yet we are constantly invited to solve the problem … through an appeal to temporality, through the processes of an emancipatory history, through a narrative that runs from here to there in time rather than in space. The temptation to drive the great bus of linear history … is especially strong in this context, given the force of claims about the emancipatory possibilities of a universalizing history that emerged in the 18th and 19th century … It works especially well as a claim about the potentialities of temporal processes that might be enabled within the state, perhaps within every state. Yet it does not and cannot work in relation to a form of political life that is already organized as a relationship between particularity and universality … Consequently, while the bus of linear history may offer a cheap ride it can only travel around in a short circuit: the endless ride from political realism to political idealism and back again … to the camp of those who assume that this is sufficient in order to engage in what we call "political theory."[22]

Again, one need not share Walker's pessimism, as indicated by his emphasis on the modal word "cannot." He highlights, nevertheless, the complex interdependencies within the semantic fields that resist the pretensions that nothing

[22] See R. B. J. Walker, *After the Globe, Before the World* (London: Routledge, 2010).

more is required than shaking the kaleidoscope of world politics in order to get from one configuration to the other. Walker also puts his finger on another sore spot: most of the arguments developed in this area are largely doctrinal and show only a vague relationship to actual practice. Thus in law notions of *jus cogens*, for example, invites fierce conceptual battles, while its impact on practice remains somewhat vexing, as the new conceptualization fails to provide an adequate solution for concrete problems.[23] It will be the task of this Meditation in sections three and four to shed a bit more light on this problem. But before I can address these questions, I should return to the problem of the power of narratives and to the tension in which they stand to spatial conceptions, such as "systems" containing the processes of change.

Systems

Traditionally, systems have operated with the part/whole distinction and they have postulated the super- and subordination of the parts in the design of the whole. This not only gave functionalism and equilibrium analysis their heuristic bite, it also conceived of the problem of order as a largely static "arrangement" of endogenous parts. Changes within systems could thus be analysed, but system-transforming processes remained out of sight. They had to be conceived as exogenous, as "shocks" that led either to the system's disintegration or to a new equilibrium.

From this brief discussion it becomes clear that this type of systems theory was either indebted to some teleological thinking, in that each part had its particular function or "end" – well captured by the organic metaphors of the "body politic" – or to some underlying design or structure arranging the parts. In this way the gravitational force among different bodies in classical Newtonian "celestial" mechanics could dispense with teleology and also serve as a template for some realist explanations of the state system.[24] Interestingly enough, while the organic metaphor had been used for the conceptualization of the "body politic," it oriented itself on the "closed system" paradigm, while in fact all biological systems are actually "open systems." They depend for their survival on exchanges with the environment, as the phenomena of photosynthesis and food intake illustrate. Thus a lot of different things seemed to be covered by the term "system" that need further unpacking.

[23] See e.g. the original "hopeful" version of the argument in M. Cherif Bassiouni, "International Crimes, Jus Cogens and Obligations Erga Omnes," *Law and Contemporary Problems*, vol. 63 (1996), 63–74. In contrast, see the more pessimistic assessment in some more recent contributions: Ulf Linderfalk, "The Effects of Jus Cogens Norms: Whoever Opened Pandora's Box, Did You Ever Think about the Consequences?" *European Journal of International Law*, vol. 18, no. 5 (2008), 853–71; Michael Glennon, "L'absurdité du droit impérative (*jus cogens*), *Revue General de Droit International Publique*, vol. 110 (2006), 529–36.

[24] See Danilo Zolo, *Cosmopolis* (Oxford: Polity Press, 1997).

In the social sciences, organization theory profited considerably from the shift in focus from the internal dynamics of the system's parts to the boundary-spanning exchanges that link systems to their environment. A further stage in systems thinking was reached when the boundary was no longer seen as fixed but was being produced and reproduced through the system(s) themselves in the process of autopoiesis. This means that the "environment" lost its residual character, and now consists largely of other systems. It is not the exchange but the "logic" of reproduction that thereby becomes the focus of attention, because all systems exist only through the process of selecting inputs from the environment and of using their "code" for the reproduction of their own elements. Systems are no longer composed of ontological givens but of *reproductive processes*. They are thus "open" but maintain themselves through operational closure, namely by transforming external stimuli or "irritations" into system-compatible elements. For example, a computer has to "digitalize" all inputs, irrespective whether they are music, mathematics, pictures, or statistical graphs. In this way, the "code" steers the selection as well as the "autopoietic" reproduction process, and different systems can be distinguished by their generative codes.

This abstract conceptualization has important implications for law under conditions of globalization, as I shall argue below. For the moment, though, I want to call attention only to the most important one: although steering takes place, it is no longer entrusted to the political or cultural "subsystems," which traditionally were supposed to fulfil this function, relying either on command (law) or value integration (culture).[25] Both systems cannot do this for the simple reason that, in the first instance, states can no longer "cage" their people or their transactions, and in the second instance because cultural systems are marred by inherent value conflicts rather than by a clear and accepted value hierarchy.

In this context legal pluralists have pointed out that a "variety" of normative systems always coexists in any given society, a situation similar to that in the international system where much of regulation takes place beyond the state and out of the sight of the "public." This leads to persistent mutual irritations of the systems, and thus provisions must be made for unblocking these interferences so that the systems can go on with their autopoiesis. This resolution of irritations – achieved through "structural coupling" – no longer necessarily orients itself on "precedents" or legislation, but seeks help from all sources in order to "go on." It is less the stabilization of expectations based on past decisions and more the use of principles, which – because of their "flexibility" – allow for even drastic changes, that now dominates the "field." Whether this "ordering" is well understood in analogy to the "running code" of the Internet, which needs only some "rough consensus" on best practices to fulfil this ordering function, as

[25] See e.g. Talcott Parsons, *The Social System* (London: Routledge and Kegan Paul, 1951).

suggested by a recent challenging book written from the private law perspective, remains of course controversial.[26]

In any case, given these new complexities it is clear that the term "functional" has also radically changed its meaning. It is no longer linked to notions of fixed functions derived from "ends," or an overall design, but it is part of the evolutionary process in which the systems are embedded. Thus, this perspective need not invoke either progress or adaptation, as the environment is not fixed but also consists of co-evolving systems. As in biology, the evolutionary process involves random changes and selection procedures but not any particular teleology, some social Darwinist misinterpretations (revived in the ideology of free markets) notwithstanding.

In a way, modern Luhmannian systems theory seems to be able to have its cake and eat it too by providing an account of proliferating "functional" systems and by placing these developments in a grand narrative of an unfolding "world society." The latter is now the last horizon within which the change from tribal segmentation to modern, functionally differentiated systems can be analysed. Within this frame the remaining "segmentary order" of territorial states, with their exclusive association of "citizens," seems like a dinosaur. It will be the task of the next section to probe these problems more deeply.

Evolution, functionally autonomous systems, the problem of a global Bukowina and of non-territorial empires

Luhmann's "mega-theory" evolved over the years by borrowing from such different sources as cybernetics, general systems theory, biology, symbolic interactionism, thermodynamics, and artificial intelligence. While it indubitably represents an intellectual achievement, it still has to prove that it forms a coherent whole, and that it can generate new insights, instead of simply recasting what is known from other sources in a new language. This is all the more important since Luhmann himself admits his "first surprise" that several key concepts incorporated into his "theory," such as "operational closure" developed by Heinz von Förster in his General Systems Theory, or the notion of "autopoietic" systems developed by Humberto Maturana and Francisco Varela in biology, were considered – by their respective authors – to be misapplied or inapplicable to social systems. Several further conceptual moves, based on this first alleged misstep, then become particularly problematic. For instance, one questionable aspect is the idea that legal communication can be reduced to the functioning of a binary code, or the suggestion that the emergence of world society can be explained in terms of the evolutionary developments from segmented to functional forms of organizations.

26 Gralf-Peter Callies and Peer Zumbansen, *Rough Consensus and Running Code* (Oxford: Hart, 2010).

Let us begin with the legal code. Luhmann insists that law has as its basic elements "programs" or norms that specify the consequences of an act in an "if – then" fashion,[27] while the "self-generating connection of legal elements"[28] is provided by the code legal/illegal. Yet some important cases fit badly into this allegedly exhaustive pattern. If I follow institutional rules by doing certain things, legal consequences follow. An example is the will I made in the form prescribed by the Wills Act. But the performative failure of not satisfying the requirement for two witnesses results not simply in an "illegal" act. Rather my actions "misfire," as Austin would have it,[29] by not leading to the desired end. They are "invalid" rather than "illegal," but such a distinction is outside of the postulated "exhaustive" dichotomy. Similarly, even if one moves outside the ambit of practices constituted by institutional rules, certain acts (while neither "illegal" nor "invalid") might affect a legal state of affairs. Thus, an inattentive husband might end a marriage without doing something illegal, or by being able to claim that the marriage had never existed.

These remarks highlight another strange element in Luhmann's theory of law, namely his conceptualization of legislation and judicial decision-making. They have to be redescribed as the system's "operational closure." According to Luhmann, not only is the code legal/illegal exhaustive of the law, but the "legal facts" also have "to facilitate as far as possible *the deductive use of legal norms*."[30] One need not be a Peircean (or an American legal realist for that matter) to doubt that "judging" entails a simple process of subsumption – since different norms make different facts "relevant" – or that the reasoning process leading to a defensible decision resembles that of an inductive inference.[31] Rather, different facts and norms are considered in their effects on one another, alternative interpretations of the facts are adduced, and other logically possible inferences are rebutted by counterexamples and interpretive legal doctrines, so that we end up with a justifiable decision. All this is a far cry from simply subsuming facts under a norm.[32]

Thus, legal outcomes are the result of operations that are quite different from logical inferences or self-referential loops of "re-entries" into the system. It is

27 Niklas Luhmann, *Oekololgische Kommunikation* (Opladen: Westdeutscher Verlag, 1986), 24, 126.

28 Niklas Luhmann, "The Unity of the Legal System," in Guenther Teubner (ed.), *Autopoietic Law* (Berlin: de Gruyter, 1988), 20.

29 See John Austin, *How to Do Things with Words* (Cambridge, MA: Harvard University Press, 1962).

30 Niklas Luhmann, "Operational Closure and Structural Coupling: the Differentiation of the Legal System," *Cardozo Law Review*, vol. 13 (1992), 1419–41, at 1430, emphasis added.

31 For a further discussion, see my *Rules, Norms and Decisions* (Cambridge University Press, 1989), particularly Chapter 6.

32 For some further thoughts along this line, see Scott Brewer, "Exemplary Reasoning: Semantics, Pragmatics, and the Rational Force of Legal Argument by Analogy," *Harvard Law Review*, vol. 109 (1996), 925–1028.

precisely because our interests differ, because our knowledge is limited, because values are conflicting, and because decisions and policies – whether of courts or legislatures – have unexpected or even perverse effects, that the ability to make clear-cut decisions by taking the simple binary code as the loadstar seems far-fetched. Nowhere does this become more obvious than in some of the most "functional" areas of law, such as in the environmental area, where "balancing" or the acceptance (or rejection) of economic standards are adduced, or, as in the case of the drafts of the International Law Commission on aquifers,[33] the law simply admonishes the parties to negotiate in good faith.

This leads me to a further question: whether the social changes we do observe – from the Westphalian settlement to the globalization of today – can be covered by the master narrative of a progressive "functional" differentiation. Here two issues arise. One is perhaps more a matter of terminology, resulting in a mistaken analogy. It concerns the imagery of a global Bukowina popularized by Teubner and misapplied to the global arena by him and Fischer-Lescano.[34] Both authors see a "global Bukowina" in regard to functional regimes in the offing and consider futile any attempt to harmonize the existing norm or regime collisions.

Let us begin with the imagery of a global Bukowina, namely the part of the territory of the old Austro-Hungarian Empire where a variety of ethnic groups coexisted in the same territory. It is hard to see why such an arrangement, which united fully segmented communities under the nominal rule of a distant sovereign, exhibits "functional" differentiation. Is this analogy then apt for highlighting the distinctive features of modern modes of governance? Is the process of functional differentiation, such as the disembedding of the financial sector from the "real economy," actually analogous to the coexistence of several segmented societies sharing the same space? I do not think so, and Teubner's more recent work on networks and "connected contracts" also seems to suggest that this might have been an unfortunate analogy.[35] After all, the Bukowina arrangement did not prove to be resilient and the wave to the future. It came apart when increasing politicization and greater Durkheimian "density" overloaded the careful management of the few "touching points" of the segmentary societies and "ethnic" strife resulted. A similar development can be observed in the decay of the millet system in the Ottoman Empire.

In short, instead of relying on a highly problematic analogy, a more fine-grained analysis is necessary to explain how actual changes came about. Instead of resorting to vague notions of functionality, or "evolution," we have to allow

[33] See Draft Articles on the Law of Trans-boundary Aquifers, 63rd Session of the GA (2008), Suppl. 10 (AS63/10), Art. 5(2).

[34] See Andreas Fischer-Lescano and Gunther Teubner, *Regime Kollision: Zur Fragmentierung des Globalen Rechts* (Frankfurt: Suhrkamp, 2006).

[35] Guther Teubner, *Networks as Connected Contracts*, ed. by Hugh Collins, transl. by Michelle Everson (Oxford: Hart, 2011).

for agency and conflict, and for mistakes and "dysfunctional" outcomes that might even get locked in. As Richard Münch suggests:

> the institutionalization of autonomous subsystems in modern society ... cannot be explained as an evolutionary process, but must be explained in terms of the struggle concerning the definition of codes and programs for the organization of social problem-solving. Existing autonomous sub-systems are not evolutionary universals, but are historically particular and varying institutions which can be established and changed in different ways.[36]

Thus particular attention should be paid to the historical struggles that are inscribed in the definitions of fields, sectors, or issue areas claiming autonomy. Here, one thinks of the struggles between science and the church, or of the "economy" and the state. Besides, functional differentiation is not akin to evolution since it does not emerge from random variation in organizational forms, especially when the necessary second step, the selection process, is never clearly specified, as is the case here. Rather, it emerges from specific struggles involving cognition and intentions of agents and thus the victories codify gains and losses, even if the results might attain *ex post* the aura of "evolutionary achievements."

The second remaining puzzle, however, is why the stabilization of expectation in interactions, so important for law, occurred largely through the growth of *the state and did not take the route of a direct functional differentiation* at a global level.[37] Moreover, one needs to explain why the differentiation process was not an even one, although certain patterns of underdevelopment and stratificatory differentiation have been noted by Wallerstein, and again what role the state played in this respect, instead of seeing in the state an anomalous relict of a segmented organization. This means that we have to explain why national societies were able to set limits to the functional logic of sectors, leading to "varieties of capitalism," *and* why, as of late, these capacities have been undermined. Here some "objective factors," such as the communications revolution and the phenomenal increase of transactions leading to a loss of control by states, are probably to blame, as are ideological factors, such as entrusting major ordering functions to "markets."

The same picture emerges when we probe the genesis of free-standing regimes. It hardly bears out the argument of evolution, or of the diffusion of norm cascades.[38] Despite a good number of case studies on the form of regimes in different issue areas, a close reading of them defies the usual grand narrative.[39]

[36] Richard Muench, "Autopoiesis by Definition," *Cardozo Law Review*, vol. 13 (1991/92), 1463–71 at 1464.

[37] Immanuel Wallerstein, *The New World System*, 2 vols. (New York: Academic Press, 1976).

[38] See Kathryn Sikkink, *Justice Cascades* (New York: Norton, 2011).

[39] See e.g. Susan Sell, *Private Power, Public Law: The Globalization of Intellectual Property Rights* (Cambridge University Press, 2004); Witold Henisz, Bennett Zellner and Mauro Guillen,

Instead, we are led back to the interplay between the domestic structures and the type of international regime that emerged.[40] In other words we have to investigate – in the sense of the 'Introduction' to these Meditations – the world political process rather than the world societal process. Intellectual property rights provide here an excellent example. Initially, a "functional" international organization, the World Intellectual Property Organization (WIPO) in Geneva, was the natural candidate for regime creation. The subsequent regime, however, did not follow this functional logic but became part of the WTO as the Agreement on Trade Related Aspects of Intellectual Property Rights (TRIPS Agreement). This at first rather odd result calls for an explanation, and it can be provided only by carefully examining some important turning points in the regime's development. The story one uncovers highlights how the United States, with the help of Europe and some other players, managed to ensconce the issue area within the WTO regime. This was achieved against the determined opposition of the developing countries and parts of the UN, which wanted a broad multilateral treaty under the auspices of the WIPO. Thus, while the distributional results of the regime are perhaps not that surprising, given the bargaining power of the USA, the placement of the issue area within "trade" *is*, since it contradicts theories that stress functional differentiation as the engine of change.

As the intellectual property rights case shows, it was not only "politics" rather than "function" that was important, but also a change in the US domestic structures (rather than in the "issue area") that accounts for the result. David Bach has provided us with a detailed analysis of what happened.[41] In the 1980s the fragmented American intellectual property regime had changed dramatically by empowering the United States Trade Representatitve (USTR) to include intellectual property criteria in its decisions for granting foreign countries access to the American market. Having hit on an institutional solution that solved the compliance problem plaguing virtually every regime, the USTR emerged as the dominant institution for aggregating interests through American trade law (amended in 1984 and 1988).[42] Subsequent lobbying by the

"The Worldwide Diffusion of Market Oriented Reform 1977–1999," *American Sociological Review*, vol. 70 (2005), 871–97; Milton Mueller, *Ruling the Root: Internet Governance and the Taming of Cyberspace* (Cambridge, MA: MIT, 2002).

40 See, however, the special issue of the Review of International Political Economy introduced by Henry Farrell and Abraham Newman, "Making International Markets: Domestic Institutions in International Political Economy," *Review of International Political Economy*, vol. 17, no. 4 (2010). See also Mathias Koenig-Archibugi and Michael Zürn (eds.), *New Modes of Governance in the Global System* (New York: Palgrave Macmillan, 2006); Daniel Drenzer, *All Politics is Global* (Princeton University Press, 2007).

41 David Bach, "Varieties of Cooperation: The Domestic Institutional Roots of Global Governance," *Review of International Studies*, vol. 36, no. 2 (2010), 561–89.

42 Judith Hippler Bello and Alan Holmer, "The Heart of the 1988 Trade Act: A Legislative History of the Amendments to Section 3012," *Stanford Journal of International Law*, vol. 25 (1988), 1–44.

Intellectual Property Committee (IPC), an organization of sixteen American CEOs, succeeded in placing intellectual property rights on the agenda of the Uruguay Round. This decision nixed all attempts of dealing with these issues through the State Department and through negotiating a multilateral treaty within the WIPO framework. Having first developed a strong domestic institutional anchor, the resulting regime reflected American interests. Furthermore, these interests were filtered through, and interpreted by, *trade institutions* rather than seen through the copyright or trademark lenses of the US Patent and Trademark Office or the US Copyright Office, which had been allies of the State Department.[43]

An analysis of the internet regime reveals similar features. The present Internet Corporation for Assigned Names and Numbers (ICANN) regime, based on a Californian private non-profit corporation assigning domain names on advice of predominantly non-state actors, neither followed the functional logic embodied in the existing International Telecommunications Union (ITU), nor did it result from some normative revolution. While the private nature of this "authority" has by now been established "globally," the regime itself remains contested. Having outflanked the "state," a de facto hegemony of stakeholders was institutionalized, thereby further marginalizing those groups and countries that cannot participate meaningfully in the actual shaping of the Internet. Some of the original pioneers with strong preferences for private ordering, such as Jon Postel, were able to use their domestically rooted leverage to create a "private" regime that now exercises control by also being in charge of the root server system, notwithstanding the objections for various "functional" UN agencies.

From such examples one might conclude that the "dominant" actor can simply have its way, and that efforts to trace regime development might add colour to the story but not fundamentally alter the "realist" plot. Such a conclusion is hasty (and an invitation to do shoddy empirical work), as the next case demonstrates: a policy controversy within the USA concerning standards for regulating the chemical industry and the implementation of environmental protection mandates.

The EU's REACH (Regulation, Evaluation, Authorisation and Restriction of Chemicals) initiative and its far-reaching information requirements concerning chemicals and their use in processes of production have been welcomed by NGOs throughout the world, but it was promptly condemned by the American federal government as too costly and unworkable due to its complexity. It engendered a national debate about the sufficiency of the standards enshrined in the Federal Toxic Substances Control Act of 1976, which is administered by the Environmental Protection Agency. Part of this debate concerned California and Massachusetts bills that were levelling up to the exacting REACH standards

[43] See Bach, "Varieties of Cooperation."

rather than remaining within the existing US regulation regarding the identification of "Substances of Very High Concern."[44] Such "independent" paths are possible in the USA since the Constitution makes this area one of shared, rather than of exclusive concern among the states and the federal government.

Environmental issues show a similar pattern of power-sharing among individual states, the federal government, and sometimes even local jurisdictions. Certain states, such as California, have tougher standards for car emissions than is required by federal law. Along similar lines, mayors of several cities, among them Seattle and Salt Lake City, have adopted official ordinances that set new "green standards" for their municipal governments. The measures were designed to abide by the Kyoto Protocol for local utility emissions, which the federal government had refused to implement. The programs were approved by the US Conference of Mayors in June 2005. By February 2006 they had been endorsed by over 200 mayors.[45]

These developments should not be overestimated in their actual impact due to the "foreign affairs preemption" doctrine[46] that US federal courts apply, thereby "controlling" the autonomy of state and local governments. But it should not be underestimated either. Precisely because federal systems allow for plural law-making, they create "diverse points of entry" for laws from abroad and for reconfiguring the nexus between the global and the local. This process might exhibit neither the clear "logic" of functionalism nor that of a Luhmannian systems theory, nor even of the teleology that the narrative of progress suggests. It shows, nevertheless, how transformative changes have decisively altered what counts as a local, a federal, or a foreign issue.

A different pattern emerges again when we look at states' attempts to transform their environment by making their laws and "practices" binding *without* asserting direct jurisdiction through incorporating those areas. Such attempts create normative hierarchies that are not sufficiently analysed by the catch-all phrase of "global governance." The efforts of the United States to embed certain accounting practices and "transparency" requirements into other legal orders, or into the qualifying criteria for assistance by international organizations, for example, are perhaps rightly considered part of a hegemonic project. Yet, the

[44] See Joan Scott, "From Brussels with Love: The Transatlantic Travels of European Law and the Chemistry of Regulatory Attraction," *American Journal of Comparative Law*, vol. 57 (2009), 899–942.

[45] See Judith Resnik, "Law's Migration: American Exceptionalism, Silent Dialogues, and Federalism's Multiple Ports of Entry," *The Yale Law Journal*, vol. 115, no. 7 (2009), 1574–670, at 1646.

[46] The *locus classicus* is *United States* v. *Pink*, 315 US 203 (1942). For more recent decisions, see *Crosby* v. *National Foreign Trade Council*, 530 UA 363 (2000), dealing with Massachusetts' boycott of Burmese goods), and *American Insurance Association* v. *Garameni* 539 US 396 (2003), addressing California's requirement that companies must disclose information from the Holocaust era if doing business in California.

US case is not unique.[47] The fact that the EU Neighbourhood Policy contains similar traits indicates that something more fundamental is at stake.

An appropriate research program would therefore have to look not only at the global processes and their abstract logic of reproduction, but would also have to examine the "laboratories" where the local and global, the concrete and the abstract meet. The resulting political order of such "laboratories" is not one of negotiation and reciprocity but rather emerges from "structural" and "productive power" in Barnett and Duvall's sense.[48] This power works through the operation of "diffuse social relations of constitution" rather than through direct impacts.

These last remarks lead me back to the discussion regarding similar issues in international law where obligations *erga omnes* and the emergence of *jus cogens* are said to be fundamentally changing the international legal order from a "practical association" to an order where "community interests" weigh in much more heavily. Thus we can remain squarely within the narrative of "progress" without having to pay heed to Foucault's sombre suggestions. Interestingly, though, these progressive changes are no longer supposed to be achieved through state practice, but are supposed to come about largely through doctrinal developments within the "invisible college" of international lawyers.[49] The high priests of the temples of justice and academia are encouraged to dispense with "inappropriate restraint"[50] and to "take every opportunity to secure that the voice of the Law of the Charter rises above the current cacophony."[51] But while a clarification of what the law "is" is certainly an important issue, the increasing distance of practice and doctrine should be as disturbing to political practitioners as it should be to lawyers.

It is one thing to be critical when courts do not do their job, such as when the ICJ declared itself incompetent to evaluate the scientific evidence in the recent *Paper Mills* litigation[52] that was germane for deciding the case. Such an abstention comes close to a denial of justice, particularly since the Court has relied on expert testimony before.[53] It is, however, quite another thing to use teleological

47 See Robert Gilpin, *War and Change in World Politics* (Cambridge University Press, 1981); Robert Keohane, *After Hegemony*, 2nd edn. (Princeton University Press, 2005).

48 See Michael Barnett and Raymond Duvall, "Power in International Politics," *International Organization*, vol. 59 (2005), 39–75.

49 See Oscar Schachter, "The Invisible College of International Lawyers," *Northwestern Law Review*, vol. 72, no. 2 (1977), 217–28.

50 See Judge Simma's separate opinion in the *Oil Platforms* case (*Iran* v. *United States* (2003) ICJ Reports, 324).

51 *Ibid.* at para. 5.

52 See *Case Concerning Pulp mills on the River Uruguay (Argentina* v. *Uruguay)* (Merits), Decision of April 21, 2010, ICJ Reports 14.

53 See e.g. the *Corfu Channel* case, where three naval experts were tasked by the Court to evaluate the visibility of mine-laying operations off the Albanian coast, even requesting a second in situ inspection when the first expert report was not conclusive. *Corfu Channel*

interpretive tools that transcend the institutional limits in the pursuit of interpretive hegemony and "tackle apparent gaps in the law, textual or doctrinal lacunae that could impede the operation of the policy or underlying normativity of the law."[54] To that extent, reaching pronouncements cast in terms of functional necessity are not innocent clarifications, but raise legitimacy questions in regard to judicial law-making. The next section addresses these problems.

The narrative of progress: the new "custom," obligation *erga omnes*, *jus cogens*

Jus cogens norms, which are exempted from derogation, are able to "trump" other norms in cases of conflict, particularly because they cannot be altered except by norms having the same status. This is in a nutshell the result of the lengthy discussions within the International Law Commission. Subsequently, *jus cogens* was ensconced in Articles 53 and 64 of the Vienna Convention on the Law of Treaties. The notion of obligations *erga omnes* has a less spectacular origin. It made its first appearance in an *obiter dictum* of the ICJ in the *Barcelona Traction* case.[55] Both concepts are, however, part of a larger debate that reaches back to the years between the First and Second World Wars. This wider debate shows some interesting twists and turns in the "development" of international law. But whatever one might think of these sometimes strange transformations, they did lead to the establishment of the notion of an *international community* as a subject endowed with rights – in the case of *erga omnes* obligations – and with some law-making capacities, as exemplified by *jus cogens*.[56]

While this assertion is rather uncontroversial, the heated debates concerning the practical implication of *jus cogens* are somewhat surprising.[57] The controversy suggests not only that the devil lies in the details, as usual, but also that perhaps inconsistent notions of *jus cogens* and of *erga omnes* obligations have become part of their respective language games. This suspicion is heightened by the fact that the paradigmatic examples instantiating *jus cogens* have

Case (UK v. *Albania)* (1949) ICJ Reports 4, para. 21; see also the order of December 17, 1948, ICJ Reports, 124.

[54] Robert Howse and Ruthi Teitel, "Global Judicial Activism, Fragmentation and the Limits of Constitutionalism in International Law," in Ulrich Fastenrath *et al.* (eds.), *Festschrift for Bruno Simma: From Bilateralism to Community Interest* (Oxford University Press, 2011), 961–74, at 962.

[55] *Barcelona Traction, Light and Power Co Ltd* (1970) ICJ Reports, 3.

[56] Out of the voluminous literature, see Alexander Orakheshvili, *Peremptory Norms in International Law* (Oxford University Press, 2006); Christian Tomuschat and Jean Marc Thouvenin (eds.), *The Fundamental Rules of the International Legal Order* (Leiden: Nijhoff, 2006). See also Andreas Paulus, *Die internationale Gemeinschaft im Voelkerrecht* (Munich: Beck, 2001); Andrea Bianchi, "Human Rights and the Magic of Jus Cogens," *European Journal of International Law*, vol. 19, no. 3 (2008), 491–508.

[57] See e.g. Linderfalk, "The Effects of Jus Cogens Norms."

changed considerably over time and some of the former super-norms are no longer even mentioned. This makes the notion of super-norms problematic for all practical purposes (the "empty rhetoric" argument[58]) and could lead to undesirable outcomes. In the following, I briefly examine three turning points of the debates.

Historically, it seems that the first argument for a *jus cogens* was made by Verdross in 1937 in conjunction with the law of treaties. States, he argued, were simply not free to conclude treaties that violated certain norms. Verdross claimed that there were two types of rules having this character. The first type consisted of discrete rules that had become compulsory over time. One of his examples was the alleged prohibition to disturb other states in their use of the high seas. The second type consisted of rules that were *contra bonos mores*, evidenced by the rules "common to the juridical order of all states." Thus at first blush the arguments seemed to address problems that traditionally, but obliquely, were dealt with under the rubrics of "custom" and "sources."

The examples Verdross provided seem strange, however, particularly if they are read in conjunction with the broader claim that no legal order can allow treaties among its members that are "in contradiction to the ethics of a certain community."[59] He considers, for example, "excessive" limitations of the police and military forces rendering a state "defenceless," as well as treaties forbidding a state to protect its nationals abroad, as somehow undermining the "moral foundations" of a community. It is rather apparent that here the dissatisfaction with the Versailles peace treaties informs the agenda.[60] In the light of later developments, such as the comprehensive multilateral regime of the Law of the Sea Treaty and the imposition of stringent disarmament conditions (in addition to "no-fly zones") as in Iraq, we would have to conclude (following Verdross) that all violate *jus cogens*.

The discussion was continued in the ILC in conjunction with the draft Convention of the Law of Treaties. The subject of *jus cogens* and the peremptory character of those norms was now based less on its "consistency with international morality" but rather on those forming the "constituent part of general principles of law," or those which give expression to the "requirements of international public policy."[61] By 1966, however, the ILC moved away from

58 See e.g. A. Mark Weisburd, "The Emptiness of the Concept of Jus Cogens, as illustrated by the War in Bosnia Herzegovina," *Michigan Journal of International Law*, vol. 17 (1995), 1–52, at 11.

59 Alfred Verdross, "Forbidden Treaties in International Law," *American Journal of International Law*, vol. 31 (1937), 571–7, at 572.

60 Kelsen later followed Verdross by suggesting that an international tribunal would probably void a treaty concluded in violation of the freedom of the sea principle, but saw nothing wrong in arrangements of reciprocal modification of diplomatic protection.

61 See Lauterpacht's report on the Law of the Treaties, UN Doc. A/CN.4/62 (1953), and his comments on Art. 15 of the draft; see also the comments by one of the later rapporteurs,

its earlier position, which had focused on the circumstances in which courts could void treaties based on public order considerations or on the recognition of evolving customary norms. It now took the more formalist approach that states could modify *jus cogens* norms if they used a multilateral treaty, as the ILC comments on this Article[62] and its wording shows.[63]

Article 50 (which with slightly different wording was to become Article 53 of the Vienna Convention) indicates: "A treaty is void if it conflicts with a peremptory norm of general international law from which no derogation is permitted and which can be modified only by a subsequent norm of international law having the same character."[64] After much debate, an insert was made: "For the purposes of the present Convention a peremptory norm of general international law is a norm accepted and recognized by the international community of states as a whole from which no derogation is permitted and which can be modified only by a subsequent norm of general international law having the same character."

In this context, the prohibition of the use of force was first mentioned by the ILC as a "conspicuous example" of *jus cogens*, while other examples provided by the delegates at Vienna were the right to self-determination, human rights, genocide, and humanitarian law. However, in the final version of the Article (now Article 53 of the VCLT) no examples were included in order to avoid the misunderstanding that this was an exhaustive list, as indeed no norm had made all of the circulated "wish lists." Weisburd suggests:

> This language clearly assumes that states are free to change *jus cogens*, at least when they use the mechanism of a general multilateral treaty to do so. The assumption that the content of *jus cogens* is under the control of states is likewise implied by the commission's statement that it planned to leave the full content of *jus cogens* "to be worked out in state practice and the jurisprudence of international tribunals."[65]

Thus, while the notion of the compulsory character of certain norms was kept, the subtext of *jus cogens* had changed considerably. On the one hand, a

Waldock, stressing the idea of an "international public order." See Humphrey Waldock, Second Report on the Law of Treaties, UN Doc. A/CN. 4 /115 (1963).

62 On the history of *ius cogens* and Article 50 of the ILC draft that became Article 54 of the Vienna Convention of the Law of Treaties, see Mark Weisburd, "The Emptiness of Concept of ius cogens, as Illustrated by the War in Bosnia Herzegovina," *Michigan Journal of International Law*, vol. 17, no. 1 (1995): 1–52.

63 The ILC comment reads somewhat cryptically: "as a modification of a rule of jus cogens would today most probably be effected through a general multilateral treaty, the commission thought it desirable to indicate that such treaty would fall outside the scope of the article." 2 Y.B. Int'l Law Commission 169.

64 See International Law Commission, Report on the second part of its 17th and 18th session, UN Doc. A/6309/rev. 1 (1966).

65 Weisburd, "The Emptiness of the Concept of Jus Cogens," at 11.

peremptory norm could overrule custom, thus imposing duties on states without their consent and even depriving them of the privileges granted to persistent objectors in customary international law.[66] Universal validity no longer depended on universal acceptance since a *jus cogens* norm received its validity from the recognition of the community of states "as a whole." On the other hand, these norms were not necessarily resistant to change, regardless of what is often implied. Finally, these norms could be invoked universally, namely by any member of the "international community" *of states*.

Sometimes this latter role was likened to the institution of an *actio popularis* of Roman law. The ICJ in the *South West Africa* case referred explicitly to this possibility in certain municipal systems, but noted that this institution "is not known to international law as it stands at present."[67] As the other provisions of the Vienna Convention concerning redress for the violations of *obligations erga omnes* and subsequent practice showed, such an interpretation is also precluded by a reading of Article 66 in conjunction with Article 65. The latter concerns the arbitration proceeding when a party has invoked a defect in consent to be bound, or a ground "for impeaching the validity of a treaty, terminating it, withdrawing from it or suspending its operation,"[68] and which does not lead within twelve months to a settlement. Otherwise the right of appeal to the ICJ, as provided for in Article 66, would not exist. Although these Articles have never been used, it seems that "the international community" still speaks through states, and particularly through states whose *particular* interests have been injured, a point that also emerges from the discussions of *erga omnes* obligations referred to below.

This interpretation seems to contradict the sometimes sweeping statements about the "fundamental character" of certain values ensconced, for instance, in human rights, since the term "fundamental" is related to a variety of rights and practices, making us wonder what the fundament of the alleged "fundamentality" really is. Thus the ICJ's use of the term "fundamental" in the *Teheran Hostage* case rests on the assessment that "there is no more fundamental prerequisite for the conduct of relations between States than the inviolability of

[66] This point was highlighted by the French delegate Hubert at the Vienna Convention, who warned that this would "create an international source of law subject to no control and lacking all responsibility" and "deprive States of one of their essential privileges … sovereign equality." As quoted in Paulus, *Die internationale Gemeinschaft im Voelkerrecht*, at 341.

[67] See *South West Africa* case (1966) ICJ Reports, 32, at 47, line 88f., echoing the advisory Opinion on Reparations for Injuries Suffered in the Services of the United Nations (1949) ICJ Reports, 174 at 181: "only parties to whom the international obligation is due can bring a claim in respect of its breach," at 181f. See a similar rejection of the *actio popularis* argument in the *Case Concerning Military and Para-military Activities in and Against Nicaragua (Nicaragua* v. *the United States of America)* (Merits) (1986) ICJ Reports, 14 at 134f.

[68] Article 56 of the VCLT.

diplomatic envoys and embassies."[69] Here "fundamental" is similar to a Kantian "transcendental condition" for a common practice that cannot be derived from an inductive examination of actual behaviour, but is nearly exclusively based on the "needs" that a practice requires for its performance. A different type of "fundamentalism" is invoked in the Advisory Opinion on the Genocide Convention. Here the court began by noting the "special characteristics of the Genocide Convention," which was unanimously approved by fifty-six states on December 9, 1948:

> The Convention was manifestly adopted for purely humanitarian and civilizing purposes. It is indeed difficult to imagine a convention that might have this dual character to a greater degree, since its object on the one hand is to safeguard the very existence of certain human groups and on the other to confirm and endorse the most elementary principles of morality. In such a convention the contracting States do not have any interest of their own; they merely have, one and all, common interests, namely the accomplishment of those high purposes which are the raison d'être of the convention. Consequently, in a convention of this type one cannot speak of individual advantages or disadvantages to States, or of the maintenance of a perfect contractual balance between right and duties. The high ideals which inspired the Convention provide, by virtue of the common will of the parties, the foundation and measure of all its provisions.[70]

The contrasting tropes elucidating the notion of the "fundamental" could not be clearer. Individual interests and the common civilizing purpose are set against each other; the instrument of contract is contrasted with the high ideals that inspire the Convention. Aggregation and balancing of interests are rejected in order to confirm and endorse the most elemental principles that also serve as guides for determining later the scope of reservations. In a nearly Rousseauian fashion the request for an advisory opinion is turned into the *aliénation totale* that the person entering into the social contract has to undergo in order to become a member of a community.[71] The rhetoric has strong natural law overtones, but not based on the concept of an ontological order of things (as the Stoics, or St Thomas would have had it), but of "nature." Since for Rousseau nature is not fixed, as the *Second Discourse*[72] makes it abundantly clear, these fundamental rights cannot be ascertained by going back to the origins or to a

[69] *Case Concerning US Diplomatic and Consular Staff in Teheran* (Order of Provisional Measures, December 15, 1979, ICJ Reports, 7 at para. 38 *et seq.*

[70] Reservations to the Convention on Genocide, ICJ Advisory Opinion (1951) ICJ Reports, 15 at 21.

[71] See Jean Jacques Rousseau, *The Social Contract and the Discourse on the Origin of Inequality*, ed. by Lester Crocker (New York: Washington Square Press, 1971), Book I, Chapters VIII and IX.

[72] Jean Jacques Rousseau, "The 2nd Discourse," in Jean Jacques Rousseau, *The First and Second Discourse*, transl. by Roger and Judith Masters (New York: St Martin's Press, 1969).

natural state. They *evolve*, leading man out of brutish existence and ignorance to enlightenment and emancipation.

Flanked by these two understandings of "fundamental," the ILC Articles on the Responsibility of States for Internationally Wrongful Acts[73] seem to be located somewhere in the in-between. "Fundamental" is neither rooted in some functional need for an *ordre public*, nor does it coincide with a purely formal notion of law-making, leaving the substance of *jus cogens* largely undefined. It also does not share the natural law overtones that are so striking in the Genocide Convention. Rather, it embodies some type of a "corporatist" idea of a community in which no single member can prevent action –thereby correcting an extreme voluntarist understanding of the international order – but the consent among less than all members also has to exhibit a *certain quality*. Since each member is a free agent and embedded in wider social contexts – such as the First, Second, and Third World of former times – this diversity has to be recognized and it needs to be reflected in a "representative" consensus supporting these norms.

Again, several things have to be unpacked. One is that universal validity can be claimed on the basis of a "fundamental" consensus reached among all relevant groups. This was a certainly a "reasonable" compromise during the Cold War when the increasing resistance, mainly from the developing world, to the policies of the "superpowers" became noticeable. These states claimed first a special status as neutrals, and later they used the General Assembly as the forum for legitimizing their agendas, supported by stable majorities, concerning issues of neo-colonialism and of different economic priorities (for example the New International Economic Order).

Second, any common enterprise that gets off the ground in international relations develops a certain "pull," even if this force is not officially recognized by Justitia, who is, after all, "blind." Thus, the EU exerts its sway over its neighbourhood and its law "migrates," as we have seen. In the same way, the ICJ in the *Reparations* case[74] laid the foundation for the claim that a part of the international community represented by the UN can act "on behalf" of all states even against non-members in circumvention of the *pacta tertiis* principle.

The third issue concerns particular rights that can be claimed when a non-specifically affected state claims to speak for the "whole." Here the ILC Draft Articles provide in Article 48.1(b) that "any state other than the injured state is entitled to invoke the responsibility of another state … if … (b) the obligation breached is owed to the international community as a whole." Crawford, the rapporteur, speaks here of an "essential distinction" between the obligations

[73] See ILC Draft Articles on Responsibility of States for Internationally Wrongful Acts (2001) GAOR 56th session, Supp. 10, 43.

[74] *Reparations for Injuries Suffered in the Service of the United Nations*, ICJ Reports 1949, 177ff., at 182.

arising *inter se*, and those owed to the international community as "a whole."[75] As essential as this distinction might be, the question is whether the notion of the community interest is broad enough to cover a right of any state to initiate proceedings, when for example gross violations of *jus cogens* are apparent, but the political processes had failed to respond adequately to them.[76] Furthermore, Crawford's position, which contradicts several ICJ judgments, is justified by his assessment: "Better to give States standing in Court to protect what they perceive as global values than to leave them only with non-judicial means of dispute settlement, whether in the guise of countermeasures, or under the rubric of the 'responsibility to protect.'"[77] But whether courts are the proper means to decide public policy questions has been subject to heated debates, both on grounds of constitutionality and effectiveness. Here the record is at best mixed.[78] In any case, as Kadelbach notes, it is only in the case of obligations vis-à-vis the international community (the ILC draft did not use the term *erga omnes*) that "a limited set of legal consequences may be invoked by third States, such as the obligation to bring the illegal behaviour and the situation resulting from it to an end, to refrain from such conduct in the future, and to make reparations for the damage to the victim state."[79]

This does not mean that states just have to stand by and do nothing. A right of monitoring or criticizing states for gross violations of accepted standards within the UN political organs – sometimes referred to as a *droit de regard* – is thereby well recognized, as it stems from their legal interests as members of the organization.[80] In this sense, in its Wall Advisory Opinion[81] the ICJ has also pointed to the General Assembly and the Security Council as the proper arenas. Here, of course, issues of hypocrisy (unevenly calling attention to

[75] See James Crawford, *The ILC's Articles on State Responsibility* (Cambridge University Press, 2002), 278.

[76] See e.g. Judge Jessup's dissent in the *South West Africa* case (1966) ICJ Reports, 51 at 374.

[77] See James Crawford, "Responsibility for Breaches of Communitarian Norms: An Appraisal of Article 48 of the ILC Articles on Responsibility of States for Internationally Wrongful Acts," in Ulrich Fastenrath *et al.* (eds.), *Festschrift for Bruno Simma: From Bilateralism to Community Interest* (Oxford University Press, 2011): 224–40, at 225.

[78] See e.g. Hirschl's comparative study of efforts by the USA, Australia, Canada and Israel to redress inequalities and traditional injustices done to native populations via court proceedings, which did not bring about the desired changes. Ran Hirschl, *Towards Juristocracy: The Origins and Consequences of the New Constitutionalism* (Cambridge, MA: Harvard University Press, 2004).

[79] Stefan Kadelbach, "Jus Cogens, Obligations Erga Omnes and other Rules – The Identification of Fundamental Norms," in Christian Tomuschat and Jean Marc Thouvenin (eds.), *The Fundamental Rules of the International Legal Order* (Leiden: Martinus Nijhoff, 2006), 21–40, at 37.

[80] See Oscar Schachter, *International Law in Theory and Practice* (Dordrecht: Martinus Nijhoff, 1985), Chapter XV.

[81] Legal consequences of the Construction of a Wall in Occupied Palestinian Territory (Advisory Opinion) (2004) ICJ Reports, 136 at para. 160.

violations or taking measures – as your terrorists are my freedom fighters) and "propaganda," rather than those concerning the overriding nature of *jus cogens*, come into play. Similarly, states, singly and in conjunction, can take countermeasures against serious breaches of *erga omnes* obligations as provided for in Article 54 of the ILC Articles on Responsibility of States for Internationally Wrongful Acts.

Thus the *jus cogens* concept, when seen through the lenses of the Law of Treaties, might not provide definite answers to the "fundamental" question, precisely because it paradigmatically starts from bilateral relations that are then "multilateralized" – even though redress and "enforcement" remain essentially bilateral (vide the WTO despite all its multilateral rhetoric) or "aggregate bilateral"[82] when others join a complaint. For that reason a more promising avenue might be to root "super-norms" in "customary"[83] international law,[84] especially in cases concerning the general prohibition on using force, genocide, and severe abuses of human rights.

But confusion abounds here also, as the issue of obligations *erga omnes partes*, for example in a multilateral convention,[85] is frequently not distinguished from *erga omnes* obligations arising out of customary law. Thus the somewhat wistful remarks of ad hoc Judge Sur in the *Belgium* v. *Senegal* case,[86] that the World Court's finding of standing on the basis of *erga omnes* is "a rabbit out of a magic hat" since the UN Convention against Torture and other Cruel, Inhuman or Degrading Treatment or Punishment (CAT) allows for reservations that appear incompatible with *erga omnes* obligations and the mechanism established by Article 22 is only optional, and should have been mandatory if the CAT had intended to entitle any state party to ensure compliance.[87] Furthermore, difficult questions of jurisdiction are thereby raised, as in the *Case Concerning East Timor (Portugal* v. *Australia)*[88] demonstrated, and state

82 I owe this term to Jan Klabbers.

83 For a discussion of custom in this context, see Michael Byers, *Custom, Power and the Power of Rules* (Cambridge University Press, 1999).

84 See Theodore Meron, *Human Rights and Humanitarian Norms as Customary Law* (Oxford University Press, 1989).

85 For a clarification see Christian Tams, *Enforcing Obligations Erga Omnes in International Law* (Cambridge University Press, 2005).

86 *Case Concerning Questions Relating to the Obligation to Prosecute or Extradite (Belgium* v. *Senegal)*, Judgment of July 20, 2012, ICJ Reports, General List 144.

87 See Inna Uchkunova, "Belgium v. Senegal: Did the Court End the Dispute between the Parties," *European Journal of International Law* website, EJIL: Talk 10/7/201.

88 *Case Concerning East Timor (Portugal* v. *Australia)*, judgment of June 30, 1995, ICJ Reports, 90. The case arose out of a dispute over resource issues and delimitation of the continental shelf between Australia and Indonesia. The latter had previously unlawfully seized the former colony of Timor from Portugal and had the territory incorporated as a province. However, Portugal had been designated by the UN as the lawful administering power, and now alleged a violation of the principle of self-determination of the Timorese and their sovereignty over their resources. The Court agreed that self-determination is a *jus cogens*

practice is all but clear and consistent, sometimes even that of the same state, as the change in Australia's position from the *Nuclear Test* case[89] to its pleadings in the *East Timor* case shows.[90]

Similarly, the ICJ in a recent decision (*Germany* v. *Italy*)[91] had to deal with the *jus cogens* character of the laws of armed conflict vis-à-vis state immunity, whereby the former must allegedly override the latter. However, the Court avoided this conclusion by arguing that there was no conflict between the procedural rules of granting immunity to another state, and the substantive norms of the law of armed conflict, since the "two sets of rules address different matters." Thus immunity rules are procedural, regulating the exercise of jurisdiction, but "do not bear upon the question whether or not the conduct … was lawful or unlawful."[92] This at first rather strange argument becomes clearer, however, when we "unpack" some of the underlying assumptions about the superiority of the "super-norms." The notion that, for example, a violation of human rights supersedes ordinary State immunity, or that a state has "waived" its rights by engaging in unconscionable behaviour, since it can no longer claim to be acting within the domain of *acta jure imperii*, is often implicit. But these inferences are problematic despite their moral appeal. Without claiming to have a definitive answer to this conundrum, the following considerations seem germane.

The argument of a supervenience would imply that the international community would no longer be bound by the obligations that the rights of the perpetrator impose upon it. While immunity certainly does not imply impunity, stripping a legal subject of its rights seems problematic. After all, we do not do this with murderers in criminal law, by making them simply *ex lex*. Here state responsibility enters the picture, as does personal criminal responsibility, and thus, as the *Arrest Warrant* case[93] suggests, even violations of *jus cogens* norms

norm implying *erga omnes* obligations, but considered the "*erga omnes* character of a norm and rule of consent to jurisdiction … two different things." Since Indonesia was not party to the proceedings and had not conferred jurisdiction, the Court concluded: "Where this is so, the Court cannot act even if the right in question is a right *erga omnes*" (*ibid.* at para. 29, at 102). Similarly the ILC Draft Articles on the Responsibility of States give "standing" to a "state other than the injured state" but allows for reparations only for the interests of the injured state (Art. 48).

89 *Nuclear Test case (Australia* v. *France)* (1974) ICJ Reports, 99 and *Nuclear Test case (New Zealand* v. *France)* (1974) ICJ Reports, 457.

90 In the *East Timor* case, Australia took a much narrower view of "standing" on the basis of *erga omnes* obligations, denying in its counter-memorial (para. 262) the general right of parties not directly affected to bring *erga omnes* proceedings.

91 See *Jurisdictional Immunities of the State (Germany* v. *Italy, Greece intervening)*, Judgment of February 3, 2012, General List 143.

92 *Ibid.* at para. 93.

93 See *Democratic Republic of the Congo* v. *Belgium* (2002) ICJ Reports, 3. There the majority held that by issuing and circulating an arrest warrant under its "law of universal jurisdiction" of 1993 charging the then Foreign Minister of the DRC with war crimes and crimes

do not necessarily defeat immunity. The argument about a "waiver" is spurious in the face of state practice, since states are very reluctant to waive immunity. Even if we argue that such a waver is "implied" when engaging in illegal activities, the argument presupposes what it attempts to prove, since in the absence of a customary rule that certain actions imply a waiver, no such attribution can be made. Finally, as Giegerich argues, the collision of a peremptory norm (such as against torture) and state immunity occurs, for example, in a tort action only if we assume that victims of a *jus cogens* violation "are entitled to an effective judicial remedy in the courts of another state."[94] This rule would arguably also have to be of *jus cogens character* (which is doubtful); otherwise a state would have to show special reasons why it is taking up the case. Thus, the inference from a wrong to a legal remedy is obviously more complicated than often assumed.

The discussion so far has shown that the normative force of certain norms is not limited to *jus cogens*, which technically belongs to the law of treaties. Instead *jus cogens* has become – perhaps unfortunately so – a *generic term* for a variety of "fundamental" norms that are rooted in "custom." Four issues arise in this context. First, in a striking reversal of the argument that legal "development" is a trajectory leading from "custom to contract," the wide variety of multilateral conventions is now taken to be an articulation of "custom." Second, these norms – especially in recent times – often concern more the articulation of standards and principles rather than specific rules. Because of their flexibility, principles allow for a more holistic approach to certain problems. As noted by judge Weeramantry in his separate opinion in the *Gabcikovo-Nagymaros* case,[95] serious environmental issues that also impact on third parties and future generations cannot be decided on the basis of the adversarial procedures that dominate ordinary *inter partes* litigation. Third, despite the great number of treaties and the fact that many states are parties to most of them, a considerable number of states still remain "outside," and there is no perfect fit of membership across the board of all treaties. Thus, embedding human rights into customary law can then also provide access for the non-members of a treaty to remedies they would not otherwise have. Finally, invoking custom might make appeals to national courts possible, as international law is *mutatis mutandis* usually part of the "law of the land." Here the litigation in the USA under the Alien Claims Tort Act in the aftermath of *Filartiga*[96] (despite its more

against humanity, Belgium had violated its legal obligation towards the DRC and that the Foreign Minister enjoyed immunity under international law.

94 Thomas Giegerich, "Jus Cogens Violations and the Jurisdiction of Foreign Courts," in Christian Tomuschat and Jean Marc Thouvenin (eds.), *The Fundamental Rules of the International Legal Order* (Leiden: Martinus Nijhoff, 2006), 202–37, at 227.

95 *Case Concerning the Gabcikovo-Nagymaros Project (Hungary* v. *Slovakia)* (1997) ICJ Reports, 7 at 117f.

96 *Filartiga* v. *Pena-Irala*, US Court of Appeals 2nd Circuit, 1980 630F.2d 876.

recent restriction in *Alvarez*)[97] comes to mind, whereby in the latter case the US Supreme Court deliberately was *not* addressing the issue of *jus cogens* and obligations *erga omnes*,[98] but limited itself to traditional "violations of the law of nations."

Yet as advantageous as such a conceptualization of the customary character of the super-norms is, it is not without problems. Take the Declaration of Human Rights as an example. It has probably the best chance of being recognized as part of customary international law, given the doctrinal support and the frequent references in court decisions both internationally and domestically. Nevertheless, the proliferation of rights in that document, such as the proviso that everybody has a "right to two weeks' paid vacations" can hardly be said to be authoritative, particularly when we realize that an ungodly number of people in the world have no jobs to begin with. Furthermore, the addressee of the obligation remains either unspecified or is attributed to an abstract "humanity." But humanity cannot act, and the important, but historically contingent, political and social institutions that we create to attend to these practical problems are largely statist.

The attempt to correct this hyperbole by switching to a "thin" version of human rights and talking only about "minimal standards" might take care of some of the problems of a distributive nature; but it will just not do with regard to "basic" human rights. Does it make sense to say that my rights to life and limb should not be guaranteed generally, but only in certain regions or on specific dates? (Tuesdays are clearly out for arbitrary arrests and bodily harm!) That cannot be right either. The whole argument that all human rights are of one cloth,[99] and that they are "mutually supportive" simply does not muster critical scrutiny.[100] Similar to the claim that "all good things come together," it is understandable only if taken as an indication of a particular faith, or as an ideology.

The last examples are illustrative of two problems of the contemporary custom and human rights discourse(s). One is that in its individualist conceptualization emphasizing subjective rights, the problem of *duty*-holder is often slighted. By making all human rights "trumps," one neglects to see that perhaps

[97] In *Sosa* v. *Alvarez Machain*; in *US* v. *Alvarez Machain* 542 US 692 (2004) the US Supreme Court held that the Alien Tort Statute provides for jurisdiction but not for an independent cause of action save in the special circumstances envisaged in the Alien Tort Statute at its creation.

[98] For a further discussion see Georg Nolte, "Universal Jurisdiction in the Area of Private Law – The Alien Tort Claims Act," in Christian Tomuschat and Jean Marc Thouvenin (eds.), *The Fundamental Rules of the International Legal Order* (Leiden: Martinus Nijhoff, 2006), 373–83.

[99] See e.g. Vienna Declaration and Program of Action (June 25, 1993) UN Doc. A/CONF157/23 (1993) para 5: "All human rights are universal, indivisible and interdependent and interrelated."

[100] See Meditations 7 and 8.

some rights have several duty-bearers, or that some rights imply duties of different degrees. The other difficulty, connected with the first, is that the need to show a link to practice has been weakened in the contemporary discussion. Now mainly the *opinio juris* invoked by scholars in their writings (usually part of a circle of true believers) seems to count. In this context another doctrinal development was significant, that is the invention of "instant custom."[101] It drastically reduced the time required for a settled practice to exist, and it also reduced the number of members that had traditionally been required for a customary rule to become binding upon non-participants, thus weakening even this criterion.

Some arguments of the ICJ's *North Sea Continental Shelf* case[102] are instructive. The judgment bestowed customary status on the practice of "a widespread and *representative*" group of states – but still on the basis of *opinio juris* – and it required only a short period of time for the transformation of a rule in a multilateral convention to become a customary norm. Similarly, not only treaties but also General Assembly resolutions could now be considered "evidence" for an *opinio juris*. This was indeed a far cry from the theory of custom advanced by Kelsen and Guggenheim, who in their earlier writings had tried to rely on state practice alone and had discounted *opinio juris* entirely. Thus, Alston and Simma observe with a certain reservation the new way of conceptualizing custom:

> What is customary about this cultured pearl version of customary law is not (at least not necessarily) its consistent application in actual state practice but the fertilizing role it plays through proclamation, exhortation, repetition, incantation, lament. For some writers practice no longer has any constitutive role to play in the establishment of customary law … After all the only task practice had to perform, the "modernists" would say, was to bring consent or *opinio juris* to the fore; and now that we have all these international bodies and above all the UN General Assembly … consent and *opinio juris* can manifest themselves more or less instantly and without the vehicle as cumbersome and demanding as actual state practice. [103]

101 See e.g. Bin Cheng: "United Nations Resolutions on Outer Space: Instant International Customary Law?," *Indian Journal of Int. Law*, vol. 5 (1965), reprinted in Bin Cheng (ed.), *International Law: Teaching and Practice* (London: Stevens, 1982), 237–62. See also Niels Petersen, "Customary Law without Custom?," *American University International Law Review*, vol. 23 (2007/2008), 275–310.

102 *North Sea Continental Shelf Cases (Fed. Republic of Germany* v. *Denmark); Federal Republic of Germany* v. *Netherlands* (1969) ICJ Reports, 3. Here the *obiter dicta* became doctrinally more important than the actual reasoning rejecting the Danish and Dutch claims that Germany had become bound by custom. It allowed, however, for the possibility of custom being created in a short time by states whose interests were specially affected, but denied that this had happened in the cases before the Court.

103 Bruno Simma and Philip Alston. "The Sources of Human Rights Law: Custom, Jus Cogens and General Principles," *Australian Yearbook of International Law*, vol. 12 (1988/89), 82–108, at 89.

The last point might actually point to another fundamental change in the notion of political practice, since much of what states do in our media-rich times is not simply "signalling" through troop movements or observable actions, which had been the tradition in European state practice. Instead, they constantly go "on record" and make declarations on virtually anything under the sun. They do so (or perhaps feel forced to do so) since they increasingly compete with "spokespersons" of advocacy groups, with "experts" employed by the media for "instant analysis," and with people interviewed in the streets. Government officials no longer have exclusive status, but must compete for sound bites and "live" spots that make the evening news.

As the *Rainbow Warrior* case,[104] the debates on NATO's air strikes in the Former Yugoslavia, the intifada, and the Iraq war all show, these *performative speech acts* invoking international law have become part of policy-making, especially in open political systems. International legal arguments often become the focal points for controversy, thus providing legal scholars with far greater opportunities for "voice" than those mentioned in the statute of the World Court (writings of the most eminent scholars). While formerly official demands or offers were largely out of view, jealously guarded by the sovereigns and their diplomats to whom the *arcana imperii* had been entrusted, modern politics is different, both domestically and externally. It would be indeed strange if the democratic and the media revolutions that have thoroughly transformed domestic politics should not also have some transformative influence on international practices.

These observations have three further corollaries. The first concerns the common assumptions that statements are largely "cheap talk" and that actions speak louder than words. There is a certain truth to this, as we think of the many New Year's resolutions we all have made and promptly broken, as they concern commitments made only to "ourselves." The implication here is that they were not serious and that we had better look at subsequent actions rather than trust announcements. The note of caution is obviously well taken, but the idea that talk *is* "cheap" is misleading. It assumes that "actions" speak for themselves, while utterances are just "descriptions" or commentaries on what is going on. Obviously, this notion is indebted to a "descriptivist" conception of language that is plainly refuted by the existence of "speech acts," whose importance for international relations analysis Onuf[105] demonstrated a long time ago. Thus, neither of the two above inferences is correct when taken literally. Not only must actions also be interpreted, but we can also "cheat"

[104] See the *Rainbow Warrior* case (two arbitrations between France and New Zealand arising out of France's sabotage of a Greenpeace ship that wanted to interfere with French nuclear tests (award of July 6, 1986) and France's later material breach of the first arbitral award (award of April 30, 1990).

[105] Nicholas Onuf, *World of our Making* (Columbia: University of South Carolina Press, 1989).

with actions too, and "motives," which we have to ascertain when we claim that someone cheats, are not directly accessible to us, and thus actions cannot speak for themselves.

The second corollary is that it is simply not true that for commitments to exist there must be some type of "reliance" by others, or some contractual bond. We can commit ourselves by "pledges" or "oaths." Actually, some of our most solemn commitments arise out of such "unilateral commitments," particularly when made together with others. This explains the normative pull of, for example, the Genocide Convention, as the World Court noted in its advisory opinion.[106]

This leads me to the third corollary, which concerns the important issue of how we should treat observations of overt behaviour when engaged in an assessment of custom. In other words, how do we decide that what we "see" is a "violation" of a customary rule, or consider it "evidence" of the non-existence of custom in a certain area? Take torture, arbitrary detention, or denial of justice, all of which are "practised" by states. Thus, noticing a "violation," an "exception," or the "non-existence" of a rule can never be based on simple observation or even on a frequency distribution of actions. As Oscar Schachter pointed out:

> Even if torture takes place in many countries it is almost always contrary to national law and not legitimized as State policy. Hence when violations … take place they are to be regarded as violations not as state practice that nullifies the legal force of the right.[107]

An indication for the correctness of such an assessment is the fact that states usually deny the actual existence of such practices rather than attack the rule or principle involved. Other such gambits include an attempt to defame the sources of such "unfavourable" information, to downplay the seriousness of the measures taken (occasional lapses or over-eager single persons), and/or to justify the measures in terms of a national emergency that allows for detentions and arrests in violation of *habeas corpus*.

The ICJ had to wrestle with this issue in the *Nicaragua* case. There we find first the traditional reference to the distinction of a mere declaration and practice itself, contained in the admonition that the Court may not disregard the essential role played by general practice.[108] But in the very next paragraph the Court focuses on the consent of the parties to General Assembly resolutions as the crystallization of an *opinio juris* without any further examination of state practice.[109] Surprisingly this came after the Court had attempted a reconciliation of these inconsistent positions by arguing that it is "sufficient" if

[106] Reservations to the Convention on Genocide (1951) ICJ Reports, 15.
[107] Schachter, *International Law in Theory and Practice*, at 336.
[108] *Military and Paramilitary Activities in and against Nicaragua (Nicaragua* v. *USA)* Merits (1986) ICJ Reports, 14 at para. 97 *et seq.*
[109] *Ibid.* at 99–104.

state conduct is consistent with such rules in general and that deviant practice should be counted as a breach of a rule and not as indication of the recognition of a new rule.[110]

The solution to this conundrum also occupied a study group of the International Law Association,[111] which in this context called attention to "the general principles of law recognized by civilized nations" as enshrined in Article 38 of the ICJ Statute. Thus, by a creative interpretative step, the concept now also covers principles of the *international legal* order rather than those of municipal law only. *Arguendo*, such a stretch can be justified at least by the intention of the drafters of this statute not to derive some principles from "functional" or natural law grounds, but from the "objectivity" the principles had gained through "recognition" by states. Having thus found a validation procedure that is directly related to state practice, there is no reason to restrict recognition to rules of domestic systems only. The surprising upshot of the argument is, then, that the norms of *jus cogens* might not be "customary" in the sense of the ICJ statute, as they do not arise out of repetition that later leads to a crystallization of a norm. Instead, what we have here is a different law-making process in which the articulation of "general principles of law recognized by civilized nations" arguably occurs by the "international community of States as a whole."

Whether such a construction "solves" the conceptual dilemmas can remain an open question since dilemmas, strictly speaking, cannot be "solved." Hence, the crucial issue is rather whether such a conceptualization lets us "go on," as discussed in Meditation 2. In this regard, two new problems emerge. The first concerns the "civilizational standard" that has always been the bane of human rights catalogues and perhaps even of international law in general.[112] The ambiguity of whether international law was to allow for coexistence of vastly different systems with different political projects, or whether it represented a missionary endeavour for a specific way of life, has always been part of the tradition of international law.

Second, one must recognize that principles need to be interpreted, and this implies not only a shift from legislation to third-party rule application, but it also calls for "courts" at the supranational level to provide their authoritative interpretation. Yet while courts can clarify issues, they cannot solve the actual political problems, as the discussion of constitutionalism above showed.

110 *Ibid.* at 98.

111 See the Report of the Committee on the Formation of Customary Law, American Branch of the ILA, "The Role of State Practice in the Formation of Customary and Jus Cogens Norms of International Law" (January 19, 1989).

112 See the discussion of international law's ambivalence in Emannuelle Jouanet, "Universalism and Imperialism: The True–False Paradox of International Law," *European Journal of International Law*, vol. 1 no. 3 (2007), 379–407.

Without a substantive entrenchment in the political process, clarifications of norms are likely to remain unheeded or, worse, become signals for unilateral action. Whatever the world community might be – a minimal *ordre public*, a practical association, or a value-based utopia – one thing seems clear: doctrines and actual practice often diverge widely and are only tenuously held together by metaphors, conceptual constructs, and narratives, instead of actual, settled practices.

Meditation 6

Cosmopolitanism, publicity, and the emergence of a "global administrative law"

Introduction

The debate of the emergence of a global administrative law follows and parallels a series of debates in international law on constitutionalization that were conducted with different emphases on both sides of the Atlantic. In the USA the "constitutional" debate – and here again we might distinguish the debates concerning the issue of "federal pre-emption"[1] and the issue of "proper delegation" of powers to administrative agencies – took place together with an "internationalist" debate that centred on both the disaggregation of the state and the emergence of governmental networks.[2] In Europe the emphasis was somewhat different in that there the European experiment played an important role. It addressed the EU's "democratic deficit" and focused on attempts to give the ordo-liberal interpretation of the EU some broader constitutional moorings. Thus both the inclusion of human rights incorporating the meanwhile extensive jurisprudence of the ECtHR as well as the push for a "constitutional treaty" aimed at improving the accountability of the European institutions and at increasing the legitimacy of the European project. At the same time this debate linked up with the discussions concerning the emergence of an "international" (administrative) law, but here was indebted more to an international and comparative law perspective than to the American tradition of administrative law.[3]

Of course all these debates also related to the more general issues concerning "liberalization" moves. The two focal points were then on the one hand the "transition" countries that had to come to terms with their communist legacy, and on the other hand the promotion of the "rule of law," which had become an explicit concern for US foreign policy – soon to be "operationalized" as an

[1] See Robert Verschick, Nina Mendelsohn, "Preemption and Theories of Federalism," Ann Arbor: University of Michigan Law School: Public Law and Legal Theory Working Paper Series (October 2007), Paper 98.

[2] See here Ann Marie Slaughter, *A New World Order* (Princeton University Press, 2004).

[3] For an illuminating discussion of the differences see Christoph Moellers and Joerg Philip Terhechte, "Europäeisches Verwaltungsrecht und internationales Verwaltungsrecht," in Joerg Philip Terhechte (ed.), *Verwaltungsrecht der Europäeischen Union* (Baden-Baden: Nomos, 2011), 1473–52.

imperative for "regime change."[4] Even the UN and some of its "functional" organizations, such as the IMF and the World Bank, seemed to be caught by the sea change by taking leave of a narrow conception of their "functionalist" mission and enlarging their agendas. In this way the neo-classical orthodoxy that had informed the Washington consensus moved towards a "post Washington Consensus."[5] The latter contained some new policies such as poverty abatement, greater accountability of governments and international organizations, the promotion of the "rule of law," and the adoption of "best practices" developed by experts in informal networks, sometimes even with the participation of members of civil society.

Everything seemed to fit like a hand in a glove: accountability could be strengthened, participation enhanced, welfare augmented (as waste and corruption could be cut), and law – even though thoroughly "deformalized" and largely cut off from its traditional sources – could provide the discursive "space" within which we could pursue the necessary global collective goods. As one of the advocates of globalizing administrative law came to the conclusion that "even if supranational governance is limited and hampered by diverging traditions, cultures, and political preferences, developing a baseline set of administrative law tools and practices will strengthen whatever supranational policymaking is undertaken."[6] Of course, this take is perhaps overly optimistic and could rightly be characterized as a caricature, especially since other studies were much more cautious for both conceptual and empirical reasons.[7] But then again, before we dismiss such a caricature, we should bear in mind that a caricature does not claim to describe reality but consciously *uses distortions for heuristic purposes*, very much in line with Weberian ideal types.[8] Nevertheless, we then have to be particularly careful not to assume that all "good things come together," but be open to the possibility that the indicators of our findings might point in different directions.

In other words, we have to face the following difficulty: even if the analysed phenomena are true singly – and here the question of "truth" can remain contestable – they *need not be true* in conjunction, unless we are ready to commit an elementary logical mistake, called the fallacy of composition. This is why pat

[4] For a further discussion see Laura Zanotti, *Governing Disorder* (University Park: University of Pennsylvania State Press, 2011).

[5] See e.g. Narcis Serra and Joseph Stiglitz, *The Washington Consensus Reconsidered: Towards a New Global Governance* (Oxford University Press, 2008).

[6] Daniel Esty, "Good Governance at the Supranational Scale: Globalizing Administrative Law," *Yale Law Journal*, vol. 115, no. 7 (2006), 1490–62, at 1490.

[7] See Pierre Hugues Verdier, "Transnational Regulatory Networks and their Limits," *Yale Journal of International Law*, vol. 34 (2009), 114–71.

[8] This is of course Weber's purpose in creating "ideal types" as he elaborated on the distinction of types based on abstractions vs. ones based on typification. See Max Weber, *Gesammelte Aufsaetze zur Wissenschaftslehre*, ed. by Johannes Winckelmann (Tübingen: Mohr, 1971).

"stories" – similar to "elegant solutions" – usually engender some unease outside of mathematics. Thus there are some good reasons why we are told to look out for *disconfirming* evidence instead of simply amassing confirmatory data,[9] as a critical stance is particularly important in practical matters.

Our unease should be heightened by the realization of some "slippage" in the overall story, such as when "regime change" is suddenly "brought under" the Kantian notion of the "democratic peace," since this conjunction – depending on the interpretation one gives to it – can be quite at odds with Kant's thesis of how a *Rechtsstaat* will have to be perfected by a "cosmopolitan law." Here is not the place to probe the mistaken interpretations of Kant's teachings[10] by making him a member of the liberal chain gang,[11] save to note that some of his ideas do not sit well with some arguments of the present global constitutional and administrative law project, which is sometimes celebrated as harbinger of a cosmopolitan law. True, Kant had insisted on "publicity" as an important defining characteristic of law[12] in general, and thus also of administrative law. But what he meant by this term seems clearly at odds with the contemporary "informality" of norm-creation by expert bodies, or by groups that do their business in mainly "confidential" settings, notwithstanding some fig leaf participation by civil society (if it exists at all).

To that that extent Nico Krisch's proposal for a "pluralist global law,"[13] which squares the circle between "publicity" – necessary for "law" (his principle of public autonomy) on the one hand – and the great heterogeneity of norms existing in international life – to which legal pluralist have pointed by asking for mutual recognition and deference (principle of toleration) – might be a noble aspiration, but one that is difficult to meet in practice. For it is one thing to argue that contestation is part of law anyhow, and to celebrate the greater flexibility of pluralism. This stance allows for and encourages accommodation,[14] instead of having a strict constitutional proviso settle this issue in advance and once and for all. But it is quite another thing to believe that this "flexibility"

[9] See e.g. Karl Popper, *Conjectures and Refutations* (New York: Harper and Row, 1965).

[10] For a criticism of the Kantian "synthesis" with Liberalism as attempted by Rawls see Raymond Geuss, "Liberalism and its Discontents," in Raymond Geuss, *Outside Ethics* (Princeton University Press, 2005), 11–28.

[11] Michael Doyle, "Kant Liberal Legacies, and Foreign Affairs," *Philosophy and Public Affairs*, vol. 12, no. 3 (1983), 205–35; and *Philosophy and Public Affairs*, vol. 12, no. 4 (1983), 323–53.

[12] See Immanuel Kant's "transcendental formulation of public right": "All actions affecting the rights of other human beings are wrong if their maxim is not compatible with their being made public." "Perpetual Peace," in Immanuel Kant, *Political Writings*, ed. by Hans Reiss (Cambridge University Press, 1991), 93–130 at 126.

[13] See Nico Krisch, *Beyond Constitutionalism: The Pluralist Structure of Postnational Law* (Oxford University Press, 2010).

[14] *Ibid.* at 249.

is likely to enable us to make "binding" decisions that can resolve collective action problems and effectively pursue common policies by defending them against hold-outs and shirkers (not to speak of the enforcement costs that are likely to explode in case of "unsettled law").

Should we then "drop" this requirement as it is at odds with modern notions of expertise and informal processes, and the therefore arguably often "irresponsible" ways of law-making and decision-making? Here the Heidelberg Project examining the exercise of public authority by international institutions and insisting on the "publicness" of the laws and of the exercises of power attains its importance.[15] But the problem remains of conceptualizing more clearly what "publicness" means under modern conditions, which cannot be settled by authentically reproducing Kant's theory. After all, the latter was tied to a – meanwhile outmoded – criterion of publicity granting the "sovereign" ample discretion and making his ministers only accountable to him. Thus the issue is a conceptual one: whether the unrestrained plucking of certain concepts from a theory, or from different theories, is a legitimate exercise of "interpretative" freedom, or whether such a move represents a highly problematic exercise in "cherry-picking," which in turn can endanger fundamental rule of law values.

As we have seen, such dangers cannot be dismissed out of hand. Treating concepts as more or less free-standing as they allegedly attain their meaning by mere reference, "mirroring" the objects of the world "out there" – while knowing that this is hardly the case in the realm of praxis – is bound to haunt us with a vengeance. Furthermore, since we know that concepts function differently when used in different contexts – Descartes' "ego" is not that of Freud, and "reason" means something different for Aristotle, for utilitarians, and for Kant – we have to pay particular attention to the problem of such linguistic "false friends." Thus despite the fact the same word is used, *the concepts* differ. Thus we would expect that a philosophy such as Kant's, which starts with duties, with an abstract notion of law, with individual autonomy, with "regulative ideas"[16] that transcend any empirical justification, should lead to some dramatically different results than one that starts with tastes and desires, with

[15] Armin von Bogdandy, Philipp Dann and Mattias Goldman, "Developing the Publicness of Public International Law: Towards a Legal Framework for Global Governance Activities," in Armin von Bogdandy, Ruediger Wolfrum *et al.* (eds.), The *Exercise of Public International Institutions* (Heidelberg: Springer, 2010), 3–32. See also Stefan Kadelbach, "From Public International Law to International Public Law: A Comment on the Public Authority of International Institutions and the Publicness of their Law," in Armin von Bogdandy, Ruediger Wolfrum *et al.* (eds.), *The Exercise of Public International Institutions* (Heidelberg: Springer, 2010), 33–49.

[16] For a useful clarification of the notion of regulative ideas, see Maeve Cooke, "The Point of Discourse," *Social and Legal Studies*, vol. 17, no. 1 (2008), 97–103.

pre-social subjective rights,[17] with a felicific calculus employed by the legislator, and with the maximization of individual happiness.

Finally, even though it might be one thing to want to "complete" Kant's dream of a cosmopolitan order, it is quite another to bring it about, as practical problems do not consist only in the "clarifications" of principles but also, more importantly, in viability concerns and the difficulties of actual realization. Here some problematic issues concerning the motivations supplied by "belief" or "faith," and the determination of the "free will," might stand in the way of getting directly from the here of the "plan" to the "there" of realization. The problem is, then, for Kant not one of individual action but one of the "*historical process*" in which freedom and necessity interact. Kant himself suggested that if we understand human actions only within the *framework of causes*, then all we can see is blind *fate*. Only *with faith* can we conceive of "providence." But if we do not have faith – then we must at least believe in "nature" and its "design"[18] – a term which he then uses. It lays the foundation for the belief in historical "progress" that works behind the actors' backs and pushes them towards the final goal. Despite the "technical" overtones contained in the term of "nature's design," it is not hard to see that the latter is actually a secularized version of the Christian eschatology at basement prices – since (due to lack of interest) the Final Judgment has been eliminated. Hope springs not only eternal, but Kant has, as he himself admitted in the *Contest of Faculties*, a foible for a happy ends in historiography.[19] Whether we nowadays want to be saddled with such a conceptual baggage is of course another matter.

[17] See Kant's Third Definitive Article of a Perpetual Peace: Cosmopolitan Right shall be limited to Conditions of Universal Hospitality, that is a right to visit but not to "right of a guest." Kant, "Perpetual Peace," at 105f.

[18] See Kant, "Perpetual Peace," First Supplement, at 108f.: "This design, if we regard it as a compelling cause whose laws of operations are unknown to us, is called fate. But if we consider its purposive function … whereby it appears as the underlying wisdom of a higher cause, showing the way towards the objective goal of the human race and predetermining the world's evolution, we call it providence … We cannot actually observe such an agency in the artifices of nature nor can we even infer its existence from them … we must supply it mentally in order to conceive of its possibility by analogy with human artifices … But in contexts such as this, where we are concerned purely with theory and not with religion, we should also note that is more in keeping with the limitations of human reason to speak of nature and not of providence, for reason, in dealing with cause and effect relationships, must keep within the bounds of possible experience."

[19] In attempting to answer the question "Is the Human Race Continually Improving?," Kant notes that human history can be narrated in three different fashions: as regressing (which he considers *moral terrorism*), as "progressing" (considered *eudemonism* or *chiliasm* [*sic*!!] which he endorses), or as standstill (which he calls *abderitism* and which he rejects). The reason for his choice – obliquely referring to the French Revolution – he gives a few pages later: "Even without the mind of a seer, I now maintain that I can predict from the aspects and signs of our times that the human race will achieve this end and that it will henceforth progressively improve without any more total reversals. For a phenomenon of this kind which has taken place in human history can never be forgotten, since it has revealed

These preliminary considerations give rise to three further questions by which we can better assess the global administrative/cosmopolitan argument. The first has to do with the issue of which debates this construct *has missed* or not mentioned, even though they seem, at least partially, germane to the administrative law project. The second question is whether there is an identifiable set of prescriptions that gives some coherence to this notion, which allows us to raise new questions for assessing the legitimacy of the identified new law-making processes beyond the state. The third question concerns the issue of "democracy" and participation, since it is the "democracy-enhancing" potential that global administrative law stresses by insuring greater transparency and accountability and by organizing a surrogate political process. It thereby makes a virtue out of the complaints about the hollowing-out of democracy through the "denationalization"[20] of politics, by identifying new opportunities for non-traditional forms of accountability and participation.[21]

It is here where the promise of global administrative law lies. But even if the identification of certain principles establishes global administrative law as a sufficiently well-articulated set of concerns and "puzzles," short of showing that it can indeed make good on its wider claim that it is "democracy-enhancing," much of its allure might be lost. Instead, people might actually conclude that for that purpose the better strategy lies in resisting the present trends, given that people often do not like what they see in the "globalized" world. While such "resistance" might not be of much help either, as we might be powerless to get the genie back into the bottle, a closer analysis might at least prevent us from barking up the wrong tree. It might very well be that democracy in the sense of a meaningful participation in making binding decisions has become a nearly non-realizable project. Both politics and legislation have meanwhile escaped domestic structures while they are at the same time not being properly covered by international law or representative global institutions. But before we jump to such conclusions and put our hope in some *ex post* judicial review of some "juristocrats" (with dubious legitimization) who are eager to "balance"[22] and tell us what we ought to want, we had better inquire a bit more closely into the actual practices within which democratic politics usually takes place. Here the

in human nature an aptitude and power for improvement of a kind which no politician could have thought up by examining the course of events in the past." "The Contest of the Faculties," in *Political Writings*, ed. by Hans Reiss (Cambridge University Press, 1970): at 178 and 184 respectively.

[20] See Michael Zürn, *Regieren Jenseits des Nationalstaats: Globalisierung und Denationalisierung als Chance*, 2nd edn. (Frankfurt: Suhrkamp, 2005).

[21] This is the sympathetic reading that Susan Marks offers in respect to the global administrative law project. See Susan Marks, "Naming Global Administrative Law," *New York University Journal of International Law and Politics*, vol. 37 (2005): 995–1001.

[22] On different notions of balancing in US and German administrative law, see Moshe Cohen-Eliya and Iddo Porrat, "American Balancing and German Proportionality: The Historical Origins," *International Journal of Constitutional Law*, vol. 8 no. 2 (2010): 263–86.

close links between constitutional law and administrative law come to the fore, as both try to regulate the exercise of public power. Both implicate each other and attain their meaning from the various links that obtain between them. This makes a brief discussion of various administrative law systems necessary (as discussed in section two), before we can try to make the case for the existence of a "world administrative law" (section 3) and probe its democracy-enhancing potential both domestically and globally (section 4). Some critical remarks on e-democracy follow in the conclusion.

Administrative law: a comparative perspective

As we have seen, the global administrative law project takes place against the background of long-standing discussions in various legal systems concerning the different "solutions" that mediate the tensions between the "sovereignty" of legislative institutions and the needs of a modern welfare state facing a nearly dizzying array of new "tasks" (*Staatsaufgaben*). Here neither the old night-watchman model, nor even that of the *Polizeystaat*[23] provides a viable template. But while the ample transfer of power to administrative agencies was everywhere the response to the social changes ushering in the "administrative state," the particular "solutions," as well as their justifications, differed markedly. They differed not only among the various legal systems – such as the common law and civil law systems – but also even within the common law family itself, as exemplified by US and English administrative practice.[24] While improper delegation and *ultra vires* provide some commonality and while certain parallels across systems can also be found – for example the decision by the French Conseil d'État in *Prince Napoleon*[25] can be read as a case analogous to *Marbury*

[23] See Hans Maier, *Die Aeltere Deutsche Staats- und Verwaltungslehre*, 2nd edn. (Munich: Beck, 1980).

[24] See e.g. the "laying" procedures by which Parliament has to submit its subordinate regulations resulting from delegated legislation for an *ex post* parliamentary review while in the US judicial review is entrusted with this task. Differences also exist in the possibility of appeal of an administrative decision. In England the possibilities for an appeal of a substantively "wrong" decision by an agency is limited to explicit grants of such a right in the authorizing legislation, as opposed to the judicial review that centres on the "*ultra vires*" problem. Only in the 1960s after the passage of the Tribunals and Inquiries Act did courts abandon their deferential attitude and subjected delegated normative powers to review in terms of principles of natural justice. See e.g. *Rich* v. *Baldwin* (1964) AC 40 HL, as quoted in Peter Lindseth, "The Paradox of Parliamentary Supremacy: Delegation, Democracy and Dictatorship in France and Germany 1920–1950," *Yale Law Journal*, vol. 113 2004): 1341–415, at 1410f.; see also Florian Becker "Die Bedeutung der *ultra vires* Lehre als Masstab richterlicher Kontrolle oeffentlicher Gewalt in England," *Zeitschrift fuer auslaendisches oeffentliches Recht und Voelkerrecht*, vol. 61 (2001), 85–105.

[25] *Prince Napoleon*, Conseil d'État Decision of February 19, 1875, Recueil 155. As in *Marbury* v. *Madison* the Conseil d'État established judicial review (against the previous presumption of political discretion for acts in the domain of the executive). It revoked a "political

v. *Madison*[26] as both dealt with the powers of governmental officials – such parallels are, at a second look, not as illuminating as first assumed. After all, the Conseil d'État is a strange creation, as de Tocqueville had noticed when he tried to explain this institution to his American friends,[27] and over the years the differences have increased. Not only does this council nowadays have to share powers with two other "supreme courts" (Court de cassation for criminal and civil matters, and since 1958 with a proper constitutional court – the Conseil Constitutionnel), it judges cases in the first instance (appeals against decrees), but also on appeal (gross negligence, legal error) and, more and more, on final appeal. It proceeds largely by adversarial rather than inquisitorial procedure and bases its decisions largely on precedents, which is an oddity in civil law systems.[28] Thus Carol Harlow is right when she points out that, for an adequate comparison, the focus on one institution would be too narrow. For her the historical record suggests that:

> administrative law is more than a command and control system centred on courts whose principles are developed in judicial review actions. It includes and even centres on the legislation set in place by government and administrators for the implementation of policy … in most systems administrative law is Janus-faced. The second perspective sits uncomfortably, however, with the rule of law ideal adopted by economic liberals and purveyed in global space through the agency of international trade law.[29]

For example, if we probe a different facet of administrative law, that is the entitlement to information, we find similar differences, even within common law legal systems. Thus the Freedom of Information Act[30] belongs in the USA as much to administrative reality as does the Administrative Procedures Act,[31] while British law, until recently (2005), treated information as proprietary and thus governmental agencies could not be compelled to divulge it.[32]

By taking this wider picture into account, we not only notice the great variety of "solutions," we also see that various historical political struggles are

appointment by Emperor Napoleon III who had made his nephew (Prince Napoleon) a high raking military officer. His name was deleted by the subsequent government of the Third Republic from the register of officers. Prince Napoleon wanted that deletion reversed but lost the case on the merits."

26 *Marbury* v. *Madison*, 5 US (1 Cranch) 137 (1803).

27 See Alexis de Toqueville, *Democracy in America* (London: Penguin, 2003), 123f.

28 See the fascinating study by Bruno Latour, *The Making of Law: An Ethnography of the Conseil d'Etat* (Oxford: Polity, 2010).

29 Carol Harlow, "Global Administrative Law: The Quest for Principles and Values," *European Journal of International Law*, vol. 17, no. 1 (2006), 187–214, at 192.

30 Freedom of Information Act of 1966 (5 U.S.C. Sec. 552, amended 1996, 2002, 2007).

31 Administrative Procedure Act, 60 Stat 237 (1946, as amended by 80 Stat. 378 (1966) and 81 Stat. 54 (1967).

32 See Patrick Birkinshaw, *Freedom of Information* (Cambridge University Press, 2010).

inscribed in them. Within Europe alone we encounter at least four different approaches to the administrative *problematique* for which paradigmatically the French administrative judge on the one hand, and the Scandinavian ombudsman (forgoing judicial review) on the other, stand at opposite ends. The British model of upholding plenary jurisdiction of ordinary courts over governmental prerogatives has already been mentioned, while the German model provides again for judicial review but not in terms of a general due process or "reasonableness" clause. It requires that all enabling legislation has to specify clearly the content, purpose, and scope of the delegation to the executive and explicitly reserves a certain domain of powers that cannot be delegated (*Grundgesetz* (GG) Article 80).

Of course, parallels to the American non-delegation doctrine can be drawn, but it is questionable again whether such a comparison is that fruitful, precisely because the practices in different systems are part of a certain tradition and have evolved in a different way. Again, a quick look at the "constitutional review" issue in France and Germany when compared to the USA is instructive. Here historical trajectories are also more telling than "structural" comparisons. Thus in France it was the inability to find a solution to governmental instability that led in the Fourth Republic to a rule by "decree" rather than legislation – despite the explicit prohibition of legislative delegation in Article 13 of the Constitution in force! This experience then weighed heavily on the constitution-makers of the Fifth Republic to prevent such a misuse of powers, while at the same time ensconcing a reserved domain for executive action (Articles 34 and 37 of the Constitution of October 1958). This attempt misfired again and the Conseil d'État took it upon itself to oversee administrative action, despite the best efforts of both de Gaulle and Debré to eliminate judicial review. Similarly the "meaning" of Article 80 in the German *Grundgesetz* is better understood if one is familiar with the flaws of the Weimar Constitution, in particular with the fatal notion of presidential rule, abetted by Article 48. It allowed for virtual wholesale delegation of powers by parliament to the president that practically eroded any discernible distinction between legislative and executive power.

This brief excursion into comparative law shows that one need not go as far as Légrand, who views law as a product of a specific *mentalité*[33] – a dubious point already made by Savigny some time before – to see that legal concepts are not free-standing entities, or "modules" that can be plugged into whatever system according to the maxim of "one size fits all." They are rather the result of historical conjunctures, of specific political compromises, and of specific trials and errors. Their "function" is, therefore, crucially related to those events and developments in which certain interests became ensconced and govern later

[33] Pierre Legrand, "European Legal Systems Are Not Converging," *The International and Comparative Law Quarterly*, vol. 45 no. 1 (1996), 52–81, at 60.

decisions. To describe these trajectories, for example, as a "levelling-up process" or "convergence" – occasioned by some inferred "needs" – or as an "evolutionary response" seems pretty heroic.

The simple truth is that history, like nature, does not have a *telos* (unless you are a believer, as discussed above) and – to make things worse – the evolutionary metaphor, although allegedly drawn from "science" rather than "religion," is not helpful either. After all, evolution is "blind" depending on two interacting processes, one of random change presupposing large numbers, the other of selection. Without specifying either one of them (as Luhmann fails to do, for example),[34] the talk of evolution becomes meaningless. This is not even to mention the "minor" problem that cultural transformations occur through conscious production, not through blind trial and error. Thus we might change and end up with different solutions or regimes without necessarily being closer to a common goal, or converging onto one "solution." While convergence might happen – and here evolutionists beware – biology would probably consider such an occurrence a rather mixed blessing, because the "requisite variety" for further trials is thereby seriously impaired. Consequently, such a process could be considered a "degenerative" rather than a productive one. From an "evolutionary perspective," we therefore should appreciate variety much more! Unfortunately, the misuse of the evolutionary metaphor in describing actually instrumental and/or teleological reasoning in judicial decision-making creates not only confusion, but "authorizes" imperial strategies.

All of these considerations seem to be pretty bad news for an attempt to distil certain abstract principles (and perhaps also some pretty substantive values) and thereby create new tools not only for the settlement of disputes in different "free-standing regimes," but also for mediating the tensions of national and international, or of public and private law. The claim that such a mediation will be "democracy-enhancing" has to fill an even taller order. It will be the task of the next two sections to provide an overview of the project and then examine its potential for a new form of cosmopolitan democracy.

Making the case

The argument for the emergence of a global administrative law has to establish not only that such a body of rules or principles exists, but it also has to demonstrate that these principles represent a set of rules that mutually support each other in safeguarding elemental procedural and substantive values inherent in the rule of law. In order to make the case for its distinctiveness and for the existence of a genuine set of administrative law principles, such a proposal therefore

[34] For a further discussion see my "Using Constructivism against some Constructivists: The Case of Luhmann's Theory of Law and its Account of Transformative Change" (mimeo September 2011).

has to distance itself somehow from the pluralist emphasis in the "governance" discourse investigating unconventional law-making processes, and it also has to keep its distance from the more ambitious attempts of the cosmopolitan turn of a constitutionalism beyond the state.

Of course no hermetic separation is possible since a new form of "constitutionalism" with a small "c" is advocated – although again with slightly different emphases. Administrative law stresses the importance of "super statutes,"[35] while constitutional lawyers focus more on "constitutional moments." Here elections and the changes in the body politic[36] allow for a remaking of the "real" constitution, outside of the formal amendment process of the constitution with a capital "C." Thus the establishment of independent regulatory agencies in the aftermath of the New Deal certainly "revolutionized" US constitutional law. These agencies are not like administrative bodies under executive control but possess independent rule-making power and have discretion and adjudicative functions for assessing particular acts, while remaining subject to judicial review. In short, they function outside the classical separation of powers scheme and of the context of the powers parcelled out to the states and the federal government by the Tenth Amendment. The question arises, therefore, whether some administrative law principles – which obviously have deep roots in the cultural and political traditions of a particular political system – can be "lifted" and applied elsewhere in the hope of doing similar work there, or whether such attempts are akin to "playing tennis with the net down," that is simply missing the point.[37]

As to disembedding these rules and principles from their political–cultural context, Carol Harlow has remarked:

> It is difficult to see it all in terms of a set of neutral apolitical concepts … (which) has been defined as a "sophisticated form of political discourse." Stripping away its skins reveals administrative law encased in constitutional law by which it is nourished and to which it owes its being. Constitutional law is in turn wrapped in, and permeated by the prevailing political and

[35] See e.g. William Eskridge, Jr and John Ferejohn, *A Republic of Statutes: The New American Constitution* (New Haven: Yale University Press, 2010).

[36] See e.g. Bruce Ackerman, "The Living Constitution," The 2006 Oliver Wendell Holmes Lectures, *Harvard Law Review*, vol. 120, no. 7 (2007), 1738–812.

[37] This metaphor had been invoked by the poet, Robert Frost when asked in 1966 whether he would not like to try his hand in free verse. "I'd as soon write free verse as play tennis with the net down." It was then used as the title for an article on the constitutional law/administrative law nexus in the US legal order by two authors who opposed the use of administrative law as "surrogate for constitutional federalism." Here Gillian Metzger's thesis that contemporary interpreters are free to substitute other criteria if those alternatives promote better public values came in for criticism since the administrative state was part of an uneasy compromise, but which nevertheless entailed Congress' primacy in delegating powers. See Stuart Minor Benjamin and Ernest A. Young, "Tennis with the Net Down: Administrative Federalism without Congress," *Duke Law Journal*, vol. 57 (2008), 2111–155.

> governmental culture. It is these deeper values which help to determine, amongst other things, when and why and where people turn to law or government. The mirror image of Légrand's notion of *mentalité* is the terminology of "background theory" or mind-set in use amongst English public lawyers to describe the deep values which infuse constitutions and legal systems. Behind rules and concepts ... lie habits, customs and ways of thought derived from historical experience. These unarticulated premises infuse both constitutional law and judicial decision making.[38]

This is not to say that legal principles or legal traditions are fixed and cannot "borrow" from other systems, but it does say that there are usually some problems with this transfer and something usually gets lost in translation. Precisely because much of the advocacy by Stewart for a reform[39] of US administrative law took place in the 1970s – against the background of the civil rights movement and a well-institutionalized representative system of government – the chances of finding a similarly hospitable environment at the global level seem slim indeed, as Stewart frankly admits.[40]

The specific historical development of US administrative law also matters as it did not occur within law itself, but outside the discipline in – *mirabile dictu* – political science. This can explain the strong process orientation that is the opposite of the abstract construction of administrative law categories we encounter in civil law systems. As Woodrow Wilson pointed out (when he still was a professor of political science at Princeton): the idea of a public administration presupposes an idea of the state and of its duties, which had arrived in the USA only after the Civil War and through industrialization. This is why "no one wrote systematically of administration as a branch of the science of government until the present century."[41] Frank Goodnow,[42] also a political scientist at Columbia, took the argument a step further by arguing that this failure was more one of legal theory and classification than of an alleged non-existence of such a branch of law covering the area that constitutional law left unattended.

Administrative law originally intended to prevent the unlawful exercise of official power against private persons, but subsequently assumed a broader scope by institutionalizing a surrogate political process in which the interests and values, which go beyond those of the persons directly impacted by the

[38] Carol Harlow, "Voices of Differences in a Plural Community," *The American Journal of Comparative Law*, vol. 50 (2002), 339–67, at 350.

[39] See Richard Stewart, "The Reformation of American Administrative Law," *Harvard Law Review*, vol. 88, no. 8, (1975), 1667–813.

[40] See Richard Stewart, "US Administrative Law: A Model for Global Administrative Law," *Law and Contemporary Problems*, vol. 68 (Summer/Autumn 2005), 63–108, at 73.

[41] Woodrow Wilson, "The Study of Administration," *Political Science Quarterly*, vol. 2 (1887), 197–222, at 198, as quoted by Oliver Lepsius, *Verwaltungsrecht unter dem Common Law* (Tübingen: Mohr Siebeck, 1997), at 24.

[42] See Frank Goodnow, *Comparative Administrative Law* (New York: Putnam's Sons, 1893).

regulation, can be represented. This stronger form of "participation" in administrative decision-making was to promote the transparency and responsiveness to social interests and values that otherwise would not be safeguarded by relying solely on electoral responses or the proper delegation of powers. Here the expansion of due process rights and of a judicial review examining whether "arbitrary or capricious" criteria had been used come to the fore. Such an assessment includes whether agencies took into consideration relevant information supplied to them and whether the responses to such evidence were indeed sufficient for buttressing their actual decisions. The burden of proof is increasingly on the agency, which can no longer simply claim discretion due to properly delegated powers.

In this context the global administrative law project attains its plausibility. In its emphasis on greater transparency, accountability, and enhanced procedural fairness, it makes a prima facie case that decisions made within, for example, a transnational "regime" would not only be more effective but also more legitimate. By improving on due process and judicial review, it is hoped that regimes also increasingly converge, as the "constitutional" elements embedded in administrative law would make themselves felt. By this "normative stealth" the existing fragmented international legal order could be amended without the cumbersome process of normal law-making. The existing "living" law, as in Kant's argument about nature's design, is put to work for the larger constitutional project. It now has an administrative tinge since it is not based on legislation (treaty-making) or dispute settlement among contending parties, but consists "of legislative and adjudicatory elements."[43]

However, aside from the traditional international administrative law developed by international organizations, and different from the cooperation of national administrative agencies making decisions on transnational concerns – such as regulating extraterritorial effects of domestic actions or engaging in cooperative regulatory equivalence determinations, or the mutual recognition of[44] standards – the new *global administrative space* is configured differently. It is no longer only one in which intergovernmental networks are representing the "disaggregated state" that Slaughter has described[45] and that Kingsbury *et al.* call "distributed administration."[46] Not only are domestic officials no longer the sole, or perhaps not even the most important part, they now interact in hybrid organizations consisting of state and private actors, as we have seen. Increasingly purely "private" networks are also producing regulatory outputs, such as the ISO standards, which are used domestically, or international organizations, such as the WTO. They can become "hard" law despite the flaw

[43] Benedict Kingsbury, Nico Krisch and Richard B. Stewart, "The Emergence of Global Administrative Law," *Law and Contemporary Problems*, vol. 68 (2004/2005), 1–63 at 17.

[44] *Ibid.* [45] See Slaughter, *A New World Order*.

[46] Kingsbury *et al.*, "The Emergence of Global Administrative Law," at 21.

of their pedigree. Thus what characterizes this new global administrative space is a common commitment to problem-solving rather than going through the cumbersome channels of formal law-making and implementation by domestic legislation.

While this argument might sit well with proponents of best practices (whatever works!), it is less convincing in the context of legitimacy since the integrity of administrative law might be affected. Domestically, challenges to the integrity of administrative law posed by pluralism, capture, and "privatization" are real enough. But administrative law here enjoys some leeway, as long as the whole process is still built around clear institutional structures and conceptions of "delegation" and review. In other words, we are not just banging the ball around in a court. Instead, we are still playing tennis, where a net is raised and rules are applied by umpires who are safeguarding the integrity of the game, instead of just insuring certain "outcomes." On the other hand, the informality of norms, the diffusions of responsibility in a multilevel governance system, and the lack of a locus for deciding on priorities and trade-offs between different sectors put severe constraints on "transposing the tools from domestic administrative law" to this new space, as the authors of global administrative law freely admit.[47]

While administrative law is thus a wide field, there is a tendency to make the output of administrative agencies the centrepiece and measure the outcomes by this yardstick. This move is not innocent, as it suggests that the "constitutional issue" of the separation of powers and legitimacy are no longer central. The observation has two implications for the global administrative law project. First, since administrative agencies are operating outside of the classical separation of powers scheme, the analogy to "free-standing regimes" comes to mind. But such an analogy raises the issue of democratic legitimacy *for both* domestic and international agencies. Second, a certain "morphology" is now available for comparison – nearly as in the old structural–functional paradigm – showing which "functions" are fulfilled by which institutional structures. Thus some international organizations possess regulative functions by having institutionalized strong tribunals, but they might lack a regime-level administrative body, such as the WTO. Others can create binding norms such as the Security Council's 1267 Committee on targeted sanctions, although it lacked in legitimacy – until the introduction of an ombudsman for de-listing requests – since some of its actions violated basic rule of law values. This legitimacy gap is also visible when binding international norms:

> adopted by treaty based regimes ... allow no, or only limited discretion in domestic implementation, short-circuiting the role of domestic administrative law. In other cases especially in horizontal methods of regulatory

[47] *Ibid.* at 53.

> cooperation, domestic implementation is accomplished through informal determinations or exercises of enforcement discretion that are not subject to procedural requirements and especially in the case of enforcement discretion, are also not ordinarily subject to judicial review. [48]

Given these "defects," the European Union seems – despite its often criticized "deficits" – like a good bet, as one of the advocates of the global administrative law program[49] admits. But if this is the hidden teleology, then the global administrative law project is much less "free-standing" than assumed, since a considerable amount of political structures have to be in place. In the EU the regime members legislate collectively, the Commission is the administrative body entrusted with regulation, the countries administer these regulations distributively through their governmental agencies, and rules regulate individuals and legal persons directly under supervision of the European Courts. Of course, the democratic deficit remains because only the Commission is entrusted with rule-making and the European parliament has no legislative initiative or delegation power. But the incorporation of a strong human rights regime – in response to the earlier criticisms in various *Solange*[50] decisions – seems to bear out the argument of "levelling up" the regulatory regime, which originally covered only the freedom of movement for goods and persons.

These plausibility arguments – so dear to functionalists and their "demand for regimes" advocates [51]– can be contested, however, by empirical findings, by conceptual and logical objections, and by being attentive to the value courts attach to political questions, such as the value of the "state" and its historical compromises. In the latter case courts might establish "margins of appreciation" for the respective member states rather than opting for uniform criteria, such as those of universal subjective rights, sometimes "found" even *praeter legem*.[52] While a full discussion of these problems is beyond the limits of this Meditation, some preliminary remarks seem in order.

[48] Stewart, "US Administrative Law," at 69. [49] *Ibid.* at 95f.

[50] For a discussion of the various twists and turns of the *Solange* jurisprudence of the German Constitutional Court, see Julian Arato's discussion of the Lisbon Judgment reviewing the previous *Solange* decisions (Maastricht etc.). Julian Arato, "A Preemptive Strike against European Federalism: The Decision of the Bundesverfassungsgericht on the Treaty of Lisbon," October 9, 2010, available at www.ejiltalk.org (accessed September 28, 2013). See also Andreas Fischer-Lescano, Christian Joerges and Arnold Wonka (eds.), The German Constitutional Court's Lisbon Ruling: Legal and Political Science Perspectives (Universitaet Bremen, Zentrum fuer europäeische Rechtspolitik), Paper 1/20010.

[51] Rober Keohane, "The Demand for Regimes," *International Organization*, vol. 36, no. 2 (1982), 525–55.

[52] Here the rather questionable jurisprudence of some recent ECJ decisions in the social area have drawn considerable criticism calling for a "check" on the Court, e.g. by a former judge of the German Constitutional Court and former President of Germany Roman Herzog. See Roman Herzog and Lueder Gerken, "Stop the European Court of Justice," available at http://EUobserver.com/7/26714 (accessed September 28, 2013).

Let us begin with the issue of "universal" standards and/or the levelling-up. At first blush the record in the EU seems to be mixed. First, while procedural justice requires impartiality, legal systems differ in granting a right to a hearing, and to a reasoned decision. For example, English law protected the right to a hearing, but access to a court could be ousted through legislation. And there does not seem to be a strict requirement of giving reasons for a decision either. Similarly, in French law the chief concern was the rights of the defence, but due process principles were not available in administrative proceedings where penalties were not involved. Here the European Court of Justice (ECJ) decisions in *Johnston*[53] and *Heylens*[54] demanded higher than national standards, as it "constitutionalized" the access principle and established effective judicial protection in administrative matters. Furthermore, since discretionary decisions are not subject to a substantive reassessment, the European Court insisted on procedural criteria allowing it to "verify whether the factual and legal elements upon which the exercise of the power of appraisal depends were present."[55]

But considering whether we are reaching a "higher level" overall might raise more difficult questions. Here questions of the legitimacy of administrative law standards, and of the proper role of judges, attain their importance. For example, in the case of the UK is the judge acting as an agent of Parliament, enforcing the latter's intent, or is Parliament itself only to legislate on the basis of a "rule of law" conception, as Lord Steyn has suggested when applying the principle of legality in administrative law cases. Or indeed are the values of administrative law free-standing and derived from common law itself, as Lord Cook has articulated?[56] This of course becomes more difficult to decide when the "European" dimension has to be taken into account. Thus while *Factortame*[57] made short shrift of the doctrine of parliamentary supremacy, the two other opinions by Steyn and Cook seem more "progressive," even though the latter squarely falls back on the common law tradition itself.

There is of course the tendency to invoke "uniformity" as the criterion for universal validity and to resort to an outcome-oriented jurisprudence when the going gets tough. "Reasonableness" might then be just a step away from "utility," raising the question of whose conception of "reason" or utility should prevail. If national rules always have to yield to community rules because of "uniformity," such a decision premise could eventually undermine the legitimacy of the

[53] Case 222/84 *Johnston* v. *Royal Ulster Constabulary* (1986) ECR 1651.

[54] Case 222/86 *UNECTEF* v. *Heylens* (1987) ECR 4097.

[55] Case C-269/90 *Technische Universitate Muenchen* v. *Hauptzollamt Muenchen Mitte* (1991) ECR I5469 para. 13.

[56] Janet McLean, "Divergent Legal Conceptions of the State: Implications for Global Administrative Law," *Law and Contemporary Problems*, vol. 68, no. 3/4 (2005), 167–88, at 178.

[57] See C-213/89 *Factortame* [1990] ECR I-2433.

legal systems of all member states and thus also of the European project itself. Kant's benign despot then seems just around the corner. Powerful constitutional courts, such as the German Bundesverfassungsgericht, have, therefore, traditionally resisted such a move.[58]

Even if we perceive a levelling-up effect,[59] its role in enhancing rule of law values is thereby not a foregone conclusion: vide the rather contorted interpretations of the ECJ in *Kobler* (brushing aside arguments of *res judicata* and judicial independence),[60] or of the ECtHR in *Osman*. There the court held that the "right to fair trial" (Article 6 of the European Convention on Human Rights) entails a tort suit in case of negligence by the police, dismissing the "striking-out" procedure that parliament had provided.[61] Thus if we assume that, for example, the "timeliness of response" is an intrinsic part of the rule of law, then allowing tort actions where they were originally disallowed means accepting the potentially unlimited expansion of tort claims, which can now be brought under the guise of human rights. In the end such a move could seriously jeopardize "timeliness" as a rule of law value. Agencies and courts will be affected as they will probably be overtaxed. The former must now devote more and more time to "documentation" (rather than to the mandated tasks), thereby decreasing the level of services, which, of course, will give rise to further complaints. Courts will then be overburdened by the claims pushed by "advocates" (not inappropriately called "ambulance chasers" in the vernacular), who sense that here a new field for lucrative services is opening up.

The idea that everything fits like a hand in a glove, and that greater rationality in administration will also result in a constitutional bonus, might be little more than an illusion. The same problematic consequences appear in other areas. If local autonomy could be strengthened by the principle of subsidiarity, and by judicially accepted "margins of appreciation," looking at something through the lens of "competition policy" and efficiency, for example, inevitably makes uniformity and centralization the preferred outcome, as the *Viking* and *Laval* decisions of the ECJ show.[62] Even if we celebrate the greater "order" these decisions imposed on the hodgepodge of European law, we should bear in mind that this comes at a price. It favours the interests of the free movement

58 See BVerf.Ger. 89, 115 October 12, 1993 (Maastricht).

59 For a still useful assessment see Juergen Schwarze, "Judicial Review of European Administrative Procedure," *Law and Contemporary Problems*, vol. 68 (Winter 2004), 85–105.

60 See Case C-224/01 *Koebler* (1986) March 1.

61 *Osman* v. *UK* (1998) 29 EHRR 245, and *Z* v. *UK* (2001) 2 FCR 245.

62 See Case C-438/05 *International Transport Workers Federation, Finnish Seamen's Union* v. *Viking Line ABP*, Judgment of December 11, 2007. Case C-341/05 *Laval un Partneri Ltd* v. *Svenska Byggnadsarbetarefoerbundet*, Judgment of December 18, 2007. For a further discussion, see Christian Joerges and Florian Roedel, "Informal Politics, Formalized Law and the 'Social Deficit' of European Integration: Reflections after the Judgment of the ECJ in Viking and Laval," *European Law Journal*, vol. 15, no. 1 (January 2009), 1–19.

of capital over those attempting to protect the rights of collective job action, ensconced both in national legislation and Article 135(5) EC.

This leads me to the last point: whether an administrative law that has been taken out of a public context and applied to more or less autonomous functional systems, is paving the way for a larger global constitutional moment. Two issues can be raised: one concerns the logical coherence of such an argument, the second addresses the issue of whether such moves will also give pride of place to such "constitutional" principles deriving from *historical experience* rather than from universal norms or overarching values. Here principles, such as checks and balances, subsidiarity (federalism),[63] threshold requirements, and so on come to mind. They largely concern constitutional design questions rather than "ultimate values" or human rights. Nevertheless, as Kant reminds us, they are intrinsically related to the functioning of democratic systems and ultimately to the "publicity" of law.

In this context one of Kant's suggestions provides food for thought, as he argued that one cannot rely on moral precepts to solve the constitutional problem, since it is only through a good constitution that "people can be expected to attain a good level of moral culture."[64] This problem is then touched upon again by the gloss that the problem of setting up a state should be possible even "among devils – so long they possess understanding."[65]

> For such a task does not involve the moral improvement of man; it only means finding out how the mechanism of nature can be applied to men in such a manner that the antagonism of their hostile attitudes will make them compel one another to submit to coercive laws … We can even see this principle at work among the actually existing (although as yet very imperfectly organized) states. For in their external relations, they have already approached what the idea of right prescribes, although the reason for this is certainly not their moral attitudes.[66]

This argument has implications for the first issue mentioned above, that of coherence: even if it were possible to take certain rules out of different systems and use them for some small "c" constitutionalism in another context, it does not follow that the resulting assembly would also exhibit these constitutional qualities. As already pointed out, unless we are ready to suspend the laws of logic, we have to realize system properties cannot simply be read off from their parts and vice versa. This leads me to the second issue: the role of historical

[63] Here the experiences with Art. 72(2) GG and its various reformulations, as well as the case law, do not seem encouraging for finding justiciable standards outside of particular "deals" between the German federal government and the Länder about reallocating jurisdictional competences. For a further discussion see Greg Taylor, "A Slow Death for Subsidiarity," *International Journal of Constitutional Law*, vol. 7 (January 2009), 139–54.

[64] Kant, "Perpetual Peace," at 113.

[65] *Ibid.* at 112. [66] *Ibid.* at 113.

experience ensconced in principles that safeguard systemic needs, such as a mixed constitution, different spheres of justice and so on. As the discussion showed, attempts of solving these problems once and for all by some form of "ideal theory" or by recourse to universal values or "human rights"[67] should make us suspicious. Furthermore, given the transformative changes of modernization, even the Madisonian "factions" might also no longer be inevitably plural, as they have long escaped the fetters of federalism and the spaces of the bounded "republics." While these principles protecting "systemic" values still embody some "lessons," it is no longer that clear what they imply for our situation.

I cannot not pursue these larger questions further here. Rather in the next section I shall take up the more limited argument about the democracy-enhancing quality of these "surrogate" processes of "participation" by private actors and groups of civil society that have become a distinct feature of global law-making.

Democracy and its institutions

What remains to be shown is whether these principles, when applied in a "reasonable" fashion, are indeed democracy-enhancing or whether they quickly become incoherent when freed from their moorings in historical institutional structures. At the most general level we notice that "reasonableness," "reason," and "public reason" are by no means self-explanatory and self-justifying. Thus "reasonableness" obviously contains both outcome-oriented criteria as well as procedural ones, but which ones should be weighing in more heavily is hardly decidable *in abstracto*. Whether, for example, the exercise of free speech "necessitates" the distribution of leaflets, which leads to littering and imposes costs not only on the city but also on particular residents, might be relatively easy to decide. We can invoke "public reason" and perhaps legal precedent for our stance. Littering is then simply one of those costs of democracy that we as members of "the public" have to bear. But such a conclusion does not follow directly from either "reason," or from the notion of "publicity." A well-ordered society under a benign despot could come to the opposite conclusion – and the despot entrusted with the public weal most certainly will do so, especially if he uses "reason" in the restricted, "modern" sense of simple goal maximization. Thus he could argue that free speech and publicness were guaranteed by the freedom of the press and the media and by the freedom of assembly, but free speech did not entail the distribution of handbills that cause "littering."

[67] For a challenging analysis stressing the importance of "criticism," see Albena Azmanova, *The Scandal of Reason: A Critical Theory of Political Judgment* (New York: Columbia University Press, 2012).

When we try to "apply" the notions of "interests affected" in order to meet the "publicness" criterion, we notice similar difficulties. No wonder that we often fall back on quite questionable pragmatic criteria, that is take those who scream the loudest or who volunteer as bona fide "representatives" of their "constituencies," and pass over the voiceless and invisible ones who might be most affected but cannot "get to the table." This example shows some shortcomings of relying solely on "private" interests and of the dangers of administrative law not infused by "public values." More importantly though, we have to realize that the "interest" of the general public is usually not represented at all, or enters rather late. In collective bargaining public interests usually come into play only when the parties reach a stalemate and an arbitrator is entrusted to "jaw-bone" them.

These last considerations also have implications for the principle of subsidiarity[68] and for the claims of cosmopolitan constitutionalism. Let us begin with subsidiarity. We notice quickly that this principle need not necessarily be "democracy-enhancing" and could perfectly well do its job among benign or dastardly potentates. Thus, the Persian Empire was ruled by "satraps," many of which were "tyrants" (in the narrower or wider sense of the word) and enjoyed great local autonomy. Their rule was limited only by the duty of transferring some taxes to the Great King, of not interfering with his "foreign policy," and of providing support in case of war, all of which fits the paradigm of subsidiarity. Apparently too much is made of this principle.

Equally important is a second observation concerning the legitimizing factor that links "subsidiarity" with the notion of an entitlement to "voice" for "common" problems. In a way this is a political version of the previous "interest" argument, as the "*res publica*" is the "common thing." However, it should be clear that the principle is indeterminate without a prior definition of a public. Thus it might very well be that that which "touches all should be decided by all" (*quod ad omnes tangit ab omnibus approbetur*).[69] But who are the "all"? Are they all humans living now, the "human race" in general (adding responsibilities and interest of future generations), or does it even comprise "planetary life" (including viruses and bacteria)? Leaving the historical political world behind, we quickly get into theological problems, such as which "interests" should be protected (those living now or those to come: is there a right to be conceived,

[68] See e.g. Matthias Kumm, "The Cosmopolitan Turn in Constitutionalism: On the Relationship between Constitutionalism in and beyond the State," in Jeffrey Dunoff and Joel Trachtman (eds.), *Ruling the World?: Constitutionalism, International Law and Global Governance* (Cambridge University Press, 2009), 258–324. See also Matthias Kumm, "Democratic Constitutionalism Encounters International Law," in Sujit Choudry (ed.), *The Migration of Constitutional Ideas* (Cambridge University Press), 256–93.

[69] For a further discussion see Friedrich Kratochwil, "Human Rights and Democracy: Is there a Place for Actual People(s)?," in Ulrich Fastenrath *et al.*, *From Bi-lateralism to Community Interests: Essays in Honor of Bruno Simma* (Oxford University Press, 2011), 488–504.

even though the right to be born is limited); or questions of species chauvinism, or even of a new version of the theodicy problem (on the basis of on what criteria should we decide which forms of life deserve protection, or can be eliminated).

It is therefore not surprising that "humanity" is chosen in order to limit the problems. But "humanity" is an equally ambiguous symbol as it usually does not stand for "all people" existing, but for a specific way of life. It embodies a civilizational standard, which an ever-expanding list of "human rights" supposedly instantiates. The fall-back on human rights, however, solves the problem only by displacing it. Thus Henry Shue,[70] who had originally made the argument for the human "right to food," quickly moved from the subjective right to the role of institutions as soon as the implications of such a subjective right became clear. True, Pedro in Colombia who, as a share-cropper, is eking out a meagre living, gets "affected" by the decision of his *padrón* to terminate his "lease" (since the owner now wants to produce flowers for the European market). Since Pedro has nowhere to go, he is clearly worse off. But most of us would argue that the problem has to be taken care of by national insurance schemes, perhaps by land reform, new local zoning laws, or the creation of cooperatives, rather than by requiring compensation from those who are several steps removed, as for example the chap in Europe who wants to give roses to his new "squeeze" on Valentine's day.

This is a useful reminder that the "interests affected" are always mediated by institutions, and that they are the result of political struggles and historically contingent arrangements rather than resulting from universal principles or values. It is here that politics becomes important as it is concerned with the "particular" and the possible, rather than with the universal or trans-historical. It is through politics that we not only decide which goods are "public," that is are goods "for" a public, but also determine who is entitled to enjoy them and who is left outside.[71] Precisely because these "common" goods are largely "club goods" (that is *are* exclusive), their provision entails choices concerning which ones, for whom, and in what order and priority they are supposed to be procured. Here questions of membership and of making binding and effective decisions arise. Law then becomes the sediment of such decisions and a powerful instrument of rule. Indeed, without a clear definition of a public, it would be difficult to justify any form of majoritarian decision-making.

Although there is nothing that would logically prevent us from expanding the particular group (of which we are a member) to "mankind," it should be obvious that such an extension is dependent on the "defining" capacity for a

[70] Shue, *Basic Rights*.

[71] For a further discussion see Friedrich Kratochwil, "El fracaso de la 'falla del mercado': vuelta a pensar en bienes 'públicos' y 'privados' con base en la riqueza de las naciones de Adam Smith, y el derecho romano," *Foro Internacional*, vol. 50, no. 2 (2011), 422–45.

public. Here something like Kelsen's normative force of facticity comes to mind, which is not derivable from universal principles justified by logic (universalization) or supreme value(s). It would involve a logical mistake of the first order to assume that since such an extension is "thinkable," it thereby has to exist in reality. This would be like saying: because I can think of a winged horse, there has to be a Pegasus (and presumably all we have to do is to look for it and catch it). Because I can think of a perfect being, God exists (Descartes), and so on.

In dealing with this issue of the constitution of a "public" obliquely, Kant speaks of the necessity of a "patriotic" attitude "where everyone in the state, not excepting its head, regards the commonwealth as a maternal womb [*sic*!], or the land as the paternal ground from which he himself sprang and which he must leave to his descendants as a treasured pledge."[72] He intimates thereby – somewhat at odds with the "constitution among devils" argument – that abstract principles and reason are *not* sufficient to solve the problem of social solidarity and of law's effectiveness. Kant not only reiterates Socrates' "noble lie" in the *Republic*[73] but also echoes Rousseau's concern with the necessary attitudinal changes in each citizen when political choices are at issue which then can claim to embody the general will (rather than being simply the summation of preferences of the *volonté de tous*).

These remarks have important implications for the issue of democracy or the "democracy-enhancing effect" of deliberations, even though actual participation in decision-making could be curtailed through representative schemes. For one, Kant, himself a republican and suspicious of the democratic riff-raff, did not consider it illegitimate[74] if some people were only indirectly represented, as long the laws passed were not in violation of the "natural laws of freedom."[75] Thus "voting" might indeed not be the only way in which individual autonomy and political freedom can be attained. But then all the more weight has to be carried by the notion of public deliberation and by argument that some surrogate processes can be used for legitimizing law-making in the international arena.

Both *topoi* are part of the cosmopolitan as well as the constitutionalization discourse and both have been used for the claim of an emergent global

[72] See Immanuel Kant, "On the Common Saying: 'This may be True in Theory, but does not Apply in Practice'" in *Political Writings*, ed. by Hans Reiss (Cambridge University Press, 1970), at 74.

[73] See Plato, *Republic*, Book III, 414b–415c.

[74] See Immanuel Kant, "Metaphysics of Morals," sections 46 and 47 in *Political Writings*, ed. by Hans Reiss (Cambridge University Press, 1970), where he adds the "attribute of civil independence" as a qualification for suffrage that rules out all those "who are obliged to depend for their living (i.e. for food and for protection) on the offices of others" while leaving open the dependence of the state but not for purposes including welfare recipients but rather "academics" drawing the line vis-à-vis mere "tutors." *Ibid.* at 139f.

[75] *Ibid.* at 140.

administrative law. It is through the inclusion of elements of "civil society" that both the democratic deficit of national legislation and of the unorthodox decision-making in international organizations and public/private partnerships, or simply private but "functional" networks, can be cured. However, a closer look suggests that not all is well and that there seems to be a strange disjuncture between the scholarly interest in these new forms of organizations and their actual practice.[76] In the discussion below I want to focus on two organizations located close to the opposite ends of the institutionalization dimension: the WTO on the one hand and the EU on the other.

Let us begin with the WTO. The pleas for a constitutionalization were originally voiced by Robert Jackson[77] in the context of curing some of the defects of the GATT/WTO framework. They were pursued later, in a different fashion, by Petersmann,[78] or Trachtman and Dunhoff,[79] or Cass.[80] But whatever the scholarly arguments were, these concerns are hardly reflected in WTO practice. Not only does the rule-making in the thirty-five committees of the WTO remain largely hidden, only to be pierced occasionally by a closer look of some scholars,[81] there also seems little interest in organizational reform, quite aside from the fact that the Uruguay Round agreements certainly did not set up a constitutional system of checks and balances. The charter did not endow a WTO body with autonomous legislative or regulatory capacity, enshrining, for example, a "right to trade" (human or otherwise),[82] nor does the organization claim that its rulings are directly applicable in the domestic legal system[83] (nor do the major trading partners allow for such direct effects). So the lack of interest in constitutional issues should not come as a surprise.

To that extent all weight has to be borne by the judicial decision of the Dispute Settlement Undertaking (DSU), in particular the Appellate Body, which according to one proponent shows a "promise" to generate constitutional

[76] See the critical remarks by Jeffrey Dunoff, "Constitutional Conceits: The WTO Constitution and the Discipline of International Law," *European Journal of International Law*, vol. 17, no. 3 (2006), 647–75.

[77] John Robert Jackson, *Restructuring the GATT System* London: RIAA, 1990). See also his "The WTO 'Constitution' and the Proposed Reform: Seven Mantras Revisited," *Journal of International Economic Law*, vol. 4, no. 1 (2001), 67–78.

[78] See Ernst Ulrich Petersmann, "Human Rights and International Economic Law in the 21st Century," *Journal of International Economic Law*, vol. 4, no. 1 (2001), 3–39.

[79] Dunoff and Trachtman, *Ruling the World?*

[80] Deborah Cass, *The Constitutionalization of the WTO* (New York: Oxford University Press, 2005).

[81] See Andrew Lang and Joanne Scott, "The Hidden World of WTO Governance," *European Journal of International Law*, vol. 20, no. 3 (2009), 575–614.

[82] See Ernst Ulrich Petersmann, "Time for a United Nations Global Compact for Integrating Human Rights into the Law of Worldwide Organizations," *European Journal of International Law*, vol. 13, no. 3 (2002), 621–50.

[83] See the Panel Report on US Section 301–310 of the Trade Act of 1974, WTDS1 52/R para. 7.72 (27 January 2000).

norms and address wider issues through its dispute resolution capacity.[84] Here particular weight is usually put on the *Shrimp Turtle* case, which emphasized that Appellate Body panels have authority to receive information from non-state actors[85] – an avenue strenuously pursued by some groups in civil society, always eager to submit *amicus curiae* briefs. This possibility, according to Cass, "lends credence to the constitutionalization claim and has significance from a democratic and constitutional design perspective."[86] But as subsequent evens show, *Shrimp Turtle* at the Appellate Body level was a swallow that did not make a summer. Disturbed by the prospects of "civic involvement," the Appellate Body issued an official Communication, urging extreme caution in accepting *amici curiae* briefs. All seventeen requests filed in a subsequent case[87] were promptly denied. The narrow construction that the Appellate Body provided was that it would only entertain arguments raised in an *amicus curiae* brief if "these arguments were taken up in written submissions … of any party or third parties"[88] (even though practice seems to be a bit more lenient – merely appending the briefs to the official submission will get them noticed at least).[89]

A similar picture emerges when we scrutinize the Appellate Board decision in *Shrimp Turtle* as to the administrative law principle of having to give notice to the affected others. As we have seen, it only held the US restrictions illegal under GATT Article XX because the USA had failed to give notice to its trade partners[90] as to the measures it had adopted. When actual "constitutional" issues were raised in other cases, such as when India asked that since it had adopted certain restrictions because of balance of payments reasons, such complaints should be submitted to another branch of the WTO as "jurisdiction was assigned to the Balance of Payment Committee and the General Council," the Appellate Body unequivocally rejected such an (arguably) inchoate "separation of powers" argument:

> After reviewing the relevant WTO texts and prior panel reports, the AB concluded that "India failed to advance any convincing arguments in support

[84] See Cass, *The Constitutionalization of the World Trade Organization.*

[85] *United States – Import Prohibitions of Certain Shrimp and Shrimp Products* WT/DS 58/ AB/R 12, October 1998.

[86] Deborah Cass, "The Constitutionalization of International Trade Law: Judicial Norm Creation as the Engine of Constitutional Development in International Trade," *European Journal of International Law*, vol. 12 (2001), 39–75, at 42.

[87] *European Communities – Measures Affecting Asbestos and Asbestos Containing Products*, Communications from the Appellate Body WT/DS1 35/9 (November 20, 2000).

[88] *United States – Investigation of the International Trade Commission in Softwood Lumber from Canada* WT/DS 277/R at 88 n. 75 (March 22, 2004).

[89] See *Mexico –Tax Measures on Soft Drinks and Other Beverages* WT/DS 308/ AB/R March 6, 2006.

[90] *United States – Import Prohibitions of Certain Shrimp and Shrimp Products* WT/DS 58/ AB/R 12, October 1998.

> of the existence of a principle of institutional balance that requires panels to refrain from reviewing the justification of balance of payment restriction."[91]

Thus, despite the fact that decisions of the DSU conform to important due process values (transparency, providing a hearing, giving reasons for its decisions, and allowing for review), as well as to more substantive standards (such as upholding legitimate expectations, establishing an ends/means test, and insisting on the least restrictive means available), they did not do much to advance democracy-enhancing elements by which administrative law is linked to constitutional concerns. Finally, although both the panels and Appellate Body arrived at their decisions through a process of deliberation, we must not forget that this type of deliberation occurs under significantly constrained conditions.

This is after all the reason why developing countries have legitimate complaints.[92] Even though they might be "participating"[93] in a much fuller sense than members of civil society, they never meet on a level playing field, as it has been pre-empted. As Andrew Lang and Joan Scott point out:

> The point here is that global administrative law does not operate in a normative vacuum; it takes shape in settings which are already populated by precepts and premises which reflect particular values and distributive outcomes. Thus to say with approval that global administrative law operates in favour of enhanced accountability is to say that it operates in favour of those rules, principles and standards which are already entrenched in the relevant regime. There is consequently a danger that global administrative law will be passive in relation to the underlying benchmarks for accountability which it serves, and as somewhat oblivious to the consequences or fairness of these.[94]

To that extent it really is not that important that many of the adopted measures, such as those taken by the important Committee on Sanitary and Phytosanitary Measures (SPS Committee), are not legally binding. The Committee also takes great pains to phrase its decisions in indicative rather than prescriptive form, using normative "shoulds" rather sparingly, while stressing its intention to "assist" the members and to "facilitate" communication. But, then again, we should remember that perhaps the "hardest" norms are those that "naturalize" an issue area by pretending that this is just the way that things "are," as in the order: "Tomorrow at eight you are here waiting for your call." Focusing largely

[91] WT/DS90/AB/R (August 23, 1999), at para. 105, as quoted in Dunoff, "Constitutional Conceits," at 658.

[92] See e.g. B. S. Chimni, "Co-option and Resistance: Two Faces of Global Administrative Law," *New York University Journal of International Law and Politics*, vol. 37 (2005), 799–827.

[93] See e.g. Robert Delonis, "International Financial Standards and Codes: Mandatory Regulation Without Representation," *New York University Journal of Law and Politics*, vol. 36 (2004), 563–634.

[94] Lang and Scott, "The Hidden World of WTO Governance," at 609.

only on the technical issues of rule-making and their character of formal "softness" or "hardness" diverts attention from the programmatic issues, from raising questions of the legitimacy of the existing agenda, and the interests which are thereby protected.[95]

As some thoughtful advocates of global administrative law admit, limiting one's attention to the existing institutions and relying on procedural discipline to improve governance, global administrative law "risks providing a patina of legitimacy without effecting any basic change, [and] diverts attention from the need for more fundamental reform … (It) may also end up sapping political accountability rather than compensating for its deficit."[96] It is at this level of agenda-setting and of institutional structure that reforms have become necessary.[97] Before we fear for the liberal character of the institution, let us remember that the reciprocal exchange of market concessions in GATT is arguably more mercantilist than liberal and free trade-friendly. It is technocratic and secretive since it is largely based on the belief that it is the openness of national "parliaments" that provides easy access for lobbying groups to protective legislation. Such defects can then only be cured – so the official ideology has it – by bringing to bear some "expertise" on the matter, entrusting it to some specialists who, far from the madding crowd, are then able to provide some "rational" solutions in "behind closed doors" meetings.

Finally, we should be aware that this form of politics is also a largely producer-driven politics. It fails to see not only to whom the benefits of free trade accrue in a time when intra-firm trade rather than arm's length trade make up the largest part of "trade," but also where the *present opposition* to "free trade as usual" originates. Since it is not the producers who have to compete with imports who nowadays call for protection, the task is no longer one of replacing "import politics" with "export politics," as was the case formerly. Rather the opposition to free trade nowadays emerges largely from non-trade concerns, such as environmental degradation, local "de-industrialization," wage dumping, issues of cultural diversity and so on, which a new political agenda has to address. Given these problems the old focus on tariffs or other impediments to trade then seems rather quaint. As Joost Pauwelyn suggests, these new trade politics have to be based on:

[95] See David Zaring, "Informal Procedure, Hard and Soft in International Administration," *Chicago Journal of International Law*, vol. 5 no. 2 (2005): 547–635.

[96] Richard Stewart and Michelle Ratto-Sanchez Badin, "The World Trade Organization and Global Administrative Law," (2009) NYU Public Law and Legal Theory Working Papers, Paper 166 at 29.

[97] See here the critical remarks by Debra Steger that the WTO still resembles a bicycle with the USA and the EU as front and back wheels, while the explosion of membership makes the present system more like a bus careening downhill with many drivers but no one certain where to go. Debra Steger, "The Culture of the WTO: Why it Needs to Change," *Journal of International Economic Law*, vol. 10 (2007), 483–95, at 484.

> a new form of "embedded liberalism," combining a world-wide general support for free markets and globalization with calls for a policy space to protect the environment, workers, consumers and citizen concerns at large, as well as to enact industrial and rural policies to boost economic development. This "new trade politics" must break with the GATT 60 years old operating system of "reciprocal exchange of market access concessions," a system that is producer driven, mercantilist and premised on a mistrust of domestic politics. Instead the operating system of "new trade politics must be consumer/citizen driven … based on proven welfare gains that come with free trade … and [it must] be fuelled by more, rather than less, input by domestic parliaments (open politics rather than closed politics)."[98]

Pauwelyn's call for a new agenda, outside the fetters of "functionality" and his plea for a politics involving actual representative institutions, is a useful reminder that appeals to legality, vested rights, and principles of good administration remain powerless to address most issues of common concern. We no longer live in the world of the former "club" of privileged members with more or less obvious, conflicting "interests." Pauwelyn puts his finger on a sore spot that we also notice when we look at the EU's policies of involving "members of civil society" in its policy-making.

In the latter case we certainly can tell a success story of European integration that leads from a narrow conception of "sectoral" cooperation, to the creation of a common market, driven by an ordo-liberal vision, to one in which the legal doctrines of "direct effect" and "supremacy" created new rights of "the people." The latter had before led only a shadowy existence as buyers and sellers, or as purveyors of labour power. But it was hoped their empowerment would finally push the process to more "participatory" modes of policy-making, which stress transparency and the involvement of groups representing new issues and concerns.[99]

The hopes for such a change were dimmed after some referenda had stopped the seemingly automatic process of integration. Nevertheless, the measures adopted after 2000 by the Commission for enhancing participation followed the trend begun in 1993 when the Council and the Commission had granted individuals access to their documents – although subject to numerous exceptions – following up on an inter-institutional Declaration on "Democracy, Transparency and Subsidiarity."[100] In this context, the issuance

[98] Joost Pauwelyn, "New Trade Politics for the 21st Century," *Journal of International Economic Law*, vol. 11, no. 3 (2008), 559–73, at 572f.

[99] See e.g. Francesca Bignami, "Three Generations of Participation Rights before The European Commission," *Law and Contemporary Problems*, vol. 68 (Winter 2004), 61–83.

[100] See Decision 93/74/EC Council December 20, 1993 OJ (L 340); Decision 94/90 Commission Decision of February 8, 1994 on Public Access to Commission Decisions 1994, OJ (L 46) 58.

of a White Paper[101] by the Commission, its subsequent "Communication on Consultation"[102] and the "Better Regulation Initiative"[103] are further milestones. The Commission broached not only the idea of "co-regulation," that is it would solicit advice from certain "target groups" before deciding on a policy initiative, it also wanted to involve them in the formulation and implementation process, by incorporating in its directives the standards developed by associations and groups of civil society. There is of course a certain tension between a wider conception of "participation" by groups of civil society "speaking for" new, more general "civic" issues (such as data protection), and a narrower conception, based on the "interests" typical of traditional corporatism.

As the White Paper itself and later developments showed, the "interest" of the Commission in involving "civil society" concerned largely technocratic issues, such as getting better information and making its decisions more acceptable to the "relevant" groups, thereby presumably saving on enforcement costs. The White Paper could not be any clearer: "Participation is not about institutionalizing protest. It is about more effective policy shaping based on early consultation and past experience."[104] Thus the fall-back to a technocratic "good management" philosophy is obvious. To leave no doubt, a subsequent "clarification" of the White Paper frankly admitted: "the guiding principle for the Commission is therefore to give interested parties a voice, not a vote,"[105] thereby clouding the issue that such a voice can only be had by well-organized groups that are "around" in Brussels and that have found favour with the Commission. While the Better Regulation Initiative also speaks of a "broad range of stakeholders," it is silent on how they are to be identified. Its emphasis on "getting rid of red tape," of getting the "job done" and avoiding "unnecessary" bureaucracy shows a clear technocratic mindset, ironically making the Brussels bureaucracy the main protagonist in the fight against "bureaucracy"![106]

It comes as no surprise that "participation" shows the usual skewed picture and did not reap the expected positive results, as a careful examination of the policy cycle in both the "sustainable development" initiative (indicated by the

[101] European Commission, *White Paper on European Governance*, COM (01) 428 final, July 25, 2001.

[102] Communication from the Commission, "Towards a Reinforced Culture of Consultation and Dialogue: Principles and Minimum Standards for Consultation of Interested Parties by the Commission," COM (02) 704 final, December 11, 2002.

[103] See EU Commission, *Better Regulation Simply Explained* (Brussels: EU Commission, 2006); see also "3rd Strategic Review of Better Regulation in the EU," Commission Communication (COM (2008) 32, January 30, 2008).

[104] *White Paper on European Governance*, at 15.

[105] Communication from the Commission, "Towards a Reinforced Culture of Consultation and Dialogue," at 5.

[106] See EU Commission, *Better Regulation Simply Explained*, at 3.

critical internal review report) and in the regulation of chemicals (REACH) showed.[107] Deidre Curtin, a long-time observer of representational issues in the EU, suggests that the consultative processes within the EU are:

> hardly a way forward in a polity which is characterized by such fragmentation at all levels and such a system of "informal politics." The EU system is arguably too diffuse and too fragmented to support the analysis that the creation of an elaborate interest-driven "talking shop" will effectively introduce more transparency and more deliberation or more consideration of the "public interest" into the policy-making process.[108]

Conclusion

At this point it is appropriate to assess some of the implications of this discussion. I began with the problem of the increasing "denationalization" of politics and its attendant democratic deficit. It is this deficit that some advocates of the constitutionalization and global administrative law debate want to "cure" by identifying a corpus of rules, sufficiently free of the "state." In this way the "rule of law" could be implemented – even in the absence of the familiar structures of political systems – by also availing themselves of new opportunities that an increasingly "pluralist" global law-making process provides. But since "rule of law" principles are rather heterogeneous, as "values," as well as organizational issues such as "checks and balances enter the picture, the crucial question is whether we are able to arrive at a set of "universal" principles that can meaningfully guide our practical choices both at the "design" level of robust institutions, and at the level of actual choices. While I consider this (still) an open question, I am not persuaded that the proposals we have seen can make good on their promises.

It might very well be a virtue to broaden our analysis to more "pluralistic" understandings of both law and politics, outside the "formal law" and outside the "Constitution" with a capital "C." But issues of power and its legitimization are thereby not solved. To say that we can leave it to "judges" or arbiters in

[107] See Patrycja Rozbicka, *Myth and Reality of EU Policy Processes and Interest Group Participation. Why are Interest Groups not as Successful as They Would Like to Be?* Ph.D. thesis in the Department of Social and Political Sciences, EUI, Florence 2011. Rozbicka comes to the following conclusions: "The results are striking. The EU political environment does not appear to be as open as its supporters would like it to be perceived. Coalition-building proves to be the most efficient element of successful interest-group campaigns. The quality and independence of the input of interest groups is questionable. And finally, it emerges that external factors, which should be irrelevant, have a major influence – both positive and negative – on groups' input transposition, depending on the situation" (Abstract).

[108] Deidre Curtin, "Private Interest Representation or Civil Society Deliberation: A Contemporary Dilemma for European Governance," *Social and Legal Studies*, vol. 12 (2003), 55–75 at 64.

various dispute resolution "mechanisms" is no answer until and unless we can find a solution to the problem of "which court" and which "judges," speaking in "whose name," shall take the case. Only then can their decision marshal assent and provide *ex post* for the resolution of a concrete dispute, but also *prospectively* inform other actors of what they need to take into consideration when making their choices. Thus in leaving the "juris-generative" role of "publics" unaddressed,[109] global administrative law is in danger of degenerating into ad hocery and technocratic rule. For a *kadi*-type of justice that works in traditional societies, common traditions are necessary, but they are no longer available to us, and appeals to ultimate values will not do. The resulting "regulatory" turn is therefore rather "jurispathic,"[110] as Ming Sung Kuo has rightly suggested.

This led me to the second part of my inquiry – the representative element in informal or semi-formal settings. Here the EU served as my foil. One crucial point emerging from the inquiry was that involving interest groups and members of civil society to cure the "democratic deficit" of decision-making is no solution, but becomes increasingly part of the problem. The reason is simple: the greatest number of the groups of civil society share the flaws of the regimes themselves, that is that they are one-issue organizations, perhaps preventing the rise of broad-based cross- sector institutions that could be making binding decisions. Furthermore, it has also become apparent that "technocratic" and functionalist styles of decision-making are not conducive to the emergence of more representative groups that could articulate a more comprehensive vision of what the "supranational" political project could be.

Finally, it seems that whatever type of civil society groups exist is not independent of the governing structures under which they evolve. Under such circumstances the move from government to governance is "fragmenting" civil society even further, as the ethos for speaking for the "whole" – observable both in Sieyes' conception of the "Third Estate"[111] and, in a different form, in Hegel (focusing on the civil servants as a "universal class"[112]) – gets increasingly lost. What remains are the interests that are no longer those of projects that need to be pursued "in common" as in the old *res publica*. Instead, what becomes "common" now are the pursuits in which we more or less universally engage in as *private* individuals. We are now shoppers, consumers, and people

[109] Ming-Sung Kuo, "Taming Governance with Legality: Critical Reflections upon Global Administrative Law," *New York University Journal of Law and Politics*, vol. 44 (2011), 55–102 at 34, available at: http://papers.ssrn.com/sol3/papers.cfm?abstract_id=1799549 (accessed September 28, 2013).

[110] *Ibid.*

[111] See William Sewell, *A Rhetoric of Bourgeois Revolutions: The Abbe de Sieyes and "What is the Third Estate"* (Durham, NC: Duke University Press, 1994).

[112] See Georg Friedrich Hegel, *Philosophy of Right*, transl. by William Wallace and A. V. Miller (Oxford University Press, 1967).

interested in gossip and "infotainment," who eagerly follow celebrities around (the latter having possibly become "spokespersons" for some "cause"), but we do not have much interest in public affairs.

As regulation increases, it seems beyond our grasp and we are content to become "subjects" again, "subjected" to virtual laws made in virtual spaces – somewhere "above" the state or "in-between" the interstitial spaces of "society" – in any case hidden from our view. And we content ourselves with being the bourgeois who loves his dogs or preserves his garden as a biotope for butterflies, frogs, or salamanders, or who just wants to make a buck as quickly as possible in the market (as this shows how smart we are) by trading via the laptop virtual goods such as options or derivatives. Besides, a "global" audience is always available by checking into various chat rooms, where one can meet like-minded "cosmopolititans." The fact that they live in Anchorage, Belo Horizonte, Mombasa, or Bhopal is then further proof of how widely "shared" these concerns are. The world is like a shop in which "ideas" and concerns can be traded, never mind that the "market," based on exit options, might never provide for those other forms of social bonding that Hirschman[113] considered necessary for social reproduction: voice and loyalty. If I do not like something, I can check out of the chat room according to my preference. Such a stance prevents the development of a serious engagement with public issues, and it also explains why most of the chat rooms on the Internet show a distinct tendency of sectarianism or radicalization over time. Since people are not forced to wrestle with the issues of realizing a common life, but prefer to spend their time with like-minded people,[114] the circle gets narrower and narrower as we "get to know" each other. (Significantly, Facebook has eliminated the "dislike" button!) Debates therefore lack both the requisite variety of arguments that a genuine deliberation about public issues requires, as well as the necessary existential seriousness that characterize "public" life.

Of course, there is a lot of uneasiness in this idyllic existence: the biotope might get touched by the electric company, which needs to build a new power grid for its "eco" electricity, the salamanders might get ironed out on a newly built road, and the market – which "cannot be fooled" as Margaret Thatcher assured us – might crash again. Then, of course, the "politics" of ire and resentment break loose, powerfully fuelled by "movements" – local, national, transnational. They now seem to be the only ones standing in for "fundamental values" so that we, enabled by the "leverage" of human rights and universal values, can catapult ourselves from our "private" preoccupations to universal concerns: preserving the planet, or safeguarding humanity. And since one

[113] Albert Hirschman, *Exit, Voice, Loyalty* (Cambridge, MA: Harvard University Press, 1970).

[114] For a further discussion of both the empirical and normative issue of "e-democracy," see Cass Sunstein, *Republic.com*, 2nd edn. (Princeton University Press, 2009).

cannot compromise on universal values, the discussion becomes shrill rather quickly. Violence ensues, spectacular actions make the headlines, and power seems to flow to those advocating "direct action." In a world where nobody is in charge, it is not surprising that the "citizen" has also disappeared. Thus there seems to be a lot more to do and at stake for democratic politics than is on the plate that is presented to us by the above-mentioned debates.

Meditation 7

The politics of rights

Introduction

Rights, and especially human rights, we are told, are fundamental. They serve as "trumps" in legal arguments[1] and are held to be of universal and trans-historical validity, identifying us as "humans" and not as a member (only) of this or that society.[2] Despite the fact that they appear at a certain time in history, their status is supposed to be based on their "transcendental" nature by either being part of a natural order of things, or by virtue of the fact that they are intuited. They can be "declared" but not "made" as are other laws, even though they need to be formulated to find their way into constitutional texts. Thus rights claims give rise to a specific "rights talk," which is, in spite of the fiction of its perennial existence, a specific modern phenomenon.[3] It reached one of its peaks by the end of the eighteenth century – after a relatively short incubation period during the English Glorious Revolution – in the American and French Revolutions,[4] and another in the post-Second World War era, particularly since the 1980s. Here the conjuncture of the "rights revolution" led first to the civil rights movement, and then to the adoption of a rights talk by transnational movements

1 See Ronald Dworkin, "Rights as Trumps," in Jeremy Waldron (ed.), *Theories of Rights* (Oxford University Press, 1984), 153–67.

2 To list just a few of the contributions antedating and taking stock of the exploding field, see Maurice Cranston, "Are there any Human Rights," *Daedalus*, vol. 112, no. 4 (Fall 1983), 1–17; H. L. A. Hart, "Are there any Natural Rights?," in Jeremy Waldron (ed.), *Theories of Rights* (Oxford University Press, 1984), 77–90; Chris Brown, "Universal Human Rights: A Critique," in Tim Dunne and Thomas Wheeler (eds.), *Human Rights in Global Politics* (Cambridge University Press, 1999), 103–27; Joseph Raz, "Human Rights," in Samantha Besson and John Tasioulas (eds.), *The Philosophy of International Law* (Oxford University Press, 2010), 321–38; Nicholas Rengger, "The World Turned Upside Down: Human Rights and International Relations," *International Affairs*, vol. 87, no. 5 (2011), 1159–78.

3 See e.g. N. E. Simmons' contribution to the modern rights debate in his "Rights at the Cutting Edge," in Matthew Kramer, N. E. Simmons and Hillel Steiner (eds.), *A Debate over Rights* (Oxford University Press, 1998), 115–233.

4 For an argument that rights are as much innovations in political practice as they are the result of conceptual changes (discoveries) and that they stand in close relation to "revolutions," see Jeffrey Wasserstrom, Lynn Hunt and Marilyn B. Young (eds.), *Human Rights and Revolutions* (London: Rowman and Littlefield, 2000).

that pinpointed gross violations of individual rights by governments worldwide. After the collapse of the main alternative utopia to the Western political project, that is "communism," the subsequent "silent revolutions" were increasingly fuelled by a "human" rather than merely a "civic" rights discourse.[5]

But despite the historical myopia, which hardly allows us to imagine a world in which rights do not play a decisive role, the "universality" of rights is usually established by amalgamating it with some notions of "natural law," or to the autonomy of the subject, a concern central to the Enlightenment. The emphasis on "reason" then provides the bridge between the subjective rights of modernity and the much older tradition of natural law, which goes back to the ontological speculations of Plato and Aristotle and later engendered the "order of things" argument and the medieval teachings of the *analogia entis*. We can also thereby link up with the Stoics, who influenced particularly Roman legal thought, and who used the trope of a "law behind the law" as guarantor of justice.[6] Since this "higher" law is supposed to pervade the "cosmos," it is "valid everywhere and at all times,"[7] thereby nobly eradicating the crucial distinction between the "is" and the "ought" and also the distinction between "what is right" and of "having a right."

It is this equivocal use of the term "right" in justifications that has made the "rights talk" in modernity the virtually exclusive source of legitimization. In the absence of God, "nature," and later the "people," rights have now become the placeholders for what was formerly the nearly unfathomable "other," the "holy," which commands respect and which is set aside and separated from the "profane." The importance of this "deep structure" influencing the at first rather technical issues of humanitarian law, trade law, or the debates on "cosmopolitanism" or on "unlawful combatants" in the war on terror, has been shown by Ann Orford and her collaborators in some fascinating studies.[8] But precisely because human rights have meanwhile attained the status of a religion for the agnostics, it should come as no surprise that many of the controversies we encounter in human rights, are also those that we find in religions. After all, ascertaining the will of God engenders conflicts in regard to doctrine, sources (tradition vs. texts), "recognized" rites and practices, interpretation and so on, quite aside from the vexing practical problems of how to deal with error, dissent (heresy), or transgression.

Thus we can also often observe a certain missionary zeal among human rights advocates and a stridency in the discourse, which Michael Ignatieff noticed

[5] See Samuel Moyn, *The Last Utopia: Human Rights in History* (Cambridge, MA: Harvard University Press, 2010).

[6] See Marcus Tullius Cicero, *The Republic and the Laws*, ed. by N. Rudd (Oxford University Press, 1998).

[7] *Ibid.*

[8] Ann Orford (ed.), *International Law and it Others* (Cambridge University Press, 2006).

when human rights are used as "idols."[9] It is then a small step to treat "dissidents" as "heretics" since they doubt the "foundational character" of human rights. In addition, branded as "relativists," they often have to suffer the *reductio ad Hitlerum*, which is a modern form of anathema. Thus the "rights talk" also obviously has a disciplining and not only an emancipatory function.

If the disciplining is left to the "community" of believers, they might *in extremis* prefer an exit from the church and splinter into "sects" rather than to engage in practices that are too latitudinarian, and which dilute the purity of the original message, be it truth, nature, God's word, humanity, whatever. But, not surprisingly, we also notice that whenever such foundational claims are raised, they are hotly contested, and the arm of public power is usually not far behind. The charge of corruption of the youth and the introduction of new gods forced Socrates to take the cup (and drink himself to death). The soul of a person denying the "natural order of things" – such as wearing men's clothes, as in the case of Joan of Arc – could only be saved by destroying the body. Today – in accordance with the norms of liberalism and its enlightened penology – perpetrators of crimes against humanity have to be convicted preferably by *supranational* courts, which now no longer exercise power in the name of a particular state or community but in the name of the universal humanity transcending any particularity and historical contingency. At least that much seems to be required by the narrative of progress.

Since under conditions of modernity power has mutated from occasional and *ex post* rectifying interventions meeting out exemplary punishment, to a much more diffuse mode of surveillance and of managing risks – as Foucault reminded us – the explosion of rights claims under the banner of human rights has also given rise to a gigantic surveillance and reporting system. It attempts to reshape societies by addressing not only their public institutions but by subjecting virtually all of social life to "capillary control." Here the campaign against smoking in terms of a "right to a smoke-free environment" – often executed in a way clearly intended to discriminate and/or humiliate – is perhaps only the most recent example of this trend.

Thus a fully fledged interrogation of the discourse on rights not only requires an investigation of the foundational claims (legitimization) that largely concern philosophical issues, but also an examination of the practices that are thereby authorized, demanded, or forbidden, constituting a particular "discipline" – both in the sense of knowledge claims and of concomitant practices – that shape the modern subject and the respective community. By finding its expression originally in a state that was supposed to put "rights" before the older notion of the common "good," the project of subjective rights is now placed in the larger horizon of the "world" and conceived as an evolving cosmopolitan order embracing all mankind.

[9] Michel Ignatieff, *Human Rights as Politics and Idolatry* (Princeton University Press, 2001).

As we shall see, the recent proliferation of rights – sometimes called the third or fourth generation of "human rights" – might have unanticipated consequences, such as empowering actors who are no longer "responsible" to anyone. Power gets diffused and is no longer bundled by specific institutions that are entrusted with making the political choices binding a discernable "public." The result might be that the former "citizens" are transformed not only into subjects of "global law," but also that they have become "clients" who must be taken care of by "helpers" and "experts." Paradoxically, the subjects no longer have to use their freedom for political action, since being loyal to the state seems passé and opportunities for exercising genuine "voice" or "loyalty" have largely evaporated. Law, celebrated as the expression of the subject's autonomy, is now being "pronounced" by a priestly class of juristocrats and servants of a utopia that no longer is beyond all time, but is "affirmed" in a cosmopolitan law that comprises the transformed versions of constitutional law, administrative law, free-standing regimes, *jus cogens*, and obligations *erga omnes*.

If this initial thumbnail sketch of the *problematique* of rights has shown one thing, it is that we here enter a conceptual minefield, where a simple clearing operation – relying on definitional fiat or on an "emerging" consensus – is unlikely to succeed. The first option is not available because when we talk about the justification of certain practices, questions of "truth" and definitional clarity are not at issue. The second alternative – to whose "pragmatism" I am personally quite attracted – articulated by Charles Beitz,[10] for example, is nevertheless problematic because it leaves too many ends untied and thus tends to displace the issues. For these reasons I have to rely here on an approach that combines criticism with "redescription," so as to illuminate why and where the puzzles of the "rights talk" arose, how they result from the language we use – the *Verhexung der Sprache* as Wittgenstein pointed out – and how we might, through some form of therapeutic redescription, overcome paradoxes and be able "to go on." Rather than being simple "errors," the problems we encounter point to genuine dilemmas that cannot be solved by looking harder at the "facts" or by "doing more of the same" – a favourite pastime of clueless "analysts" and administrators in cases where the intended outcome is not reached.

If radical uncertainty exists, if genuine dilemmas abound, and if no absolute foundations are in sight despite the attempted recourse to a (bare-bone) "humanity," then the pathos of having discovered "nature's design" (Kant), of knowing the "end of history" (Fukuyama), or of making "man the measure of all things" becomes stale. It can quickly turn into despair, or even rage, as our very existence seems suspended over an abyss. But then the only way out is to give up on the obsession that a meaningful life is possible only when we can build on ultimate certainties, which also have to be "eternal" and unchanging, since only in this way could our fears of insignificance and meaninglessness

[10] Charles Beitz, *The Idea of Human Rights* (Oxford University Press, 2009).

can be assuaged. Such a realization, however, requires more than a few changes in the concepts we use, and some substantive adjustments in our practices. Such a reorientation is more "existential" and it will not result in a new "theory" in which we can see the things as they "really" are. The "view from nowhere" – God's view, in modernity recast as an epistemological ideal – remains unavailable to us. The turn in our thinking it entails also does not result in an alternative comprehensive "program" of action, precisely because life has largely become a "do it yourself game without instructions," as the former templates have lost their exemplary pull.

These initial remarks seem to have three corollaries. One is that the reflections I offer are neither to be taken as "affirmations" of rights, nor as their "rejection." Given that rights have become so central in our tradition and in our practices, it would indeed be difficult to conceive of a "world" in which they had no place. Nevertheless, as some critics of rights[11] as well as some of their staunch defenders have pointed out, a world that consisted only of rights, in which the respect for one's fellow members depended solely on the ability of making strident "querulous claims,"[12] would not be a society most of us would like to live in. There is something to Bernard Williams' suggestion that systems of morality, in which rights have become virtually the only source of obligations, tends to discourage autonomy and cooperation among the actors and makes "blaming" others and "the system" the predominant mode of discussing common problems.[13]

The second corollary is that our largely instrumental understanding of law might be alright as a first cut, but is misleading in that it suggests that rights are just instruments with which we "work" on a pre-existing world, like a chisel on stones, instead of bringing to the fore their constitutive function and their role in structuring the "meanings" of the social world. Here the analysis necessarily becomes historical, as we have to get the question right before we can understand why and how rights provided an "answer," and this analysis has to precede the further explication of rights by, for example, a Hohfeldian typology. Thus even the well-elaborated concept of the right to one's body – which entails in our world a constitutional, perhaps even a "human right" to abortion – would not make any sense for members of a Neolithic tribal society and neither could it be sensibly used as a yardstick for criticizing their social arrangements, or those of Ancient Egypt.

This leads me to the third point – and perhaps the most controversial part of this Meditation – the doubt it casts on the proposition that issues of "validity"

[11] See e.g. Bernhard William, *Ethics and the Limits of Philosophy* (London: Fontana, 1985): 177.

[12] Jeremy Waldron, *Nonsense Upon Stilts: Bentham, Burke, Marx on the Rights of Man* (London: Methuen 1987), 196.

[13] Williams, *Ethics and the Limits of Philosophy*, at 172. See also Mary Ann Glendon, *Rights Talk: The Impoverishment of Political Discourse* (New York: Free Press, 1991).

can be meaningfully discussed only if we silently assume, or explicitly postulate, that there are "universal" standards. This position seems to me unpersuasive. It mistakes the particular historical answer that emerged in Western philosophy to the sophists' challenge to existing knowledge and morality, as the "only" possible answer. In the case of "natural law" the "answer" involved a reference to, and a grounding in ontology, whereby "true being" was considered as "unchanging." However, it should be obvious that this answer was quite at odds with that of the pre-Socratic speculations, as it is with that of modernity, which severed the link between the "is and the "ought." While the last argument seems to rebut "universality" as an unchanging a-historical standard, it does not by itself dispose of the notion that a definite (although no longer a-historical) standard is necessary, such as "utility," or even better Kant's notion of the free will determining itself according to the requirements of reason. Whether such a standard is actually required and helpful when we reason about rights or value conflicts will be discussed more fully in Meditation 8.

In order to elaborate on these claims, my argument takes the following steps. In the next section I address briefly the issue of natural law and show why and how natural law and natural right claims differ fundamentally. This demonstration intimates that the long historical "tradition" of "human rights" is not only an invention, but also one that muddies the waters. It does not allow us to inquire why some pre-modern societies – the medieval one to boot – could do without the notion of subjective rights. It also leaves us in the dark as to why and how the individual rights claims, based on "intuition" or nature, were an intrinsic part of the *political projects* of the American and French revolutions, as well as of the "fashioning" of modern subjectivity. A detailed examination of these problems represents the third part of this Meditation ("The paradoxes of claiming rights"). In section four I address the wider issue of how modern subjectivity and its particular links to society and the "world" created the semantic field in which "natural" or human rights could emerge and be action-guiding. We can thereby also see *the preconditions for human rights to function in different cultural contexts*, instead of taking simple "empirical" references (such as frequency counts to human rights in public discussions) as an indicator of their ability to convey meaning and direct action. I conclude with some brief remarks that set the stage for Meditation 8.

The archaeology of "right(s)"

Although some rights are said to be "human" or natural, predating or transcending society, they are also an integral part of the way we think about justice and about organizing a polity under law. Here questions of how law, which is "made" instead of "found," can be legitimated[14] is well exemplified by the debate

[14] For a general discussion see Christian Meier, *The Greek Discovery of Politics*, transl. by David McClintock (Cambridge, MA: Harvard University Press, 1990).

on whether laws are valid by nature (*physei*) or by legislation (*thesei*) in fifth- and fourth-century BC Greece, around which the tragedies and the Platonic and the Aristotelian responses to the sophistic challenge revolve. Aristotle provides two classical answers in his *oeuvre*. One is in his *Politics* where the "law is king" thesis (*nomos basileus)* is elaborated[15] – which later, as we have seen, becomes the classical *topos* for "rule of law" arguments. The second one can be found in his *Rhetoric* where he provides a particular interpretation of Antigone. This version has attained canonical status, probably due to its closeness to the subsequent Stoic speculation and Cicero's writings, but which is not well supported by the text.

Aristotle relies in the *Rhetoric* largely on other authorities such as Alkidamas, who stated in his Messenian oration: "God sent all men forth free; none has nature created a slave."[16] Being part of his discussion about different genres of speech – in this case, pleading before a court – Aristotle seems simply interested – as any good advocate has to be, in regard to his client – in strengthening Antigone's case, thereby nobly keeping his teachings about the "slave by nature" to himself.[17] But in doing so he actually also does considerable violence to the Sophoclean text.[18] He argues:

> Just and unjust acts are defined in relation to two kinds of law and in relation to persons in two ways: by law I mean on the one hand particular law and on the other general law, "special" being that one defined by each group in relation to itself, this being either unwritten or written down, and the general law being that of nature. For there is something of which we all have an inkling, being universal, right and wrong, even if there should be no community between the two parties, nor contract, to which Sophocles' Antigone seems to be referring in saying that it is just, though forbidden, to bury Polynices, as it is naturally right:
>
> Not from yesteryear, nor just today,
> Lives this command, but always. Whence it came
> None knows …
>
> …
>
> Furthermore, justice in relation to the person is defined in two ways. For it is defined either in relation to the community, or to one of its members what one should or should not do. Accordingly it is possible to perform just

[15] Aristotle, *Politics*, Book I, Chapter V (1254a7–1255a3).

[16] Aristotle, *Rhetoric*, Book I, XII, 2–5 at 1378b2-3, ed. and transl. by J. H. Freese (Cambridge, MA: Harvard University Press, 2006), 139.

[17] Aristotle, *Politics*, 12546 16–21. This argument was then used by Sepulveda against Las Casa, arguing that the Amerindians were slaves by nature. See John Crow, *The Epic of Latin America*, 4th edn. (Berkeley: University of California Press, 1992).

[18] For a good discussion of the various interpretations of Antigone from Sophocles to Anouilh and Lacan, see Françoise Meltzer, "Theories of Desire: Antigone Again," *Critical Inquiry*, vol. 37 (Winter 2011), 169–86.

> and unjust acts in two ways, either toward a defined individual or towards the community. The adulterer and mugger wrongs one of the individuals, the draft dodger the community.[19]

Since this passage is somewhat difficult, several things need unpacking. It should be clear, though, that the discourse is not about individual rights but rather about "what *is* right." Second, when Antigone appeals to "customary" standards, she claims that this custom imposes duties on specific people. She feels bound by the customary rules – "which Hades requires"[20] as she says – since she is the only one left to bury her brother, as all other members of the family have died. Thus her motive is not the vindication of her rights under a general "human rights" law, but issues from a duty to the gods of the underworld among which she also counts "justice"(!). Third, her loyalty is to a family member who transgressed the law of the city that forbade the burial of persons killed in "revolutionary" action. Antigone's brother Polynices had engaged in such action, and was killed as result of it.

This fact pattern does not easily square with Aristotle's claim that the more universal has to take precedence (so to speak as a reversal of the *lex specialis* rule). Rather we see here the "tragic" conflict when two different sources of law claim applicability and impose incompatible obligations on an actor. If anything, Creon's law invokes the more "universal" standard of equal treatment by the law, which unites all citizens, and which is applicable to all "cases similarly situated." Only in this way could the particular privileges of the noble families, which had enjoyed customary immunities, be overridden. Significantly, Antigone's other brother Eteocles, who was also killed but in defence of the city, is given an honourable burial by Creon, who refuses the same treatment to Polynices on the grounds "that the base should not fare as do the brave."[21]

This last remark hides a fourth problem. The criterion of "universality" becomes problematic when it invokes "custom." As we know from discussions of "custom" in international law, it requires not only considerable evidence but also some form of proof that a particular practice is considered "obligatory." But there is something even more implicit in Antigone's claim, that is that the "old" is the "original," the pristine, which deserves respect since everything subsequent is only an instance of "decay." Here a "return" to the pristine, to the golden age, or the return (revolution) to the original rights of Englishmen in 1688, fits this template. Of course, this assumption sits uneasily with the previous ontological assumption of the "true" (valid) as "unchanging and eternal."

Finally, from all of the above arguments it is quite obvious that Antigone is not speaking the language of "rights," but of "right" or "wrong." As H. L.

[19] Aristotle, *Rhetoric* 1373b, transl. by H. L. C. Lawson Tancred (London: Penguin, 1991), 125.
[20] *Antigone*, verse 519. [21] *Antigone*, verse 520.

A. Hart reminds us, "having a right" is to put forward a specific claim that does not simply coincide with the distinction of right and wrong. Thus the Ten Commandments are based on this distinction, but are so based without any conferral of "rights."

> Codes – and natural law arguments fall into that category – might prescribe certain duties and characterize actions as good or bad, right or wrong or appropriate or inappropriate, but do not involve notions such as the exercise of or claims to "subjective" rights. Rights deal with entitlements and justifiable interferences and thus they are different from other moral principles that consider the moral worth of actions either because the latter satisfy the requirements of good will, virtue, or are conducive to certain ends (happiness). Rights address questions of when, how, and why, it might be legitimate for one actor to limit the freedom of other(s) and determine their actions either as forbearances or demands which might justify coercion (including taxes!) in cases of non-compliance. On the other had it is clear that "having a right" might thereby entail being justified in doing the "wrong thing." An important feature of this justification is that the required actions by other(s) is not based on some moral quality of the required action but that it results simply from the "constitutional" requirement that a "certain distribution of human freedom will be maintained if (the claimant) is allowed to determine how that other shall act."[22]

To that extent rights can be said to be possessed by or to "belong" to individuals – analogous to property rights. But before we consider this simply a feature of liberalism's possessive individualism,[23] we should take note that Kant makes a similar distinction in his *Rechtslehre*, where he distinguishes between obligations arising out of *officia juris* and those arising out of *officia virtutis*. While the latter have moral worth only if they are informed by the moral principle of the good will, the former do not require that the will shall be so determined.[24]

This has several implications. The first is that the assertion of a "right" implies that we inquire how the duty that is owed to the right holder arose, and that means that it is not enough to derive the duty from the benefits that result from certain actions, or are in accordance with general principles of "justice." If I promise Peter and Mary to take care of their children and the family dog while they are out of town, I owe this duty *to them* and not to Emilia, or Martin, or to Ulysse the canine, even though it is they who benefit from my care. Thus the obligation I incur is again not based on the quality of the action to which I commit myself – to be present and, for example, read an "emancipatory" bed-time

[22] Hart, "Are there any Natural Rights," at 80.

[23] C. B. Macpherson, *The Political Theory of Possessive Individualism* (Oxford University Press, 1962).

[24] Immanuel Kant, *Rechtslehre*, transl. by W. Hastie as *Immanuel Kant: The Philosophy of Law* (Edinburgh: T. and T. Clark, 1887), Prolegomena, sec. II: The Division of a Metaphysics of Morals, pp. 20–6.

story to Emilia, or prepare Ulysse's din-din – but it is to the promisees and it is only they who can modify or rescind my obligations.

This feature limits on the one hand the notion of "natural rights," as they are not the result of some voluntary action or institutional arrangement but arise out of the mutual recognition of all persons as free agents in a natural state of liberty. However, in spite of the fact that "rights" stand in a close relation to "possessions," the *fundamental* rights to life and liberty are different from other property rights as they are not "alienable." Rather they constitute the transcendental conditions of human agency *tout court*. All other notions entailing more substantive entitlements have then to be linked to this bare-bone conception of rights. Whether such extensions can be made by simply postulating additional human rights of different "generations" – all of which of "equal" worth and "mutually reinforcing"[25] – is a different question, which I leave aside for the moment.

On the other hand it also clear that a whole host of "special obligations" arise out of the mutual undertakings to which we are committed. It is here that "political obligations" arise that are badly conceived if they are derived from general values or universal principles, as has become the habit in recent human rights talk. This mistake has a long tradition, as the Antigone example showed, but I think H. L. A. Hart is right when he points out that if people engage in common projects and restrict their liberty by accepting common rules, they are entitled to expect that the other participants will impose the same restraint on themselves. However, things might quickly get more complicated:

> The rules might provide that officials should have authority to enforce obedience and make further rules and this will create a structure of legal rights and duties, but the moral obligation to obey the rules in such circumstances is *due* to the cooperating members of this society, and they have the correlative moral right to obedience. In social situations of this sort (of which political society is the most complex example) the obligation to obey the rules is something distinct from whatever other moral reasons there might be for obedience in terms of good consequences (e.g. the prevention of suffering); the obligation is due to the cooperating members of the society as such and not because they are human beings on whom it would be wrong to inflict suffering. The utilitarian explanation of political obligation fails to take account of this feature … both in its simple version that the obligation exists because and only if the direct consequences of … disobedience are worse than obedience, and also in its more sophisticated version that the obligation exists even if this is not so, if disobedience increases the probability that the law … will be disobeyed on other occasions when the direct consequences of obedience are better than those of disobedience.[26]

[25] See e.g. Philip Alston and Mary Robinson (eds.), *Human Rights and Development: Towards Mutual Reinforcement* (Oxford University Press, 2005).

[26] Hart, "Are there any Natural Rights," at 85f.

Thus rights not only give rise to specific second order powers and immunities, but the issue also arises whether such further normative structures can be coherently justified within the rights discourse itself – and here the "will" theory of rights and the "interest" theory of rights represent two different if not necessarily opposing versions[27] – or whether the rights talk needs to invoke other values such as "justice." In other words, the question arises of which "functions" a discourse of rights serves. If we had an answer to this question, we then could perhaps derive from it a "correct" notion of "rights" that could command universal respect. To that extent one would have to show that the human rights talk has indeed become the universal moral discourse, having more or less overcome "previous" conceptualizations of moral and social ordering.[28]

But, conversely, this also would imply that the charge of Western intellectual "imperialism" would have to be rebutted by showing that "other" ways of conceiving of the ordering the social world – such as through Asian values, Confucian duties, or tradition (Sharia law)[29] – were actually either "saying the same thing" (even if cast in a different language), or represent a sufficiently large area of "overlapping consensus" so as to provide a new "utopia" that is sufficiently robust to inform our contemporary social and political projects.

While of course such a task is daunting, not only for an essay but for a lifetime project, the bitter truth is that it probably cannot be implemented, at least not in a straightforward fashion. But saying that there might be no definite answer to the questions it raises – as is the case in all "deep" questions such as: "why is there something and not nothing"? "what is the meaning of life"? and so on – does not mean that nothing at all can be said. I think the fear of being otherwise condemned to have to listen to the idle chatter of the id arises only if we think that there has to be a "final" word, so that we can dispose of all errors and misconceptions once and for all, since we finally see things as they "are." Somehow this attitude still underlies many of our debates, instead

[27] See the spirited debate between Kramer, Simmonds, and Steiner on the one hand and the more recent challenges by Wenar and Sreenivasan. Matthew Kremer, Neil Simmonds and Hillel Steiner, *A Debate over Rights* (Oxford University Press, 1998); Leif Wenar, "The Nature of Rights," *Philosophy and Public Affairs*, vol. 33, no. 5 (2005), 223–52; Gopal Sreenivasan, "A Hybrid Theory of Claim Rights," *Oxford Journal of Legal Studies*, vol. 25, no. 5 (2005), 257–74; Matthew Kramer and Hillel Steiner, "Theories of Rights: Is there a Third Way?," *Oxford Journal of Legal Studies*, vol. 27, no. 2 (2007), 281–310.

[28] I explicitly use the terms moral and social in this context since "rights" bridge both realms – which is part of their "success" but also explains the confusion they often engender. Thus the "right" of a judge to sentence a criminal and deprive him of his liberty is a power entrusted to the official and is not a right in the sense that it either belongs to the person (rather than the office) or that it is alienable (although certainly not a "natural right" either) or even that its exercise is discretionary, as some rights (such as privileges) are.

[29] Here the Saudi protest in 1948 during the Drafting of the Universal Declaration provides the first inkling of the much larger resistance that was to emerge from the theocratic counter-project of an Islamic Republic in Iran.

of realizing that the very notion that debates have to end would mean that we have nothing more to say. In that case "silence" is then the just price paid for grasping the truth, and "history" can end in an everlasting blissful present. But we know that this view is mistaken. As the apocryphal story of a wise man who was challenged to state one non-analytical truth shows, such substantive "truths" are not easily available, as he just answered: "this too shall pass." Thus we had better take Wittgenstein's advice "to go on" by patiently examining the language games and forms of life they engender, to engage in "redescriptions" of things that puzzle us and stop us in our tracks, and to accept contestation rather than "clear and distinct ideas." I shall avail myself below of this alternative in order to clarify some of the puzzles of the rights talk. Instead of asking what rights "are" – an attempt that leads only as far as the above discussion adumbrated – I am interested in tracing the circumstances when "rights" claims emerged as powerful elements in the political and moral (justificatory) discourse.

The paradoxes of claiming rights

The above discussion has shown some overlaps between notions of natural law (it is right that) and natural rights (having rights as "natural" entitlements). Both discourses are foundational in that they invoke some form of direct intuition of either an ontological order, or some ultimate values, or interests that we all share. This is why natural or human rights are held to be "self-evident" and can only be "declared." Nevertheless, the distinct logic of natural rights and their role in social and political life cannot be adequately grasped when our narratives link the Stoic speculation with the Declarations of the Rights of Man, or the American Declaration of Independence, for example. Such a "storyline" does not pay attention to the important conceptual differences. Thus the practice of *claiming rights* not on the basis of social status, but as the "birthrights" of men (unfortunately only "men" originally) in their state of natural liberty and equality, usually remains unexamined and obscure, in particular the close relationship of "rights" to a certain political project.

The latter link of course engenders a certain paradox. On the one hand the rights, which are claimed as natural rights, have to be "above" politics and its historical contingencies, while on the other hand the shift from natural law to natural rights is beholden to a specific form of revolutionary politics. This is the case in Holland, where Grotius defined first "natural rights"[30] as being separate from God's will and belonging to individuals qua persons. A second coincidence of rights claims and revolution is observable in England in the 1640s and ended in the settlement of the Glorious Revolution by the Bill of Rights (1689).

[30] See Knud Haakonsen, *Natural Law and Moral Philosophy: From Grotius to the Scottish Enlightenment* (Cambridge University Press, 1996).

After that the American, and then the French Revolution are crucial for the articulation of the modern understanding of human rights. In addition, one could argue that the politics of rights to self-determination ignited the struggle against colonialism,[31] and that later the civil rights revolution in the USA transferred this political struggle to the global level by the 1970s. Thus the Helsinki Accords with their "basket III" provisions, as well as the later "silent" revolutions dissolving the Soviet bloc and continuing in the Arab Spring, also exhibit the close connection of rights thinking and revolutionary politics.

As opposed to this dynamism the first declarations on human rights after the Second World War, such as the one on Genocide and the Universal Declarations of Human Rights, stood rather outside the main political events that defined the Cold War. Both of them are perhaps better understood as a revival of natural law thinking after the atrocities of the Nazi regime had been exposed, and the potential for "totalitarianism," making the "state" the ultimate judge of right and wrong, had become obvious. Article l of the Declaration simply states: "All human beings are born free and equal in dignity and rights. They are endowed with reason and conscience and should act towards one another in a spirit of brotherhood."[32] But as Michael Ignatieff correctly points out, the Declaration "enunciates rights; it does not explain why people have them"[33] and – one could add – what they can "do" with them. The point of clarifying standards of decency was obviously important after the episode of unprecedented barbarism, but the dynamism that the politics of individual rights engendered is thereby hardly captured. Apparently the "restatement" in the Declaration was for most of the drafters only a set of moral exhortations, as no enforcement was attached, and neither were they linked to any political program. As such, the Declaration did little to cure the myopia of postulating standards of decency, while turning away its gaze from ethnic cleansing, and the existing racial and gender inequalities and oppressions at home.

Perhaps this also explains why the victims, who had either been suppressed as minorities, or had become stateless, or, still worse, were members of a group that had been subject to mass murder, were largely indifferent to the Declaration. They appear to have shared "the disdain for the powers … to enforce human rights in any elementary or general sense."[34] Given also the dismal experiences with "minority protection" under an international regime, the loss of status by being deprived of citizenship and becoming, legally speaking,

[31] Here one has, however, to realize not that individual rights were seen as foundational but that the "right to self determination" was considered the "prerequisite of the full enjoyment of all fundamental Human Rights." See the Final Communiqué of the Bandung Conference in George M. Kahin, *The Asian African Conference: Bandung, Indonesia April 1955* (Ithaca: Cornell University Press, 1956), 80.

[32] Ignatieff, *Human Rights as Politics and Idolatry*, at 77. [33] *Ibid.*

[34] Hannah Arendt, *The Origins of Totalitarianism* (San Diego/New York: Harcourt Brace and Co., 1976), 292.

a stateless "non-person," or of being expelled because of one's "ethnic" origin, the victims mistrusted anything short of national guarantees. Rather, they all opted for being protected by their national "mother country," or for the creation of their own state. Here the darker side of the original "Rights of Man" comes to the fore. They were conceived to be inalienable as they were formulated against governmental interference, but the experiences of the two World Wars were a stark reminder to the victims that people who were no longer "subjects" because they lacked a government could not fall back on a minimum status of rights attributed to their "humanity," since there was no authority left to speak for them. Formerly such understandings were outside of politics, and entrusted to religious or status groups. But now, when all other social institutions had lost their power to the state, these institutions showed little inclination to assume some authority by carrying the brief for those who "fell out" of the "normal." The tragic result was that those few who did advocate "human rights" were marginal figures politically speaking: some philanthropists, idealists, or lawyers. Here the Polish lawyer Raphael Lemkin (1900–1959) comes to mind. He coined the term "genocide" and campaigned for its proscription. As Hannah Arendt remarked when recalling these years:

> The groups they formed the declarations they issued showed an uncanny similarity in language and composition to that of societies for the prevention of cruelty to animals. No statesman, no political figure of any importance could possibly take them seriously: and none of the liberal or radical parties in Europe thought it necessary to incorporate into their program a new declaration of human rights.[35]

Two remarks concerning Arendt's take on the Declaration are in order. One concerns her point about the importance of having the "right to have rights," protected by political institutions rather than merely postulated as a moral appeal. It is well taken and explains the, at first, rather strange inclusion of a "right to nationality" in the Article 15(1) of the Declaration. The other (connected) point is her characterization of the group of politically more or less marginal "philanthropists" who were the authors of the Declaration. Even if we disagree with this judgment and tend perhaps to "remember" these facts differently – considering Eleanor Roosevelt an important person, for example – Arendt's look back is thereby not necessarily invalidated. It rather accurately reflects the mood of the post-Second World War era and of the early Cold War, as Donnelly also suggests.[36] We should not forget that the twentieth anniversary of the Declaration was even celebrated by the UN in Teheran, where the shah – certainly not an ardent adherent of subjective rights – used human rights for

[35] *Ibid.*

[36] Jack Donnelly, "The Social Construction of International Human Rights," in Tim Dunne and Nicholas Wheeler (eds.), *Human Rights and Global Politics* (Cambridge University Press, 1999): 71–102.

his purposes by crediting the Persian emperor Cyrus with their invention, and his own regime with the fulfilment of this promise.[37] It also shows us how different the project of "human rights" became in the 1970s and 1980s. It contributed to the break-up of the Soviet bloc, to "transitions" both in Eastern Europe and Latin America, and to some imperial projects in the new millennium. But it also suggests that the anti-colonial movement was really not a human rights struggle and that the tragedy in the Balkans seems to repeat the experiences of the inter-war and post-Second World War period, rather than being resolvable by advancing a human rights agenda.

Several conceptual issues have to be considered if we are to understand the politics of natural or human rights. First, these rights are not "granted" by a superior who derives his legitimacy from the traditions of a status society. They are rather quasi "birth rights" belonging equally to all persons and they serve now – on the contrary, and reversing the order of priority – as the *foundation* of any "society." To that extent the "naturalness" of these rights no longer roots them in teleology, exemplified by a form of the Aristotelian "good life" of the polis, but their naturalness is based on the equality of human beings as sensuous creatures in a state of natural liberty. Such a conceptualization has important implications for the semantics of politics, as it reconfigures the meanings of several key concepts. While even with the emergence of the rights discourse "happiness" is still the goal of all practical action, it is no longer tied to a "superior" way of life (*vita contemplativa*), but becomes the "pursuit" of happiness, that is the continuous satisfaction of desires. Governments are no longer divinely ordained institutions – as exemplified by the *Dei gratia* principle – but are instead devices for "securing" the rights of the subjects, acting as "trustees" rather than exercising rule qua original possession.

Furthermore, these rights, as claim rights of the subjects themselves, are not simple statements about what "is right" all things considered, even though they appeal to some direct moral intuition that is allegedly universal. As Alexander Hamilton asserted in 1775 when the debate among the colonists, who originally claimed their "constitutional rights" only as Englishmen, had come to an impasse as the colonies found themselves at war with their mother country: "The sacred rights of mankind are not to be rummaged for, among old parchments, or musty records. They are written as with a sunbeam, in the whole volume of nature, by the hand of divinity itself."[38] These rights can therefore not be a privilege or result from an act of legislation. They can only be "declared" and they must later be "claimed." Both are speech acts and this characteristic is a significant feature of the rights discourse. Thus the "declaration" and

[37] Moyn, *The Last Utopia*, at 2.

[38] Alexander Hamilton, "The Farmer Refuted" (February 23, 1775) in Harold C. Syrett *et al.* (eds.), *The Papers of Alexander Hamilton* (New York: Columbia University Press, 1961), vol. I, 122.

the subsequent "claim" imply some commitment by the subjects to "stand "on their rights, rather than asking humbly for redress when something has gone wrong.

It is this yoking of the assertion "rights" with their "declaration," based on a moral intuition, that gives the natural rights discourse its force and shows its close connection to modern "revolutionary" politics, thereby also radically changing the very meaning of "revolution" itself. Of course, "rights" were not unknown before the natural rights revolution. But these rights were then either property rights or immunities from otherwise general obligations. They were certainly not natural, but since they attached to the representatives of certain estates, they were not personal either, but "corporate." Thus, under the last Tudors the "speaker" of Parliament still had to "petition" the monarch to grant the commons their ancient privileges, such as to speak freely on matters of common concerns without the fear of arrest and further punishment (which was the penalty for such a crime of meddling in the ruler's "prerogative"), and of having access to the ruler (right to be heard). As David Zaret points out:

> When those representatives spoke out in support of the liberties and rights of English subjects, which they did (increasingly) … they were resisting what they perceived as an encroachment on privileges and immunities of the Commons. In this discourse, the prevailing corporate perspective on society subsumed references to individual rights. Subsequently, several principal rights commonly found in enumerations of human rights – e.g. individual rights to rule under law, security of life and property – grew out of these traditional privileges and immunities.[39]

In this context it is interesting that a new understanding of parliamentary powers evolved that linked the established taxing powers of the Commons to non-fiscal matters, a move that was answered by strident counter-assertions of royal prerogatives.

In this struggle the medieval institution of the *petition* played an important role. The Parliament's Petition of Rights (1628) responded to the assertion of the royal prerogative of raising taxes and quartering soldiers with a reminder that the "fundamental liberties" of English subjects were being abused, such as protection from arbitrary arrest, institution of martial law, and taxation without parliamentary approval. "Rights" became increasingly "birthrights," but they were still only birthrights of English*men*! Given the revolutionary situation after the beheading of King Charles I, the tyranny of the Long Parliament, and the ensuing political mobilization, the "orderly" petition was transformed and used by Pym, his allies, and opponents as a political weapon. They all tried

[39] David Zaret, "Tradition, Human Rights, and the English Revolution," in Jeffrey Wasserstrom, Lynn Hunt and Marilyn B. Young (eds.), *Human Rights and Revolutions* (London: Rowman and Littlefield, 2000), 43–58.

to whip up support for their respective political agendas by collecting thousands of signatures and forcing Parliament to address these issues.

While printing petitions violated traditional norms and parliamentary privileges, it became routine after 1641, and all factions used them in their attempts to enlarge the arena in which the controversies of a deeply divided the society could be aired. Interestingly enough, "the people" and public opinion on the one hand, and "reason" on the other, foreshadowed their legitimizing power. Appeals to "reason" had more radical implications, as the following incident demonstrates. In 1640 the Leveller Richard Overton, who had been imprisoned by the Long Parliament for violating parliamentary privileges, made an "Appeal to the People." While admitting the lack of precedent for such an act, he justified it "by reason," which is "the fountain" of all precedents and must be invoked against all "betrusted" power that has betrayed this trust because: "By natural birth all men are equal and alike born to like property and freedom."[40] Here an appeal is made to natural rights as intuited by reason and no longer dependent on specific birthrights that traditionally accrue to Englishmen.

Of course, in the subsequent settlement, which we call the Glorious Revolution, neither this radical form of a universal birthright, nor Overton's call for a radical egalitarian property regime were heeded. Rather the "ancient rights" of Englishmen were affirmed. Consequently, the catalogue of rights reads more like a list of particulars indicting some of James II's policies. But the prohibition of cruel and unusual punishment, and that of excessive bails, later become part of the US Constitution and are now arguably also "human rights." It seems strange that there is in the British Bill of Rights neither a concern with the "purposes of government" nor with certain subjective rights that we consider "fundamental," such as the freedom of conscience. But we should remember that the Bill of Rights was above all a statement of the terms under which William and Mary were to rule and keep England a protestant country. Nevertheless, some fundamental changes had occurred, as is evidenced by the explicit listing of the "right" to petition the king. While the medieval petition was narrowly circumscribed, conceived as an a-political instrument for conveying information about some grievance or public "ill" that needed the attention of the authorities, it did so without a reference to "reason," to peoples' rights, or to the "will of the people" articulated in public opinion. However, it became a powerful new weapon in the armoury of politics when it was transformed into an "appeal" that linked rights and reason. It thus provided new, external criteria of justification that far exceeded those of traditional "grievances," which were limited to internal criteria such as inequity, corruption, or oversight.

It is of course tempting to see in the American and French Revolutions the logical conclusion of the triumph of natural rights, which in turn could then serve as the foundation for the "rights revolution" of universal human

[40] *Ibid.* at 55.

rights. But such a storyline is historically and conceptually too simple. It is true that the framers of the Declaration of Independence and the authors of the Constitutions spoke the language of rights.[41] But the initial remonstrances against British taxation in the aftermath of the Seven Years War were still phrased in the traditional idiom of the "rights of Englishmen," and were only later followed by appeals to "natural rights." When war ensued, the colonists found themselves in a "state of nature" and could claim their "natural rights" again.[42] Here the importance of the link to "revolutionary" politics becomes visible.[43]

The vocabulary of natural rights, while far from being universally shared in the colonies,[44] nevertheless had a significant impact on the political discourse. In this context the collection of essays *Cato's Letters,* which had been written by the English pamphleteers John Trenchard and Thomas Gordon in the 1720, and which had been widely circulated in England and America,[45] became

[41] See e.g. the protest by the Massachusetts Whigs concerning the salaries of judges in the Bay Colony, when the king wanted to tax the colonists for the administration of judges while the colonists, who had traditionally paid the salaries themselves, feared that this could weaken the "rule of law." They protested this royal move by a circular issued by the Boston Committee of Correspondence (November 20, 1772). Since here the traditional rights of Englishmen could not be invoked, as a king could certainly pay his servants according to traditional constitutional understandings, the circular claimed that the royal salary violated the "Natural Rights of the Colonists as Men." James Hutson, "The Bill of Rights and the American Revolutionary Experience," in Michael Lacey and Knud Haakonssen (eds.), *A Culture of Rights: The Bill of Rights in Philosophy, Politics and Law 1791–1991* (Cambridge University Press, 1991), 62–97, at 67.

[42] See Wilson's and Hartley's speeches of November 28, 1787 and November 30, 1987 at the Pennsylvania ratifying convention, as quoted in Hutson, "The Bill of Rights," at 70.

[43] While the leaders of the colonists such as Adams, Wilson, and Jefferson maintained that Parliament had no power to legislate in the colonies as they were not represented in London and part of the settlement contained in the Bill of Rights was the prohibition of taxation without the consent of the governed. Since the colonies had their own legislatures, the colonists were connected to England only by their allegiance to the British Crown. The British argument was that the colonies were part of the realm and subject to parliamentary legislation even though the colonies were only "virtually" represented in Westminster. When the requests by the First and Second Continental Congresses were answered by British retaliatory measures, such as the "Proclamation of Rebellion" and the Prohibitory Act of February 1776, which envisaged criminal prosecutions of individuals, and the blockade of ports declaring American ships to be enemy vessels.

[44] See e.g. John Philip Reid, *Constitutional History of the American Revolution* (Madison: University of Wisconsin Press, 2003), who stresses the common law rather than the notion of natural rights in the making of the Constitution. See also his provocative "The Irrelevance of the Declaration," in Hendrik Hartog (ed.), *Law in the American Revolution and the Revolution of Law* (New York University Press, 1981).

[45] See Bernard Bailyn, *Pamphlets of the American Revolution, 1750–1776*, vol. 1, 1750–1765 (Cambridge, MA: Belknap Press of the Harvard University Press, 1965). See also his *The Ideological Origins of the American Revolution* (Cambridge, MA: Harvard University Press, 1967).

important. They had popularized John Locke's version of "natural rights," in an interpretation much more akin to the Levellers' position than to the notion of rights endorsed by the Glorious Revolution.[46] Finally, it did not take long for one of the members of the Constitutional Convention, James Wilson, who was a lawyer and had just been appointed to the new chair of jurisprudence at the College of Philadelphia, to distinguish British from American rights-thinking, taking Blackstone and Burke as his sparring partners. Thus in Wilson's view the:

> British held rights to be a kind of communal property to be granted to individuals, and they held individuals "nothing what society frames." It is as a contrast to this view that he formulates the well-known "American" idea of human beings as carriers – in society and out of it – of certain inalienable natural rights, and of civil society and its government as the means "to secure and to enlarge the exercise of the natural rights of its members."[47]

Nevertheless, even the American Bill of Rights, which became part of a constitution, focuses more on the safeguards insuring the proper exercise of governmental powers than on an explication of natural rights. This becomes clear from the federalist/anti-federalist controversy,[48] from the inclusion of the, in a way, strange Ninth Amendment – which many constitutional scholars argue was originally to be read in conjunction with the Tenth Amendment[49] – and the (for us) strange absence of relying on courts to safeguard constitutional rights. The reason for this was that the peoples' natural rights were supposed to be safeguarded by state constitutions. As Edmund Randolph stated at the Philadelphia Convention, "We are not working on the natural rights of men not yet gathered into society, but upon the rights modified by society."[50]

In this context it is also not surprising that Madison later thought that the first eight Amendments found their systemic place in Article 1, section 9 between clauses 2, 3 and 4 of the Constitution, that is in the section explicitly

[46] For a further discussion of the controversies among constitutional historians espousing the "irrelevance" thesis (not "natural rights" but common law was important), or the "succession thesis" ("natural rights" became important after the colonists became radicalized) and in favour of an "amalgamation" thesis (that both were sources for the colonists), see Michael Zuckert, "Natural Rights in the American Revolution," in Jeffrey Wasserstrom, Lynn Hunt and Marilyn B. Young (eds.), *Human Rights and Revolutions* (London: Rowman and Littlefield, 2000), 59–76.

[47] Haakonssen, *Natural Law and Moral Philosophy*, at 310f. The quotes refer to James Wilson, "Lectures on Law," in *Works*, ed. by James De Witt Andrews, 2 vols. (Chicago: Callaghan and Co, 1896), vol. II, 303 and 307.

[48] See e.g. Hamilton's dismissal of the need for a bill of rights in *Federalist* 84. See Clinton Rossiter (ed.), *The Federalist Papers* (New York: Mentor, 1961), 510–20.

[49] Raoul Berger, "The Ninth Amendment," *Cornell Law Review*, vol. 66 (November 1980), 1–26.

[50] As quoted in Hutson, "The Bill of Rights," at 90.

limiting Congress' legislative powers. This explains not only the persistence of slavery, in spite of the universalist rhetoric of "natural rights" in the Declaration of Independence, it also explains the exemption for raising such issues and pointing to the political "compromises" outside the constitutional framework. Finally, it also foreshadowed the future debate on questions of "state rights" and "citizenship" and of the rights thereby conferred, since citizenship had been left largely undefined by the Constitution. When this issue was "resolved" by the Supreme Court in its infamous *Dred Scott* decision, it led to the Civil War. And indeed it was through the Fourteenth Amendment, originally imposed on the defeated South after the Civil War, that issues[51] of "civil rights" could be vetted only after the Second World War. By then natural law or natural rights arguments – once thought to be indispensable – had largely fallen out of favour. Thus, in a way, the Arendtian argument, suspicious of the proliferation of enumerated human rights and focusing instead on the "right to have rights," seems to have much more force than is usually assumed.

"Universalism," on the other hand, had its way on the other side of the ocean where the American experiment had been followed with keen interest.[52] As one of the French deputies remarked during the opening days of the deliberation on a Declaration of Rights of Man and the Citizen (August 1789): "The Americans have set a great example in the new hemisphere; let us give one to the universe."[53] Again, antedating the revolution was an intense preoccupation with "rights" that markedly shifted their "source" from the rights and privileges conferred by societal status to some form of self-evidence, or some deeply held belief. As Diderot wrote in his 1775 contribution on *droit naturel* for his *Encyclopaedia*: "The use of this term is so familiar that there is almost no one, who would not be convinced inside himself, that the thing is obviously known to him. This interior feeling is common both to the philosopher and to the man who has not reflected at all."[54]

There is, of course, the ambiguity that attaches to the French term "*droit*," which means both "law" and "right," but the appeal to some form of deeply held belief that does not need "reflection" clearly marks this contribution as part of a new discourse on universal "natural rights." This interpretation is also confirmed by the political consequence that the passage of the French

[51] On the fate of the Bill of Rights in the development of the Constitution – stressing its eclipse after its passage – see Michael Kammen, *The Machine that Would Go of Itself: The Constitution in American Culture* (New York: Knopf, 1987).

[52] For a detailed account of the "Atlanticist" dimension of this transformation, see Richard Palmer, *The Age of the Democratic Revolution: A Political History of Europe and America*, 2 vols. (Princeton University Press, 1959 and 1964), particularly vol. I, chapter 5.

[53] Matthieu de Montmorency, August 1, 1789, as quoted in Lynn Hunt, "The Paradoxical Origins of Human Rights" in Jeffrey Wasserstrom, Lynn Hunt and Marilyn B. Young (eds.), *Human Rights and Revolutions* (London: Rowman and Littlefield, 2000), 3–17 at 8.

[54] As quoted in Hunt, "The Paradoxical Origins of Human Rights," at 9.

Declaration had. By subsequent action of the new National Assembly those rights were extended to all males, including Protestants and Jews, and finally even to the colonies, which had originally been exempted from their reach. After the slave revolt in Haiti, they were given effect and slavery was abolished in February 1794.

Given this considerably more "universal" conceptualization and acceptance, two puzzles remain. One is the status of women, which had been discussed in the salons, and a Declaration of the Rights of Woman and the Female Citizen had been drafted by Olympe de Gouges in 1791.[55] In addition, there was the discovery of the new "interiority" that had been celebrated in popular novels that had *women* as their protagonists: Rousseau's *Julie, ou la Nouvelle Heloise* (1767) and Richardson's *Pamela* (1740), both of which had taken their audiences by storm.[56] The other is the strong and rather naïve belief that "natural rights" can easily be squared with the supremacy of the nation as a lawgiver and guarantor of rights.

Addressing the first puzzle, that is the status of women, I am at a bit of a loss. Feminists have usually pointed out that the "abstract" notion of rights invites their improper limitations, as women were considered too emotional and in need of rational "guidance." But something more seems to be going on, as the language of rights might be "gendered" and, by extolling an adversarial ideal, it is hard or impossible to give voice to issues of compassion and degradation.[57] The second puzzle is easier to address, as Madison did not put his faith in the belief in natural rights, but in a more sociological approach, enhanced by some insights from republican theory. When rights are no longer defences against a tyrannical sovereign but against "the people" who have became the power holders, the threats to individual rights come from the majority. As Madison wrote in a letter to Jefferson:

> Wherever the real power of Government lies, there is the danger of oppression ... In our Government the real power lies with the majority of the Community, and the invasion of private rights is *chiefly* to be apprehended not from acts of government contrary to the sense of its constituents, but

[55] See Joanne Scott, *Only Paradoxes to Offer: French Feminism and the Rights of Man* (Cambridge, MA: Harvard University Press, 1996).

[56] See Ian Watt, *The Rise of the Novel: Studies in Defoe, Richardson, Fielding* (Berkeley: University of California Press, 1967). Lynn Hunt, *The Family Romance of the French Revolution* (Berkeley: University of California Press, 1992). See also Nicole Fermon, *Domesticating Passion: Rousseau, Woman and the Nation* (Middleton: Wesleyan University Press, 1997).

[57] See e.g. Carol Pateman, *The Sexual Contract* (Oxford: Polity, 1988) and its review by Susan Moller Okin, "Feminism, the Individual and Contract Theory," *Ethics*, vol. 100 (April 1990), 658–69; see also Okin's version of a humanist liberalism in her "Liberal Humanism," in Nancy Rosenblum (ed.), *Liberalism and the Moral Life* (Cambridge, MA: Harvard University Press, 1991), 39–53.

> from acts in which the Government is the mere instrument of the major member of the constituents.[58]

Thus rights might be, at first sight, only "parchment walls," but when combined with properly managed "factions," which "check and balance," they safeguard individual liberty while also allowing for an effective government. Nevertheless, the "solution" is distinctly political rather than "legal." This is why we see here little of what a contemporary student of rights would expect: the enforcement of rights through judicial review, which is nowadays the standard instrument for advancing "human rights."

Underlying this preference for the "judicialization" of rights is the belief that the "defence of individual rights to the exclusion of everything else … embodies something like the moral theory of Immanuel Kant"[59] when we enter the realm where individuals are treated as "ends" in themselves. The common law tradition was originally somewhat more sceptical about such propositions, as Bentham's scathing remarks about natural rights being "rhetorical nonsense," or "nonsense on stilts" indicate.[60] Civil law countries, on the other hand, seem to have been more at ease with shifting power from representative institutions to juristocrats through the growth of administrative, and later of constitutional courts. Admittedly, the differences between legal systems might become less pronounced over time, and the debates in Great Britain about a Human Rights Charter showed that the advocacy of rights, rather than the traditional voting into power a government[61] that has the "right" political priorities, has won ground.[62]

But before we celebrate these trends as proof of a "final" breakthrough to the "rule of law," we had better be careful with our assessment. Even for a liberal theory, judicial review – especially when it engages with policy questions entrusted to "other branches of government," or when it decides hypothetical conflicts outside of case and controversy (as was done by the Hungarian

[58] Letter to Jefferson, October 17, 1788, in *The Papers of James Madison*, ed. by William Hutchinson *et al.*, vol. XI (Charlottesville: University of Virginia Press, 1977): 297–300 at 297f.

[59] Alan Ryan, "The British, the Americans and Rights," in Michael Lacey and Knud Haakonssen (eds.), *A Culture of Rights: The Bill of Rights in Philosophy, Politics and Law 1791–1991* (Cambridge University Press, 1991): 366–439 at 377.

[60] Jeremy Bentham, "Nonsense on Stilts," in Jeremy Waldron, *Nonsense Upon Stilts* (London: Methuen 1987): 29–60.

[61] See e.g. Hume's argument in his *History of England*, which relied more on sociological reasons than on rights for explaining the success of the settlement after the Glorious Revolution. See David Hume, *The History of England: From the Invasion of Julius Caesar to the Revolution in 1688*, 6 vols. (Indianapolis: Liberty Classics, 1983–85).

[62] See e.g. the spirited defence of rights by Dworkin against utilitarian considerations in his *Law's Empire* (Cambridge, MA: Harvard University Press, 1986): 285–91.

supreme court by admitting *actiones populares*) – does raise issues of legitimacy.[63] Furthermore, there is scant evidence for the proposition that, for example, the US Supreme Court has in times of crisis protected individual rights better than the British political system based on parliamentary democracy. Both systems tend to react with visceral responses to crisis situations and are prone to buttress governmental policies in clear violation of basic rights.[64]

Finally, we had better also ponder the perverse phenomenon that "basic" rights need not necessarily be opposed by authoritarian regimes, especially if they concern the individual "pursuit of happiness," that is enjoyment of property and consumption. Coercion and the abridgement of civil rights is then justified by the "exceptional circumstances" and by reliance on the implied or "tacit consent" of the governed. Thus, despite his murderous instincts and Caesarian delusions, even Hitler seems to have had a strange obsession with legality.[65] Of course such concerns did not derive from his respect for individual rights but rather from his appreciation of the propaganda value of having the law on one's side. It was paired with his realization that modern bureaucracies can only function as instruments of domination if they operate in a "rational legal" mode. Both insights can explain some strange combination of a politics of repression and legality. Reviewing some recent cases of authoritarian dictatorships Rolando Gaete has pointed out:

> Dictatorial regimes can be co-opted into human rights systems by offering them the right to use emergency clauses … They must operate through the rule of law, that is by legal commands, generating a legal environment within which municipal courts can be deferential without embarrassing the legal profession too much … Some dissenting judges can be expected to voice isolated independent opinions … but instead of undermining the regime, the toleration of these critical opinions proves that the courts are truly independent. An "independent" judiciary and a Constitutional Bill of Rights can be tolerated by a modern dictatorial regime operating under martial law or emergency legislation. Judiciary and Bill of Rights do not cease to exist. They simply become irrelevant.[66]

But even in far less problematic circumstances putting one's trust largely in "the law," without too much concern for the necessary political framing conditions, seems rather myopic. Judicial review involves a significant shift of power from Parliament to the courts, and allows them to change constitutional reality by routine decisions, while disabling parliaments (or making it very difficult for

[63] See Jeremy Waldron, "The Core of the Case Against Judicial Review," *Yale Law Journal*, vol. 115 (2006), 1348–406.

[64] See above ftn. 59.

[65] Alan Bullock, *Hitler, A Study in Tyranny* (New York: Harper, 1964).

[66] Rolando Gaete, *Human Rights and the Limits of Critical Reason* (Brookfield: Dartmouth, 1993), 91.

them) to make such constitutional choices. The question is then not only the simple Schmittian problem of *quis judicabit*, but also the one of *quis custodiet ipsos custodes* (who is watching the watchmen). This dilemma (inevitably?) sets the stage for "mission creep," since courts have the competency to decide their own competency and they cannot refuse rendering a decision, unless excused by jurisdictional limitations or the finding of (in)admissibility. This creates great difficulties in well-institutionalized systems in which foundational doctrines of "the people" and their sovereignty delineate the bounds of sense. It is much more difficult if these institutions are "above" a constitutional framework that yokes law and politics, occasional calls for constitutionalization notwithstanding. But it seems even more difficult if "speaking what the law is" (*juris dictio*) is done in terms of some "natural" and universally valid rights. At a minimum this would presuppose a coherent "theory" of rights and, as a complement (not replacement), a theory of authority.[67] Finally it would have to provide a reflection on which type of subject and of politics are presupposed by such a theory. It is to the latter problem that the next section is addressed.

Subjectivity and natural rights

The upshot of the argument so far points to the historical character of claims buttressed by some "higher" forms of validation and to the strong conceptual links between moral notions and political projects. In a way it can be read as a criticism of natural, or human rights, but it should not be understood as a simple "unmasking" of the rights talk that camouflages some ulterior motives. Rather, my intention was to probe the semantic field, which is reconfigured and imparts new meaning to its elements in this process.

"Rights" need not, therefore, necessarily "correspond to some "given" ontological order, fixed "nature," or essence – in spite of the strange insistence on their self-evidence – but they follow, as instruments of justification, a certain grammar in structuring a discourse. They also need not be conceived as an individual's "possession," as if the natural rights we ascribe to a person as a moral agent have to be brought along like suitcases when s/he leaves the state of nature and arrives at the big city of Cosmopolis. As with all rights, natural rights are not about the "things" we have, but about the social relations that are thereby mediated and that co-constitute "subject" and "society." Their validity is not established by correspondence to some (eternal, a-historical) "truths" but by the coherence with other notions and decisions, considered to be right when vetted in accordance with certain argumentative practices and understandings. As Dworkin correctly points out, the contemporary judicial practice of rights is hermeneutical and thus "need not assume that rights have some metaphysical

[67] This is sometimes called the problem of "licence," as rights might be abused or be in conflict so that their "trump" character can no longer be used to settle the issues concerned.

character."[68] As such, our present way of using them "departs from older theories that do rely on that supposition"[69] and (mis–)conceived them as "a set of timeless rules stacked in some conceptual warehouse awaiting discovery by judges."[70]

To that extent we can remain critical by attempting to discover the presuppositions of different forms of rights talk, without having to buy into the assumptions of their unchanging nature or eternity – as for example Article 79(3) of the German Basic Law – or exposing ourselves to the opprobrium of "relativism," because we allegedly hold the view that "anything" goes. I do not think that this conclusion "must" follow, as such an inference is based on certain metaphysical assumptions that have become untenable. It does, however, put the burden of proof upon me to specify more explicitly whether and under what circumstances the discourse of rights "makes sense." In other words I have to give more substance to Habermas' suggestion that each historical period has a dominant mode of justification based on a typical "moral practical insight."[71] And it is this ability of law to create "meaning" by linking to other symbolic orders, such as myths, ontological speculations, endowing customs and traditions with validity, and establishing "facts" (institutional facts) that is nowadays an often overlooked dimension of law, because we tend to privilege a managerial perspective. The latter focuses on the role of law in dispute resolution and in shaping policy questions, but thereby also opens up law to colonizing moves by economics, transforming it into some form of cost/benefit calculation. Before we can enter this debate, it is necessary to sketch the larger picture or particular world-view that enables law to sustain a discourse on rights. In other words, what are the enabling conditions of this discourse that structure the relations not only to others (society) but also to "the world"?

As we have seen, "rights" hardly played a role during the Middle Ages since, in a society dominated by social rank, the powers and privileges of the person were thereby specified. Thus one did not need a general concept of individual rights. When in the emerging "cities" – which often became "republics" – the rights of the citizen had to be ascertained, they derived from their status as a member of a corporation.[72] Similarly, the person was seen as an "actor" – the old imagery of his "role" in mastering his life is conveyed by the metaphor of a person who, as in the theatre, speaks through a mask (persona from *per-sonare*, that is sounding "through" a mask). He was, however, not conceived as the

68 Ronald Dworkin, *Taking Rights Seriously* (Cambridge, MA: Harvard University Press, 1978), Introduction at XI.

69 *Ibid.* at XII. 70 *Ibid.* at 15.

71 Juergen Habermas, *Legitimization Crisis* (London, 1976), 87.

72 For a further discussion see Richard Dagger, "Rights," in Terrence Ball, James Farr and Russell Hanson (eds.), *Political Innovation and Conceptual Change* (Cambridge University Press, 1998), 292–308.

maker of his own fortune since he was not the author of the script. He could act on the world, but his "destiny" was somewhere else and his fate depended on how well or badly he played his role. The play, or the order in which he acted, however, was provided by the creator. This distinction of the creator and the creation, and the gulf that opens up when God is seen as the creator and not part of nature itself, also stakes out an agential space for the person. By assigning man a role, setting him just below the angels and giving him "freedom to choose," establishes, according to Pico della Mirandola, the "dignity of man."[73]

Here is not the place to trace the shifts from the emphasis on choice and free will – powerfully reinforced by the notion of original sin and of the means of redemption – to a secularized version of doing God's work *within* the world, which Weber[74] and Troeltsch,[75] and in a different way Hannah Arendt,[76] have examined. Crucial for this new conception of agency (and of duties), however, was the increasing devaluation of contemplation and of withdrawal from the world, even though human destiny remained – even for Protestantism[77] – anchored in the transcendent. Mariano Barbato has used here the figure of the "pilgrim" (in contrast to the later model the *homo faber* or *homo economicus*) in order to explore the practical implications of this world-view.[78] Thus there is an obligation for the believer to practise brotherly love, which widens the horizon and includes others, even if they are "afar" and not part of the familiar. They are now becoming an object of normative interest, and not only of curiosity, such as the fabulous animals that are said to inhabit the unknown depths of the oceans or the uncharted areas of the earth. But this new awareness is not a call for uniting humanity (aside from propagating the faith, or seeking one's fortune in the "new world").

For the latter project various arrangements emerged, ranging from brutal suppression and enslavement, as in the Americas, to strictly regulated restrictive contacts (Japan). Law played a key role here, as the "Spanish school" of international law shows, but it did not give rise to the assertion of universal subjective rights. As Heinrich and Pacini point out:

> The call to brotherly love is not a universal ethic for action in the world. Despite the individual's independence from this world … through its

[73] Giovanni Pico della Mirandola, *On the Dignity of Man*, transl. by Charles Glenn Wallis (Indianapolis: Hackett, 1998).

[74] Max Weber, *The Protestant Ethic and the Spirit of Capitalism*, trans. by Talcott Parsons (New York: Scribner's, 1958).

[75] Ernst Troeltsch, *The Social Teachings of the Christian Churches*, trans. by Olive Wyon (New York: Macmillan, 1992).

[76] Hannah Arendt, *The Human Condition* (University of Chicago Press, 1958).

[77] See e.g., the treatise by the puritan John Bunyan, *The Pilgrim's Progress from this World to that of Which is to Come* (Oxford University Press, (1678) 2008).

[78] Mariano Barbato, *Pilgrimage, Politics and International Relations* (New York: Palgrave Macmillan, 2013).

> transcendence to the redemptive, no conception of human rights can emerge in this correlation: this image of the world fails to promote the sense of self-determination necessary to direct independent reflection back toward the world order of the present (temporal) sphere.[79]

In short, this conception contrasts sharply with two other world images that view man as embedded in "nature" or as an autonomous actor – as in the enlightenment project – where the subject has truly become the "measure of all things." In the former case (man being embedded in nature) the image of the world and the self are understood largely in terms of how part and whole fit together. Such a semantic field does not allow for an independent reflection on the world as a potential manifold of "possibilities" and on the choices of the agent in "making" it. Rather such an understanding sets limits to self-chosen "wilful" actions, which is crucial for a conception of a "right." Instead, in this world:

> we would see ourselves as agents whose actions conform to and reflect our knowledge about fundamental processes of the natural life system. In such a world, perseverance and acceptance of fate are the norms that would bear most strongly on our lives, for they sustain the life cycle.[80]

In any case, "rights" remain foreign in such a discourse since they do not easily connect with other concepts that could lend strength and coherence to the semantic field and to the notion constituting the "subject."

Thus while in contemporary politics objections to "human rights" were sometimes couched in terms of Asian "values" – which exposed their proponents immediately to ridicule from "universalists" – the objections did "name," I think, a genuine conceptual problem. It becomes especially visible in the ecological area, where "Western" scholars combat problems of nature's degradation through a slew of regulatory measures, or even through the ascription of "rights" to "protected species." Some Asian scholars, such as Onuma Yasuaki,[81] are highly critical of this Western "rightism" and seek a "trans-civilizational perspective" to "overcome West-Centric, Judiciary-centric deficits in international legal thought." Others more interested in the ecology, such as Yol Yung Hwa, argue that a complete rethinking of "man in nature" has become necessary[82]

[79] Dieter Heinrich and David Pacini, "The Context of Autonomy: Some Presuppositions of the Comprehensibility of Human Rights," *Daedalus*, vol. 112 (Fall 1983), 255–77, at 259.

[80] *Ibid.* at 258.

[81] Onuma Yasuaki, "A Transcivilisational Perspective on Global Legal Order in the 21st Century: A Way to Overcome West-centric and Judiciary-centric Deficits in International Legal Thought," in Ronald St Macdonals and Douglas Johnston (eds.), *Towards World Constitutionalism* (Leiden: Martinus Nijhoff, 2005), 151–89.

[82] See e.g. Yol Yong Hwa "The Way of Ecopiety: An Essay in Deep Ecology from a Sinitic Perspective," *Asian Philosophy*, vol. 1, no. 2 (1991), 127–40. See also his *Transversal Rationality and Intercultural Texts* (Columbus: State University of Ohio Press, 2010).

and he and some of his colleagues search for solutions within Buddhism and some Far Eastern traditions. Not surprisingly, they blame the "anthropocentric" notion underlying Western humanism for the present misery, and not only its degenerations, as exemplified by neo-liberalism's hedge fund hogs and consumption freaks.

Whether this is a viable alternative that can lead to some further debates across this divide remains to be seen, as notions of stewardship, or of a responsibility to future generations, of respect for the creation, for example, are appearing in the Western world. In any case, Brian Tamanaha points to "daunting complications" that arise when "bills of rights":

> are transplanted from a Western society onto a non-Western culture in a manner that conflicts with prevailing views. In situations like this, Western theories (like Dworkin's) that assume a match between background morality and law are plainly inapt. The law will not match the morality of society and there will be no overarching coherence. There is no standard formula for dealing with a situation like this other than to tread with care.[83]

The correlation of self and world image most conducive to the adoption of "rights" is, of course, the project of the enlightenment that centres on the moral autonomy of the subject. Thus not only do actions issue from the agent, but the norms guiding his conduct also have *their source in the subject*. This presupposes a new conception of the "self" and of the world. As a first step, self-reflexivity becomes the site where radical doubts can be assuaged and the toxic criticism of the sceptics can be refuted. Here the Cartesian "self" provides a *fundamentum inconcussum*. However, as we have seen, the problem remained how the *res cogitans* and the *res extensa*, concept and object, were related. It was still "solved" in a "theological" fashion that entailed the assumption of a pre-existing world that was brought by the subject "under" the appropriate concepts, whereby a benign God guaranteed their "fit." Of course, such self-awareness in a given world was not able to generate norms for conduct, as they are not natural facts. Thus norms were either unreflectively followed – as in the case of Descartes' "traditionalism"[84] – or one had to fall back on some natural law conception – as in the case of Locke where the influence of Cicero on him is well documented.

[83] Brian Tamanaha, *On the Rule of Law: History, Politics, Political Theory* (Cambridge University Press, 2004), 138.

[84] See e.g. Descartes' argument for a resting place while rebuilding his own (philosophical) "house" by indicting the "meddling and restless spirits who being called neither by birth nor fortune to administer public affairs" but who dream of "reforming the State." Instead, he suggests following three maxims, the first being "to obey the laws and customs of my country, adhering firmly to the faith in which, by the grace of God I have been educated from my childhood and regulating my conduct in every other matter according to the most moderate opinions." *Discourse on Method*, transl. by F. E. Sutcliffe (London: Penguin 1962), at 38 and 45 (2nd and 3rd Discourse).

> Autonomy thus conceived became the backdrop for a type of theory that is explicitly based on the conditions and needs of life (Locke). From these basic needs legal entitlements were derived that not even the power of the state could violate … Difficulties arise for this type of theory however as soon as reason is introduced to explain the universality, reciprocity and obligatory nature of rights since reason is not inherent in the set that gave rise to the theory.[85]

In other words the issues of "reason" and of the "will" remain problematic, as reason is concerned with the ordering of sense impressions and with and calculating the means for attaining the subject's goals. But in later "liberal" thought it is apparently powerless to impose even a lexical ordering on different goals, so that "the *pursuit* of happiness" imposed by desires – not its attainment in a state of rest – becomes the crucial ordering problem. Such a constant "pursuit" of satisfaction cannot consist only in getting "more of everything," in spite of the Hobbesian anti-Aristotelian slant suggesting that much. It consists in, and thus presupposes, some notion of a "successful life," that is one with worthwhile pursuits. As Joseph Raz put it: "we care not merely about our having our wants satisfied, but about having reasonable wants. We value our lives, judge them to be successful, in proportion to their being occupied with worthwhile pursuits."[86] Liberalism thus attempted in various ways to circumvent the problems of its incoherent notion of utility (in both the personal and interpersonal realm) and its deficient conception of motivation – reducing reason to a slave of passion. It espoused a theory of moral sentiments (Hume, Smith), of higher and lower pleasures (Mill), or fell back on a notion of "*reasonableness*," rather than (instrumental) "reason."

Another way of dealing with these difficulties is, of course, the attempt of implicating the autonomous "self" in the "making" *of the world*, as Rousseau had already suggested and Kant had systematically explored. In that case "the world" is no longer "given" but remains undefined as a range of possibilities. It is the horizon in which the indeterminate "things in themselves" appear but which can be given form and definiteness only through the self in the act of appropriation through reason. Here neither survival nor happiness provide the natural parameters for human action, as such a conception still remains beholden to some "natural needs." Instead, the experience of radical freedom makes it necessary that the subject determines itself. Instead of a historically contingent list of rights, which were supposed to be remedies to certain "abuses" and which could then be claimed against the government, the generative force of autonomy made it necessary that this freedom as self-determination is recognized as *the core duty* of individuals. But it also represents the central task

[85] Heinrich and Pacini, "The Context of Autonomy," at 262.
[86] Joseph Raz, "Liberating Duties," *Law and Philosophy*, vol. 8 (1989), 3–21 at 14.

for governments, which are not to provide goods or happiness, but are tasked, above all, to secure the integrity of self-determination.

The discourse of rights is then transcended, as rights are inferred from duties (not the other way around) and "rights" are neither derivable from a natural order of things, nor from any list of particulars that form a "catalogue" based on certain historical experiences, prudential considerations, or needs. Rights follow rather from the formal criteria that the free will imposes upon itself in the light of reason. But such a project ultimately also needs the *Rechtsstaat* in which such a project can unfold, and beyond that a shared understanding about the institutional framework within which the states themselves interact. History can only supply the solution for the last problem when it is considered in a "cosmopolitan intent" and humanity has become its subject. As Kant reminds us that in this project "rights," rather than overcoming politics, require a *particular kind of politics*, and not just some legal "theory" or professional or "moral" expertise for policy advice. They need for their realization the "*moral politician*" who can seize the moment and create the necessary institutions.[87]

Given the dependence of "rights" on politics – which might cause a certain uneasiness among liberals – it is, of course, easy to fall back on metaphors of rights as "trumps." But this presupposes that one plays a certain card game – and even here the question of when to use which card will require skill and a sense of timing. But politics, particularly international politics, is seldom a well-structured game with fixed trumps or accepted umpires. Conflicts abound and collective action problems cannot be "solved" through decrees. Thus the real question remains how a political project framed by the discourse of rights can be made to "stick" as our interests widen and "society" and the world we live in become ongoing concerns, while familiar communities lose their unquestioned standing and their integrating force. It will be the task of the last two Meditations to address these issues.

[87] See Immanuel Kant, *Zum Ewigen Frieden* (Berlin: Preussische Akademieausgabe): 372; see also Martti Koskenniemi, "Miserable Comforters: International Relations as a New Natural Law," *European Journal of International Relations*, vol. 15 (2009), 395–422.

Meditation 8

The limits and burdens of rights

Introduction

The previous Meditation was concerned with the emergence of the human rights talk and its politics. By investigating its grammar and by showing its heterogeneous sources I tried to counteract the quasi-theological narrative within which this talk is frequently embedded. In addition, I intended to point to specific interactions between political processes and law that account for the hegemonic character of the rights talk in modernity and post-modernity. Not only are rights everywhere, policy problems, as well as general moral questions, are also increasingly phrased in terms of "the right to." They are displacing former conceptions of the *salus publica*, of the police powers of the state, of civic or personal virtue, or even of duties that we owe to ourselves or to others. This leads not only to a certain impoverishment of the political and perhaps even moral discourse which Glennon[1] and Gilligan[2] have noted, but also as to some conceptual puzzles which Waldron[3] addressed.

The rights talk is also responsible for the phenomenal explosion of rights, from animal rights to the right of receiving a "promotion"[4] at work. There is apparently little concern with the embeddedness of such remedies in certain specific social structures and with the heuristic costs of a conceptual stretch, when the modern factory worker is taken as an a-temporal "universal" paradigm. But such an ideal type certainly does not sit well with that of self-employed professionals, who probably cannot even fathom what a right to promotion would entail. Similarly, resisting the tendency of assigning rights to

[1] Mary Ann Glennon, *Rights Talk: The Impoverishment of Political Discourse* (New York: Free Press, 1991); see also the "communitarian" criticism by Michael Sandel, *Liberalism and the Limits of Justice* (Cambridge University Press, 1982).

[2] Carol Gilligan, *In a Different Voice* (Cambridge, MA: Harvard University Press, 1984).

[3] Jeremy Waldron, "A Right to Do Wrong," in Jeremy Waldron, *Liberal Rights* (Cambridge University Press, 1993), 63–87.

[4] See Article 7c of the Additional Protocol to the American Convention on Human Rights in the Area of Economic, Social and Cultural Rights, which James Griffin considers a case of unacceptable extension. James Griffin, "Discrepancies between the Best Philosophical Account of Human Rights and the International Law of Human Rights," *Proceedings of the Aristotelian Society, New Series*, vol. 101 (2001), 1–28 at 23.

animals has to do with the inaptness of protecting all things by rights. After all, "claiming" or "standing on one's rights" is central to the notion "having rights" both in terms of agency, which is thereby constituted, but also in terms of the duties that are then assigned to others.

While transferring the "claiming" of rights to "others" has been a well-established practice – particularly if the persons are minors, or incapable of claiming the rights themselves (as the sick or the poor) – the fact remains that such a transfer of claiming power changes rights significantly. It creates "clients" (instead of claimants) and sometimes not even that, since only advocates for certain noble "causes" are pleading their case. Finally, what shall we make out of a "right to peace," as desirable as peace is? Does this "human right" conflict with the "inherent right" of self-defence, and is a government that is exercising this right as part of a "humanitarian mission" – in accordance with the "Right to Protect" – violating the "human rights" of its people? Does advocating a "robust peace-making mission" infringe on the injunction of the International Covenant on Civil and Political Rights, which provides in Article 20(1) that "any propaganda for war shall be prohibited by law"? Similarly the African Charter of Human Rights states in Article 23(1) that all people have the "right to national and international peace and security."[5] Is this how the apodictic statement in the Vienna Declaration and Program of Action of 1993 [6] that "All Human Rights are universal, indivisible and interdependent, and interrelated" plays out in practice?

While to some of us this overabundance of rights might seem like progress – and thus the dilemmas are left to "further developments" – for others it tends to be rather an indicator of a pathology.[7] Since both parties can, as usual, cite some evidence buttressing their point of view, coming to an assessment is then difficult. It is difficult not only because of the nature of the rights *problematique* itself, which cuts across different fields ranging from ethics, to law, politics, and policy, but also because we have to attend to problems that implicate each other conceptually and practically, since the individual, the state, and the world community are linked in complex ways. Thus the "cosmopolitan project"[8] raises a whole host of problems, such as: what is owed to us and what do we

[5] *Ibid.*

[6] See Vienna Declaration (1993), para. 5, as quoted in Jack Donnelly, "The Social Construction of Human Rights," in Tim Dunne and Nicholas Wheeler (eds.), *Human Rights in Global Politics* (Cambridge University Press, 1999), 71–102, at 89. It was adopted by a World Conference on Human Rights, and represented a move towards universality (against cultural relativism) and a "normative deepening" of the concept of human rights. Donnelly, "The Social Construction of Human Rights."

[7] See e.g. Onora O'Neill, "The Dark Side of Human Rights," *International Affairs*, vol. 81, no. 2 (2005), 427–39; David Kennedy, *The Dark Side of Virtue* (Princeton University Press, 2004), especially Chapter 4.

[8] For a useful anthology of various schools of "cosmopolitanism," see Garrett Wallace Brown and David Held (eds.), *The Cosmopolitan Reader* (Oxford: Polity, 2010).

owe to others, be they friends, citizens, or particular persons with whom we are involved in specific common undertakings, but who remain "strangers"? These complications make it hard to use conventional strategies of "bracketing." Instead, it seems that we have to find "simultaneous" solutions, as rights are relational concepts operating not only on different levels, but whose implications seem also to "escalate" over time, as we shall see below.

We are also confronted with substantially more demands when distributional questions are cast in the language of rights, such as the "right to food" or subsistence. The prospect of facing billions of desperately poor "humans" who are no longer satisfied with the benign neglect of the privileged, or with their charity, but who call attention to their needs by insisting on their "rights," overtaxes us, even if we are sympathetic to their plight. Here our imagination, experience, and capacity all get challenged, as we fear escalating demands. After all, Feinberg reminded us "When that to which one has a right is not forthcoming, the appropriate reaction is indignation; when it is duly given there is no reason for gratitude since it is simply one's own, or one's due that one received."[9] We therefore resort to defensive strategies, such as repression and amnesia, and concentrate on the "business at hand" (that is, "us"), or even blame the bearers of bad news, since we are also irked by those who have the "radical chic" of becoming advocates of the downtrodden.

No such intractable issues seem to be involved when we deal with the classical human rights, which define us as free agents and assign duties to others that require, at first blush, only "non-interference." Although conceptually some difficult problems arise when my liberty of action conflicts with yours, somehow we do not feel as threatened, since socialization and some well-settled practices – such as good fences make good neighbours – mostly solve these issues pragmatically. In the event that no solution is available, those problems then become the mainstay of lawyers, providing them with an endless stream of income.

But even classical "negative" rights, such as the right to be left alone or to be free from torture, are not that simple and can generate mushrooming obligations. Thus your right imposes upon me the duty not to do anything that would jeopardize your bodily integrity and it enjoins the government from using torture in "fulfilling its duty" of protecting the citizens. But it also might engender duties to become proactive in ensuring that torture is not resorted to, to prosecute acts of torture, to rescue people from torture (as part of a mandated international undertaking), or to provide victims with asylum, and so on.[10]

Thus the distinction between negative and positive rights is misleading, and so might be the notion that each right has only one duty-bearer, or that we

[9] Joel Feinberg, *Social Philosophy* (Englewood Cliffs: Prentice Hall, 1973), 59.

[10] This point is well made by Jeremy Waldron, "Rights in Conflict," *Ethics*, vol. 99 (April 1989), 503–19.

are able to separate some core rights that will never conflict with one another. Instead, we must face the problem of trade-offs when rights conflict. We probably cannot even rely on some "lexical priority," as Rawls suggested,[11] so that we attend to some of them first, before the less important ones can be satisfied. Actually we might end up with two plagues upon our house: one of indeterminacy, that the notion of "rights" was supposed to overcome by clearly establishing which of my interests have to be "taken care of" by which duty-bearers. Second, we will have to "weigh" rights, and utility here once provided the handy yardstick, even though rights were "invented" (as Bentham correctly perceived) as a defence against overeager legislators, using the "felicific calculus" for justifying their policy choices.

A closer examination through the Hohfeldian pairs, and through an "interest theory" of rights, can clarify some issues, even though no "solution" to several other dilemmas is available. This is also a useful reminder that the rights discourse cannot claim to be comprehensive moral theory but attains its persuasiveness from the overlap with other discourses, such as Kantian ethics, utilitarianism, and even virtue ethics. The issue of the "abuse of rights,"[12] which has been a standard topic in both virtue ethics and legal praxis in civil law countries (and more recently also in international (environmental) law[13] – points in the same direction. It also suggests that the resonance and persuasiveness of the rights discourse are deeply connected with certain habits and particular practices, rather than with resolving certain conceptual puzzles abstractly. Here Hegel's remarks in his *Philosophy of Right*, criticizing Kant's insistence on rights even in intimate relationships, were intended to show the limitations of the rights approach when applied to all spheres of human conduct. More recently Waldron tried[14] to counter this Hegelian criticism of Kant by arguing that even in the intimate sphere rights are a useful fall-back position when love has run its course, and the former partners have become strangers to each other and want to "move on." Such a position will certainly resonate with the young (or not so young) professionals in the Western world, precisely because this is what we do. We call the lawyer and not the priest, rabbi, or the head of the clan to settle the issue. But things are, unfortunately, a bit more complicated in other contexts, particularly in traditional societies.

[11] Rawls creates such a lexical ordering by giving "political rights" precedence over rights of economic opportunity, and equal opportunity having precedence over social and economic rights derived from the "difference principle." See John Rawls, *Theory of Justice* (Oxford University Press, 1971), at 243 and 298 respectively.

[12] Michael Meyer, "When Not to Claim your Rights: the Abuse and Virtuous Use of Rights," *Journal of Political Philosophy*, vol. 5 no. 2 (1997): 149–62.

[13] See e.g. Michael Byers, "Abuse of Rights: An Old Principle, A New Age," *McGill Law Journal*, vol. 47 (2002): 389–431.

[14] See Jeremy Waldron, "When Justice Replaces Affection: the Need for Rights," in Jeremy Waldron, *Liberal Rights* (Cambridge University Press, 1993): 370–91.

This is of course no (knock-out) argument against divorce, as it indeed provides a solution in some hopeless situations, but it does not necessarily invalidate the wider point that Hegel wanted to make.[15] This objection need not be cast in the language of "*Sittlichkeit*" that is equally set apart from calculation as it is from passion, as Hegel did. It can equally be made in terms of the perverse incentives such a solution fosters. The "war of the roses," fuelled by the insistence on one's "rights" and by adversarial proceedings, is frequently not simply motivated by an attempt "to get out," but is used to "get even" or, better still, to "get everything" (to quote Ivana Trump). Thus any move to "naturalizing" this familiar practice, deriving from it some notion of human dignity, or even reason itself, is questionable and should be resisted. Instead, what comes into focus is the dependence of "rights" on particular background conditions, such as settled practices and even notions of human flourishing (or domination!), which are crucial[16] for a discourse on rights.

From these initial remarks the steps of my argument are as follows. In the next section I begin with the traditional distinction of negative and positive rights. In section three I address the problem of conflicts among rights. Having demonstrated that some of the more serious problems cannot be answered by the two predominant "theories" of rights, that is the interest theory and the will theory of rights, I turn my attention to the issue of whether the rights discourse can be identified with a special approach to morality *tout court*, as Mackie[17] suggested and Dworkin attempted to work out in his interpretive legal theory. Section four is then devoted to a discussion of some special rights, that is rights to common goods and problems of political participation. Here I want to focus in particular on Waldron's "right to rights," as he articulates a political rather than a philosophical solution of the rights *problematique*. While rejecting some of the Waldron's wider claims, I also suggest that the problems cannot be solved philosophically, even though both Dworkin and Habermas have attempted to do so by providing for a "right answer," or for "truth" conditions of the normative propositions of law. By showing that such an attempt has to postulate a universal reason able to define an Archimedean point – a hope that most philosophers have given up – I prepare the way for the last Meditation, which deals with drawing and redrawing the bounds of sense.

15 See G. W. F. Hegel, *Elements of the Philosophy of Right*, ed. by Allen Wood, transl. by H. B. Nisbet (Cambridge University Press, 1991), paras. 75, 161, 162.

16 See Chris Brown, "Universal Human Rights: A Critique," in Tim Dunne and Nicholas Wheeler (eds.), *Human Rights in Global Politics* (Cambridge University Press, 1999), 103–29.

17 See e.g. J. L. Mackie, "Can there Be a Rights-based Moral Theory?," in Jeremy Waldron (ed.), *Theories of Rights* (Oxford University Press, 1984), 168–81.

The burdens of rights

If the above analysis is correct, then the classical distinction between negative and positive rights is not very useful and rather an impediment to understanding. True, rights are first of all guarantees of a sphere of personal autonomy and of possessions that impose duties of non-interference on others. But enforcement mechanisms are never costless; and neither are the institutions taking care of the assignment of property rights, or of dispute resolution, charged with inuring that I can "stand on my rights." In addition, rights are not all of the same cloth, as Hohfeld has shown.[18] They contain liberties, privileges, powers, and liabilities, which all impose different obligations on "others," so that the simple correlativity of rights and duties is a rather special case. As any simple hypothetical can show, things become complicated rather quickly.

Assume that I, as a "big brother," have taken on special responsibilities for Rick, a troubled youngster, who is walking the fine line of the law similar to Justice Holme's "bad man." Rick himself knows that he is troubled and asks me to "help" him when in need. One day I see him from afar as he is running down the street with something in his hand. He recognizes me, waving his hands for help while dashing into an apartment of a house I happen to own. A few seconds later a policeman with his gun drawn turns around the corner, huffing and puffing, and we hear the slam of a door. The officer walks up to the door, knocks on it, identifies himself as the police, and demands that the door be opened. He receives no answer. After repeated warnings the officer – having the stature of a Green Bay Packer – kicks down the door and enters the building. Then I hear a few gunshots and when the policeman reappears, I see a handcuffed and hurt Rick being packed into an arriving police car. I run across the street while Rick casts a spiteful look at me and yells: "You did not help me!"

Although we all understand that Rick's *cri de coeur* is rather misplaced, it is useful to consider more closely which types of rights are at issue here. At the most obvious level my special obligations to Rick are easily overridden by my duty not to interfere with the "public" official in the course of his work. He has, in Hohfeldian terms, a "privilege" or "licence" that confers upon him an exemption from a general duty, such as not breaking down the doors of houses he does not own, and I, as the owner, will probably not be able to collect damages from the police or the community, as officers enjoy an "immunity" for their official acts.

But if the officer had the "privilege" to break down the door, did he not also have a "duty" to exercise this privilege? After all, the "powers" invested in him are not like those I have possessing a "licence" to drive my car wherever I want, but which leaves it up to me whether I want to go somewhere or stay home.

[18] See Wesley Hohfeld, *Fundamental Legal Conceptions*, ed. by Walter Wheeler Cook (New Haven: Yale University Press, 1919).

Actually, my "right" to drive contains two privileges, that is to drive and not to drive. The powers of the policeman, on the other hand (or those of the judge for that matter, who later sentences Rick for an attempted armed robbery), that is their "privilege," is one of a special kind. As "powers," the officials' privileges imply the ability to alter or modify, within a set of rules and circumstances, the "rights" of others. But they are not discretionary. Only rights that are "paired powers" – or paired privileges – endow their bearers with discretion concerning some action. Rights that are paired powers are thus both authorizing and discretionary.[19] Furthermore, rights over objects, such as over property or over one's body, are first-order privileges (that is against others not to infringe upon them), while "powers" as "rights over rights" are second-order entitlements, which are either exercised (as privileges and powers) or just enjoyed (as claims and immunities).

Applied to our hypothetical case, this means that the policeman can deprive Rick of his liberty to move freely by arresting him. Similarly, the judge can send him to prison, provided the attempted robbery can be proven, and Rick was the actual perpetrator and not just a bystander walking in on an attempted robbery. In the latter case Rick just would have made the mistake of running away when the police arrived and of having later bolted the door because he was afraid of the officer, particularly since he had a pop gun in his possession. While both officials had to exercise their power, the factual circumstances *do matter* and can lead to entirely different outcomes. Thus the police officer obviously could not let Rick go, claiming that he had the privilege to do so, but the judge *has to* let Rick go if the charge cannot be proven. At best her or she can, in light of the circumstances, decide that only a charge of "resisting arrest" can be made "to stick." This has little to do with "discretion" (giving Dworkin his due), but it shows that the discussion of "rights" is always only part of the story, as the complex interaction of facts and norms, and not only of the structure of norms (rules vs. principles, conflict among rules and so on), is at issue. To that extent the decisions to bring different norms into play involve judgements and appraisals that remain contestable. But this does not mean that such decisions are "arbitrary," that is unconstrained, although the "right answer" thesis cannot be maintained either, even in rather "simple" cases (such as this hypothetical example) or in highly complex "constitutional cases."

The upshot of this argument is that all rights, whether *in rem*, against specific persons, the state, or as claims to particular common goods such as political participation,[20] are actually mediations by which social relations are ordered through specific institutional rules. Consider in this context the following example. When Peter beats up Paul, we usually do not consider this a violation

[19] Leif Wenar, "The Nature of Rights," *Philosophy and Public Affairs*, vol. 33 (Summer 2005), 223–52 at 231.

[20] *Ibid.*, especially 230ff.

of Paul's "human" rights, and rather assess this to be an "assault." But if John, a policeman, is doing the same thing and the "state" does not intervene, or fails to punish him for having acted without cause or for having used excessive force, then not only Paul's civil rights but potentially also his human rights have been violated. Far from being "free-standing" and "pre-social," human rights show their close links to society and to institutionalized "public power."

The effects of rights are somewhat different if new groups of claimants are constituted by law and whose members are thereafter entitled to certain benefits. Then the public is charged with new expenses that go beyond the maintenance of the public order, and the implementation of those rights depends upon additional taxes.[21] They are levied on virtually all members of society (not only citizens but resident aliens as well) in order to assist even "illegals," at least for the abatement of certain hardships (such as access to schools for children, and for health care due to public health concerns).

Here Michael Ignatieff has perceptively described the situation in a modern welfare state in which we all "are responsible for each other, but we are not responsible *to each other*,"[22] as in times when family bonds or status groups had to shoulder this task, or when providing the benefit was being left to "charity":

> My encounters with them [the pensioners he sees in his street] are a parable of moral relations between strangers in the welfare state. They have needs, and because they live within a welfare state, these needs confer entitlement-rights in the resources of people like me. Their needs and their entitlements establish a silent relation between us. As we stand together in line at the post office, while they cash in their pension checks, some tiny portion of my income is transferred into their pockets through the numberless capillaries of the state. The mediated quality of our relationship seems necessary to both of us. They are dependent on the state, not upon me, and we are both glad of it. Yet, I am also aware of how this mediation walls us off from each other.[23]

It is clear from the above discussion that the basis of the assignment of "rights" has shifted over time. On the one hand, rights were supposed to secure a domain for freedom for the individual and his autonomous will. On the other hand, if the function of rights was viewed as the means of safeguarding certain important basic "interests" such as subsistence and well-being – otherwise the free will determining itself might indeed be hollow – some important consequences follow. Not surprisingly, a debate has pitted advocates of a "will theory of rights" against those defending a conception of an "interests theory of rights," which ended, as most debates do, somewhat inconclusively. In addition, it is

[21] Cass Sunstein, *After the Rights Revolution* (Cambridge, MA: Harvard University Press, 1990).

[22] Michael Ignatieff, *The Needs of Strangers* (New York: Vintage, 1984), 10.

[23] *Ibid.* at 9f.

not quite clear whether this dichotomy[24] is able to accommodate certain other types of rights – also considered "basic" – such as participatory political rights, or whether claims to certain "common goods" can even be pressed into the scheme of individual "basic" or even "human" rights. Some further discussion seems in order.

Let us begin with "subsistence" rights, which emerged in the 1970s and 1980s and carried over into the new millennium in the writings of Peter Singer,[25] Charles Beitz,[26] Thomas Pogge,[27] Henry Shue,[28] Onora O'Neill,[29] Thomas Nagel,[30] and Amartya Sen and Martha Nussbaum[31] (to name just a few). Obviously, the respective participants emphasized different aspects of the problem of "global justice" that would require the assignment of rights. They identified the *scandalum* of mass starvation and general misery in certain parts of the world, while the "developed" countries enjoyed previously unknown levels of abundance. Thus moral issues, questions of distributive justice, of "development," and of basic needs were raised and interacted in these espoused positions in different ways. But a common thread in these debates was the challenge to our usual complacency with a "politics," by calling attention to our enabling "cooperation" in this sorry state of affairs,[32] and to some serious flaws in our philosophical vocabularies and disciplinary understandings.[33]

In this context two problems were of particular importance: one concerned the issue that our moral vocabularies, which work pretty well in the case of individual choice, rather quickly come to an end when applied to "global

24 In this context see the argument by Matthew Kramer and Hillel Steiner, "Theories of Rights: Is there a Third Way?," *Oxford Journal of Legal Studies*, vol. 27, no. 2 (2007), 281–310 (affirming the appropriateness of the classical dichotomy), and the challenge by Gopal Sreenivasan, "A Hybrid Theory of Claim Rights," *Oxford Journal of Legal Studies*, vol. 25 (2005), 257–74.

25 See e.g. Peter Singer, "Famine, Affluence and Morality," in Peter Lasslett and James Fishkin (eds.), *Philosophy, Politics and Society*, Fifth Series (Oxford: Blackwell, 1979), 21–35; and his *Practical Ethics* (Cambridge University Press, 1979).

26 Charles Beitz, "Justice and International Relations," *Philosophy and Public Affairs*, vol. 4 (Summer 1975), 360–89; see also his *Political Theory and International Relations* (Princeton University Press, 1979).

27 Thomas Pogge, *World Poverty and Human Rights* (Oxford: Basil Blackwell, 2002).

28 Henry Shue, "Mediating Duties," *Ethics*, vol. 98, no. 4 (1988), 678–704.

29 Onora O'Neill, "Life Boat Earth," *Philosophy and Public Affairs*, vol. 4 (Spring 1975), 273–92.

30 Thomas Nagel, "Poverty and Food: Why Charity is not Enough," in Peter Brown and Henry Shue (eds.), *Food Policy: The Responsibility of the United States in Life and Death Choices* (New York: Free Press, 1977), 54–62.

31 Martha Nussbaum and Amartya Sen, *The Quality of Life* (Oxford: Clarendon, 1991).

32 See Henry Shue, *Basic Rights, Subsistence and American Foreign Policy* (Princeton University Press, 1980).

33 Here an early warning had been voiced by Alfred Hirschman concerning our "paradigm" of economic development (see Alfred Hirschman, "The Search for Paradigms as a Hindrance to Understanding," *World Politics*, vol. 22, no. 3 (1970): 329–43. See also Amartya Sen, *On Economic Inequality* (Oxford: Clarendon, 1973); and his *Poverty and Famines: An Essay on Entitlements and Freedom* (Oxford: Clarendon, 1981).

problems." Even the criterion of "minimal altruism," for example, could imply some disturbingly far-reaching obligations when applied to the problem of global hunger. Originally this principle was designed to demarcate those acts that can be required from us, such as sharing some food of which we have enough, from those of asking for some heroic efforts (acts of super-rogation), such as of rescuing a person while risking one's own life. However, Peter Singer drew the radical conclusion that global justice did not involve super-rogation but that:

> we ought to give until we reach the level of marginal utility – that is the level at which, by giving more, I would cause as much suffering to myself or my dependents as I would relieve by my gift. This would mean of course that one would reduce oneself to very near the material circumstances of a Bengali refugee.[34]

The prospect of pauperization of course did not provide strong incentives for the privileged, quite aside from the fact that the "moral" value of such a proposition is also highly debatable,[35] since it shows some egregious lack of understanding the sources of poverty and its concomitant political and social implications. Here several issues are raised, ranging from overpopulation to the ruin of subsistence agriculture through "food aid" and one-sided "industrial" policies. It is not surprising that Fishkin's contribution in his *The Limits of Obligation*[36] debunked such a stance and initiated a second round of the debate. Having shown that Singer's position was hardly tenable, one could now conclude that we might not have any obligation, as Fishkin came close to suggesting.

Second, it is here that the move from "duties" to "rights," and from a "will approach" to rights to an "interest" approach appeared to be helpful. While duties are of course directly action-guiding, "rights" need not be so, as we have seen. Thus general "rights" are either assumed to be solely "negative" à la Nozick,[37] or they are "imperfect duties" since they are not assigned to specific duty-bearers. But this conceptualization seems, at first blush, to be a nearly fatal blow to arguments for certain subsistence rights *outside of properly constituted communities* to which this imposition of duties can be assigned. Humanity as such cannot act and thus cannot be the duty-bearer, as Onora O'Neill has argued. Consequently, there seems to be little to a human "right to food," aside from making what Feinberg[38] has called a "manifesto claim," that is identifying a problem that needs collective attention. In a recent restatement of her position O'Neill writes:

34 Singer, "Famine, Affluence and Morality," at 33.

35 Singer modified his position somewhat in his *Practical Ethics*, at 163f.

36 James Fishkin, *The Limits of Obligation* (New Haven: Yale University Press, 1982).

37 Robert Nozick, *Anarchy, State and Utopia* (New York: Basic Books, 1974).

38 Joel Feinberg, "The Nature and Value of Rights," in Joel Feinberg, *Rights, Justice and the Bounds of Liberty* (Princeton University Press, 1980), 143–55.

> the claim that rights must have counterpart obligations asserts the exceptionless logical point that where anyone is to have a right there must be identifiable others (either all others or specified others) with accurately corresponding obligations. From a normative view of rights, obligations and claimable rights are two perspectives on a single normative pattern: without obligations there are no rights. So while obligations will drop out if we read human rights "claims" merely as aspirations rather than requirements, so too will rights, as usually understood. Unsurprisingly, aspirational readings of human rights documents are not popular. However, such readings at least offer an exit strategy if we conclude that claiming rights without counterpart obligations is an unacceptable deception, and find that we can't develop an adequate normative account of obligations and rights.[39]

While from a Kantian standpoint the wilful uptake of an obligation constitutes a "perfect duty," and while owing others only respect for their moral autonomy might be a tenable position, from the point of view of an "interest theory" of rights this stance seems less convincing. Besides, given the increasing interdependencies of modern life, especially in the economic sphere, we might be engaged with "strangers" in more ways than we think. Such common engagements, especially if they lead to some pathology in "development," might give rise to special obligations, on the basis of participation in common institutions. Thus even the IMF and the World Bank recognized as of late that their "functionally" defined mission cannot be pursued in splendid isolation from other economic and social problems. In the context of "development," mere "supervision" of monetary policy is unlikely to succeed, if poverty abatement and institutional reform remain unaddressed. It was then no accident that the "right" to subsistence[40] was raised in conjunction with a critique of certain US policies and of the institutional structures that they had created. Henry Shue's logic of his "mediating duties" is, therefore, worth pondering. Starting out from an interest theory of rights, Shue suggests:

> One should not in any case leap from universal rights to universal duties. It is true that an alleged right means nothing unless duties to fulfil it have been assigned to definite people, so that some claimant or representative of a claimant could call upon them. Yet in order for everyone to have a certain right, such as a right to food, it is not necessary for everyone else to have all the duties required to fulfil the right – it is necessary only for some others to have each of the duties required. On the side of duties there can be a division of labour … For every person with a right and for every duty corresponding to that right there must be some agents who have been assigned that duty and who have the capacity to fulfil it. We have no reason to believe,

[39] O'Neill, "The Dark Side of Human Rights," at 431.

[40] For the purposes of my argument here I leave out part of Shue's plea for "security," which he considers equally basic.

however, that everyone has burdensome duties towards everyone else even if everyone else has meaningful rights.[41]

While Shue's argument goes a considerable way in showing how "imperfect" duties can become (near) perfect duties (in a Kantian sense) via the mediation of institution, there still remain some problems of implementation. Shue himself is clear that his "enjoyment of the substance of a right" should be guaranteed only against "standard threats." Thus despite the fact that his starting point is human needs – and that needs are potentially limitless – he rather narrowly circumscribes the "level" of enjoyment of those rights. Nevertheless, the devil lies in the detail, which any "interest" theory of rights has to face. For example, if Shue argues that there is no duty (and thus no right) to provide open-heart surgery, but at the same time postulates as a criterion for recognizing a "basic right" the *functional role of a right* to a "threat to an individual's life," then this criterion seems hopelessly indeterminate.[42] It seems that any standard that we consider "reasonable" is highly context-sensitive and probably more "culturally" and politically determined than derived from any "human" right.

Of course we encounter similar difficulties in the provision of the Covenant on Economic, Social and Cultural Rights, where we find a "right to health" (not only health care) and to "adequate food." While the latter might be clearer in so far as a minimum caloric intake is guaranteed thereby – having of course to make allowances for special needs, such of the sick and undernourished, or pregnant women – the former is rather vague. Is it the best attainable health care – which can be minimal and vary also from society to society – or is it the best available health care in accordance with contemporary medical possibilities? If it is the latter, then it is utopian, since "how can everyone have a right to the best?"[43] I think, therefore, that the problem lies deeper than simply assuming that careless drafting of the document is to blame.

This brings me to some equally important points about the role of institutions in mediating duties. First, while the existence of common institutions might help us in conceiving of duties to "strangers," they are also part of the problem. Like property regimes in general, they are not "neutral" and their function is precisely to protect certain interests and to background others, or even make them "invisible" to the participants in common undertakings. Thus the WTO might be a "multilateral" institution, guaranteed by the multilateralization of the most favoured nation (MFN) clause, and thus doing business according to "universal" rules that protect free trade. But that does not mean that trade is now "fair," or that all countries have the same pull in getting their

[41] Shue, "Mediating Duties," at 689.

[42] For a good discussion of Shue's impact nearly thirty years after the publication of his *Basic Rights*, see the collection of essays in Charles Beitz and Robert Goodin (eds.), *Global Basic Rights* (Oxford: Oxford University Press, 2009).

[43] O'Neill, "The Dark Side of Human Rights," at 429.

interest recognized or put on the agenda. Even when developing countries are "winning a case" before the DSU, they hardly have equal "enforcement" capacity since "sanctioning" has remained entirely bilateral in this "multilateral organization."

Second, what still needs to be explained is how poverty by itself can generate responsibilities to subsistence on the basis of common institutions. Such an argument might turn less on involvement per se than on a variety of (contestable) factual assertions about what "explains" the particular outcome and what steps could alleviate the problem. The jump from the fact of participation in a joint endeavour – even if it is more profitable for some than for others – to the conclusion that a definable and claimable moral right exists vis-à-vis other participants, seems compelling only if we presuppose beforehand that inequality and thus differential benefits represent an unjust enrichment. Otherwise, something more seems to be required than involvement and benefit. Without some plausible account of how and why a particular practice is reasonably connected to the dismal outcome – and such an assessment will depend on practical experience as well as on our "theories" – no definite assignment of duties seems justified. Particularly since poverty abatement is such a highly complex problem, rushing to a "solution," such as assigning the duty of ensuring food supplies to "benefiting" countries for example, might in the end help the "victims" little, and actually do considerable harm. It also can hardly be required morally as a strict duty if certain "perverse" effects, such as a slump in domestic food production, can be foreseen. This does not mean of course that we ought not to think about these problems and attempt to identify possible ameliorating strategies.[44] However, rights thinking is not that helpful here.

There are also decisive differences between state and international institutions that have to be considered precisely because the technical term of "institution" hides these differences. The mediation by state institutions is a result of their capacity to aggregate various still free-floating concerns into a hopefully coherent set of policies. But the question remains whether the many free-standing regimes in international politics, which could generate such "duties beyond borders," can similarly aggregate these duties short of being in something like a world state. Such an aggregation would presuppose *both the authority and capacity* of deciding among competing or even conflicting "rights" and "levels" of satisfaction. This is already extremely difficult domestically, as "property rights" frequently bar certain desirable social policies, or no funding is available, and thus the level of the enjoyment of rights is always up for political

[44] See e.g. Thomas Pogge's proposal for institutional reform of the existing international economic legal order, precisely because of its effectiveness and sustainability, which other redistributive schemes lack. Thomas Pogge, "The Role of International Law in Reproducing Massive Poverty," in Samantha Besson and John Tasioulas (eds.), *The Philosophy of International Law* (Oxford University Press, 2010), 417–35.

grabs. To expect something even resembling such a mediation in the face of the "fragmentation" of the international legal order seems more than heroic.

In short, as soon as we talk about "policies" we are pretty far removed from individual rights. The issue of rights recedes into the background and, similar to the notions of "right" and "wrong," they are soon overwhelmed by the logics of various policy machineries, supposed to "implement" the agreed-upon policies. Since "human" rights are not directly claimable by the "owners," as *states* are usually only obliged to "ensure" that these policy objectives are being respected, no implementing policies are in place and thus individuals cannot "stand on their rights." International organizations and free-standing regimes can then continue with their business as usual, as they are not "responsible" either. They occasionally seek "inputs" from members of "civil society," consulting them at their pleasure, but do so mainly for purposes of enhancing "compliance." Or if they are involved in the distribution of goods and services, they cannot be "claimed" since they come from donations and charity rather than from an authoritative allocation that is bound by right claims. Whatever the case is, even the most ardent "cosmopolitan" activists and members of "civil society" have to admit that they are still without even the "right of petition" and certainly cannot appeal to some public authority to "set things right."[45]

Conflicting rights

If rights are trumps, then they provide some remedy against arbitrary and high-handed actions of governments. They are also designed to cure infringements on my sphere of liberty by others where they are not simply conceived as agent-relative, minimal side-constraints, requiring only omissions by all other actors.[46] But when we consider rights as protecting important interests that impose duties on others, things change and the facile distinction between negative and positive rights breaks down, as we have seen. For example, my right of free speech ought to not only prevent the government from curtailing it, it also imposes on me the duty to refrain from interfering with it, such as with the assembly of some people on a "speakers corner" in my street, even though my right to privacy, or of the enjoyment of my property is thereby affected, as the jeers one hears make reading in my garden a doubtful pleasure. Similarly, I cannot claim compensation from anyone when a lucrative business deal could not be consummated because I could not get to the signing of the papers in time due to a demonstration that caused a traffic jam.

Here not only do the various "interests" or "goods" have to be identified, since only certain "interests" merit such attention, but a "theory" identifying

[45] See e.g. Alan Boyle and Christine Chinkin, *The Making of International Law* (Oxford University Press, 2007).

[46] This seems to be the position of Robert Nozik in *Anarchy, State and Utopia*, at 28f.

those interests also has to provide for some way in which these different "goods" protected by rights can be assessed.[47] In this context the metaphor of weighing and balancing re-enter the picture, although originally "rights" were supposed to counteract the "felicific" calculus that would have allowed the visiting of misery on one person, if overall happiness was thereby enhanced. Thus poor Rob, who is not enjoying life anyway due to his social isolation and depression, could be designated as an "organ donor," so that Bill, Susan, and Whitney could benefit from various transplants.

There are, therefore, several problems that need to be addressed. One is of course a clear conception of the difference between making a decision according to overall utility calculations (the "greatest happiness," or perhaps the "greatest happiness to the greatest number"), and of a proper "weighing of rights" when they compete or conflict. The second is that the creation of "privileged groups" of claimants (and perhaps also allowing someone to claim these special privileges on behalf of others, such as for animals or "the earth") requires in democratic societies special authorizations through representative institutions. To claim such privileges on the basis of "human rights" alone therefore creates certain practical (insufficiency of funds) and theoretical (no taxation without representation) problems. These issues have to be addressed, particularly since "right claims," far from being "secure" and incontrovertible, appear to be subject to rescission and substantial modifications as soon as some of the "background" conditions change. If this suspicion is correct, then the notion of "founding" morality on "rights" becomes incoherent and thus the hope that a theory of rights is "the answer" will be disappointed.

Let us begin with the idea of rights as trumps, that is virtually indefeasible grounds that protect a certain interest. Justice Black's idea of free speech being "absolute" seems to fit this description, but does not hold up under closer scrutiny. Mill had already suggested that crying "fire" in a theatre or inciting a riot in front of the house of a corn dealer is not an exercise of free speech. The somewhat strange interpretation of the First Amendment, bringing not only "commercial" free speech under its penumbra, but also of decreeing that certain actions "are" free speech (such as "flag-burning"), could also be read as a somewhat contorted history of the concept rather than as a triumphalist account safeguarding "liberty." Add to this the recent decisions concerning campaign financing and your enthusiasm is dampened even further.[48] Dispensing with

[47] For a general discussion see Joseph Raz, *The Morality of Freedom* (Oxford: Clarendon, 1986).

[48] Super PACs were the result of a Supreme Court decision allowing unlimited spending for "independent expenditure only committees," which may not contribute to a candidate or party in a specific election but can engage in unlimited spending for political "caucuses" independent of an election. See *Citizens United* v. *Federal Election Commission*, 558 US 310 (2010).

campaign financing limitations, the Supreme Court decisions allow Super PACs to buy up virtually all publicity time and thus to drown out other opinions. Since oligopolies are known to be detrimental and justify limitations on the exercise of property rights, it is not clear why the buying-up of television time, which is a "public good" (but not in the economic sense as there is rivalry of consumption!), does not impinge on my ability to exercise my right (and that of many others) of getting a hearing.

Thus while certain "trade-offs" of "interests," and of rights protecting them, are obscene – such as the above organ donor example – not all of them are. Some, tragically enough, cannot be avoided – such as having to decide which of three or four children I shall rescue when their boat has capsized, because I can save only one. Other choices again might be less "tragic" but are perhaps equally problematic, as when we send young men and women abroad to fight for their country – often for rather dubious adventures, even when couched in "humanitarian" terms – and when we as decision-makers and as citizens alike assuage our pangs of remorse by holding on to the principle *volenti not fit injuria*, and hope for the best. After all, those having chosen this "career" also "knew" what they were getting into. Still other cases of inter-right conflicts raise vexing issues of prioritization, such as how much money to allocate to education, to police protection, welfare, or even to the courts (safeguarding important due process rights).

These are all well-known problems sitting uneasily with the Dworkian notion that rights are simply "anti-majoritarian immunities," as articulated in his *Taking Rights Seriously*.[49] And it is also not surprising that a more structural, or "reason-constraining" view of rights emerged in his later work, as Raz[50] and Regan[51] have pointed out. Dworkin attempted to link these different versions to an overarching notion of the "moral independence" of the individual, while acknowledging that "in our political culture there are *two* major sources of claims of individual rights i.e., "equal concern and independent commitment to basic freedoms."[52] Thus there remain sufficient doubts about the existence and viability of this final synthesis, even though Dworkin reiterated that "equal concern" and "personal liberty" (and thus presumably the two conceptions of rights) do not conflict in the way Isaiah Berlin had feared. They are, according to a recent statement by Dworkin, "thoroughly integrated" and form part

[49] See Richard Pildes, "Why Rights Are not Trumps" *Journal of Legal Studies*, vol. 27 (1998): 725–63; see also Dworkin's "Two Conceptions of Rights," *Journal of Legal Studies*, vol. 29 (2000), 309–15.

[50] Joseph Raz, "Professor Dworkin's Theory of Rights," *Political Studies*, vol. 26 (1978), 123–37.

[51] Donald Regan, "Glosses on Dworkin: Rights, Principles and Policies," *Michigan Law Review*, vol. 76 (1978), 1213–64.

[52] Ronald Dworkin, *Freedom's Law* (Cambridge, MA: Harvard 1996), 73.

of his effort to defend "the metaphysical independence of values."[53] But then again, he himself admits somewhat wistfully that that might strike outsiders as a "Procrustean" solution.[54]

In any case, the first conception of rights (immunity view) lets us think of them as personal possessions that allow individuals to act, regardless of what the government or the majority considers "right." The rights the owners possess provide an "all-purpose shield" against outside interferences. On the second view, rights can be infringed under certain circumstances but not on the basis of an all-purpose, superior necessity, or a "general good" argument. Rights no longer simply entitle; rather:

> they channel the kinds of reasons upon which the state can constitutionally act in diverse institutional and other contexts. Conceived in this way rights are still ultimately justified on the grounds of the individual interests they promote, but these interests are distinct … from the way interests are conceived in the immunities conception. There is no general state of duty of non-interference with such rights, but a duty not to interfere for certain reasons.[55]

In these circumstances courts are called upon to "balance" the conflicting rights and to attribute to individuals and to the government which powers, freedoms, or claims they validly hold. While this might be a far cry from the original notion of subjects claiming their rights, it is also far from the idea that a legislator has to consult only the felicific calculus for arriving at the "right" decision. Furthermore, there exist some importance differences in various legal systems for tackling this task. Thus the balancing of US courts, particularly of the Supreme Court in exercising judicial review,[56] and the use of a "proportionality" test by German courts are perhaps the best examples. A different test of "reasonableness," originally articulated in *Wednesbury*[57] for English and Commonwealth systems of yore, required *from the claimant* some proof that an official had acted irrationally before a court would grant judicial review.

The proportionality test, however, has in the meantime made great inroads into the common law and has left its mark on both the administrative and constitutional law practice of the Eastern European "transition" states.[58] It has

53 Ronald Dworkin, *Justice for Hedgehogs* (Cambridge, MA: Harvard University Press, 2011), at 4 and 9 respectively.

54 *Ibid.* at 5.

55 Richard Pildes, "Dworkin's Two Conceptions of Rights," *Journal of Legal Studies*, vol. 29 (January 2000): 309–15 at 312.

56 Here the Court developed the doctrine of "strict judicial scrutiny." See e.g. Richard Fallon, "Strict Judicial Scrutiny," *UCLA Law Review*, vol. 54 no. 5 (2007): 1267–337.

57 See *Associated Provincial Picture Houses Ltd.* v. *Wednesbury Corporation* (1948) 1 KB223 (UK).

58 For an extensive discussion see Alec Stone Sweet and Jud Mathews, "Proportionality Balancing and Global Constitutionalism," *Columbia Journal of Transnational Law*, vol. 47 (2008/2009): 73–164.

influenced the jurisprudence of the South African, Canadian,[59] and Israeli[60] Supreme Courts and increasingly replaces the traditional standards within different European legal systems. It also has been adopted by the EU, the European Convention on Human Rights and its Court[61] and the WTO,[62] and thus has arguably also become part of the "new constitutionalism"[63] in international law. In the USA the impact of the "proportionality" criterion[64] explains some of the heated debates between those who saw in balancing "the ultimate rule of law"[65] and those who considered its "dark side," that is interpreted it as a threat to constitutionally protected individual rights.[66] Needless to say, that "proportionality" thereby also became part of the larger controversy on the appropriateness of using "foreign" sources of law.[67]

Originally the proportionality test emerged from the practice of the Prussian Supreme Administrative Court after the codification of the Prussian General Law (*Preussisches Landrecht*) of 1794. By the 1880s the "police" powers of the government became the subject of scrutiny, since ministerial accountability to parliament had not been institutionalized in the second German Reich and remedies were sought through administrative law measures. The decisions of this Court significantly influenced legal doctrine and, through the appointments of scholars who had developed those ideas further in the period between the First and Second World Wars, it also has shaped the German Constitutional Court's jurisprudence. In its famous *Apothekenurteil* of 1958 the doctrine received its classical form by focusing on the criteria that judges have to observe when deciding conflicts between individual rights and public policy:

59 Dieter Grimm, "Proportionality in Canadian and German Constitutional Law Jurisprudence," *University of Toronto Law Journal*, vol. 57 (2007), 383–97.

60 See e.g. the former president of the Israeli Supreme Court Aharon Barak, "Proportional Effect: The Israeli Experience," *University of Toronto Law Journal*, vol. 57 (2007), 369–82.

61 See Steven Greer, *The European Convention on Human Rights* (Cambridge University Press, 2006).

62 See Joel Trachtman, "The Constitutions of the WTO," *European Journal of International Law*, vol. 17 (2006), 623–46.

63 See Alec Stone Sweet, *Governing with Judges* (Oxford University Press, 2000).

64 Moshe Cohen-Eliya and Iddo Porat, "The Hidden Foreign Law Debate in Heller: Proportionality Approach in American Constitutional Law," *San Diego Law Review*, vol. 46 (2009), 367–415, taking issue with Justice Bryer's attempt to introduce proportionality to the US constitutional discourse. For a general discussion see also Moshe Cohen-Eliya and Iddo Porat, "American Balancing and German Proportionality: the Historical Origins," *International Journal of Constitutional Law*, vol. 8 (2010), 263–86.

65 David Beatty, *The Ultimate Rule of Law* (New York: Oxford University Press, 2004).

66 See e.g. the review of Beatty's book by Vikki Jackson, "Being Proportional about Proportionality," *Constitutional Commentary*, vol. 21, no. 3 (2004), 803–59.

67 See e.g. Justice Scalia in *Printz* v. *United States* 521 US 898, 921 n.11 (1997). On the debate in the aftermath of *Roper* v. *Simmons* 125 S Ct 1183 (2005) where Justices Scalia, Thomas, Rehnquist and O'Connor dissented from the majority, which based its decision on an emerging international "consensus." See also see Jeremy Waldron "Foreign Law and the Modern Jus Gentium," *Harvard Law Review*, vol. 119, no. 1 (2005), 129–47.

> The purpose of constitutional right should be to protect the freedom of the individual while the purpose of the regulation should be to ensure sufficient protection of societal interests. The individual's claim to freedom will have a stronger effect … the more his right to free choice of a profession is put into question; the protection of the public will become more urgent, the greater the disadvantages that arise from the free practicing of professions. When one seeks to maximize both … demands of the most effective way, the solution can only lie in a careful balancing (*Abwägung*) of the meaning of two opposed and perhaps conflicting interests.[68]

While at first blush there seems not much difference between proportionality and balancing, since in both cases some "maximization" is invoked (even if considerably modified, as Alexy[69] suggests), there are some notable differences even if they are not immediately obvious. Thus there is for example a difference between the structured assessment of proportionality and an open-ended mandate "to do the right thing," or to "take everything into account."[70] When fully articulated, "proportionality" involves four steps and within each step a different "test" has to be administered.

At the first stage the judge has to ascertain that the government is constitutionally authorized to take measures in the area in which the case falls (legitimacy test). At the second stage the test concerns the "suitability" of the measures taken, that is they must be rationally related to the policy objective. In the third step the "necessity test" is designed to ascertain whether the adopted measure was the "least restrictive means" by which the objective could be reached. Only at the fourth stage does an actual "balancing" between competing rights or "goods" (*Rechtsgüter*) occur, what is called "balancing in the strict sense."[71] But even here "proportionality" need not involve a comparison among incommensurable values. As Cohen-Eliya and Porrat suggest:

> There is a nice example that may explain this claim. Consider a dog show in which there are different contests: the best bulldog, the best schnauzer and so on. However, there is also a final contest for the best dog overall. Comparing one schnauzer with another can make sense, but how are we to compare bulldogs and schnauzers? Proportionality, so the argument goes, provides a solution: we take the bulldog that won the bulldog show and the

[68] BVerfG June ll, 1958 7 BverfGE 377(404f), as quoted in Sweet and Mathews, "Proportionality Balancing and Global Constitutionalism," at 107f.

[69] See Robert Alexy, *A Theory of Constitutional Rights*, transl. by Julian Rivers (Oxford University Press, 2002). See also his "Constitutional Rights, Balancing and Rationality" *Ratio Juris*, vol. 16 (2003), 131–40.

[70] Frederick Schauer, "Balancing, Subsumption and the Constraining Role of Legal Text," *Law and Ethics of Human Rights*, vol. 4, no. 1 (2010), 34–45 at 36f.

[71] See Mattias Kumm, "Political Liberalism and the Structure of Rights: On the Place and Limits of the Proportionality Requirement," in Stanley Paulson and George Pavlakos (eds.), *Law, Rights, Discourse: The Legal Philosophy of Robert Alexy* (Oxford: Hart, 2007), 131–66.

> schnauzer that won the schnauzer show and ask with respect to each one how close it came to the ideal bulldog or schnauzer in terms of the standards for its respective species. Similarly, the proportionality test assesses each value in its own terms without the need to compare incommensurable values, and then asks with respect to each one how close the infringement in the case was to the core of this value.[72]

Although there is a point to this argument, I am not so sure whether the analogy of the dog show holds. After all, there is an independent metric for each breed and the one that receives the highest marks automatically wins the "best dog" contest. In the other case, there is, for example, one metric of "security" and another of "personal liberty." But in the case of a particular proposal both metrics can be influenced negatively and positively. Does it follow that, for example, the security concern should win out if the proposal adds thirty points on the ideal scale of "security" and takes only ten points off the ideal "liberty scale"? That does not seem right, as the incommensurability issue raises its ugly head. Nevertheless, the advantage of this four-step process is that justices can no longer make assessments only according to their own valuation, even though there remains some subjective element in the final judgment. The difference can be seen when we compare such a four-step appraisal with the Naulilaa award of 1928, where the tribunal made only a distinction between a "thicker" and "thinner" version of proportionality in addressing the justifiability of German reprisal against Angolan (Portuguese) military installations and civilians. The German actions had occurred in response to the killings of three German officials who had erroneously crossed the border of the Portuguese colony during the First World War (December 1914). As the tribunal reasoned:

> Even if it could be considered that international Law did not require that a reprisal would have to be proportionate to the offence, one would surely have to consider such reprisals which are wholly disproportionate with the act which gave rise to them as being excessive and illegal. Thus in the present case ... there was an obvious disproportion between the incident at Naulilaa and the six acts of reprisals which followed.[73]

By using a proper proportionality test judicial law-making is not camouflaged but subject to certain exacting requirements that have to be met *coram publico*. This does not dispose of the "second order" legitimacy problem, given that "the law" applicable to the dispute could not have been known by the parties when the dispute arose, but it does provide an open procedure by which judges acquire a coherent, practical means of responding to these basic legitimacy

[72] Cohen-Eliya and Porrat, "American Balancing and German Proportionality," at 269.

[73] Naulilaa Arbitration Award, as quoted in Georg Nolte, "Thin or Thick? The Principles of Proportionality and International Humanitarian Law," *Law and Ethics of Human Rights*, vol. 4 (2010), 244–55 at 249.

questions.[74] To that extent "balancing" does seem to have solved some of the puzzles that remained from the old controversies about *Interessenjusrisprudenz* in Germany and the identification of the variety of social interests that impinge on the law, as identified by Roscoe Pound[75] in the United States. The latter in particular never transcended the stage of identifying different interests, as it developed no adequate method for dealing with conflicts.

Two problems remain. One is the issue of comparability of the two methods of "weighing," which is a general problem familiar from comparative law, that is whether what is going on in two (or more) different systems is really comparable, as discussed in a previous Meditation. In the present case we then have to assume that the "discourse on balancing" signals that a particular analytical process commences. This "discourse/process" assimilation then guarantees that references to "balancing" are "taken as reliable indicators which supplies the *tertium comparationis*, even though the language of balancing might mean very different things at different times and in different places."[76]

The second and more difficult problem is whether this technique can be treated as "free-standing," so as to be available to "courts" that are not part of a constitutional structure and law-making constraints. This seems to be a concern when considering the "dispute resolution mechanisms" in the international arena, as it is not clear when supranational courts should, for example, grant "margins of appreciation" to different systems for dealing with "policy" problems. It also raises questions of what counts as evidence when these free-standing courts engage in such appraisals. Thus, can a Human Rights court simply ignore the specific agreement between two governments that concerns the treatment of a convicted person who is being returned to his own country? Is it sufficient if the convict alleges that he will become a potential victim of abuse at home, therefore claiming a "right" of stay in the host country, even in violation of local (constitutional) law? Similarly, why should convicted felons retain their right to vote in the presence of existing prescriptions to the contrary?[77] In these cases Juvenal's question of *quis custodiet ipsos custodes* shows its bite.

There seems to be the widespread perception among jurists that "of course" judges are the appropriate body to resolve this conundrum. As Lord Denning once so aptly put it in the debate on the adoption of a Human Rights Charter:

[74] Sweet and Mathews, "Proportionality Balancing and Global Constitutionalism," at 80.

[75] See e.g. Roscoe Pound, "A Survey of Social Interests," *Harvard Law Review*, vol. 57 (1943), 1–39.

[76] Jacco Bomhoff, "Genealogies of Balancing as Discourse," *Law and Ethics of Human Rights*, vol. 4, no. 1 (2010), 108–39 at 113.

[77] See *Hirst* v. *United Kingdom* (2006) 42 ECtHR, 41.

> You need not fear! The judges of England have always in the past – and always will be – vigilant in guarding our freedoms. Someone must be trusted. Let it be the judges.[78]

This call to arms is remarkably self-serving. First, even if we accept Lord Denning's "Whig interpretation" of history, the conclusion simply does not hold, as the fortunate outcome might be the result of the British Constitution upholding parliamentary supremacy, not of judicial review. Second, it seems to rely for its force on a version of the "father knows best" argument, or of the benign despot whom Kant feared. Third, until and unless we are told why judges are of a different timbre than the rest of us, who, as bankers, priests, teachers, accountants, scientists, or whatever, can all become corrupted unless proper safeguards (checks and balances) exist, we can only take this as an act of faith. Finally, it assumes that there are some things in which we simply have to trust. But this is a strangely Bodinian or Hobbesian argument that the invention of "rights" was supposed to counteract.

Rights, justice, and the "right of rights"

The argument so far has shown that the notion that rights are "absolute," or can serve as unequivocal "trumps," is problematic even if we are only seeking an answer to the problem of how to delineate spheres of non-interference. Such problems become particularly virulent, as we have seen when we consider distributional issues, that is decide on what the "rich" owe to the "poor" and through which strategies these human rights, rooted in needs, can be fulfilled. Thus if rights are not treated as simple direct claim rights, whose non-fulfilment would automatically constitute a wrong, they become a "goal" within a system in which fulfilment and non-realization of rights are incorporated into the evaluation of a state of affairs. Then a different system for appraising various options emerges. This system has been called by Sen a "goal-rights system"[79] in which non-fulfilment of certain rights is accepted, as long as the overall performance of the system provides basic liberties and welfare gains. To that extent, for Sen, rights should not be understood as individual claims to goods, as is the case for Shue,[80] but they address a "range of human capabilities." This approach stresses the importance of different types of human concerns, but also emphasizes the overall "quality of life" and of the agent's choices, instead of focusing only on the commodities and their "level" of supply.[81]

78 As quoted in Jonathan Morgan, "Law's British Empire," *Oxford Journal of Legal Studies*, vol. 22, no. 4 (2002), 729–46 at 730.

79 Amartya Sen, "Rights and Agency," *Philosophy and Public Affairs*, vol. 11 (1981), 3–39 at 15.

80 See Shue, "Mediating Duties," at 23.

81 See Amartya Sen, *Inequality Reexamined* (Cambridge, MA: Harvard University Press, 1992), Chapters 4 and 5. See also his *Development as Freedom* (New York: Anchor Books, 1999).

Although some, such as Rawls, considered this "capability approach" an "unworkable idea,"[82] the program developed by Sen and Nussbaum had significant impact on policy.[83] It informed the UN Development Program and its more than 500 Human Development Reports[84] assessing different countries in terms of a Human Development Index. In short, their approach (and I neglect here some differences between them) is not a simple utilitarian maximization of satisfaction. Sen also resisted a strict lexical ordering of rights in which subsistence rights have priority over certain political rights. He did so by noting that no democratic regime has suffered in recent times from hunger, as did the Soviet Union and China. Perhaps Sen makes too much of this argument, since his native India is certainly more democratic than either of the other two, but did suffer from such plagues, even if they were less severe than the devastation visited on the Soviet Union by Stalin's policies or on China by Mao's "Great Leap Forward" or by the "Cultural Revolution." Nevertheless, this type of "rights consequentialism" does improve on some of the perplexities created by claim rights to a "minimum" of commodities. Such "minimalism" leaves not only "special needs" largely unattended – for example, those of a pregnant woman, paraplegic, or nursing mother – it also fails to prioritize emergencies to the detriment of "normal" rights-based distributions. After all, we all are familiar with the dilemmas doctors face under battle conditions, for example, when they have to "economize" on the available medicine, giving it perhaps not to those who most need it, but to those who have the best chance of surviving. Thus neither rights nor needs provide us with universally applicable criteria for meeting these challenges.

This realization has two consequences. On the one hand, it shows us that right claims are easily defeasible as soon as some of the parameter conditions change. As Dorsey points out:

> what sense does it make to say that A has a right to minimal decency (so that non-fulfilment entails a great moral wrong) although depending upon resource availability, the state behaved rightly in non-fulfilment … Resource scarcity makes a claim right to a minimally decent standard implausible. And because most of the problems, to which the theory of global justice must be sensitive, are of this kind … the failure of claim right views is a tremendous blow to the applicability of the rights talk to global justice.[85]

[82] John Rawls, *The Law of Peoples* (Cambridge, MA: Harvard University Press, 1999), 13.

[83] See e.g. Martha Nussbaum, *Women and Human Development: The Capabilities Approach* (Cambridge University Press, 2000); see also her *Creating Capabilities: The Human Development Approach* (Cambridge, MA: Harvard University Press, 2011).

[84] For an assessment see Ingrid Robeyns, "The Capability Approach in Practice," *Journal of Political Philosophy*, vol. 14, no. 1 (2006), 131–76.

[85] Dale Dorsey, "Global Justice and the Limits of Human Rights," *The Philosophical Quarterly*, vol. 55, no. 221 (October 2005), 562–81 at 568.

Dorsey here echoes a criticism about the "rights talk" that Tushnet raised nearly forty years ago in another context. Taking issue with the general assessment of rights as an undoubtedly "good thing," he tried to show that rights are actually quite unstable and indeterminate, so that relatively small changes in the background conditions make it "difficult to sustain the claim that a right remains implicated."[86] He takes as his hypothetical example the right to an abortion:

> The contemporary right to reproductive choice has, as a matter of contingent technological fact, two components. A woman who chooses to have an abortion today necessarily chooses two things: to remove the foetus from her body and to destroy the foetus. All the arguments that support the right to reproductive choice apparently implicate only the first decision. The technology of reproduction, however, has now neared the point where the two choices are independent. If the choices were independent there would no longer be a right to reproductive choice in the sense that interests us today. No one would care about a woman's decision merely to remove a foetus from her body, because the act would not have the consequence, i.e. the death of the foetus that troubles many people today. If the removed foetus had some caretaker available to it, the mere act of removal would be morally inconsequential.[87]

The point here is not to reopen the abortion debate but to show that supposedly "basic" rights alter their meaning under changing background conditions. We might – even in Tushnet's "advanced" world – keep the old arrangement, where the choice stays with the woman, but we would now have to justify the destruction of the foetus in terms of perhaps "ownership," similar to the claim that we own our eyes, kidneys, or bone-marrow, all of which we can donate or not. But then again, the foetus is not an integral part of the host's body and "ownership" could possibly also be asserted by the father. Conversely, the state might intervene and claim "guardianship" in order to facilitate later adoption. There is no need to speculate further, but we can see how things could soon get out of hand and insisting on a presumed "inalienable" right might quickly lose its force.

This observation also points to two paradoxes in regard to the role of rights in creating and abating conflict. On the one hand rights, especially if they are in conflict, are supposed to remove the issue from the terrain of warring interests and place them at a higher level of "objectivity," that is of rights that we ought to respect. The first paradox is of course that the intended de-escalatory move might strengthen the resolve of the contending factions. Now not just certain interests, subject to bargaining and compromise, but "rights," that is fundamental entitlements, are at issue. This paradox is then disguised by what Douzinas calls "institutional moral intuitionism." In this situation courts are entrusted

[86] Mark Tushnet, "An Essay of Rights," *Texas Law Review*, vol. 62, no. 8 (1984), 1363–403 at 1363.

[87] *Ibid.* at 1366.

with a decision and use "rights" as "foundational" constructs that are "imaginative interpretations of a particular political, legal and moral history"[88] in order to buttress support. Thus what once was the main instrument for combating the state by placing its power at the command of individuals who insisted on their moral autonomy, has now brought back the state in order to relieve individuals from their quandary of conflicting subjective rights.

Furthermore, since morality and law are now intertwined via "rights" in a specific way of argumentation, the second (Tushnet's) paradox appears. Precisely because law and morality have become so closely amalgamated, rights themselves have become hostage to particular factual and historical interpretations that undermine their normative pull and action-guiding function. To that extent the notion that rights could provide us with a fully fledged moral theory seems rather far fetched indeed.[89] What we have instead is the continuous proliferation of rights, as the former "constructs" lose their power and the only defence against their corrosion is the creation of still more rights. Since modern human rights are also increasingly parasitic on this understanding of rights as "interests" grounded in certain "values," they participate in a metaphysics of subjectivity that is now linked in a strange way to legal positivism.

The difference of modern rights to the pre-modern notion of *ius* could not be more pronounced, especially in the "interests" version of rights. When paired with legislative initiative, or in the case of human rights with the drafting skills of activist lawyers, the proliferation of special beneficiaries seems unlimited:

> Classical right or jus was a limitation on individual excess; modern rights have no inherent limit in them: they are the legalization of desire and as such the sanctification of individual limitlessness. Rights do not derive from objective nature but from individual desire … Subjectivity founds rights … The law translates desire into right and turns it into the cornerstone of the social bond. Desires are posited by individual wills, rights are their formal recognition and pre-conditions of humanity: the more rights an individual has, the more human he is … If a new object of desire gets couched in legal terms, if a new claim crosses the threshold of popular acceptability, its full legal recognition is a matter of time and legal recognition turns into another "essential" human characteristic. At the limit, all desires will become legalized, all interests will give rise to enforceable claim and full humanity will be achieved, a state which Villey, Strauss and Legendre believe will lead

[88] Costas Douzinas, *The End of Human Rights: Critical Legal Thought at the Turn of the Century* (Oxford: Hart, 2000), 246.

[89] See e.g. J. L. Mackie's argument trying to develop Dworkin's proposal for a rights-based moral theory, "Can there Be a Rights-based Moral Theory?"; for a thoughtful critique see Joseph Raz, "Right-Based Moralities," in Jeremy Waldron (ed.), *Theories of Rights* (Oxford University Press, 1984), 182–200. See also the useful discussion by Evan Simpson, "Rights Thinking," *Philosophy*, vol. 72, no. 2 (1997), 29–58.

to the total dissolution of the social bond and will not be far removed from total inhumanity.[90]

One need not share the author's pessimism, as money might run out, putting an end to such hypertrophic growth, and trends can also discontinue as other fashions become dominant. Nevertheless, the dystopian Foucauldian potential of "biopolitics" is not only imaginary, particularly since the last generation of "rights," such as a "right to development," to "ecological stability," or to "peace," cannot be predicated of individuals. Here society at large has to demand from the government particular policies in order to procure some public or communal good, even though the insistence on subjective rights has paradoxically undermined the *res publica*, the common thing.

Two further points are worth considering in this context. One is that since this procurement is connected with new surveillance and risk management techniques, it is not difficult to see that the results, in all likelihood, are detrimental to a robust conception of individual liberty that rights were supposed to protect. However, unless one radically reconceptualizes "autonomy" in relational terms (as Jennifer Nedelski has proposed)[91] rather than treating it as accoutrements of natural liberty, such an option does not seem to exist for the standard liberal account. The other point is that certain "communal goods" should not be dealt with in terms of constituting individual entitlements, but neither should they be conceived along the lines of Marx's analysis in the Jewish question.[92] There he argues that the "egotist" nature of the "rights of man" separate him from his community and make him an "isolated monad," reinforcing his alienation. Finally, communal rights should also not be treated in terms of the too narrow conception of classical "public goods," that is those that are non-rivalrous in consumption and non-excludable, and that therefore lead to "market failure."[93]

In the subsequent discussion I want to keep the first problem in abeyance, since I hope by criticizing the second and the third problems we get some hints of answering the first question of how to conceptualize "communal rights."

The Marxian point is obviously mute since the "Rights of the Citizen" do involve the individual in common affairs, and even the individual right to a fair trial does require communal efforts. The third problem deserves further

90 Douzinas, *The End of Human Rights*, at 241f.

91 See her fascinating analysis in Jennifer Nedelski, *Law's Relations: A Relational Theory of Self, Autonomy and Law* (Oxford University Press, 2011).

92 See Karl Marx, "On the Jewish Question," in Robert Tucker (ed.), *The Marx–Engels Reader*, 2nd edn. (New York: Norton, 1978), 26–52.

93 Mancur Olson's classical treatment of the problem in his *The Logic of Collective Action* (Cambridge, MA: Harvard University Press, 1996) followed Samuelson's original framing as an instance of "market failure." The subsequent discussion showed that this "one size fits all" paradigm represents a rather poor analytical tool. For a further discussion see e.g. Elinor Ostrom, *Governing the Commons* (Cambridge University Press, 1990).

scrutiny because a closer analysis shows that there are actually very few collective or public goods – perhaps public lighting might be one. Most of the traditional "public goods" are either "club goods," that are excludable (such as security, toll roads and so on), or are goods that were traditionally in ample supply, such as clean air, which gets more and more polluted and for which we now create pollution markets.[94]

But how are we then to think of certain "common goods" that avoid the problems of the collective goods interpretation? A "common good" in a non-economistic sense would be one that we not only enjoy together – even if enjoyment remains personal – but in which our enjoyment derives from the common undertaking. Waldron gives the conviviality at a party as an example.[95] In that case our enjoyment also depends on the perception that others enjoy themselves, that is our utilities interact and we can begin to form what Bratman[96] calls some collective intentions. A good conversation, the enjoyment of team sports, of dancing, of playing a string quartet are other instantiations. Can this phenomenon be adequately expressed in the language of "subjective rights"? It does not seem so. If what is distinctive about rights is that their duty-imposing character on others occurs on the basis that a certain "interest" of an individual serves as a sufficient reason for this imposition, then it is difficult to see how this could be the case. Claims to promote the common good presuppose:

> a justificatory discourse that does not proceed to the establishment of social duties from any conception of the importance of the interest of a single individual, taken on its own. The importance of promoting a communal good stems from its worth to members of the community in question taken together. It would be odd then to claim such a good as an individual right (or even as a right of all individuals). Such a claim would mislead one's audience about the way in which the importance of the good was to be understood.[97]

This argument points to an Arendtian position in regard to "rights," since the right to participation is, so to speak, the primary right, or a "right on rights" that puts all members of a community under obligation. They have to take their participatory duties seriously in the face of inevitable disagreements about what the "right" answers to our common problems are. Such questions cannot

94 For a further analysis see my "El fracaso de la 'falla del mercado': vuelta a pensar en bienes 'públicos' y 'privados' con base en la riqueza de las naciones de Adam Smith, y el derecho romano," *Foro Internacional*, vol. 50, no. 2 (2011), 422–45.

95 Jeremy Waldron, "Communal Goods as Human Rights," in Jeremy Waldron, *Liberal Rights* (Cambridge University Press, 1993), 339–69 at 355.

96 See Michael Bratman, *Intentions, Plans and Practical Reasons* (Cambridge, MA: Harvard University Press, 1987); see also his *Faces of Intentions* (Cambridge University Press, 1999).

97 Waldron, "Communal Goods as Human Rights," at 360.

be left to some juristocrats but have to be decided by an authoritative act of the "public," precisely because:

> [A] substantive theory of rights is not itself the theory of authority that is needed in the face of disagreements about rights … [It] is no good saying that when people disagree about rights, the view which should prevail is the truth about rights or the best account of the rights we have. Each theorist regards his own view as better than any of the others … So this way of settling a social choice in the face of disagreement would reproduce exactly the disagreement that called for an authoritative rule in the first place … This is one of Thomas Hobbes' contributions to political philosophy: any theory that makes authority depend on the goodness of political outcomes is self-defeating, for it is precisely because people disagree about the goodness of outcomes that they need to set up and recognize an authority.[98]

For Waldron this means that these choices should better be left to legislation. Despite my sympathies for Waldron's "political" solution, I think he claims too much. For one, his own reference to Hobbes shows that "the people" might transfer these powers to a sovereign. Unless he claims – following Rousseau – that the "sovereignty" of the people can never be legitimately transferred, his preference for legislation over judicial law-making is vulnerable to the counterargument that, for better or worse, the people can transfer these powers and authorize judicial review.

But this argument is not quite right either, in that the "highest courts" do actually decide by a *political decision mechanism*, that is voting, sometimes by the smallest of margins. This makes the "right answer" or best fit argument a quite dubious construction, particularly when the "the majority" often settles on the same decision but for different axiological and normative reasons (concurring opinions). Furthermore, Waldron does have a point concerning the "secondary legitimacy" problem created by judicial decision making, as judicial decisions lack in "author-based legitimacy" as Michelman suggested, and we have seen in a previous Meditation. Thus for democratic theory there is a basic problem when the law to which the people are subject does not issue from their collective choice. Some courts recognize this point in various "deference" arguments, such as political questions, separation of powers, exacting standing requirements, or allowing for "margins of appreciation" in human rights adjudication. The problem is, however, that most courts, especially in the supranational realm, are not "bound" to apply such doctrines. Because of the self-referential character of law, we have to face the paradox that only law can determine what the law is. To that extent the tendency to invoke "ultimate" foundations, such as "natural law," "humanity," "society," or "functions,"

[98] *Ibid.* at 323.

becomes understandable when used to deal with that conundrum (despite the fact that such "foundations" cannot deliver what they promise).

Here both Dworkin's[99] and Habermas'[100] attempts of providing their legal theories with such ultimate foundations are instructive. Both attempt to create a vantage point that allows them to reject positivism on the one hand, and on the other hand give an account of law as a distinct social practice that is superior to other ways of settling disputes. Dworkin proceeds by a criticism of other theories, such as those of positivists such as Coleman and Raz, or of pragmatists such as Rorty or Sunstein, and by claiming that his interpretive approach provides a "better account" because of its "fit" with the actual reasoning underpinning legal decision-making. Even if we grant some, or even most of his criticism, his claim is thereby not established. For one thing, the notion of "fit" supposed to provide the criterion remains rather elusive.[101] Second, the attempt itself of trying to give truth conditions for legal proposition might be mistaken, as it is not an epistemological problem to begin with. Thus it is one thing to claim, as Dworkin does, that the positivists' notion of law as "settled" is problematic, since "moral" considerations do figure prominently in legal reasoning. It is, however, another thing to assume that moral principles can specify the truth conditions for the propositions of law if his interpretive approach is used. For Dworkin:

> A proposition of law is true … if it flows from principles of personal and political morality that provide the best interpretation of other propositions of law generally regarded as true in contemporary legal practice.[102]

Thus giving a proper account of law – getting its "point" – is to provide a coherent "theory" not only for a particular legal system but of "legality" itself. Again while this might indeed be what we are after – and Brunée and Toope's[103] proposal comes to mind here – it does not settle the issue of whether this can be done in the fashion Dworkin proposes. Here ambiguities abound. What does it mean to say that the best account is one that provides the "best interpretation" of the propositions of law generally regarded as true in practice?

99 See Dworkin's recent restatement of his approach to jurisprudence by answering some of critics and likening his work with that of Rawls in his *Justice in Robes* (Cambridge, MA: Harvard University Press, 2006).

100 See Jürgen Habermas, *On the Pragmatics of Social Interaction* (Cambridge, MA, MIT Press, 2001). See also his *Theory of Communicative Action*, 2 vols, transl. by Thomas McCarthy (Cambridge: Polity Press, 1989–91).

101 See e.g. the criticism of Dworkin's reformulation in his recent *Justice in Robes* by Richard Nobles and David Schiff, "The Emperor's New Clothes," *Modern Law Review*, vol. 70, no. 1 (2007), 139–60.

102 Ronald Dworkin, *Justice in Robes* (Cambridge, MA: Harvard University Press, 2006), 14.

103 Jutta Brunée and Stephen Toope, *Legitimacy and Legality in International Law* (Cambridge University Press, 2010).

Aside from the ambiguity of the term "personal morality" – which will understandably raise some eyebrows (unless of course we assume the obviousness of an impersonal (?) morality), the same ambiguity plagues the notion of "practice." If practice means what judges do, then the positivists and their way of reasoning have to be included. In that case Dworkin has gained at most a Pyrrhic victory in proving them wrong since he must now include them in the pantheon. If on the other hand he means that all legal propositions have to be justified by moral considerations, then this would be a tall order to fill (and an absurd one to boot). After all, that is why we created law – to settle certain issues so that we can go on and not be constantly burdened with showing why the application of a certain rule, such as a time limit for filing appeals, or zoning laws and speed limits "truly" serve the common good and are compatible with morality in general.

The upshot of the above criticism is that in dealing with a practice, theoretical standards specifying truth conditions seem inappropriate. They cannot supply the foundations as they inevitably entail paradoxes. It was this point that convinced Wittgenstein that "solutions" have to be found somewhere else – contrary to his original attempt in the *Tractatus* – and not in a theory of "truth." In the case of Dworkin this means that a "settled" law is required in order to generate competing accounts of contested law.

Similar problems plague Habermas' attempts to tackle validity problems as truth claims by means of applying his discursive ethics approach. He grounds the validity of norms, especially of higher order principles, in the discursive procedure in which their *Rationalitätspotential* (that is their "reasonableness") can be tested. They become "valid" through the assent they are able to command and the duties they then can impose. Quite aside from the fact that not everything that is valid has to be true – assent in Habermas is not the reason why we are bound, as in contractual obligations, but because "*reason itself*" demands our assent – this move comes at a price. If we take his earlier ideal speech situation, then we also have to assume ideal participants *and* – what is even more difficult to assume – coherence among higher order norms. If there is, however, a multiplicity of equally valid principles that have contradictory implications, then the "truth" test does not dispose of their inability to structure our actions and assign duties. Since trade-offs have to be made, at issue is less their status as "true" norms, but the criteria by which we decide in conflict situations. If we assume a less exacting requirement, such as that of assent by "reasonable" people who share a common *Lebenswelt*, the question of their "transcultural" status – so important for human rights – becomes an issue. Finally, Habermas is aware that discourses might not only validate but also *undermine* the validity of norms! But like all adherents of the "enlightenment" he discounts this problem. "Norm cascades" apparently happen only in one way, that is pointing to ever greater inclusiveness and "progress."

This does not mean that agreement cannot arise, although it will be more fortuitous than expected. But it does mean that these problems cannot be solved philosophically via epistemology, and the construction of "truth claims" and any "theory" of law or rights, which relies on such props, is ill-served. It may be sufficient to maintain, as Christine Chwaszcza[104] has done, that human rights are articulations of "standards of legitimacy for sociopolitical and legal institutions." That of course makes them contestable and this circumstance explains the loss of much of the pathos that is usually part of the rights talk; but this might be preferable to buying into some implausible constructs, which at the beginning of modernity made sense, but whose intellectual purchase has been debased in the meantime. How under those circumstances the bounds of sense then have to be drawn or redrawn, that is when we no longer expect that the three Kantian questions of "what can we know," "what shall we do," and "what can we hope" can all be answered from an Archimedean point, is the topic for the next Meditation.

[104] Christine Chwaszcza, "The Concept of Rights in Contemporary Human Rights Discourse," *Ratio Juris*, vol. 23, no. 3 (2010), 333–64.

Meditation 9

The bounds of (non)sense

Introduction

The upshot of the last Meditation was neither that rights work as simple trumps, nor that a "theory" of rights is coextensive with morality, nor that a theoretical "foundation" can be given for law and its practice, as certain paradoxes appear. Paradoxes are not simply perverse effects resulting from unintended consequences or from aggregation problems, but are rooted in logical impasses, as for example Russell[1] has shown. This realization has disturbing implications for getting at the "truth" of any matter, as "truth" is neither a simple matching operation, as we have seen, nor is it unequivocally guaranteed by logic. Thus we usually take for granted that at least the "truths" contained in analytical statements (bachelors are unmarried men) are reliable, closely followed by those that derive conclusions from premises via rigorous deductions. But our confidence seems somewhat misplaced.

Consider the status of analytical truths, as in the example of the bachelor who is an unmarried man. It is not as clear-cut as it appears. Suppose we deal with a man who is living with a woman, perhaps even having a child with her. We might not consider him a bachelor, although "technically" speaking he might be if the legal system does not recognize a common law marriage. Thus the distinction between analytic and synthetic statements itself is problematic, as Quine pointed out.[2] Similarly, against the optimism that scientific progress is insured if one uses the proper method – which Thomas Kuhn and the "history of science,"[3] as well as the "sociology of science" exemplified

[1] The paradox runs as follows. There is a barber in a town where all men shave themselves or are shaved by the barber. The barber shaves only those who do not shave themselves. But what about the barber? If he shaves himself, then this violates the assumption that only those who do not shave themselves are shaved by the barber. If he does not shave himself then this violates the assumption that everyone in the town shaves himself. Thus the barber shaves himself if he does not shave himself and does not shave himself if he shaves himself. See Badredine Arfi, *Rethinking International Relations Theory via Deconstruction* (London: Routledge, 2012): 39.

[2] Willard van Orman Quine, "The Two Dogmas of Empiricism," *The Philosophical Review*, vol. 60 (1951), 20–43.

[3] Thomas Kuhn, *The Structure of Scientific Revolutions* (University of Chicago Press, 1962).

by Bourdieu[4] and Latour[5] or Knorr-Cetina[6] corrected – Kenneth Boulding reminds us that there remain puzzling *conceptual* problems concerning "truth":

> The problem of what constitutes truth in mathematics, in logic, and in deductive processes is surprisingly difficult, especially in the more sophisticated inquiries. Elementary mathematics and logic are true enough for most practical purposes. But we have to go beyond Euclidean geometry in the physical sciences and we should go beyond Cartesian algebra in the social sciences. For in social systems, minus-minus does not make plus; not doing harm is not the same thing at all as doing good. There is need to go beyond Aristotelian logic when the reality is probabilistic. Goedel's proof that no system of deductive reasoning can be self-sufficient suggests that we should not take mathematics and logic for granted. There are problems too in quantification, where the reality of which we are trying to form an image is topological rather than quantitative. Used mechanically, without reference to the field of inquiry, quantification can be quite misleading. For instance, a consumer price index used mechanically can accelerate inflation.[7]

In a way these reflections lead us back to the beginning of these Meditations where I proposed a Wittgensteinian approach to deal with the failure of traditional "theoretical" efforts in regard to problems of praxis. If we now have to realize that not even formal logic can make good on its promises of providing unequivocal yardsticks for guiding our actions. Instead, as paradoxes make these choices indeterminate, the problem of "de-paradoxification" becomes crucial and takes the place of traditional epistemology. Several attempts have been mentioned in passing.

Derrida suggests that the puzzles can be solved when we give up on the notion of language as a referential system, and understand it instead as a *semiotic system* in which the meaning results from the properties of a system of signs, rather than from reference. Following up on that insight, his method of "deconstruction" shows the ultimate arbitrariness of our language. In a similar, but more "constructive" fashion Luhmann's system theory attempts to focus on the process of the closure of systems that reproduce themselves "autopoietically" while maintaining at the same time their openness. Lyotard, especially

[4] Pierre Bourdieu, *Science of Science and Reflexivity*, transl. by Richard Nice (Cambridge: Polity, 2004).

[5] Bruno Latour and Steve Wolgar, *Laboratory Life: The Social Construction of Scientific Facts* (Los Angeles: Sage, 1979); see also Bruno Latour, *Science in Action: How to Follow Scientists and Engineers Through Society* (Cambridge, MA: Harvard University Press, 1987).

[6] Karin Knorr-Cetina, *The Manufacture of Knowledge* (Oxford: Pergamon, 1981).

[7] Kenneth Boulding, "The Optimum Utilization of Knowledge: Some Central Concepts," in Kenneth Boulding and Lawrence Senesh (eds.), *The Optimum Utilization of Knowledge* (Boulder: Westview, 1983): 1–19 at 6.

in his "middle period,"[8] wrestles with the same problem. His emphasis on language, on knowledge production, and on the end of "grand"- or "meta"-narratives, shows his critical engagement with the conceptual frameworks that misrepresent a reality that is not "there" but always in the making. American pragmatism from Pierce to Dewey and Rorty could also be mentioned[9] and so could the thinking of Arendt and Heidegger.

In the previous Meditations I have also tried to show that practical reason has certain ways of overcoming some of the perplexities created by logical paradoxes. Thus some dilemmas that are irresolvable in logic can be solved by utilizing "time" as a means of dissolving the paradox that, for example, one cannot be ruler and be ruled at the same time, a problem that "rotation" and "the rule of law" dissolves in a way. Similarly Burrian's ass – where a donkey is indifferent between two heaps of hay and thus starves to death – seems rather easily resolvable in practice. Since the ass is already motivated by his "desire," that is hunger, the logical problem of indifference does not inhibit action and a random walk between the heaps will do the trick. Only when we assume that the problem is purely one of logic does the paradox of undecidability arise.

The last example has an important further lesson. It draws attention to the often unstated background conditions that frame paradoxes. Thus the famous paradox whether an omnipotent God can make a stone so big that he can no longer lift it, extends the meaning of "omnipotent" to all states of affairs. But while it is not nonsensical to include under one description all things one "cannot" do – such as for human beings to fly like birds, or eating one's cake and having it too – collapsing the distinction of possibility and impossibility and bringing both under the concept of "omnipotence" leads exactly to the loss of the discriminatory power on which "meaning" depends. In the former case of flying like a bird, the distinction is embedded in "field-dependent" criteria of an empirical state of affairs. In the latter case the problem is *conceptual*, and as such no discrimination is allowed because "omnipotence" suddenly covers both sides of the distinction.

Dissolving paradoxes thus entails simply examining and abandoning some or all of the commitments that created the contradiction. Here no straightforward solution, such as the mechanical avoidance of self-referential terms,

[8] See Jean-François Lyotard and Jean-Loup Thébaud, *Just Gaming*, trans. Wlad Godzick (Minneapolis: University of Minnesota Press, 1985), translation of *Au juste: conversations* (Paris: Bourgois, 1979); Jean-François Lyotard, *The Postmodern Condition: A Report on Knowledge*, trans. Geoff Bennington and Brian Massumi (Manchester University Press, 1984), translation of *La condition postmoderne: rapport sur le savoir* (Paris: Minuit, 1979); Jean François Lyotard, *The Differend: Phrases in Dispute*, trans. Georges Van Den Abbeele (Manchester University Press, 1988), translation of *Le différend* (Paris: Minuit, 1983).

[9] See my discussion in "The Points to Ponder about Pragmatism" in Harry Bauer and Elisabetta Brighi (eds.), *Pragmatism in International Relations Theory* (London: Routledge, 2009), 11–25.

seems promising, as the same paradoxes can re-emerge in hetero-referential circumstances, as Gyula Klima shows in his reciprocal liar's paradox:[10]

> DWORKIN: "What Raz is saying is true."
> RAZ: "What Dworkin is saying is false."

Second, as modern system theory has shown and as we have observed in law, self-reference allows the closing of the legal system while keeping it open for outside influences. Derrida is right about the "groundlessness" of law, but it does not follow that his endless "deconstruction" is "productive" in the sense of being able to show us how "to go on." Instead, he resembles in his efforts a "logocentric" cat that is endlessly chasing its tail. Although he most forcefully opposed privileging logic, does he not in the end remain under the spell of that very logic which he so artfully attacked in his *On Grammatology*?[11] Furthermore, from the fact that law cannot "ground" itself as it pretends to do, it does not follow that it is "violence." Law is certainly about "power" and *Herrschaft* (*dominium*), but power is something different from violence. As Hannah Arendt suggested, power emerges from people acting together, committing themselves to certain projects, and enforcing these commitments against opportunists or other types of "law-breakers." This has little to do with "terror" or violence, which entails "inflicting a wound" on individual or social integrity. As Arendt states:

> Power is indeed the essence of all government, but violence it is not. Violence is by its nature instrumental: like all means it always stands in need of guidance and justification through the end it pursues … Power needs no justification, being inherent in the very existence of political communities: what it does need is legitimacy … Power springs up whenever people get together and act in concert, but it derives its legitimacy from the initial getting together, rather than from any action that might follow.
>
> Politically speaking the point is that loss of power becomes a temptation to substitute violence for power.
>
> Terror is not the same as violence; it is, rather, the form of government that comes into being when violence, having destroyed all power, does not abdicate, but on the contrary remains in full control. It has often been noticed that the effectiveness of terror depends almost entirely on the degree of social atomization.[12]

One wished that some of these basic distinctions would have resonated with Derrida and lots of trees could have been saved. Again the main mistake here is

[10] Gyula Klima, "Consequences of a Closed, Token-Based Semantics History and Philosophy of Logic," *History and Philosophy of Logic*, vol. 25 (2004), 95–101, as quoted in Oren Perez, "Law in the Air. A Prologue to the World of Legal Paradoxes," in Oren Perez and Gunther Teubner (eds.), *Paradoxes and Inconsistencies of the Law* (Oxford: Hart, 2006), 3–39 at 9.

[11] Jacques Derrida, *On Grammatology* (Baltimore: Johns Hopkins University Press, 1974).

[12] Hannah Arendt, *On Violence* (New York: Harcourt, Brace, Jovanovic, 1970), 51–3.

that the inference depends on an exclusive dichotomy so that we are seduced to believe that if we show that something is not white, it has to be black. It seems strange indeed that someone dedicated to the study of signs seems to fall back on the very props he tries to debunk. A "productive" de-paradoxification would entail not only insights gained from the deconstruction, exposing the links that exist among the signs, but from finding new distinctions and new links that "let us go on." But this requires a different mode of analysis, one that is as far from the traditional epistemological ideal as it is from mere deconstruction, precisely because both do not seem to be able to overcome the fascination with the philosophical tradition, its tools, and traumas.

In this Meditation I want to interrogate the traditional strategies for knowledge generation and adumbrate an alternative for creating "useful" knowledge that is not based on some theoretical ideal, or on abstract universal principles and values, but takes into account the distinct nature of practical problems and the diagnostics that they require. The source for this type of knowledge is rooted for Aristotle in practical wisdom, which allows us to orient ourselves, but which does not determine our choices in a necessary, law-like manner. Thus I shall take issue with the usual way of proceeding by assigning to philosophy or (analytical) ethics the "clarification" of the foundational principles, and to "practitioners" the application of them to the problems of the "real world." This makes for a nice division of labour between theorist and professionals, who, in most cases are not really much interested in what "the other" had to say. The result then is that we get two pathologies for the price of one. An often unreflective knowledge of what "works" sits uneasily with the elaborate ethereal principles supposedly guiding action, but which have been distilled without much concern for what the actual problems were to which they are supposed to supply the answer.

My plea here is for a "diagnostic" that avoids most of these problems and that is both attentive to the constitutive role of the "observer" and to the context of the "question" s/he asks. Thus explanations are not free-standing, as positivism tends to assume, nor are the "answers" or proofs (corroborations) they tender. As the philosopher of science Bas Van Frasssen argued:

> The discussion of explanation went wrong at the very beginning when explanation was conceived as a relationship like description: a relation between theory and fact. Really it is a three-term relation between theory fact and context. No wonder that no single relation between theory and fact ever managed and fit more than a few examples. Being an explanation is essentially relative, for an explanation is an answer (in just the sense that being a daughter is something relative: every woman is a daughter and every daughter is a woman, yet being a daughter is not the same as being a woman). Since an explanation is evaluated vis-a-vis a question, which is a request for information. But exactly what is requested by means of the interrogative "why is it the case that P?" differs from context to context. In addition the

> background theory plus data relative to which the question is evaluated ... depend on context. And even what part of that background information is to be used to evaluate how good the answer is qua answer to that question is a contextually determined factor.[13]

Given that the constitutive role of the inquiring subject must be reflected upon, and given the contextual nature of framing the question, the traditional dichotomy between falsehood/error and "truth" are too indiscriminate to map the bounds of sense. Relying on such an approach is hardly the *via regia* to knowledge. This is particularly true when we try to master the "unknown" future, by either amassing additional facts (we know what we do not know), or by attempting to insure ourselves by managing "risks," or even transforming the unknown/unknown (uncertainty) into calculable bets. Here the question of "right/wrong" becomes entirely self-referential, as Keynes' beauty contest shows. The person who guessed right what the others are likely to choose "is" right, although this insight is difficult to bring under the description that "truth" is a matching operation between a pre-existing "world" and its corresponding description.

The loss of the "world out there" as the ultimate yardstick creates anxieties that the "abolition" of the traditional conception of truth must lead to an "anything goes" attitude and ultimately to "relativism." This problem is particularly vexing in the realm of praxis since there the creation of "reality" is bound up with notions not only of true or false, but with right or wrong, error and misrepresentation, or even telling lies, which in turn link to the notions of justice, responsibility, and freedom. Given these complexities, the only way that seemed promising to traditional thinking was to map as fully as possible an end-state, a utopia, and then to reason backwards from there, that is combat the problem of time and radical uncertainty by the development of an ideal theory that was supposed to serve as a loadstar. To that extent the advocacy of a diagnostic that eschews "ideal theories" – both in the form of value-based utopias and in the sense of methodologically driven axiomatic approaches – is doubly frightening, since it gnaws on the ropes of the two anchors we seem to have: "the world out there" and "logic." It is therefore not surprising that such arguments are treated more like a transgression and sacrilege than as a criticism of the mantras concerning the nature of knowledge. Nevertheless, I shall defend the view that a Wittgensteinian redescription of practical action "works" by alleviating the anxieties while opening our eyes to the idea that the traditional props are poor security blankets.

From these initial remarks the argument below takes the following steps. In the next section I critically address the case for "ideal theory," as proposed in different ways by Rawls and by neo-classical economics, particularly since both

[13] Bas C. Van Fraassen, *The Scientific Image* (Oxford: Clarendon, 1980), 156.

have impacted on law either through the "institutional design" argument, or through the "law and economics" approach. In section three I examine in this light the recent "turn" of one of the main proponents of the latter approach and ask whether Richard Posner's recent "conversion" to a Keynesianism, which he originally vehemently opposed, is "productive" in the sense that this "refutation" allows us to understand our present predicament of, for example, the financial crisis better. Some important issues of how knowledge and action relate to each other are thereby raised. Section four is then devoted to making the case for a diagnostics that eschews ideal theorizing by proposing an alternative.

Ideal theory and its flaws

It might seem strange to pair Rawls, the moral philosopher, with some economists dedicated to rigour and prediction. For one, although both are "normative," the norms constituting a social order have to satisfy *special criteria*, such as equal concern, natural liberty, the binding nature of freely entered commitments and so on, while other "ideal theories" can be based just on assumptions, pure abstractions, or on criteria of logic. Second, Rawls' attempt is – at first blush – directed at Kant's rigorism – and thus his own "ideal theory" is explicitly devoted to the correction of this flaw, thereby attempting to give Kant's project of freedom and reason a more "realizable" form. But then again, despite Rawls' intention to "present a conception of justice that generalizes and carries to a higher level of abstraction the familiar theory of the social contract as found, say in Locke, Rousseau and Kant,"[14] he might share a surprisingly large part of the vocabulary and analytical instruments with "formalists" engaged in ideal theorizing.

In all fairness, over the years Rawls has modified his position considerably in the direction of a more empirically based model of "political justice,"[15] exemplified by the importance he accords later to the "overlapping consensus" existing in concrete societies, and to "reasonableness" as opposed to the "true" and the "rational" *tout court* of his earlier work. But the question remains whether these adjustments leading from a moral to a more political notion of "justice" have eliminated the paradoxes of ideal theorizing, or whether they have only displaced them, as the debate between Habermas and Rawls[16] seems to suggest (whereby of course Habermas might see the splinter in Rawls' eye without noticing the beam in his own). After a careful analysis of the conceptual adjustments and their discussions, Albena Azmanova concludes:

[14] John Rawls, *A Theory of Justice* (Oxford University Press, 1972), 11.

[15] John Rawls, *Political Liberalism* (New York: Columbia University Press, 1993).

[16] See Juergen Habermas, "Reconciliation through the Use of Reason: Remarks of Rawls's Political Liberalism," *Journal of Philosophy*, vol. 92 (1995), 109–31; John Rawls, "Reply to Habermas," *Journal of Philosophy*, vol. 92 (1995), 132–80.

> for both authors the validity of just rules depends on epistemic authority that is itself independent of world-views. Thus notwithstanding their declared trust in citizens' mutual reason-giving practices, when it comes to the generation of principles of justice, Rawls and Habermas resort to procedural devices outside the actual practices of public debates.[17]

To that extent the "displacement" interpretation seems more appropriate. In any case, I am not interested here in a "history of thought" or in the "development" of particular thinkers, but with a mode of thinking that they – at least at certain times – employed. Thus Rawls himself admits his closeness to rational choice, which then provides a justification for his "ideal theory" approach in the *Theory of Justice*. Only in this way, he argues, will we be able to arrive at principles that free and rational persons, "concerned to further their own interests,"[18] will accept, and that can then define the fundamental terms of their association. He proposes, therefore, a particular procedure, that is he constructs a choice situation in which the actors have to select the principles of justice. They decide behind a "veil of ignorance," that is without knowing what their personal assets are – since they are morally irrelevant – and in ignorance of their future position in the system (thus preventing the incorporation of particular interests in the "constitutional" order). In addition, the "reflective equilibrium," that is a going back and forth between our convictions and the conditions of the choice situation, led Rawls to "*assume* that eventually we shall find a description of the initial situation that both expresses reasonable conditions and yields principles which match our considered judgment, duly pruned and adjusted."[19]

Since Rawls admits that this theory of justice is "part, perhaps the most significant part, of rational choice"[20] and that "the concept of rationality must be interpreted as far as possible in the narrow sense, standard in economic theory, of taking the most effective means to given ends,"[21] one really has to wonder how this can be accomplished in view of the moral dimension on the one hand, and the vexing equilibrium selection problem[22] on the other. Our confidence is further undermined when efficiency and effectiveness are mixed up, or when the "contract" becomes not only hypothetical (as in all social contract constructions), but loses all relations to any form of interactive communication and bargaining. Since each participant is "equally rational and similarly situated,

[17] Albena Azmanova, *The Scandal of Reason* (New York: Columbia University Press, 2012), 102.

[18] Rawls, *A Theory of Justice*, at 11. [19] *Ibid.* at 20. [20] *Ibid.* at 16. [21] *Ibid.*

[22] Since there are various equilibrium concepts and many games have multiple (Nash) equilibriums, "rational" players will have difficulties in settling on one solution. The Folk theorem addresses the same problem. For a further discussion see John Harsany and Richard Selden, *A General Theory of Equilibrium Selection in Games* (Cambridge, MA: MIT Press, 1988).

each is convinced of the same arguments,"[23] with the result that "unanimous agreement can be reached."[24]

At this point one justifiably gets nervous. After all, why should anyone feel obliged by a contract in which the ineluctable difference of preferences among actors prevents a joint preference ordering (exemplified by Arrow's theorem) is substituted by an assumption of a unique solution? It is precisely this dilemma of the multiplicity of views and of preferences that cannot be reduced to an algorithm that gives contracts – construed as a "meeting of *wills*" – its legitimacy.[25] Gone is not only Rawls' original commitment to "reasonable empiricism" – on which he insisted against Kant's metaphysical presuppositions – gone is also the coherence of his own position. After all, he had opposed utilitarianism and preferred a deontological system of rules because in utilitarianism the impartial spectator is the only one perfectly rational person who decides on the maximization of happiness and thus (inappropriately) extends to society "the principle of choice for one man."[26] But by a strange twist we have now arrived at the same position. Not only is the choice of principles unanimous, it can also be seen as the choice of one person, any person taken at random. In elaborating on the "original position," Rawls states:

> Therefore we can view the choice in the original position from the standpoint of one person taken at random. If anyone after due reflection prefers a conception of justice, then they all do, and a unanimous agreement can be reached.[27]

It seems then only fitting that these principles "are always chosen" when one enters the original position. Furthermore, since the parties need not, and do seem unable to "learn," one has to ask oneself how such a construction, denuded of all politics and historical experience, can be of any help in dealing with our predicament. Besides, one suspects that here some form of backward induction is used so that the (otherwise quite implausible) stipulation of the "original position" yields the principles one wants. In other words, the trick here is making it appear that such a procedure can provide solutions that are justified by a purely formal, impartial, and therefore universal point of view. As John Gray suggests:

> The point then is not that Rawls's construction of the original position is designed only to yield end-state principles, nor yet that his list of alternative principles of justice is far from exhaustive (which Rawls readily admits), but that Rawls's reasoning becomes viciously circular in so far as he can give

23 Rawls, *A Theory of Justice*, at 139. 24 *Ibid.*

25 See my discussion in "The Limits of Contract," *European Journal of International Law*, vol. 5, no. 4 (1994), 465–91.

26 Rawls, *A Theory of Justice*, at 26f. 27 *Ibid.* at 139.

> no good reasons for accepting stipulations regarding the original position other than they allow him to derive the outcome he wants.[28]

The later extension of a (modified) original position to deal with issues of justice in international relations reinforces this suspicion. On the one hand we want to be tolerant and Rawls suggests that there are "decent peoples" who might not have adopted the principles of the original contract, which had yielded "liberal principles" for their domestic order. But we also want to be sure that no (radical) alternative emerges from the deliberations taking place now at the higher, international level. Thus only the representatives of liberal states are admitted to such a meeting![29]

One does not need much imagination to perceive that such efforts have more to do with articulating an imperial project than with facilitating interactions across different political projects. The illusion that all that is necessary is the clarification of first principles (or ascertaining their universality) conveniently forgets that abstract principles will have to be interpreted, and that this places the actual power in the hands of those interpreting them. So quite different from the notion that these principles do most of the work in our moral reasoning, they actually do very little. Furthermore, relying on such a procedure fundamentally misunderstands our moral perplexities. Ideal theory is of little help when we no longer deal with the question of whether or not a duty exists, but face instead a *conflict of duties*. Here Kant's rigorism is hardly persuasive, as his answer to the question whether one can lie to a person who is pursuing my friend who is hiding in my house shows. Despite my knowledge of the pursuer's bad intentions, the duty of truth-telling on demand is paramount for Kant, as he assumes that all situations can be given one and only one appropriate description.

Similarly, analytical philosophers and political theorists have spent an awful lot of time and effort on whether a "right of humanitarian intervention" exists, while paying only the scantiest attention to the question of how this would play out in practice. Questions such as what type of right that responsibility to protect (R2P) would be, which type of duties would follow, how (differential?) duties could be assigned to specific actors, and under what circumstances would they have to be exercised – all of them were largely left unanswered. It is as if the ascertainment of the existence of this right also disposed in one fell swoop of all other questions. This has led to entirely scholastic debates whose artificiality becomes evident when, after having decided (despite the problematic legal situation and the lack of solid evidence) that an intervention against Iraq is "justified," wishful thinking could take over. The "liberation of Paris" is invoked as a precedent that had to fill the gaps and take care of objections.

[28] John Gray, "Social Contract, Community and Ideology," in John Gray, *Liberalism: Essays in Political Philosophy* (London: Routledge, 1991), Chapter 3 at 32.

[29] See John Rawls, *The Law of Peoples* (New York: Basic Books, 1993).

But, as the little story below suggests, proceeding in this fashion is courting disaster.

When I mentioned to a proponent of the invasion of Iraq that the Iraqi population would probably not react in a way similar to the Parisians at the end of the Second World War, he replied: "So you must think that the Iraqis do not want democracy and a decent life of free markets and Human Rights?" When I objected that these terms are unlikely to resonate in the same way and result in the same outcome, since we are dealing in Iraq with a deeply divided society, torn by all types of conflicts, his response came quickly and contained the usual knock-out argument: "Then you are saying that the Iraqis are not human, not capable of living a 'decent' life? You are just a racist!" Needless to say, our relations have soured. But more importantly the reference to "decency" (and thereby to the necessary *indecency* of the opponent) liberates the speaker from any further doubts and from engaging with genuine dilemmas.

It is also not just accidental, as Rawls uses the term "decency" in *The Law of Peoples*.[30] Simply casting the devils out – with whom even Kant still wanted to found a republic – and now calling them "outlaw states" might be "true" in a way, as (some) supporting evidence for such a designation can always be procured, but it does not address the practical political problems that such a choice of words and strategies entails. Even if one (mistakenly) believes that our "categorizations" are unproblematic tools, readied by universal reason for our march through history, such decontextualization of "naming" should be resisted. History is certainly no court of law and no laboratory in which something that worked once before could be simply repeated, because most of the time the enabling parameter conditions no longer obtain. But such "historicist" objections are, quite understandably, "deflating" the political project of certain "liberals" who, better than some other "decent people," have apparently gotten things just "right." Consequently, no further questions arise as to the principles and institutions that are appropriate.

In the context of criticizing this approach, Raymond Geuss provides a telling illustration. He mentions the (possibly apocryphal) encounter of Rawls with a visiting European historian, to whom Rawls handed a draft of a paper about "Modern politics since the Treaty of Westphalia in 1548."

> When the historian mentioned that the accepted date was 1648 Rawls replied mildly: "Oh really?" and changed the offending digit with a single stroke of the pen. Despite myself, I cannot help finding this rather sublime. From the view of the original position, the difference between the 16th and the 17th century is completely insignificant, actually invisible. Of course one tries to get things right, if one can, but nothing in the work depends on

30 There he distinguishes (in descending order?) between liberal, decent, outlaws, burdened societies, and benevolent absolutism. *Ibid.* at 4f.

> this type of correctness. No further part of the paper needed to be changed apart from that one digit.[31]

The historical amnesia induced by such attempts urges us to accept that the question "what is the correct conception of justice" *is the* basic question, and that the stipulation of a specific institutional structure is the appropriate "answer" to it. But given the problem of violence, of genocidal activities, of state-perpetrated terror and so on, is not security of equal importance, standing in complex relations to justice and equality? In the face of the present misdistribution of resources and of pervasive market failures, is not the belief in market efficiency a myth? Under such circumstances can the "lexical ordering" of priorities, which Rawls defends, still be maintained? Is the answer to *the* "basic" question an appropriate response to the problems we have to confront? Are the remedies to the breakdown of trust and the difficulties of mastering collective action problems really resolvable when relying on some highly problematic notions of rationality and motivation (getting the incentives right), while refusing to analyse the havoc such a regime can create, as evidenced by repeated disasters? In short, the only thing history teaches us, is that there is never only *one* question, and that the necessary remedies can never be derived from it alone. Instead, any serious analysis presupposes, as a first step, a recognition of the historicity of our social world and of *getting the questions right*, and that means – among other things –understanding what the participants of the political game consider relevant, instead of silencing such an endeavour by the force of assumptions.

The latter problem has of course become one of the main problems in economic analysis, especially since the "efficient" market hypothesis turned out to be more of a "hype" than a hypothesis for the simple reason that it is tautological and thus true by definition. Against all evidence, in the happy world of ideal theory "bubbles" cannot exist, as the rational actors with full information will always bring the market back into equilibrium. In this way this construct could justify the debt binge of the 1980s, and later the more substantial subprime debt crisis, which is, of course, not to say that this was the only reason. It does, however, explain why we were so careless with both "disconfirming" evidence that we promptly discounted instead of searching for possible "problems" that loomed on the horizon and required remedial action, but which was not forthcoming.

The other problem is the conceptual confusion in that "the market" is supposed always to function in the same way, despite the fact that markets for goods are obviously different from those supplying health care, or those of banking or of finance. While the goods sector conforms more or less to the

[31] Raymond Geuss, "Neither History nor Praxis," in Raymond Geuss, *Outside Ethics* (Princeton University Press, 2005), 29–39 at 39.

demand and supply nexus regulated by a price mechanism under competitive conditions, the others do not. In financial markets the price does not stand *for* some real phenomenon such as a good traded; rather the price *is* the product. Financial markets mediate options (promises) on goods that are usually not yet in existence, are frequently not owned by the seller, who promises to supply them at a certain time for a given price, and that are sold to a buyer, who usually does not want ever to possess them either. He is also most likely to never get them, having hopefully made a handsome profit by saddling somebody else with that option. Thus, different from product markets where all, or at least some, can "win" as the actors there are in a positive sum game, in option markets we have pure zero sum transactions. What drives such transactions is certainly "interest" – the magic wand of economics – but contrary to product markets no value is being created; simple redistribution is at issue. The only point is, therefore, to "play" the market, which functions then more like a casino than as a coordinating mechanism for production and distribution.

This gives rise to further befuddlements when "efficiency," supposedly uniting all types of markets, is invoked. Unfortunately, as in the case of the term "market," efficiency also means different things. Efficiency in product markets means allocative efficiency, which steers resources via the price signal to efficient use, that is maximum output. Of course, technology and investment in human capital are thereby neglected. But this "oversight" leads to a long-term "inefficiency" that eventually shows up as "non-competitiveness," just as Schumpeter predicted.[32] Thus what we are actually after when we invoke "efficiency" is what Douglas North has called an "adaptive" rather than a purely allocative form of "efficiency," because only the latter incorporates Schumpeter's concerns and promises long-term growth.[33]

There remains – somewhere in-between these two conceptions – the Keynesian notion of efficiency concerning the welfare losses caused by market downturns, due to lack of effective demand (the so-called Okun gap). Thus if a Keynesian intervention distorts market prices – a point Friedman always made – but thereby stimulates demand, standard economic analysis seems to lack an appropriate tool for assessing the implications of these two different conceptions of efficiency. And then there is the case of health care where huge positive externalities may obtain (such as when vaccinations are available and mandatory), which, however, in the absence of some "public" enforcement cannot be realized. So much for the argument that the interventions of the "public hand" always have to be "distorting"! Nevertheless, a whole host of other dilemmas have then to be faced (allocation of scare organs, general public health and

[32] See Joseph A. Schumpeter, *Capitalism, Socialism and Democracy* (London: George Allen and Unwin, 1961).

[33] Douglas North, "Economic Performance through Time," *American Economic Review*, vol. 84 (June 1994), 359–69 at 367.

prevention vs. intervention, compulsory insurance vs. freedom of choice and so on). A comparison across health care systems will therefore have to involve multiple dimensions so that the meaning of one single efficiency criterion is difficult to understand. Consequently, contestation rather than convergence on one "true" model is to be expected.

Now it could be that there is a common core to all notions of efficiency since the word "*efficere*" means "making," "creating something," "bringing it into existence." But it might be better to think that we have here at best a "family resemblance" instead of some essential property since attempts at harmonizing the conceptual divergences have not been very successful. This difficulty has, of course, not prevented most economists from claiming that efficiency is the key to all social understanding, thereby issuing warnings against (political) interference.

Ironically, financial markets, considered to be the closest to the frictionless competitive market, are most dependent on political decisions and on external factors, such as technology and *doxa*. They do not spontaneously evolve but have to be "made" by "removing" all interferences with capital flows, so that trading can be carried out by supercomputers in milliseconds. Proponents of frictionless markets have to find legislators who believe that their special knowledge supports their claims and that, for example, interfering with the magic "natural rate of unemployment" is going to backfire. They must ask for fiscal restraints, but they also have – because of "cost considerations" – to baulk at "onerous" disclosure requirements (because in their world information is free and costless). Thus when consumers buy harmful products, they "must" be maximizing their utility. The advocates are also dependent on political sponsors to allow "freedom" for often fraudulent manoeuvrings with opaque financial instruments. If traders make some exorbitant gains, they have to convince others that their earnings "must" mean that they contributed the same amount of value to the economy. As in the world of true love, reality proves nothing, and given the self-generating capacity of expectations, the "theory" will fit reality as soon as "the world" has been "fitted" to the theory and the "incentives" have been set right. Of course, some "unfortunate" accidents occur, and do so quite often. For the theorists these remain, however, mysterious despite their frequency exactly because they are not part of the ideal of market rationality. Here the theological roots of this "ideal" are suggestive.

Similar to the former version of the theodicy, God's plan – symbolized by the *manus gubernatoris* of the scholastics – had to be discovered in the historical world, despite pervasive existence of evil. It is not accidental that Adam Smith later appropriated this metaphor for the "market"[34] and this hand is – like God – "invisible." From there it was a small step to argue that someone

[34] See Stefan Adrianopoulos, "The Invisible Hand: Supranatural Agency in Political Economy and Gothic Novel," *English Literary History*, vol. 66, no. 3 (1999), 739–58.

who understands the market not only understands the "economy," but holds the key to understanding all forms of social interaction. The economist Gary Becker has ventured into a variety of fields ranging from education to family planning – thus even children become "commodities" – to the production of knowledge, to the "market" of marriages and divorces. All areas of life are supposed to be subjected to the critical assessment of the relation between investment and expected gains (calculated by using "shadow prices").[35]

Such an approach relieves the "student" from any actual inquiry, or from acquiring knowledge of other disciplines, or of historical events, as nothing new can be discovered. What remains is the dogmatic claim that an economic perspective provides – because of its "power" – a unique, coherent, and thus superior account of what holds the social world together. In such a world unexpected "events" have little place, as rational actors can, despite their limited knowledge, anticipate future states and make them part of their present calculation. Even the unknown future can be transformed into a decision under risk since random changes that introduce instability into the system as a whole, can be managed by "risk-offsetting" investments.

Why this argument, based so obviously on wishful thinking, is taken as a gospel is somewhat puzzling. After all, we know that not all systems tend towards equilibrium but have, if positive (rather than negative) feedback loops obtain, *systemic grounds* for instability. To that extent not all "disasters" are simply external shocks, analyzable analogously to rare natural catastrophes, but are system immanent. Thus even if stabilization mechanisms might be able to stabilize some deviations through "offsetting investments," the resulting outcome is unlikely to be a stabilization of the system. Here the work of Charles Perrow[36] and of heterodox economists like Mandelbrot[37] becomes relevant, the upshot of which is that the knowledge generated by orthodox economic theory might not only be contestable but also actually wrong – with ominous implications for policy advice derived from these models. The patterns that emerged from Mandelbrot's analysis resembled volatile oscillations familiar from fluid dynamics. Mandelbrot discovered odd periodicities such as "Joseph effects" (seven good years and seven lean ones) that combine with "Noah effects," that is deluge-like catastrophic events.[38] Instability is thus systemic rather than exogenous and – perversely enough – the measures of "securitizing" volatility by certain "offsetting investments" contribute to greater systemic volatility.

[35] Gary Becker, *The Economic Approach to Human Behavior* (University of Chicago Press, 1976).

[36] Charles Perrow, *Complex Organizations* (New York: McGraw Hill, 1986).

[37] Benoît Mandelbrot, "The Variation of Certain Other Speculative Prices," *The Journal of Business* (Jan 1967), 393–413; Benoît Mandelbrot and Richard Hudson, *The (Mis)-behavior of Markets: A Fractal View of Risk, Ruin and Rewards* (New York: Basic Books, 1974).

[38] For a more extensive discussion, see Joseph Vogl, *Das Gespenst des Kapitals*, 4th edn. (Zurich: Diaphanes, 2010), Chapter 6.

Finally, allocative efficiency can only obtain when we make decisions based on fixed budgets. But since financial markets operate with future expectations, there is no limit for financing needs. In addition, these "expectations" create perverse incentives for traders to reap profits through fees, and for inventing new instruments that become riskier and riskier, making crises all the more likely. Thus the notion of an (allocative) efficiency and equilibrium is meaningless under these circumstances; and worse still, financial markets cannot meet the criteria of a Schumpeterian or a Keynesian notion of efficiency either.

This raises the general question of whether the conceptual framework of a general equilibrium model is still able to accommodate these "anomalies" or whether we actually deal with systems that are fundamentally different. Such systemic instabilities are not uncommon in nature and can be observed, for example, when "synchronous lateral excitation" has to be taken into account, as in the case of engineering suspension bridges. As we had to find out, the synchronization of the steps of only 156 pedestrians was enough to nearly lead to the collapse of London's Millennium Bridge in 2000.[39]

Analogous phenomena could be observed in the case of the last financial crisis, as Hyun Song Shin suggested.[40] Certain instruments can destabilize the system despite the "securitization" of the risk of single instruments by bundling risky and well-performing papers. Similarly, if value is created by guessing correctly how others will value an option or stock – Keynes' famous beauty contest – their price will rise without this rise being based on any change in the fundamentals, and the price will fall if others sell and thereby force others also to sell. This interdependency of valuations not only violates the independence of decision-making, necessary if the market is supposed to be "efficient"; it also shows that the play between demand and supply will here not follow an equilibrating logic. But this is just another way of saying that the formation of bubbles and catastrophes (crises) is intrinsic to such "markets." Of course, this does not mean that all destabilizing effects are internal and that there are no external shocks that can be devastating, as the OPEC oil price increase showed, and which gave us the "impossible," that is stagflation. But it does suggest that Minski's analysis that blames most of the instability on factors internal to the financial system[41] attains considerable persuasiveness.

Of course there arises a "further" question: even if we "explain" certain disequilibria, particularly in financial markets, by their sensitivity to information – given the self-generative force of expectations – there still remains a further problem, that is the "fiduciary" issue. In every transaction we need not only to know the "prices" but must also "trust" that the products actually deliver what they promise. This is the case for "goods" where warranties, not only to solve

[39] *Ibid.* at 158.

[40] Hyun Song Shin, *Risk and Liquidity* (Oxford University Press, 2010), 1–6.

[41] Hyman Minsky, *Stabilizing an Unstable Economy* (New Haven: Yale, 1986).

the information problem but also clearly to allocate responsibilities for restitution or repair. In financial markets this problem is supposedly solved by "rating agencies." But even if we assume that the agencies "know" more than all others, and are not part of an insider trading scheme – indeed a heroic presupposition given the existing perverse incentives – there is no "warranty" that allocates fiduciary duties (despite some recent attempts by the EU Commission in this respect). If the information is, as the agencies claim, just some private opinion sold to unwitting clients, the fiduciary duties are left hanging. But how one could ascribe such responsibilities in automated computer trading schemes remains even more mysterious.

The suspicion that we are dealing with rather disparate problems that "ideal theory" amalgamates under some idealized notion of a market is heightened when we consider the following. Friedman's monetarist theory has little to do with the theory of exchanging goods – despite Friedman's own belief in the "market"[42] – and it is also far from the logic of the pricing option model developed by Black and Scholes.[43] In the latter case the circulation no longer occurs through the exchanges of goods or through compensations that "settle" debts, but through the proliferation of debts within an indefinite time frame. The relevant question is then why concrete, that is finite human beings, should *not* be worried (even if their time horizon includes the next generations) that under such conditions debt will devour an ever-increasing amount of the inherited and created wealth. Furthermore, since the burst of speculative bubbles can lead to potentially catastrophic losses and to credit crunches that are reflected in substantial increases in interest rates, it is not clear how the "productivity" of the real economy will be able to outpace the rise in debts and interest rates. After all, it is one thing that in Fama's world[44] (here *nomen est omen*, as "fama" does not only mean "fame" but also "rumour") "historicity" does not exist, as the future can only be thought of as a continued process of optimization as all events and states of the (social) world have their known or insurable price. It is another thing and takes some doing to trust such "predictions" in the face of continued instability.

Nevertheless, the dominant response to such criticisms has been that there is a "continuity" in the economy, that occasional disturbances should not be taken as refutations[45] of the dominant paradigm, thereby preventing us from

42 See e.g. Milton Friedman and Rose Friedman, *Free to Choose* (London: Secker and Warburg, 1980).

43 Fischer Black and Myron Scholes, "The Pricing of Options and Corporate Liabilities," *Journal of Political Economy*, vol. 81 (1973): 637–54.

44 Eugene Fama, "The Behavior of Stock Market Prices," *Journal of Business*, vol. 38 no. 1 (1965): 34–105. Eugene Fama and Merton Miller, *The Theory of Finance* (New York: Holt Rinehart and Winston, 1972).

45 See e.g. Robert Shiller, *The New Financial Order: Risk in the 21st Century* (Princeton University Press, 2003): 1–2.

"getting the questions right" and at the same time muting any suggestion that the record should give us some good reasons to think more seriously about the aggravated moral hazard problems created by the information-sensitive financial markets. They – nearly systematically – invite conspiratorial and criminal activities such as insider trading, misuse of funds, and corruption. Here the Kerviel case of 2010 is emblematic of the dubious practices in which traders are engaging – in all likelihood with the full knowledge of their superiors – who use them later as scapegoats for the 5 billion lost for the Société Générale. A similar picture emerges from the investigations by the US District Attorney for Southern Manhattan that uncovered a network of hedge fund managers, rating agencies, and bank officials who engaged in insider trading.[46] And to round out the set, the recent manipulation of the LIBOR rate by some banks seems to drive home the same point. However, all this disturbing news is treated as mere "exceptions," as they are attributed to a few black sheep.

At this point the widely shared assumption among orthodox economists that any governmental intervention is not only useless but deeply subversive of our "freedom," not only for us as *homines economici* (which is already doubtful enough), but as *persons tout court*, seems rather heroic. Attack is then considered the best defence and the absurdity of conclusion is covered up by confronting us with a false dichotomy. In his programmatic statement *Capitalism and Freedom* Friedman wrote:

> Fundamentally, there are only two ways of coordinating the economic activities of millions … One is central direction involving the use of coercion – the technique of the army and the modern totalitarian state. The other is the voluntary cooperation of individuals – the technique of the market place.[47]

We need not engage in the deconstruction of these bold assertions, as nearly all the classical (and misleading) *topoi* are here assembled in a potent ideological mix. But one should at least be sensitive to the fact that this argument is based on a false dichotomy since "firms" in the market rely on "imperative control" and not free exchanges. But never mind; there is the "fundament," that is the "free" exchange that forces upon us the existential choice between good and evil, freedom or serfdom, a move that is buttressed by traditional logic via the excluded middle, and thus everything follows from that.

Given this rather pathetic parody, Charles Schultze, chairman of the Council of Economic Advisors under President Carter, might have hit on something when he once confided in Robert Kuttner, a syndicated columnist writing on economic affairs: "When you dig deep down economists are scared to death of being sociologists. The one great thing we have going for us is the premise that individuals act rationally in trying to satisfy their preferences." Kuttner draws

[46] Wolfgang Hetzer, *Finanz Mafia* (Frankfurt: Wochenend, 2011), Chapter 4.

[47] Milton Friedman, *Capitalism and Freedom* (University of Chicago Press, 1962), 1.

from this the conclusion: "this helps explain why the profession tends to marginalize, even ostracize, those who posit that motivation is more complex and that non-economic factors matter."[48] To hope under these circumstances that the ideal of professionalism will be able to set things right then seems equally heroic.

Colonization or illumination?

The upshot of the above argument is that ideal theory is not likely to make good on its promises and is actually a hindrance to understanding. This objection is not new and has been made by "heterodox" economists, in particular in the context of "development," or the formation of preferences (Hirschman,[49] Sen[50]), and by students of the history of science alike.[51] Precisely because science is not simply a monologic demonstration but also a social practice, what "*counts*" as knowledge and gets processed and promulgated by the fraternity of scientists is the important thing. Here paradigmatic understandings, intellectual hegemonies, or plain and simple repression or concealment by both producers and "users" of knowledge (what is known but is *not to be known publicly*) have to be taken into account.

The interaction between knowledge production and organizational diffusion is also decisive for comprehending the colonization moves of certain disciplines in other fields. Given that the key terms of orthodox economics are ambiguous and notions of "rationality" and "interest" tell us little about how preferences arise or "trump" myopic conceptions of interest, the prospects for colonization do not seem to be the best when viewed epistemologically. Furthermore, given that "prices" depend upon a general medium of exchange that also serves as a measure and store of value, it is surprising that economic thinking has made considerable inroads into other disciplines, such as law and politics. After all, the latter's disciplinary understandings are closely tied to the notion that "powers" or "liberties" should not become fused into one universal yardstick. This would not necessarily preclude that certain areas of law are perhaps more amenable to a treatment in terms of the law and economics model[52] since we have seen that "balancing" (the "trade-offs" of economics) has become an important part of adjudication, although as we have seen there is no one-to-one translation and the analogy might be problematic. But disciplinary resistance should

[48] Robert Kuttner, *Everything for Sale* (University of Chicago Press, 1996), 41.

[49] Albert Hirschman, *The Passion and the Interests* (Princeton University Press, 1977).

[50] Amartya Sen, "Rational Fools: A Critique of the Behavioural Foundations of Economic Theory," *Philosophy and Public Affairs*, vol. 6, no. 4 (1977), 317–44.

[51] Howard Margolies, *Paradigms as Barriers: How Habits of Mind Govern Science Beliefs* (University of Chicago Press, 1993).

[52] See e.g. Guido Calabresi, *The Costs of Accidents: A Legal and Economic Analysis* (New Haven: Yale University Press, 1970).

form, when all of law is subjected to such a move. In responding to the first observation we could take tort law as an easy case, since the purpose of tort law is to minimize social costs "defined as the sum total of accident costs, administration costs, costs of properly allocating accident losses by means of insurance, and accident prevention costs of both the insurer and the victim."[53] Criminal law, on the other hand, seems to provide a harder case and could serve as an indicator for addressing the second observation.

Let us begin with tort law. Faced with this daunting task of minimizing social costs, "the law" has to develop both liability rules and rely on efficient enforcement mechanisms. Practically this means that the conceptualization of "fault" is approached as an optimization problem that can be solved via a marginal cost analysis. Thus a person is at fault and liable if she has neglected to apply an additional unit of care, even though the cost to her was less than the marginal benefits to the victim. In this way we could reduce the total amount of the expected damages. The so-called Learned Hand formula[54] then provides the yardstick for a socially optimal level of care. While such a formula seems "reasonable" and fair, there are at least two major difficulties.

One is that no clear rules are then possible, since damages are assessed only *ex post* and the costs, instantiated in the rules, are not available to the parties *ex ante*. Thus the outcome seems more like a Weberian *kadi*-justice than one of formulating rules that allow for prospective ordering. While such a possibility is thereby not excluded, for it to occur, both judges and insurers would have to be perfect maximizers and agree on the same accounting scheme in order to set the optimal level of care. Here the assumption of complete and costless information raises its ugly head. We all know, of course, that such an assumption is "unrealistic," as it is "ideal." But it turns out also to be logically *incoherent*, as soon as we try to relax this stringent assumption. This leads us to the second problem. If information is not costless, then the question arises of how long and at what cost we are going to search. However, the resulting "augmented" decision problem does not let us determine the "optimal level of search" so that we can converge on an optimum level of care. It was precisely for these reasons that we tried to "economize" and use short cuts by inventing rules in the first place! Our hope was that they would at least help us in our calculations by identifying fewer and more manageable factors that we have to take into consideration. Thus property rules relieve us from worrying about the needs of others and of social optima that could be relevant when "needs" are adduced to "solve"

[53] H. B. Schafer and A. Schoenberger, "Strict Liability vs. Negligence," in B. Boukoukaert and G. De Geest (eds.), *Encyclopedia of Law and Economics*, vol. II (Cheltenham: Edward Elgar, 2000), 598.

[54] This formula has been incorporated into US tort law. See Stephen G. Gilles, "The Invisible Hand Formula," *Virginia Law Review*, vol. 80 (1994), 1015–54.

the distribution problem. As Conlisk points out,[55] the idealized assumption of an optimum providing us with firm guidance has to fall down when the "costs" for solving the augmented decision problem are included.

It is therefore no surprise that the genuflection before the ideal has little to offer to either a "theory" of law or to the actual practice of judging. If we do not want to fall back on idiosyncratic reasons of the judges, as the realists suggested, we need some consensual "rules of thumb" by which we, as potential tortfeasors and judges alike, can assess how to proceed. These rules need not be unequivocal or incontestable, and they certainly will not be universal, showing instead the traces of "traditions" and (criticizable) "common sense." But unfortunately, that is all we have and we must make do with it.

Things are not getting better when we turn to the "hard case" of criminal law. As we shall see, there is a good reason why law separates spheres and distinguishes criminal liability from torts. To that extent attempts to eradicate these boundaries have some mind-boggling implications for non-cognoscenti. Thus the upshot of Posner's introduction of cost–benefit analysis into criminal law[56] led – in the ironic rendition of his thesis by one of its critics – to the startling conclusion that "rape should be legalized if rapists would be willing to pay more to rape (victims) than they (the victims) would pay to avoid rape."[57] Posner himself admits that his case was "weak" because only non-coercive consensual transactions "can create wealth and be … efficient."[58] Nevertheless, he admonished us not to take a "too narrow view of market alternatives" and gives to the rapist – who would "not get as much pleasure from consensual sex" – the avuncular advice that, even in the absence of market alternatives, "it does not follow that there are no other avenues for satisfaction"[59]. In lieu of "furtively stalking women," our poor chap could, for example, "engage in productive activities in which people get compensated."[60] So when all is said and done – after all the convoluted arguments that no market exists, but should, even though it really does not create wealth, and so on – the young man should simply get a job and enjoy the pay cheque!

Nevertheless, with perhaps somewhat less grandiose aspirations of having found the "theoretical hammer" that makes the whole world look like a nail,[61] the problem of how to provide the highest possible levels of welfare,

[55] John Conlisk, "Why Bounded Rationality?," *Journal of Economic Literature*, vol. 34, no. 2 (1996), 669–700 at 690.

[56] See Richard Posner, "An Economic Theory of Criminal Law," *Columbia Law Review*, vol. 85 (October 1985), 1193–231.

[57] Cass Sunstein, *Legal Reasoning and Political Conflict* (Oxford University Press, 1996): 15.

[58] Posner, "An Economic Theory of Criminal Law," at 1198.

[59] *Ibid.* at 1199. [60] *Ibid.*

[61] See e.g. Posner's prolific writings ranging from animal rights, to ageing, public intellectuals, plagiarism, "sex and reason," and, of course, to regulation.

either through regulation or through market mechanisms, has been a genuine issue in economics itself. The older welfare economics, pioneered by Pigou,[62] was later challenged by Coase in his seminal article "The Problem of Social Costs."[63] Coase challenged Pigou's faith in the beneficial consequences of governmental intervention in the event of "market failure." His main line of attack was that Pigou did not consider the costs of this strategy when compared to alternatives, particularly in the face of the possibility of *governmental failure*. Thus courts, central banks, and governmental regulators seem to be unable to improve on economic outcomes, which individuals without governmental interference could negotiate. Under the assumption that these negotiations were uncoerced, readily available, and without transaction costs, Coase argued that individuals will arrive at better solutions than those provided by governmental intervention.

This Coase theorem provided the foundation for Richard Posner's manifesto against governmental regulation, presented in his article "Natural Monopoly and its Regulation," and for the sweeping deregulations over the next decades.[64] The assumption of costless transactions was of course heroic, but fitted well with the penchant for "ideal theory" based on "unrealistic assumption" à la Friedman. Nevertheless, something must have gotten lost in the translation of Coase's theorem into the plain and simple deregulation message of Posner. When Posner presented his views at a conference, purportedly basing his argument on Coase, the latter reacted rather viscerally:

> My first reaction on reading Posner's paper was one of amusement … as I studied the paper with more care [I] ceased to be amused. Posner says that the first part of his paper describes "the conception of the field (the new institutional Economics) held by Ronald Coase. Reading this part … recalled to my mind Horace Walpole's opening remark in his book on *King Richard the Third*: "So incompetent has the generality of historians been for the province they have undertaken, that it is almost a question, whether if the dead of past ages could revive, would be able to reconnoitre the events of their own times, as transmitted to us by ignorance and misrepresentation." I have only one foot through the door, but should the final yank come before this piece is published, Horace Walpole's words would apply to Posner's highly inaccurate account of my views.[65]

[62] A. C. Pigou, *The Economics of Welfare*, 4th edn. (New Brunswick: Transaction Books, 2002).

[63] Ronald Coase, "The Problem of Social Costs," *Journal of Law and Economics*, vol. 3 (1960), 1–44.

[64] Richard Posner, "Natural Monopoly and its Regulation," *Stanford Law Review*, vol. 21, no. 3 (1969), 546–643.

[65] Ronald H. Coase, "Coase on Posner on Coase," *Journal of Institutional and Theoretical Economics*, vol. 149 (1993), 96–98 at 96.

Posner was not rattled by this criticism and argued that he knew Coase better than Coase himself.[66] Thus apparently we are not only moving in an "ideal" world based on unrealistic assumptions, but in a world in which Humpty-Dumpty's rule applies:

> "When I use a word," Humpty-Dumpty said in a rather scornful tone, "it means just what I choose it to mean – neither more nor less."
>
> "The question is," said Alice, "whether you can make words mean so many different things."
>
> "The question is," said Humpty-Dumpty, "which is to be master – that's all."[67]

But then again, there is perhaps hope, since Posner has, as of late, discovered Keynesianism and admittedly read the *General Theory* for the first time.[68] In his new book, entitled *A Failure of Capitalism*,[69] he has come to the conclusion that capitalism has not only failed, but "that excessive ideologically motivated regulation"[70] is to blame, and he noted "the pernicious effect of competition and ultimately deregulation on bank safety."[71] Suddenly massive governmental bailouts, such as that of the auto industry by the US administration, are all right,[72] the danger of public works programs becoming a "permanent drain on the federal budget is less serious,"[73] and "more government intervention in the economy and … higher taxes are not necessarily a bad thing."[74] These are astounding admissions, given Posner's original stance.

Although this would not be the first time that a Saulus gets transformed into a Paulus and that the joy is the greatest when a prodigal son returns home, we should be careful not to conclude that the exchange of one theory for another necessarily solves the problem of how to generate and assess useful knowledge. After all, there are numerous ways of being wrong and whether governmental interventions have debilitating effects, as Friedman *et al.* have argued, is still an open question. Answering it will depend not only on a "theory" but also on what people have tried before and what they are ready to do now. Even when we see that the financial market has by virtually all accounts refuted the "efficient market" hypothesis, such a realization does not answer the question

[66] Richard Posner, "The New Institutional Economics Meets Law and Economics," *Journal of Institutional and Theoretical Economics*, vol. 149, no. 1 (1993), 73–87 at 73; see also Richard Posner, *Overcoming Law* (Cambridge, MA: Harvard University Press, 1995), Chapter 21.

[67] Lewis Carroll, *Through the Looking Glass* (London: Penguin, 1994), 100.

[68] See Richard Posner, "How I Became a Keynesian," *The New Republic*, September 23, 2009.

[69] Richard A. Posner, *A Failure of Capitalism: The Crisis of '08 and the Descent into Depression* (Cambridge, MA: Harvard University Press, 2009).

[70] *Ibid.* at 306. [71] *Ibid.* at 130. [72] *Ibid.* at 164.

[73] *Ibid.* at 171. [74] *Ibid.* at 226.

of how we can create institutions that work reasonably well without creating perverse effects.[75]

In the next section I attempt to defend the view that for such purposes our conventional mode of "theorizing," or reflecting critically upon the practical problems, is ill-equipped for this job and that some important conceptual changes are required. It is not an optimum derived from axiomatic assumptions that provides the yardstick, but expectations, more like those we have of an effective medicine, should be the criterion. We take the medicine when it betters our overall health without restricting us too much in our daily pursuits, or overwhelming us with side effects. However, as we will see, even the analogy to medicine might still be too limited since "health" is dependent on "natural" facts, although what represents "normal" good health (and what should be classified as a disease) is obviously also subject to cultural conditions (vide the high levels of smoking in older movies, long after its dangers had been publicized). To the extent that the social world is one of artifice, praxis confronts us with even more exacting problems.

The case for a "diagnostics"

The proposal for a non-deal "theory"[76] has to meet several initial challenges before it can be elaborated. As usual, what is being discussed under this rubric contains several different issues. Sometimes when we used the term "ideal" we just want to contrast it with the "real." Thus when the painter Giotto could draw perfect circles by free hand on which a compass did not improve, this still was not the "ideal" circle of geometry. Similarly, we can assume certain states of the world although they hardly obtain, such as a perfect vacuum or absolute zero in temperature. In a second way we use "ideal" when we deal in practical contexts with some (normative) assumptions, such as rational action and the *homo economicus*. The third use of "ideal" is to have these normative constructs satisfy more exacting criteria, such as *moral* ones by, for example, including equal concern, respect for the natural liberty of others, perhaps even some "virtues" such as benevolence and altruism and so on.

The common procedure in "ideal theorizing" is, however, in a way always the same: it starts with abstract principles and assumptions, hoping that their clarification will help us in solving concrete problems after we have found a solution "in principle." But in the case of practical problems that involve a moral dimension, this creates great difficulties. As Kant suggested and Albena Azmanova

[75] For an interesting discussion of various approaches to the institutional "design" problems, see Robert Goodin (ed.), *The Theory of Institutional Design* (Cambridge University Press, 1996).

[76] For a clear exposition of the issues involved, see David Wiens, "Prescribing Institutions without Ideal Theory," *Journal of Political Philosophy*, vol. 20, no. 1 (2012), 45–67.

has thoroughly investigated, we encounter here the "scandal of reason,"[77] that is the paradox that reason cannot provide a "theory" of judgment by which the universal principles can be applied.

This recognition has several corollaries. First, it should be obvious that a "non-ideal" of reflection on problems of praxis *does not deny* the importance of "ideals" or values, but proposes a different way of realizing them. To put it simply, this approach is neither some form of political (or scientific) "realism" at basement prices, nor is it an endeavour, such as analytical ethics, which elaborates on the principles of morality. A non-ideal approach to acting *does* take values seriously but proceeds by not providing ideal targets against which the actual order can be assessed, but by identifying *specific failures*. It diagnoses them, and prescribes a remedy that need not be universally applicable but that might "work" because of "local" or historical conditions. Since the ideals are not conceptual truths that can be postulated or introduced by assumption, they must be derived from *actual historical experience* and they must be *realizable under actual non-ideal conditions*. This has important implications for both our understanding of human action and for creating institutions, as Alex Wendt has pointed out in a much-underappreciated article.[78]

Second, these realizations have led from Aristotle to the present to a critical reflection on "second-best" solutions[79] for which he assembled actual constitutions and engaged in comparisons that provided the background for his reflections on stasis and for its "solution," that is the idea of a "mixed constitution." Similarly, speculations about "second-best" markets have been advocated,[80] as opposed to "idealizations" that base institutional design on complete and costless information. In the same vein, Sen's recent work on justice has to be mentioned, as he explicitly rejects ideal theory à la Rawls.[81] In short, if small changes in initial conditions, for which an institution was designed, for example, result in considerably different outcomes, then institutional borrowing and the transfer of "best practices" becomes problematic and needs careful scrutiny.

[77] Azmanova, *The Scandal of Reason*.

[78] Alex Wendt, "Driving with the Rearview Mirror. On Rational Science and Institutional Design," *International Organization*, vol. 55 (Autumn 2001), 1019–49.

[79] See e.g. his discussion of the distinction between the "best man" and the "best citizen" and his distinction of the best constitution and the best possible constitutions, given particular circumstances. For the substitution of "satisficing" for "optimizing," see Herbert Simon, *Models of Man* (New York: Wiley, 1957).

[80] The "second-best" approach suggests that, since various factors contribute to price distortions, the correction of one distortion by introducing market elements (as in health care) is not likely to improve the overall outcome. Second-best markets thus function with a variety of institutional structures to which market forces have adapted. See K. Lancaster and R. G. Lisey, "The General Theory of the Second Best," *Review of Economic Studies*, vol. 24, no. 1 (1956), 11–32.

[81] Amartya Sen, *The Idea of Justice* (Cambridge, MA: Harvard University Press, 2009).

Third, here another difference comes to the fore: although such an approach also implies a "design" problem for institutions, it does not compare it to, or evaluates the outcomes in accordance with, some unique standard based not only on idealization, but often on *demonstrably false* or incoherent assumptions.[82] Ironically the latter constructs are then justified by their pragmatic value of making "predictions" possible even though we do not know why we hit it right, as outcomes are usually overdetermined. Furthermore, since the focus is now no longer on a unique best outcome to which the existing order has to aspire, but has been shifted to the broader question of "as compared to what," the requirement for a rational ordering can no longer be understood as a goal/means relationship or a simple optimization procedure. Rather, given the multiplicity of values issuing in different arrangements, the problem is now of finding an acceptable range of value realizations for which political agreement has to be sought, since no purely logical solution is possible. Enter politics, since the alleged paralysis of scepticism cannot be overcome by a flight to ideal theory, as we have to act, despite our limitations and the fallibility of our knowledge. Not "truth" but "responsibility' and the "art of the possible" in acting together now become the decisive elements.

Such an approach is obviously open to the objection that it might set its eyes too low (and thus represent a right-Hegelian bias in that the existing is the "reasonable"). Another objection could be that it lacks a clear specification of the "goal" and that it therefore cannot provide a blueprint, or a map, for where we want to go. Finally, one could argue that non-ideal theory's dependence on "local" conditions misunderstands morality, whose task is to clarify universally valid standards. Thus, singly and in conjunction, these objections seem powerful enough to stop this project even before it can get off the ground. Luckily (or, unfortunately for those making this pitch) I think none of the objections can be sustained. Let us look a bit closer at the problems involved.

If feasibility is a decisive criterion for solving practical problems, the costs of measuring the actual state of affairs by the yardstick of universally valid standards has to be compared to those of drawing on a possibly "impoverished set" of feasible alternatives. But if the idea of one supreme value (such as human dignity or of consistently ordered values) leads to contradictions and paradoxes, as I have shown, the argument of setting one's eyes high loses much of its persuasiveness. It leads, at best, to interminable, undecidable debates, if not to open conflict. We had such debates in the field, for example, when we tried to assess the impact of economic sanctions and came to the conclusion that they "do not work."[83] While they certainly disappointed our expectations, we soon

[82] See e.g. Friedman's instrumentalist approach to theorizing in Milton Friedman, *Essays in Positive Economics* (University of Chicago Press, 1953).

[83] See Daniel Drenzer, *The Sanction Paradox: Economic Statecraft and International Relations* (Cambridge University Press, 1999) for a good discussion of the sanction debate. See also

learned that "force" also has severe limitations when compared to our "normative" expectations of how they are supposed to work. As Baldwin pointed out, much of the discussion had an ethereal quality, since the yardstick was never clear and the hidden assumption that sanctions – any type of sanction – could bring us back to the *status quo ante* is an impossible idea to sustain. Thus what we need instead is a carefully constructed contingency framework that allows for comparing the various strategies and outcomes.[84]

The second objection, that no coherent road map is presented, is somewhat off, in that most of idealized theorizing never bothers to do this to begin with. It rather "solves" this problem by assumption, or by a vaguely articulated "theory" of progress. True, the diagnostic approach is retrospective, as it starts with identified ills, but this does not mean that thereby no "future" states are being considered, particularly when the set of options is assessed and comparisons are supplemented by counterfactual reasoning.

Finally, while "morality" requires from us the impartial assessment of the affected interests, it does not require that such an assessment must be made in terms of allegedly universal values. As the Antigone example and the hypothetical of blaming stone-age dwellers for not realizing human rights showed, such attempts are largely scholastic and unproductive. It seems to me no accident that virtually all "utopias" sooner or later fall back on the social arrangements with which their proponents are familiar, that is they derive their plausibility from their own "parochial" way of life.

Impartiality among different political projects, however, *is* required when we deliberate and try to assess and identify the advantages and benefits of certain arrangements. Here we cannot make decisions based on idiosyncratic criteria, such as withholding benefits from people with red hair, or suspending *habeas corpus* on Wednesdays since it is (as all academics know) an extraordinary, perhaps even loathsome day – because it cuts in on the weekend on both sides! But impartiality is always limited to those interests that are actually "represented." This, of course, does raise further issues of access, of voice, of exit or loyalty, and of possibilities for advocacy, discussed previously. But nothing in these discussions seems to require impartiality *among all possible* claims.

These few preliminary observations have again several corollaries. One, since the advocated approach shifts the attention from the "ideal" to the identification of a perceived "ill" or disappointment, it is more concerned with the diagnosis of a problem and with finding a solution rather than with identifying an optimum or equilibrium. This seems more fruitful, since given the strategic environment, different equilibriums might exist that all satisfy the "rationality"

Meghan L. O' Sullivan, *Shrewd Sanctions* (Washington DC: Brookings, 2003), asking for "flexibility" and "wise choices" rather than some purely technical assessments.

84 David Baldwin, "Power Analysis and World Politics: New Trends vs. Old Tendencies," *World Politics*, vol. 31 (1979), 161–94.

criterion, but no obvious "best" solution is available. (This is why even Rawls' choice behind the veil of ignorance has to transform the choice problem to that of a single "rational" actor, exploding thereby the idea of a "contract.")

Two, since all efforts in ideal theorizing is spent on getting to the point where "all" see the problem in the same way, we lose sight of several fundamental problems. In view of the indeterminacy of "logical" solutions even in well-defined games, as multiple equilibria exist, settling on one of the equilibriums even in games of coordination will involve "politics" rather than "rational demonstration." Thus "politics" emerges precisely because *binding decisions* have to be made in the absence of a compelling algorithm for choice. To start from the assumption of a veil of ignorance or to assess the possibilities in terms of absolute impartiality, which then provides us with a compelling solution, fundamentally misrecognize the problem of political practice. Finally, the realizability problem that ideal theory places in the second phase, that is in the application stage, while suggesting that we have to attack the "design" problems first, by finding the "right" principles, misunderstands what is at stake.

Beginning with the analysis of a "problem," rather than with the blueprint of higher order principles, has some further advantages. Since there is no actual blueprint from which institutions diverge but only a set of feasible, but problematic alternatives, attention is not restricted to this divergence, but to the more complicated issues of comparing and choosing between feasible alternatives, which makes the analytical enterprise more "useful." Thus, one educational system might score high on having prestigious universities and research facilities, but restricts access to them to members of a *nomenklatura* and their friends. Another system might score rather poorly on the "checklist" of excellence, but has great coverage and provides considerably better opportunities of access. Now consider a country that has to choose within budget constraints. It would hardly be helped by an ideal blueprint, but in studying "feasible" alternatives, certain trade-off and possibilities emerge. In any case, such an engagement necessitates not only a critical appraisal of different systems, but also a *conscious reflection on the very criteria we use* when we judge different alternatives, a problem that blueprint analysis tends to marginalize. In addition, the appropriate methodological tools are no longer those of building grand theories, but of identifying "cases," of keeping one's eyes open for surprises, rather than clearing the ground right at the beginning and dispensing with ambiguities through clear-cut definitions and "operationalizations" of the key terms.[85]

[85] For a valuable collection of essays on the different epistemological and methodological issues involved in case studies, see Charles Ragin and Howard Becker (eds.), *What Is a Case? Exploring the Foundations of Social Inquiry* (Cambridge University Press, 1992). See also Charles Ragin, *Fuzzy Set Social Science* (University of Chicago Press, 2000).

Such a critical engagement also prevents a too facile identification of a hierarchy of values (rather than raising our awareness of their conflicting nature), as it draws our attention to the historical situatedness of the identification of a problem and of its solution. This counteracts on the one hand the *hybris* of the "end of history" speculations and of "best practices" that Dewey criticized in the libertarians' preferences. According to Dewey, libertarians:

> put forward their ideas as immutable truths good at all times and places … [They] hold that social change can come about in but one way, the way of private economic enterprise, socially undirected, based upon and resulting in the sanctity of private property … [and] have been blinded … to the fact that their own special interpretations of liberty, individuality and intelligence were themselves historically conditioned and were relevant only to their own time.[86]

In other words, the myopia created by the ideal theory does not let its proponents see how its very ideal of liberty is thereby perverted.

But having problematized one's "designs" also prevents another equally disastrous mistake of dismissing critical reflection and just "getting things done." Since "theory" or criticisms do not help anyway, professionals on the ground frequently believe that they are at least in possession of certain techniques and practices that "work." While this rather "a-theoretical" bent, or outright hostility to theory seems at first to be the exact opposite to ideal theory, it is actually part of the same mindset. Here ready-made "solutions" are again in search of problems and we get, therefore, a similar pathology of decision making. The only difference is that this "garbage can model" of deciding seems[87] even *less* reflective, and it is usually touted by "practitioners" on the ground, rather than by philosophers espousing their "view from nowhere." The result is, however, that again the framing conditions of the solution remain out of sight and thus the "answer" drives out any concern of what the question was. "Peace-keeping" and "humanitarian intervention" are perhaps the most striking examples, as discussed previously.

It is cold comfort that things are not necessarily better when "practitioners" on the ground work together with other "professionals" providing new justifications via their expertise in risk-management. The war on terror has shown that by linking formerly separate ways of assessing and combating threats, new serious problems have been created by this "synergy." The "securitization" moves, which erased the boundaries between the police, intelligence

[86] John Dewey, *Liberalism and Social Action* (Amherst: Prometheus Books, (1925) 2000), Chapter 2 *passim*, as quoted by Wiens, "Prescribing Institutions without Ideal Theory," at 58f.

[87] For an exposition of this pathology of organizational decision-making, see Michael Cohen, James March and Johan Olsen, "A Garbage Can Model of Organizational Choice," *Administrative Science Quarterly*, vol. 17, no. 5 (1972), 1–25.

services, and the military, have engendered new forms of "cooperation" under the umbrella of the neutral-sounding term of "governance." But it has also dissolved the conceptual grid of criminal responsibility, imminent danger, and of the laws of war, which allowed through status ascriptions (combatant) the infliction of harm, while also protecting "civilians" and narrowly circumscribing the discretion of preventive action. As Oliver Kessler and Wouter Werner point out, traditionally:

> (T)he capture and killing of individuals … (was) governed by at least three different rationalities for wrongful behaviour, imminent threat and institutionalized danger (or combatant status) … the framing of the war on terror – and specifically policies of targeted killing – echoes structures of governance that bypass these rationalities of responsibility, immediate threat and institutionalized danger. In doing so the war on terror introduces fundamental uncertainty as an element of legal reasoning. The result is that … individuals are killed on the basis of informal determinations of responsibility, unchecked characterizations of imminent threats and disputed status of the laws of war.[88]

While these remarks link back to David Kennedy's warning of the "darker" side of professionalism, they all show the need for a critical reflection that is not driven by either the fetishization of formal rigour, or by declaring or clarifying ultimate values that have to be maximized. This approach requires instead an engagement with the actual practices and perverse effects that need correction.

Peace, health, or justice are certainly "goods," but they are not commodities that can be straightforwardly maximized, like money or possessions. As Terry Nardin reminded us some time ago:

> A just person, strictly speaking, is not one who promotes "good ends" but rather one who respects certain limits defined by morality and law in pursuing particular ends … Even peace is better regarded as a constraint than as a purpose, for to respect the value of peace is not to achieve as an end the avoidance of all uses of force. It is rather to act on the principle that force is to be used only in authorized ways … and to do so in the manner that will restore regular and amicable relations afterward.[89]

Perhaps Nardin's use of "constraint" might still be somewhat misleading, precisely because it conjures up associations with the process of production, in which "matter" constrains the creator of an artifact. It thus neglects the productive power that emerges from the "acting together" of people that Arendt

[88] Oliver Kessler and Wouter Werner, "Extrajudicial Killing as Risk Management," *Security Dialogue*, vol. 39 (2008), 289–308 at 291.

[89] Terry Nardin, *Law, Morality and the Relations of States* (Princeton University Press, 1983), 13.

has rightly stressed.[90] Thus, peace and justice *are* "common goods" but not in the narrow technical sense of being instances of "market failure." This characterization tells us only that one way of providing them will not work, but leaves us in the dark as to how we are supposed to realize them. They also cannot be "produced" – unless we use the term metaphorically – but rather must be "cared for." They must be cared for not by fantasies of perfect health or omnipotence that changes the human condition by the stroke of a pen or the thump of a gavel. Heidegger's contrast of *Sorge* and *Gelassenheit* with the compulsions that emanate from conceiving the world as a *Gestell*, as an agglomeration of fabricated things,[91] comes to mind here. This alternative way of focusing on our predicament is rooted in praxis and the appropriate attitudes for acting, for "making" the world, rather than in assuming that discovering or "seeing" the world "out there" which circumscribes our existential problem.[92] Praxis directs our attention to the *Aufgaben*, that is tasks that are given and entrusted to us, which must be "taken care of" – by correcting again and again the problems that come up because our understandings and capacities are limited – while we strive to go on with our individual and collective projects.

90 For a good discussion of Arendt's reception, see Lewis P. Hinchman and Sandra Hinchman (eds.), *Hannah Arendt: Critical Essays* (Albany: SUNY Press, 1994).

91 There is no good equivalent in English for this German concept, only that it is a "thing" and that it has been "put" there (*stellen*). I also do not want to enter into the discussion of whether earlier work (*Sein und Zeit*) and the writings following his "*Kehre*" are compatible formulations. For a further excellent discussion see Dana Villa, *Arendt and Heidegger: The Fate of the Political* (Princeton University Press, 1996).

92 Interestingly, the context of emotion and cognition is hardly ever addressed in "science" (where "invention," i.e. asking a question, remains a purely "psychological" problem exogenous to the logic of discovery) or in the dominant and totally implausible "desire plus belief" model of rational action. Some notable recent exceptions are Martha Nussbaum, *Upheavals of Thought: The Intelligence of Emotions* (Cambridge, Cambridge University Press, 2001); Jonathan Mercer, "Rationality and Psychology in International Politics," *International Organization*, vol. 59, no. 1 (2005), 77–106; Jonathan Mercer, "Emotional Beliefs," *International Organization*, vol. 64, no. 1 (2010), 1–31; Janice Bially Mattern, "A Practice Theory of Emotion for International Relations," in Emanuel Adler and Vincent Pouliot (eds.), *International Practices* (Cambridge University Press, 2011), 63–86.

INDEX

CAMBRIDGE STUDIES IN INTERNATIONAL RELATIONS

118 *Ayşe Zarakol*
After defeat
How the East learned to live with the West

117 *Andrew Phillips*
War, religion and empire
The transformation of international orders

116 *Joshua Busby*
Moral movements and foreign policy

115 *Séverine Autesserre*
The trouble with the Congo
Local violence and the failure of international peacebuilding

114 *Deborah D. Avant, Martha Finnemore and Susan K. Sell*
Who governs the globe?

113 *Vincent Pouliot*
International security in practice
The politics of NATO–Russia diplomacy

112 *Columba Peoples*
Justifying ballistic missile defence
Technology, security and culture

111 *Paul Sharp*
Diplomatic theory of international relations

110 *John A. Vasquez*
The war puzzle revisited

109 *Rodney Bruce Hall*
Central banking as global governance
Constructing financial credibility

108 *Milja Kurki*
Causation in international relations
Reclaiming causal analysis

107 *Richard M. Price*
Moral limit and possibility in world politics

106 *Emma Haddad*
The refugee in international society
Between sovereigns

105 *Ken Booth*
Theory of world security

104 *Benjamin Miller*
States, nations and the great powers
The sources of regional war and peace

103 *Beate Jahn (ed.)*
Classical theory in international relations

102 *Andrew Linklater and Hidemi Suganami*
The English School of international relations
A contemporary reassessment

101 *Colin Wight*
Agents, structures and international relations
Politics as ontology

100 *Michael C. Williams*
The realist tradition and the limits of international relations

99 *Ivan Arreguín-Toft*
How the weak win wars
A theory of asymmetric conflict

98 *Michael Barnett and Raymond Duvall*
Power in global governance

97 *Yale H. Ferguson and Richard W. Mansbach*
Remapping global politics
History's revenge and future shock

96 *Christian Reus-Smit*
The politics of international law

95 *Barry Buzan*
From international to world society?
English School theory and the social structure of globalisation

94 *K. J. Holsti*
Taming the sovereigns
Institutional change in international politics

93 *Bruce Cronin*
Institutions for the common good
International protection regimes in international security

92 *Paul Keal*
European conquest and the rights of indigenous peoples
The moral backwardness of international society

91 *Barry Buzan and Ole Wæver*
Regions and powers
The structure of international security

90 *A. Claire Cutler*
Private power and global authority
Transnational merchant law in the global political economy

89 *Patrick M. Morgan*
Deterrence now

88 *Susan Sell*
Private power, public law
The globalization of intellectual property rights

87 *Nina Tannenwald*
The nuclear taboo
The United States and the non-use of nuclear weapons since 1945

86 *Linda Weiss*
States in the global economy
Bringing domestic institutions back in

85 *Rodney Bruce Hall and Thomas J. Biersteker (eds.)*
The emergence of private authority in global governance

84 *Heather Rae*
State identities and the homogenisation of peoples

83 *Maja Zehfuss*
Constructivism in international relations
The politics of reality

82 *Paul K. Ruth and Todd Allee*
The democratic peace and territorial conflict in the twentieth century

81 *Neta C. Crawford*
Argument and change in world politics
Ethics, decolonization and humanitarian intervention

80 *Douglas Lemke*
Regions of war and peace

79 *Richard Shapcott*
Justice, community and dialogue in international relations

78 *Phil Steinberg*
The social construction of the ocean

77 *Christine Sylvester*
Feminist international relations
An unfinished journey

76 *Kenneth A. Schultz*
Democracy and coercive diplomacy

75 *David Houghton*
US foreign policy and the Iran hostage crisis

74 *Cecilia Albin*
Justice and fairness in international negotiation

73 *Martin Shaw*
Theory of the global state
Globality as an unfinished revolution

72 *Frank C. Zagare and D. Marc Kilgour*
Perfect deterrence

71 *Robert O'Brien, Anne Marie Goetz, Jan Aart Scholte and Marc Williams*
Contesting global governance
Multilateral economic institutions and global social movements

70 *Roland Bleiker*
Popular dissent, human agency and global politics

69 *Bill McSweeney*
Security, identity and interests
A sociology of international relations

68 *Molly Cochran*
Normative theory in international relations
A pragmatic approach

67 *Alexander Wendt*
Social theory of international politics

66 *Thomas Risse, Stephen C. Ropp and Kathryn Sikkink (eds.)*
The power of human rights
International norms and domestic change

65 *Daniel W. Drezner*
The sanctions paradox
Economic statecraft and international relations

64 *Viva Ona Bartkus*
The dynamic of secession

63 *John A. Vasquez*
The power of power politics
From classical realism to neotraditionalism

62 *Emanuel Adler and Michael Barnett (eds.)*
Security communities

61 *Charles Jones*
E. H. Carr and international relations
A duty to lie

60 *Jeffrey W. Knopf*
Domestic society and international cooperation
The impact of protest on US arms control policy

59 *Nicholas Greenwood Onuf*
The republican legacy in international thought

58 *Daniel S. Geller and J. David Singer*
Nations at war
A scientific study of international conflict

57 *Randall D. Germain*
The international organization of credit
States and global finance in the world economy

56 *N. Piers Ludlow*
Dealing with Britain
The Six and the first UK application to the EEC

55 *Andreas Hasenclever, Peter Mayer and Volker Rittberger*
Theories of international regimes

54 *Miranda A. Schreurs and Elizabeth C. Economy (eds.)*
The internationalization of environmental protection

53 *James N. Rosenau*
Along the domestic–foreign frontier
Exploring governance in a turbulent world

52 *John M. Hobson*
The wealth of states
A comparative sociology of international economic and political change

51 *Kalevi J. Holsti*
The state, war, and the state of war

50 *Christopher Clapham*
Africa and the international system
The politics of state survival

49 *Susan Strange*
The retreat of the state
The diffusion of power in the world economy

48 *William I. Robinson*
Promoting polyarchy
Globalization, US intervention, and hegemony

47 *Roger Spegele*
Political realism in international theory

46 *Thomas J. Biersteker and Cynthia Weber (eds.)*
State sovereignty as social construct

45 *Mervyn Frost*
Ethics in international relations
A constitutive theory

44 *Mark W. Zacher with Brent A. Sutton*
Governing global networks
International regimes for transportation and communications

43 *Mark Neufeld*
The restructuring of international relations theory

42 *Thomas Risse-Kappen (ed.)*
Bringing transnational relations back in
Non-state actors, domestic structures and international institutions

41 *Hayward R. Alker*
Rediscoveries and reformulations
Humanistic methodologies for international studies

40 *Robert W. Cox with Timothy J. Sinclair*
Approaches to world order

39 *Jens Bartelson*
A genealogy of sovereignty

38 *Mark Rupert*
Producing hegemony
The politics of mass production and American global power

37 *Cynthia Weber*
Simulating sovereignty
Intervention, the state and symbolic exchange

36 *Gary Goertz*
Contexts of international politics

35 *James L. Richardson*
Crisis diplomacy
The Great Powers since the mid-nineteenth century

34 *Bradley S. Klein*
Strategic studies and world order
The global politics of deterrence

33 *T. V. Paul*
Asymmetric conflicts
War initiation by weaker powers

32 *Christine Sylvester*
Feminist theory and international relations in a postmodern era

31 *Peter J. Schraeder*
US foreign policy toward Africa
Incrementalism, crisis and change

30 *Graham Spinardi*
From Polaris to Trident
The development of US Fleet Ballistic Missile technology

29 *David A. Welch*
Justice and the genesis of war

28 *Russell J. Leng*
Interstate crisis behavior, 1816–1980
Realism versus reciprocity

27 *John A. Vasquez*
The war puzzle

26 *Stephen Gill (ed.)*
Gramsci, historical materialism and international relations

25 *Mike Bowker and Robin Brown (eds.)*
From cold war to collapse
Theory and world politics in the 1980s

24 *R. B. J. Walker*
Inside/outside
International relations as political theory

23 *Edward Reiss*
The strategic defense initiative

22 *Keith Krause*
Arms and the state
Patterns of military production and trade

21 *Roger Buckley*
US–Japan alliance diplomacy 1945–1990

20 *James N. Rosenau and Ernst-Otto Czempiel (eds.)*
Governance without government
Order and change in world politics

19 *Michael Nicholson*
Rationality and the analysis of international conflict

18 *John Stopford and Susan Strange*
Rival states, rival firms
Competition for world market shares

17 *Terry Nardin and David R. Mapel (eds.)*
Traditions of international ethics

16 *Charles F. Doran*
Systems in crisis
New imperatives of high politics at century's end

15 *Deon Geldenhuys*
Isolated states
A comparative analysis

14 *Kalevi J. Holsti*
Peace and war
Armed conflicts and international order 1648–1989

13 *Saki Dockrill*
Britain's policy for West German rearmament 1950–1955

12 *Robert H. Jackson*
Quasi-states
Sovereignty, international relations and the third world

11 *James Barber and John Barratt*
South Africa's foreign policy
The search for status and security 1945–1988

10 *James Mayall*
Nationalism and international society

9 *William Bloom*
Personal identity, national identity and international relations

8 *Zeev Maoz*
National choices and international processes

7 *Ian Clark*
The hierarchy of states
Reform and resistance in the international order

6 *Hidemi Suganami*
The domestic analogy and world order proposals

5 *Stephen Gill*
American hegemony and the Trilateral Commission

4 *Michael C. Pugh*
The ANZUS crisis, nuclear visiting and deterrence

3 *Michael Nicholson*
Formal theories in international relations

2 *Friedrich V. Kratochwil*
Rules, norms, and decisions
On the conditions of practical and legal reasoning in international relations and domestic affairs

1 *Myles L. C. Robertson*
Soviet policy towards Japan
An analysis of trends in the 1970s and 1980s